THE MUSICIAN'S MIND

THE MUSICIAN'S MIND

Teaching, Learning, and Performance in the Age of Brain Science

Lynn Helding

ROWMAN & LITTLEFIELD
Lanham • Boulder • New York • London

Published by Rowman & Littlefield
An imprint of The Rowman & Littlefield Publishing Group, Inc.
4501 Forbes Boulevard, Suite 200, Lanham, Maryland 20706
www.rowman.com

6 Tinworth Street, London SE11 5AL

British Library Cataloguing in Publication Information Available

Library of Congress Cataloging-in-Publication Data

Name: Helding, Lynn, 1960–, author.
Title: The musician's mind : teaching, learning, and performance in the age of
    brain science / Lynn Helding.
Description: Lanham : Rowman & Littlefield Publishing Group, 2020. | In-
    cludes bibliographical references and index. | Summary: "The Musician's
    Mind translates the latest cognitive and neuroscience research into clear,
    compelling concepts that enlighten the central pursuits of musicians' lives:
    teaching, learning, and performance. No matter your instrument or level of
    musical ability, this book will show you new ways to optimize your mind's
    creative power and wellbeing"—Provided by publisher.
Identifiers: LCCN 2019043511 (print) | LCCN 2019043512 (ebook) | ISBN
    9781538109946 (cloth) | ISBN 9781538109953 (paperback) | ISBN
    9781538109960 (epub)
Subjects: LCSH: Music—Psychological aspects. | Music—Performance—
    Psychological aspects.
Classification: LCC ML3830 .H3 2020 (print) | LCC ML3830 (ebook) | DDC
    781.1/1—dc23
LC record available at https://lccn.loc.gov/2019043511
LC ebook record available at https://lccn.loc.gov/2019043512

♾ ™ The paper used in this publication meets the minimum requirements of
American National Standard for Information Sciences Permanence of Paper
for Printed Library Materials, ANSI/NISO Z39.48-1992.

CONTENTS

PREFACE

Of Systems Breakdowns and Musicians' Brains

Systems breakdowns—whether of marriages, hip joints, or laptops—are little disasters that interrupt normal function. In scientific brain research, however, systems breakdowns are seen as priceless opportunities for studying intact systems. According to this reductionist viewpoint, not only does devastation in one part of the brain reveal how it must have operated when it was healthy, but insights are also gleaned by observing how the healthy components compensate for the diseased ones.

Both the birth of brain science and the creation of this book owe some of their origin story to breakdowns. In the case of brain science, it was the gruesome accident of railroad worker Phineas Gage, who blasted out his left frontal brain lobe when gunpowder and a tamping iron collided on the job. In the case of this book, the breakdown occurred within my instrument.

As a music student pursuing an operatic career the early 1980s, I had acquired a healthy and solid classical vocal technique through work with my first voice teacher. With the certainty provided by some performance kudos and a few major singing competition wins under my belt, I left home to pursue further music studies at a renowned school of music. But after only six seeks in my new teacher's studio, I began to lose my voice, most often immediately following my voice lessons. Logic directed me to tell my teacher, but that only generated a scolding that

I wasn't practicing hard enough, that I must actually practice *more*. Dutifully following this directive, I rapidly spiraled into vocal distress.

So began my long education into voice physiology and the scientific principles of vocal production, begun by voice teachers Ralph Appleman and William Vennard in the 1960s and masterfully propelled forward by voice pedagogue Richard Miller in the 1980s. With the help of an excellent voice technician who espoused Miller's systematic vocal technique, I quickly regained my instrument, convinced that voice science could bridge the gap between what Miller had dubbed "the historic Italian school of singing" and the current century and, more importantly, that voice science could answer age-old questions and settle tiresome debates. (What *is* breath support, anyway?)

In my burgeoning teaching career, I eagerly heeded Miller's exhortation that, as teachers, "we owe it to our students to be able to take advantage not only of everything that was known 200 years ago, but also of everything that is known today" and ramped up my efforts in what I came to call "the Doctrine of Accumulation."[1] That doctrine was simple: the more you know about the physiology of the voice and the way that vocal acoustics work, the better you can sing and teach singing. It seemed to me, then, that *what* one knows matters most.

A similar mode of thinking can be found within the pedagogies of almost every musical instrument (at least for the classical instrument families that comprise the traditional American music conservatory), even though the standard teaching method in those schools is based on the European master-to-apprentice model, wherein technical knowledge is bequeathed to students in highly personal, subjective, and idiosyncratic ways. Yet for every ten music teachers like this who do not teach the physiology of the body parts that it takes to drive their instruments, there is at least one who is sold on the idea that knowledge of the biomechanics of the wrist, the delicate facial muscles that construct an embouchure, or the components of respiration are critical to advancement, self-care, protection from harm, and recovery in the event of a systems breakdown. This type of knowledge is, in my view, vital for effective and humane music teaching. Indeed, many in our profession would do well to heed the ancient Hippocratic oath of physicians: *Primum non nocere*, "First, do no harm."

Yet regardless of which method music teachers choose—an empirical one, based on their own artistic experience, or a scientific one, built on a base of knowledge accumulated by many people over time—the transference of that knowledge from teacher to student ultimately hinges on the ability of the student to absorb it. Indeed, such a knowledge base is virtually worthless to the student if they cannot understand it. Unfortunately, this truth provides the perfect rationale for science-averse teachers to eschew science or "evidence-based" pedagogies altogether.

Nevertheless, there are a number of musicians within every instrument family who earnestly pursue the science behind their instruments, propelled by a combination of fascination with facts and concern for their students and bewitched by the Doctrine of Accumulation. Eventually, though, many who reach the far shore of knowledge with their priceless cargo intact will discover that they cannot get their goods to market—they cannot install their treasures with equal measures of speed and success into their students' minds—and are stymied by the realization that *what* one knows as a musician is no guarantee whatsoever of teaching success.

This revelation occurred to me in stages. The first stage was acceptance of its truth, which allowed a different question to reveal itself, the urgent question of "How?" Assuming one possesses the knowledge in the first place, *how* might we first plant and cultivate that knowledge within our individual students and then propagate it within the studio and even beyond to others who might benefit by it?

The second stage of revelation occurred to me at the National Center for Voice and Speech, where I had gone to study at the Summer Vocology Institute. Dr. Katherine Verdolini Abbott, in the midst of her course on motor learning theory, made an offhand comment that *what* teachers and clinicians know about the voice does not necessarily transfer to *how* to train it. This insight hit me like a thunderbolt. With the power of a spiritual conversion, I realized that, while scientists pursue knowledge for the sake of knowledge (and, admittedly, artists pursue art for art's sake), teachers—and especially artist teachers—are lodged in an entirely unique domain. We simply do not have the luxury to merely accumulate knowledge or artistic experience; we must figure out *how* to transfer both into our students. In the pursuit of the question "How?" I came to realize that the "what" of voice science was missing both the delivery system and the receptacle for that knowledge: the human mind.

These realizations fortuitously coincided with the 1990s' presidentially decreed Decade of the Brain, which was intended to "enhance public awareness of the benefits to be derived from brain research" and to "encourage public dialogue on the ethical, philosophical, and humanistic implications of these emerging discoveries."[2] This initiative spurred explosive growth in that decade in both the cognitive and neurosciences, which was first ignited in the 1950s by the aptly named cognitive revolution. As I dove headlong into this research, I proposed cognitive science as a logical place of rapprochement for voice science and vocal art because they had been at odds for over a century.[3] I later came to propose that a paradigm shift in all music pedagogy must occur in response to the cognitive revolution, a shift in emphasis from how well teachers teach to how well students learn; a shift from *what* musicians know to *how* to train them.[4]

This book is a result of more than nine years of research that follows these lines of thinking. It is my hope that readers will find this research as illuminating, stimulating, and useful as I have in my life as an artist, a musician, and a teacher. Toward that end, I offer the following navigational thoughts.

Intended Readership: This book is intended for all musicians, at all stages of their learning-teaching-performance journey, as well as for those who teach, love, and nurture them.

Musical Genres and Styles: Similarly, this book is intended for musicians of all musical genres and styles. In cognitive terms, the biggest division is between written and oral practices. The ability to read musical notation is a hallmark of Western classical music, yet the ability to improvise based on memorized musical components is fundamental to many other musical styles. These diverse practices seem to demand different mental gymnastics, depending on whether the musician is accessing memorized material as a canvas for creation or cognitively processing musical notation in the act of recreating the written work of a composer. In both cases, the brain is evincing its *network connectivity*, currently thought to underpin all complex cognitive tasks. Once again, cognitive science offers a fruitful arena for rapprochement between many diverse musical genres and styles.

Cognitive Science: Many disciplines are now housed under the heading *cognitive science*, specifically *neuroscience, cognitive psychology, neurobiology, neurophysiology, neurolinguistics,* and *evolutionary* *psychology*. Thus, a founder of the field has suggested the field would be more appropriately named the *cognitive sciences*, opining that the plural form would signify its interdisciplinary nature. Nevertheless, the blanket term *cognitive science* is the primary term used throughout this book.[5] This choice intentionally reflects the focus of this book, which is cognitive science (how the brain processes information) and not neuroscience (a branch of biology focused on the anatomy and physiology of brain structure). Thus, the reader will rarely encounter the names of brain structures in this book, and graphics featuring the brain sliced up like a side of beef are nonexistent.

Experts and Expertise Studies: Much of the information in this book about fruitful practice methods comes from the fields of motor learning and the relatively new field of expertise studies. Why should we study experts? Mostly because of the clear-eyed observation that experts seek continually to improve. That is why they are experts. And improvement demands practically all of the attributes that are eschewed by a "don't-think-just-do-it" mentality: that is, self-reflective thinking, planning ahead, predicting and weighing results, and monitoring physical actions. So this book is not intended for the casual musician but rather for both experts and students of expertise—let us call them "expertise-seekers." How far the learner chooses to travel on the continuum from beginner to mastery is ultimately a personal choice, yet it is my opinion that very committed amateur musicians can gain much from this book to aid their pleasure in music-making.

Terminology: I am a singer trained in the Western classical tradition and have sung and performed in several different vocal styles: opera, choral, early music, musical theater, and jazz. As a child, I also received training in piano, percussion, viola, and guitar. Throughout this book, I have used the generic term *musician* to stand for both singers and instrumentalists and also have delineated them when necessary. Likewise, use of the word *athlete* in the chapters on motor learning refers to all motor performers, not just those in the world of sports. Therefore *athlete* refers to musicians and dancers, as well as to runners, skiers, basketball players, and so forth.

Pronouns: Cognitive and motor learning principles as they apply to music teaching, learning, and performance are best illustrated through imagined scenes and stories; therefore, the use of pronouns is unavoidable. I have attempted an even distribution of *him/his*, *her/hers*, and *they* throughout the book.

NOTES

1. Richard Miller, "The Singing Teacher in the Age of Voice Science," in *Vocal Health and Pedagogy*, 3rd ed., ed. Robert Sataloff (San Diego, CA: Plural, 1991), 7–10.

2. U.S. Library of Congress, "Project on the Decade of the Brain," January 3, 2000, www.loc.gov/loc/brain/.

3. Lynn Helding, "Voice Science and Vocal Art: In Search of Common Ground," *Journal of Singing* 64, no. 2 (November/December 2007): 141–50; Lynn Helding, "Connecting Voice Science to Vocal Art: Motor Learning Theory," *Journal of Singing* 64, no. 4 (March/April 2008): 417–28.

4. Lynn Helding, "The Missing Brain," *Journal of Singing* 66, no. 1 (September/October 2009): 79–83.

5. George A. Miller, "The Cognitive Revolution: A Historical Perspective," *Trends in Cognitive Sciences* 7, no. 3 (March 2003).

ACKNOWLEDGMENTS

I would like to acknowledge the following institutions, organizations, and people who have supported my research:

- Dickinson College
- The University of Southern California Thornton School of Music
- Westminster Choir College of Rider University
- The National Association of Teachers of Singing
- The Voice Foundation
- The Van Lawrence Fellowship
- The National Center for Voice and Speech and its Summer Vocology Institute
- The Pan American Vocology Association
- At Rowman & Littlefield—Natalie Mandziuk, acquisitions editor; Michael Tan, assistant editor; Kellie Hagan, senior production editor; and John Shanabrook, copyeditor

I wish I could say thank you to every single person in my life who ignited my synapses. But I cannot, so my profoundest thanks are given to those whose influence carved a deep neural pathway. For that, I say thank you to

- My parents, Robert and Joanne, for providing what is now known as free-range parenting but which they just understood as a normal childhood. This was fundamental to everything that came after. How can one issue a sufficient enough thank-you for that?

Instead, I regularly weep with gratitude because normal is sadly neither average nor common.

- My brother, for teaching me how to fight like a boy. That knowledge has come in real handy.
- My piano teacher, Mrs. Braxton, for insisting on three piano lessons a week.
- My middle school English teacher, Mrs. Bradshaw, who taught me how to write.
- The late Esther England, for teaching me how to sing in the way that I wanted to be heard.
- Don Carey, for "emotion and meaning in music" long before I discovered Leonard Meyer.
- Ingo Titze, for opening a door to walk on the wild side with science.
- Kittie Verdolini Abbott, for exposing me to my Holy Grail, motor learning theory, and sharing your draft motor learning chapters with our vocology class.
- The late Paul Kiesgen, for enthusiastically supporting my belief in cognitive science as the third pillar of voice science.
- Don Miller, for challenging me on the worth of cognitive science in the field of voice science. Here is your answer.
- Meredith Mills, for making me laugh myself silly.
- Chris Arneson, for honoring my ideas yet urging me to always keep it practical. Let me know how that worked out, won't you?
- Scott McCoy, for encouraging me to publish my writing and then doing so himself.
- Dick Sjoerdsma, for sharing my enthusiasm about the human mind, handing me a column to write, then being the best eagle eyes a gal ever had. I am a better writer because of your stringency and interest in my work. You made *Mindful Voice* truly a "desirable difficulty."
- Lynn Maxfield, for taking over that column and for his clarifying graphic, a revised version of which is reprinted in this book by permission.
- Eric Hunter and Manuj Yadav, for generous e-mail discussions on the nature of sound.
- All my students, past and present, who continually motivate me to answer the question "How?"

- Melissa Treinkman, for reading the chapters on learning and for being an insatiable learner yourself. You are exactly the kind of graduate student I hoped to find when I finally earned the honor of teaching them.
- Kristin Rothfuss Erbst, for enlightening me as to the difference between the master's-degree mind and the doctoral-degree mind (and the vast territory in between).
- My USC Thornton School of Music teaching and learning colleague Beatriz Ilari, for reading the chapter "How Learning Works," reminding me of the centrality of emotion, and then giving it her seal of approval.
- My USC Thornton colleagues Peter Erskine, Rod Gilfry, William Kanengiser, Stephen Pierce, and Antoinette Perry, for their good work on the Thornton Musicians' Wellness Committee and for sharing their wisdom about music performance anxiety.
- Cindy Dewey, because she thinks that anybody who researches the brain must be really smart. You are my sister from another life.
- My children, Claire and Keanan, for keeping it real. As the Skin Horse said, "*Real* is a thing that happens to you, after a child has loved you for a long, long time. And it doesn't happen all at once, either. You become. It takes a long time, and doesn't happen often to people who break easily, or have sharp edges, or who have to be carefully kept." Thanks, kids, for filing down the sharp edges and keeping it really real.
- Ah, Blake Wilson. As Salman Rushdie wrote, "Our lives are not what we deserve; they are, let us agree, in many painful ways, deficient. Song turns them into something else. Song shows us a world that is worthy of our yearning, it shows us our selves as they might be, if we were worthy of the world." And so, *meine Seele, mein Herz,* you truly are *mein guter Geist, mein bess'res Ich.*

INTRODUCTION

A New Enchantment

The human brain is the superstar of the new millennium. How this homely, wrinkled lump of cranial tissue was sprung from its hidden attic room within the human skull and emerged a pop-culture phenom reads like a Cinderella fable.

The story begins in the waning decades of the nineteenth century, when physiological explanations for human behavior began to surpass philosophical accounts. Leaders of the then-nascent field of experimental psychology felt called to rescue psychology from philosophy, marry it to the emerging field of biology, and legitimize its progeny (psychological phenomena) through scrutiny in a proper scientific laboratory, not a psychoanalyst's risqué chaise longue. These experimental psychologists, particularly in the American school, soon cleaved brain from mind and banished the latter and its by-products, emotion and introspection, from serious scientific inquiry. Thus the ephemeral mind was shunted to the outer rings of mainstream psychology, while the material brain, in thrall to the authority of science, served out its serf-like drudgery throughout the cold-war era of behaviorism.

But at the dawn of the 1960s, the brain was emancipated by the new cognitive science. And so began its Pygmalionesque transition. By the 1990s, the brain was reunited with the missing mind and, gussied up in the day-glo colors of neuroimaging, debuted as the belle of the ball at the start of its namesake era, the presidentially decreed Decade of the Brain.

Imaging technologies such as fMRI, PET, and MEG can now illuminate the brain in real time as it negotiates the attributes of human behavior (like language processing), the sublime creations of human culture (like music), and the scourges that exploit our neural hardware (like gambling and pornography addictions). The transubstantiation of the brain's heretofore hidden activities into fixed images, at once thrilling and disturbing, makes manifest the mantra of the new science of mind: The mind is what the brain does.[1]

Practically from the moment of their inception, the gaudy fMRI "brainbow" images proved too promiscuous for confinement to academe. The persuasive power of what two psychologists have dubbed "neurobabble" and its "cousin, brain porn," have sparked the new field of neuromarketing, which seeks to exploit these images' dual powers of fascination and authority to sell everything from Coke to cars to political candidates.[2] And just as a cunning young starlet might morph from a hottie hawking merchandise to a high-class artiste, the shrewdly managed brain has even become the subject of a book-length portrait collection.[3]

Yet the brain's popularity is not confined to its photo ops. A quick Internet perusal of worldwide headlines on any given day reads like the peregrinations of a media darling: "Scientists Locate 'God Spot' in the Human Brain" or "Breast-Feeding Feeds Babies' Big Brains." Yes, even "Attack of the Teenage Brain!!"[4]

The megastar brain flits among research topics as lithely as a popstar changes escorts, but like a true diva, it outshines every associate within its orbit, even one as attractive as music. The brain's partnership with music generated the field called the *cognitive neuroscience of music*, which, as its name suggests, is compounded of cognitive psychology and neuroscience and devoted to the scientific study of the neurobiology of music. Within this constellation, music is valued primarily for its ability to offer "a unique opportunity to better understand the organization of the human brain."[5] True to form, the brain steals the spotlight.

THE BRAIN ON MUSIC

Two pillars of investigation within the cognitive neuroscience of music are (1) music and emotion, and (2) the perception and cognition of musical structures. The current state of this research is reflected in the title of a popular book on the topic (*This Is Your Brain on Music*), and its narcotic overtones bespeak the way in which the elements of musical experiments are delivered to their subjects: from the outside in. This research is largely conducted along a one-way path, funneling a channel of recorded musical sound (itself previously produced by unseen music-makers) and injected through the conduit of the human ear to its final destination, the human brain.[6] With a few notable exceptions, research-ers use the information gleaned in order to infer how *listening* to music affects the brain, not how the brain might influence the way we *make* music—let alone how we might improve our music-making.

Throughout this book, I flip these priorities by first stepping back from the sensational brain hype to a more reasoned consideration of what is known about the brain so far. I focus on cognition, specifically, how humans learn, and so the guiding question is be "How?" How might the current state of brain science make us better musicians? As you shall see, this question is largely absent from the cognitive neurosci-ence of music, perhaps because neuroscientists consider the evolution-ary question "Why?" in regard to music making much more compelling:

> More fascinating than how people make music (and greater myster-ies, perhaps) are why people make it, why others listen and how a beat of any sort can have such a profound impact on the body and the brain.[7]

Undoubtedly, some musicians will agree with science journalist Eliza-beth Quill, who wrote that statement, and find such questions fascinat-ing. For those people, there are several excellent books that consider these questions. It is equally certain that many more musicians have already answered the question "Why?" for themselves, and that answer probably has something to do with emotion and meaning.

Quill herself acknowledges "music's tendency to get charged with cultural, religious and emotional meaning" and notes that these very attributes "may complicate things for scientists seeking its roots and benefits," while at the same time allowing that these complications are what make pursuing the questions "worthwhile."[8]

Yet not all cognitive scientists find the question "Why?"—in regard to music at least—a worthy one. A total eclipse of music as "useless" was proffered by cognitive psychologist Steven Pinker in his now-infamous comments on the status of music within the human condition. For Pinker, the pure pleasure gleaned from music can only be explained by its dismissal as so much "auditory cheesecake": sweet but empty.[9] Those were fighting words for evolutionary psychologists, who took on the challenge of revealing the evolutionary roots of music, as if proving music's function might prove its worth.[10]

But musicians need no such evidence. We already know music's inherent worth. Yet in much current research on music and the brain, the endgame is not to explain music's power "to soothe a savage breast" but to defend music's *usefulness*—to prove the power of music to, in Quill's words, "provide a mental boost" for such implicitly higher-order computations as "improved understanding of grammatical rules and sharper auditory perception."[11]

THE "MOZART EFFECT"

The lines of inquiry described by Quill labor in the shadow of the so-called Mozart effect, a now thoroughly discredited scientific legend that listening to classical music makes you smarter.[12] And while serious scientific researchers were suspicious from the start that merely listening to classical music could boost cognitive performance (it doesn't), some were then, and yet remain, enthusiastic about the cognitive benefits of active engagement with music through music lessons and performance. A leader in this corner of research is Canadian composer and cognitive psychologist Glenn Schellenberg.

In 2004, Schellenberg conducted an important experiment to test the hypothesis that music lessons promote intellectual development.[13] The children in Schellenberg's study who received music lessons showed, on average, a 2.7-point boost in IQ over the kids in control groups. If that seems statistically insignificant, researcher Schellenberg himself notes that this was only a "small increase" in IQ.[14] Despite the unequivocal and provocative title of the article ("Music Lessons Enhance IQ"), Schellenberg's written conclusion at the end of the paper is more somber: in the process of formal education, he writes that "extra-curricular experiences such as music lessons appear to play a role."[15]

In fact, there are many well-known factors besides music lessons that can cause a boost in test scores, starting with the phenomenon that instruction of *any* kind can boost IQ.[16] A second known factor in positive academic achievement is a low student-to-teacher ratio.[17] Indeed, a distinguishing characteristic of music instruction is the one-on-one paradigm: children who take lessons once weekly receive a weekly dose of undivided adult attention. This factor has been suggested as one correlational link between music lessons and the higher IQ scores and improved school performance noted in musical kids.

A third and significant correlation is a ubiquitous factor in the lives of scheduled children: parents. It is well known that "children with high IQs are more likely than other children to take music lessons because better educated and more affluent parents tend to provide music lessons for their children."[18] These special adults who will drive kids to lessons, oversee instrument upkeep, and foot the bill for musical activity are also apt to help their children with homework, require healthy physical activity, and ensure adequate rest, all factors that boost academic success.

Parents' reason for providing music training for their offspring may be for the sheer love of music or for cognitive enhancement, but chances are it is for the latter. In two recent Gallup polls, 88 percent of adults surveyed said they believe that music-making boosts a child's overall intellectual development (along with other benefits, such as self-discipline, enhanced creativity, and the ability to work well with others).[19]

Yet a recent study that made headlines found that "there is very little evidence supporting the idea that music classes enhance children's cognitive development."[20] Despite the habitual caution of researchers to the lay public that "correlation does not equal causation" (or, just because certain events line up does not mean that they cause or even influence each other), this study, in the words of one of its authors, ignited a "media firestorm."[21]

And so it goes in the Mozart effect wars. Given that music-making demands many cognitive skills and at high intensity, it would be fairly amazing if at least some permanent cognitive benefits were not realized with practice, over time. Indeed, there is very promising research that shows a direct connection to music training and brain plasticity—in effect, "softening up" the brain to make it more pliable (or "plastic") for receiving information.[22] Still it remains difficult to determine the causal effects of music training on cognition. Even Schellenberg has allowed that the many underlying factors that influence children's intellectual achievements are so complex and interconnected that future experiments on the music-to-cognition connection "could find that there is no clear winner or loser."[23]

Nevertheless, research by Schellenberg and others is regularly seized upon as definitive by arts-industry trade groups and other arts supporters because the vast majority of the general public believes that art makes you smarter. This belief has become, in the words of arts education researchers Ellen Winner and Lois Hetland, "almost a mantra" among parents, teachers, and politicians, while the ability for arts classes to improve kids' scores on standardized test is "practically gospel among arts-advocacy groups."[24]

Despite the understandable desire to wield scientific research in defense of the arts, the impulse to do so is wrong-headed. Hitching arts training to gains in unrelated fields obfuscates what the arts can actually provide. The arts, indeed the broad scope of the humanities, teach creative thinking, a commodity all the more prized as it becomes more rare due to the heavy influence of standardized testing within our current educational systems in the United States and the emphasis on STEM topics (science, technology, engineering, and mathematics). It makes no sense to measure the value of something precious simply by how it may boost parameters within entirely different domains. I do not value my second-born child because he provided ballast to my first (even though it is true that he did); I cherish him simply in and of himself.

The measure of the value of music has less to do with cognitive enhancement—even if music does prove to provide it—and more to do with a broader enhancement of human experience. As literary scholar Joseph Carroll describes it,

> art, music, and literature are not merely the products of cognitive fluidity. They are important means by which we cultivate and regulate the complex cognitive machinery on which our more highly developed functions depend.[25]

We should promote music's intrinsic worth and value not because music makes us smarter but because music makes us better. And in order to make better music, as teachers, learners, and performers, musicians can reap the benefits of the most recent discoveries in cognitive neuroscience.

MUSIC AND THE MIND

Chapter 1, "Science, Art, and the Missing Mind," begins by surveying modern psychology, whose outsize influence on everyday life was advanced under the banner of behaviorism during much of the twentieth century until behaviorism was challenged and largely overthrown in the 1960s by the so-called cognitive revolution. According to some educational reformers, behaviorist principles still underlie many teaching environments today to the particular detriment of such attributes as creative thinking, perseverance, and internal motivation. An in-depth look at this is in order, for musicians' lives depend upon these very attributes.

And while the cognitive revolution provided the impetus for what *New York Times* opinion writer David Brooks calls our "new enchantment" with brain science, such upheavals should generate caution as we navigate this enchantment; it is wise to heed the ancient warning caveat emptor.[26] Even though creativity is generally culturally valued and individually sought, human creativity per se is not always directed toward positive ends. Studies of the dark side of human personality have shown that the very divergent thinking that marks creativity may also engender behavior that is "morally flexible," which in turn opens the door to antisocial or even harmful acts.[27]

When human ingenuity teams up with psychological acuity, the human qualities we hold most dear can bear bitter fruit, and so it is with music. The very thing that musicians love can be weaponized by means of psychology's dark arts. As disturbing as it is to see our muse commandeered for harm, musicians should not spare themselves the knowledge that the U.S. military has alchemized the elements of music in order to inflict damage on its enemy combatants. Largely due to the investigative work of musicologist Suzanne Cusick, as you shall see, the pain potential in music goes well beyond amped-up volume or pitch levels.

The insidious value of music as an instrument of torture lies in its ability to penetrate the mind and infect the prisoner with "earworms," yet leave no visible trace.

I will move from that dark corner to consider the historic milestones in education and philosophy most significant for musicians, namely C. P. Snow's 1950s *two cultures controversy* (on the nexus of art and science) and Howard Gardner's *multiple intelligence theory* (MI theory), which in the early 1980s took the first crack at previously unquestioned notions of intelligence. MI theory paved the way for the more expanded view of human competencies that we currently enjoy, creating a space for emotion after its long exile by rationality and producing calls for a culture in which science and art are revered as equals.

Thus girded by cautious enchantment and inspired by the dawn of a new age of understanding more amenable to the artistic temperament, in chapter 2, "Groundwork: At the Foothills," I debunk popular conceptions about the brain and move on to consider the real brain gains from current research that are most applicable to musicians.

Chapter 3, "How Learning Works," amalgamates current cognitive research with the overabundance of learning theories to provide a clear and concise basic primer on how human cognition works by focusing on cognition's three main building blocks: *attention, learning,* and *memory*. These are the necessary components common to two of the basic types of learning from standard psychology, *declarative* and *procedural*. Declarative learning (colloquially known as *book learning*) is required for mastering Western classical music yet is arguably less important for other musical genres, particularly those that do not require the ability to read musical notation. However, procedural learning (also known as *muscle* or *motor learning*) is essential to all genres of music performance, for it forms the core of any musician's life: technique. Regardless, no learning is possible without the critical prerequisite of *attention*; thus, attentional aides are considered in light of recent research on what boosts attention and what is harmful to it. The chapter ends with the paradigm shift in our understanding of human change via *neurogenesis* (brain-cell growth) and *neural plasticity*, the brain's amazing ability to transform itself.

Chapter 4, "Learned Movement: Motor Learning," goes more deeply into procedural learning, or motor learning (ML). ML research advanced rapidly through support by the U.S. military during World War

II; indeed, psychological experts' rise to prominence during the twentieth century was largely abetted by the war effort. But by the mid-1960s, progress in ML theory had slowed as the cognitive revolution drew researchers away from previous fields of inquiry and toward newer and more tantalizing areas of research, such as verbal learning, information processing, and memory studies.

After a brief hiatus, ML research was reborn in the 1970s, when the field of sports psychology took off. Today, thanks to advances in neuroscience (and funding from the multi-billion-dollar-per-annum sports industry), ML research is thriving. New research on the organization of practice schedules, the timing of feedback, and the quality of practice have revolutionized sport and led to optimized performance in the physical realm. This research is directly applicable to music learning and performance.

In this chapter I also consider two sides of the popular maxim "Go with the flow," known in ML research as the *theory of attentional focus*. New insights indicate that the key difference between the brain of a beginner and the brain of an expert is the depth of the *motor plan* in their respective brains. Experts may be able to "relax and go with the flow," but how can beginners do so when they have, in the early stages of motor learning, no flow with which to go?

Of particular note throughout this book is the vital difference between learning and performance. While one leads to the other, they inhabit distinctly different domains, yet their conflation is common, to the detriment of both. Their vital link is *practice*. In chapter 5, "Performance Studies," I consider practice as a valuable deposit into a future account of automatic recall. Musicians will want to know how much practice time is required (Is it really 10,000 hours?) and whether those hours carry a quality rating (they do)—which is why an artless tally of the hours one spends at a keyboard is far less important than the quality of intention within those practice hours. Psychologist K. Anders Ericsson, an expert on expertise, has dubbed this *deliberate practice*. I consider how the concepts of deliberate practice can revolutionize music practice, even if becoming a bona fide expert is not necessarily one's goal. I also consider some of the hottest topics in both popular science and popular parenting media, including that troublesome notion called *talent*. I consider psychologist Robert Bjork's concept of *desirable difficulties*, which takes its name from a necessary component of learning:

struggle. Yet this necessity has been withheld from many, particularly among those to whom the talent label was most strongly affixed. The aversion to struggle, combined with the cultural phenomenon of self-esteem theory, created a potent combination that is blatantly toxic to learning. This toxicity is especially evident in sports and music, two arenas that share motor learning as a fundamental component and in which American kids spend the majority of their extracurricular energy. Children who are yoked to the talent myth and fed big dollops of praise soon develop what social psychologist Carole Dweck has termed a *fixed mindset* that, unless exchanged for a *growth mindset*, stunts progress throughout the life of the learner.

Whether historic and modern musical luminaries were guided by a talent account or a growth mindset, one thing is certain: all had to log a minimum of 10,000 practice hours—even the child prodigy Wolfgang Amadeus Mozart. That his success in achieving this magic number had something to do with his papa Leopold has inexplicably remained buried in the so-called expertise literature, which has long shown that a primary component to success in many endeavors (particularly sports and music) is parental involvement.

Übermom Amy Chua dealt perhaps the first nationwide blow against self-esteem theory in her now-infamous parenting memoir, *Battle Hymn of the Tiger Mother*, whose debut was preceded by an excerpt released in the *Wall Street Journal* under the provocative headline "Why Chinese Mothers Are Superior."[28] Yet her book is as much about raising musicians as it is about raising kids. Much of Chua's small volume is devoted to reprints of detailed notes she took while sitting in on her daughters' music lessons and the daily practice directives she devised for them by the dozens. Now that the Tiger Mom firestorm is history, the musical education and accomplishments of Chua's daughters merit a rational look by musicians through the composite perspective of what we currently know about attention, deliberate practice, neural plasticity, synaptic strengthening, and self-esteem theory.

Chapter 6, "Mind Games," begins with an overview of the autonomic nervous system and our current understanding of the human stress response, based largely on the work of neuroendocrinologist Robert Sapolsky. This chapter includes new information from the nascent field of music-performance-anxiety research as well as two particularly weird phenomena that especially bedevil experienced performers: (1) the so-called ironic effect, described as that inexorable pull "in a direction precisely opposite" the intended one, which results in (2) "choking," the inexplicable mistakes made in public performances by seasoned professionals.[29] Research on the latter has largely been funded by the sports-entertainment industry, which has a lot riding on cures for choking. The research is both fascinating and hopeful for musicians, particularly for those chokers who seek alternatives to pharmacological treatments. On the upside of games the mind can play, the marvel of mirror neurons holds promise as an effective "no-practice" practice routine for injured musicians.

Evolutionary psychologists note that attention is an adaptive behavior; without it, the human race would not have survived. Yet attention as a human resource is under an attack so severe that journalist Maggie Jackson has tied its demise to a "coming dark age."[30] Chapter 7, "The Digital Brain," first considers the bad news: digital media has the power to effect devastation upon attention, memory, and social interaction. Given that the centerpiece of a musician's life is public performance, which in turn is undergirded by thousands of hours of deliberate practice—and that both these activities demand loads of attention from both the doer and the receiver—a sobering look at the fragmentation of attention is in order, including the cultural harm of mass inattention as revealed in the section titled "Who Cares If You Listen? The Problem of Audience Attention." Yet while musicians are just as vulnerable as anyone else to the addictive qualities of technology, we are also uniquely positioned to combat its pernicious side effects and champion Jackson's optimistic "renaissance of attention."

I end this exploration of the new brain science in chapter 8, "Emotion, Empathy, and the Unification of Art and Science," with a final look at the importance to art and artists of emotion's rescue because emotion links to empathy, which is a cornerstone of civilized culture. I circle back to Snow and consider whether calls for a fourth culture might herald a new age in which art and science are, at long last, equal partners. Author and inspirational speaker Daniel Pink has dubbed this possibility "The Conceptual Age," and he envisions a new world order guided by "nonlinear, intuitive and holistic" thinkers. If Pink is correct that "the wealth of nations and the well-being of individuals now depend on having artists in the room," then musicians should plan to take their rightful place there.[31] This book can help prepare the way.

NOTES

1. Steven Pinker, *How the Mind Works* (New York: W. W. Norton, 1997), 24.

2. Christopher Chabris and Daniel Simons, *The Invisible Gorilla* (New York: Crown, 2010), 142.

3. Carl Schoonover, *Portraits of the Mind: Visualizing the Brain from Antiquity to the 21st Century* (New York: Abrams, 2010).

4. Fox News, "Scientists Locate 'God Spot' in the Human Brain," March 10, 2009, www.foxnews.com/story/0,2933,507605,00.html; MSNBC, "Breast-Feeding Feeds Babies' Big Brains," March 29, 2011, www.msnbc.msn.com/id/42330417/ns/health-kids_and_parenting/; and Dennis Palumbo, "Attack of the Teenage Brain!!" Huffpost, May 25, 2011, www.huffingtonpost.com/dennis-palumbo/attack-of-the-teenage-bra_b_173646.html.

5. Isabelle Peretz and Robert Zatorre, eds., *The Cognitive Neuroscience of Music* (New York: Oxford University Press, 2003), preface.

6. Daniel J. Levitin, *This Is Your Brain on Music: The Science of a Human Obsession* (New York: Penguin, 2006).

7. Elizabeth Quill, "A Mind for Music," *Science News* 178, no. 4 (August 14, 2010): 17.

8. Ibid.

9. Pinker, *How the Mind Works*, 528–34.

10. See David Ball, *The Music Instinct: How Music Works and Why We Can't Do without It* (New York: Oxford University Press, 2010); and Steven Mithen, *The Singing Neanderthals: The Origins of Music, Language, Mind and Body* (London: Weidenfeld & Nicolson, 2005).

11. Quill, "Mind for Music."

12. See Adrian Bangerter and Chip Heath, "The Mozart Effect: Tracking the Evolution of a Scientific Legend," *British Journal of Social Psychology* 43, no. 4 (December 2004): 613; and Christopher Chabris, "Prelude or Requiem for the 'Mozart Effect'?" *Nature* 400 (August 1999): 826–27.

13. E. Glenn Schellenberg, "Music Lessons Enhance IQ," *Psychological Science* 15, no. 8 (August 2004): 511–14. His research team announced free lessons to children in exchange for being part of a study on the cognitive benefits of music training. A total of 144 six-year-olds were selected and then randomly divided into four subject groups of 6 kids each: two groups received music instruction (keyboard or voice), and two control groups received either drama lessons or nothing. Lessons were given over a thirty-six-week period, and at the conclusion of instruction, each child was administered an intelligence test before entering the first grade and then again the following summer. As might be expected, all of the children evinced a significant increase in

full-scale IQ simply due to the fact that they had been in school. However, the kids who got music lessons showed, on average, a 2.7-point boost in IQ over the kids in the control groups.

14. Ibid., 513.

15. Ibid., 514.

16. Stephen Ceci and Wendy Williams, "Schooling, Intelligence and Income," *American Psychologist* 52 (1997): 1051–58.

17. Ronald G. Ehrenberg, Dominic J. Brewer, Adam Gamoran, and J. Douglas Willms, "Class Size and Student Achievement," *Psychological Science in the Public Interest* 2, no. 1 (May 2001).

18. See Gael I. Orsmond and Leon K. Miller, "Cognitive, Musical and Environmental Correlates of Early Music Instruction," *Psychology of Music* 27, no. 1 (April 1999): 18–37; and Schellenberg, "Music Lessons Enhance IQ," 511.

19. Samuel A. Mehr, "Music in the Home: New Evidence for an Intergenerational Link," *Journal of Research in Music Education* 62, no. 1 (2014): 79. See also NAMM, "NAMM Global Report," 2011, 175, www.nxtbook.com/nxtbooks/namm/2011globalreport/UPI; UPI, "Poll: Music Education Is Important," April 21, 2003, www.upi.com/Top_News/2003/04/21/Poll-Music-education-is-important/UPI-99891050959298/#ixzz35CK0oZUx; and NAMM, "New Gallup Survey by NAMM Reflects Majority of Americans Agree with Many Benefits of Playing Musical Instruments," April 29, 2009, www.namm.org/news/press-releases/new-gallup-survey-namm-reflects-majority-americans.

20. Samuel A. Mehr, Adena Schachner, Rachel C. Katz, and Elizabeth S. Spelke, "Two Randomized Trials Provide No Consistent Evidence for Nonmusical Cognitive Benefits of Brief Preschool Music Enrichment," *PLoS ONE* 8, no. 12 (December 11, 2013): e82007.

21. Samuel A. Mehr, "Miscommunication of Science: Music Cognition Research in the Popular Press," *Frontiers in Psychology*, https://doi.org/10.3389/fpsyg.2015.00988.

22. Krista L. Hyde, Jason Lerch, Andrea Norton, Marie Forgeard, Ellen Winner, Alan C. Evans, and Gottfried Schlaug, "The Effects of Musical Training on Structural Brain Development: A Longitudinal Study," *Annals of the New York Academy of Sciences* 1169 (2009): 182–86.

23. E. Glenn Schellenberg, "Long-Term Positive Associations between Music Lessons and IQ," *Journal of Educational Psychology* 98, no. 2 (2006): 466.

24. Ellen Winner and Lois Hetland, "Art for Our Sake," *Boston Globe*, September 2, 2007, www.boston.com/news/globe/ideas/articles/2007/09/02/art_for_our_sake . See also Lois Hetland, Ellen Winner, Shirley Veenema, and Kimberly M. Sheridan, *Studio Thinking: The Real Benefits of Visual Arts Education* (New York: Teachers College Press, 2007).

25. Joseph Carroll, "Steven Pinker's Cheesecake for the Mind," *Philosophy and Literature* 22, no. 2 (October 1998): 481.

26. David Brooks, "The Social Animal," TED Talk, March 2011, http://blog.ted.com/2011/03/14/the-social-animal-david-brooks-on-ted-com/.

27. Francesca Gino and Dan Ariely, "The Dark Side of Creativity: Original Thinkers Can Be More Dishonest," *Journal of Personality and Social Psychology* 102, no. 3 (2012): 445–59.

28. Amy Chua, *Battle Hymn of the Tiger Mother* (New York: Penguin Press, 2011); and Amy Chua, "Why Chinese Mothers Are Superior," *Wall Street Journal*, January 8, 2011, http://online.wsj.com/article/SB10001424052748704 111504576059713528698754.html.

29. Daniel M. Wegner, "Ironic Processes of Mental Control," *Psychological Review* 101, no. 1 (1994): 34.

30. See Maggie Jackson, *Distracted: The Erosion of Attention and the Coming Dark Age* (Amherst, NY: Prometheus Books, 2009).

31. See Daniel Pink, *A Whole New Mind: Why Right-Brainers Will Rule the Future* (New York: Penguin, 2005).

SCIENCE, ART, AND THE MISSING MIND

WHAT REVOLUTION?

If you were neither alive nor sentient in the last half of the previous century, you no doubt missed the revolution. If you were alive, adult, and aware, you can still be pardoned for not noticing, for even the revolution's footsoldiers and architects have claimed they were oblivious to the so-called cognitive revolution as it rolled out and are only aware of its significance in hindsight. Nevertheless, given the brain's current star power, key players have jostled for the bragging rights to have known the brain back in the dowdy, black-box days of behaviorism and to lay claim to having engendered its starring role in the cognitive revolution.

According to renowned developmental psychologist Howard Gardner, the scholars who attended a symposium titled "Cerebral Mechanisms of Behavior" at the California Institute of Technology in 1948 stood "at a critical juncture of scientific history."[1] While Gardner acknowledges that cross-fertilization among American and British scholars of the mind was occurring with increasing frequency throughout the 1940s and 1950s, he singles out this symposium as a major harbinger of the revolution because it featured two of its most radical and vital components: new theories of human information processing and a robust challenge to behaviorism, the ruling orthodoxy in psychology at that time. But harbingers seldom receive the accolades that the main event enjoys.

According to psychologist Steven Pinker, the official birthday of the revolution occurred over a decade later, on the opposite coast of the United States. The Massachusetts Institute of Technology (MIT) was the setting, and 1956 was the "annus mirabilis" for a symposium on information theory that would come to be acknowledged as "the start of the modern scientific study of the mind"—and the beginning of the cognitive revolution.[2] On the occasion of the MIT symposium's fiftieth anniversary, science writer Jonah Lehrer invoked the swashbuckling image of "a group of brash young scholars" who "introduced a series of ideas that would forever alter the way we think about how we think."[3]

The late psychologist George Mandler preferred the term *evolution*, and he observed (as a player in the [r]evolution himself) that there was little "radical rooting out of previous dogmas." Rather, behaviorism, according to Mandler, "faded because of its failure to solve basic questions about human thought and action, and memory in particular." Mandler and others believed that talk of revolution overly romanticizes what was simply the natural progression of psychology. "Much was said in colloquia and in congress corridors," wrote Mandler, "but the written record does not record a violent revolution."[4]

Indeed, George Miller, himself one of those brash young scholars, asserted a sentiment common to revolutionaries when, in hindsight, they consider their historic moment: "At the time, of course, no one realized that something special had happened, so no one thought that it needed a name," he reminisced. "That came much later."[5]

Some psychologists have argued that, besides the notable exception of the founding of modern psychology itself, revolution in psychology is a myth, and furthering the cognitive revolution storyline is actually harmful to the field.[6] Some have defensively sniffed that the other *-isms* that cognitivism supposedly overthrew (notably behaviorism) are still alive and kicking, even as cognitivism currently dominates the field.[7] Yet others have summarily dismissed the entire revolution narrative as simply "banal."[8] Despite these seemingly arcane debates among experts, understanding the evolution of psychology does matter to the layperson, if for no other reason than the privileged position of power and influence in American life that this field exerts. Like the saga of America itself, the rise of modern American psychology begins with its divorce from Europe.

By the mid-twentieth century, experimental psychology, having ditched the pesky mind, was finally solidly situated as a natural science. Thus it was positioned to harness, as did science en masse, its suddenly elevated social status, borne of the realization that, if science could make a nuclear bomb and unleash its terrible power, science was equally capable of offering defense and protection. So began what historian Ellen Herman has termed "the romance of American psychology," the field's meteoric rise to power during the years of World War II and its cold-war aftermath through organized consortiums of academic, political, civilian, military, and governmental persons and entities.[9]

The influence of the psychological establishment on American public policy, begun under duress during the war years, is now so ubiquitous in twenty-first-century life as to be virtually unremarkable. Its reach into our private lives is evidenced by the sustained, robust consumption of self-help and how-to books, with diet and parenting guides topping the list. Psychology in the present era is not just an academic discipline or a professional association but, as Herman argues, nothing less than "the creed of our time."[10]

And what about that revolution? While scholars within the psychological establishment debate the details of location and birthdate, should the rest of us care whether a bona fide revolution birthed our current worldview or not?

We should care for at least two reasons. First, if a revolution occurred, we might well wonder, the way civilians in wartime do, if we are securely located in its aftermath. Even more significant is the very reason for any revolution's existence in the first place, namely, the entity against which it reacts. In the case of the cognitive revolution, that antagonist was behaviorism. And understanding the effects of behaviorist psychology is key to understanding our motivations and weaknesses as they currently play out in all our arenas of musical endeavor and accomplishment, whether as students, teachers, parents, or practicing musicians.

MINDLESS BEHAVIORISM

At the dawn of the twentieth century, American experimental psychology was on a quest to join the natural sciences by systematizing observation through "experimental introspection" as a method to crack the code of consciousness, itself guilelessly described by psychology historian Daniel Robinson as the thing that "every man, woman and child know to be true during every waking hour of daily life."[11] (Spoiler alert! In spite of this grand effort, consciousness per se yet remains the Holy Grail of brain science.) As the century progressed, instead of a focus inward on this quest, many forces from both within psychology and outside the discipline combined to abandon philosophy, inexorably supplanting *introspectionism* and *mentalism* with *behaviorism* as the dominant school of psychological thought. While, as Robinson notes, it is "difficult to isolate the factors responsible for the early success of behaviorism," it is germane to this chapter to identify a few of them.[12]

The great waves of immigration into the United States at the turn of and into the early decades of the twentieth century corresponded with massive, indigenous population shifts away from rural agrarian life to urban life. The resultant population growth in many American cities was explosive—and unnerving to their longer-term occupants. At the same time, novel theories of education and child development combined with the influence of Darwinism and laid fertile ground for a new psychology that shifted focus away from the individual to consideration of the citizenry as a whole. And with that, the enticing promise (and, some argued, the necessity) of controlling group behavior came into view.

The observations of the German psychologist Kurt Koffka, arriving at Cornell University in 1924 as a visiting professor, offer a keen outsider's perspective on the American intellectual climate at the time, which he found

> chiefly practical; the here and now, the immediate present with its needs, holds the centre of the stage. . . . In science this attitude makes for *positivism*, an overvaluation of mere facts and an undervaluation of very abstract speculations, a high regard for science, accurate and earthbound, and an aversion, sometimes bordering on contempt, for metaphysics that tries to escape from the welter of mere facts into a loftier realm of ideas and ideals.[13]

Early behaviorists, sparked by John B. Watson's 1913 dictum *Psychology as the Behaviorist Views It*, eschewed the products of the mind (Koffka's "ideas and ideals") as too ephemeral for serious scientific study and thus dismissed the mind altogether as unknowable. They endeavored to join psychology to the ranks of the sciences by transforming the field from its preoccupation with interior, hidden mental states into a discipline strictly confined to directly observable behavior. And once a thing is observable, it is but a short path to measurability, the sine qua non of scientific credibility.

American behaviorism fed upon each of the cultural predilections that Koffka had enumerated; the exaltation of "mere facts" was exactly behaviorism's allure. In the chapter "The Danger of Science" in his 1935 book, *Principles of Gestalt Psychology* Koffka cautions that erecting a rational system of psychological knowledge would necessarily require cherry-picking only those facts that "would most readily submit to such systematization." His prediction that we might all "pay for science by a disintegration of our life" was a warning both plaintive and prescient: a catastrophic second world war soon followed, marked most terribly by an enemy that wielded eugenics as one of its motivating ideologies. [14]

Consequently, during the years that followed World War II, psychological theories that hinged on genetics or heritable traits were quietly shelved, while *environmentalism* (the "nurture" half of the ancient nature-versus-nurture debate) ascended. Onto this primed platform stepped behaviorism's most famous and ardent purveyor, the late Harvard psychology professor B. F. Skinner (1904–1990). Skinner picked up where Watson and followers had left off, advancing a more rigorous and spartan school of behaviorist thought, one that did not "regard itself as under any obligation to speak of brains or minds." [15]

By behaviorist principles, future behaviors of an organism are necessarily shaped by the positive and negative consequences that the organism experiences the first time around, whether pigeon, rat, or child. The practice of manipulating those consequences, *operant conditioning*, came to be one of Skinner's most famous (and infamous) contributions to science—not to mention to the training of the family dog. And since behaviorists saw virtually no behavioral distinction between animal or human, the basic tenets of operant conditioning were soon enthusiastically applied to controlling behavior in group settings like prisons and classrooms.

Behavioral control systems are based upon a set of assumptions, the most critical being that organisms choose their behavior voluntarily.

Since positive behavior is rewarded and negative behavior brings unpleasant consequences, behaviorists believe that positive behavior tends to be repeated while negative actions will be avoided. This all made rational sense until psychologist Martin Seligman discovered in the mid-1960s that some of his animals that were repeatedly subjected to the "unpleasant" consequence of pain in the laboratory chose a third and unexpected path: they simply crumpled and gave up. Even when offered an opportunity to escape, these animals chose the path of no resistance. Seligman dubbed this response *learned helplessness*, a principle that opened the door to research on depression, which in turn spawned cognitive behavior therapy and the positive psychology movement.[16]

Still, behaviorism could not explain why people do not always choose the sensible path of reward; it could not explain why some folks will irrationally subject themselves to repeated "unpleasantness." It turns out that people cannot be judged and predicted by outward behavior alone; people do not always choose their pain.

Yet behaviorism reigned as the dominant school of psychology in America for so much of the past century that anyone who received a standard-issue education during that time is likely the product of an educational system based largely on behaviorist psychology. And despite the currently held view (which incidentally hews to the revolution storyline) that "the cognitive movement dethroned behaviorism and brought the mind back to psychology,"[17] critics like progressive-education scholar Alfie Kohn maintain that our culture remains completely "marinated in behaviorism."[18] Kohn has made a singular career of blasting behaviorism, particularly the ubiquitous use of what he calls "goodies" (candy, praise, financial rewards) to "incentivize" behavior. Kohn has long argued that these behaviorist principles, still common practice among parents and teachers, have spawned multiple generations of schoolchildren who have grown up so addicted to incentives, praise, and prizes that they find little joy in discovery, little intrinsic worth in learning for its own sake, and therefore little reason to pursue a goal without the promise of immediate reward.

Yet research by psychologist Carole Dweck and others has shown that such incentives are actually not the primary forces that stimulate human endeavor and creativity. Furthermore, these "goodies" are not only ineffective motivators, but in children they can actually cause regression of the very motivations they are intended to ignite, devolving into a negative cascade that has been cleverly dubbed "the inverse power of praise" (a subject I will return to in chapter 5). [19]

If these incentives are so ineffective, why do they persist? Indeed, as early as the 1950s, behaviorism had already "come to be labeled by its opponents as a narrow, rigid, dogmatic and authoritarian system," yet these opponents operated primarily within the rarefied world of academe. [20] Even after the knowledge brokers declare an entire theoretical system passé and move on, the rest of society remains stuck, often for decades, in the wake of their abandoned -isms. Kohn asserts that this is so for behaviorism because B. F. Skinner lives on through his "surviving minions," who ply operant conditioning techniques on so many levels of modern life that behaviorism is now deeply embedded in the American psyche. "Behaviorism," Kohn insists, "is as American as rewarding children with apple pie." [21] If Kohn is right, then all of us ought to take more than just a passing interest in behaviorism's overthrow. And more critically, we ought to be alert to what new theories of learning are erected in behaviorism's place.

THE NEW SCIENCE OF MIND

Whether the cognitive revolution started intentionally or inadvertently, at a west- or an east-coast conference, a new intellectual environment was spawned at the mid-twentieth-century mark, after which similar interdisciplinary symposia flourished. By 1960, the Center for Cognitive Studies had been founded at Harvard, and similar centers quickly followed at universities across the United States. As a field, cognitive studies was conceived as cross-disciplinary from its inception and included researchers and scholars from the fields of psychology, linguistics, philosophy, biology, mathematics, anthropology, pediatrics, history, psychiatry, and psychoanalysis. This amalgamation, cognitive science, now includes neuroscience, sociology, education, and artificial intelligence as well and has recently come to be more broadly defined as "the New Science of Mind." [22] In turn, calls to fund a Decade of the Mind coalesced into an international initiative to build upon the progress made during the 1990s' Decade of the Brain. [23]

Like the many fields it encompasses, this new science of mind can be seen from multiple perspectives as a foil to behaviorism, as a new horizon in psychology, or as what *New York Times* opinion writer David Brooks has grandly anointed "the new humanism" and "a new enchantment":

> It's in the study of the mind, across all these spheres of research, from neuroscience to the cognitive scientists, behavioral economists, psychologists, sociology; we're developing a revolution in consciousness. And when you synthesize it all, it's giving us a new view of human nature. And far from being a coldly materialistic view of nature, it's a new humanism, it's a new enchantment.[24]

Brooks, like many nonscientists, often uses the word *revolution* when referring to this new science of mind, but at least one expert, psychologist Justin Barrett, has scolded that "we should get our 'revolutions' straight. What Brooks refers to as a 'cognitive revolution' is predominantly non-cognitive."[25]

Barrett's comment is technically correct. As he explains it, "the Cognitive Revolution was, first and foremost, about cognition and not about brain activity"—in other words, it was about brain function (cognition), not brain cells (neuroscience). Cognitive science owes its birth to the insight that computer processing can be harnessed as a metaphor for understanding human problem-solving, though the field is still mainly concerned with studying human information processing rather than consciousness per se, both the Holy Grail and the stickiest wicket in the new science of mind. However, the trope of revolution is simply too attractive for those outside scientific disciplines who, like Brooks, have understood the magnitude of this sea change in psychology and have begun to imagine what it portends for all of us, both individually and as a society.

Critics from within the academic psychological establishment argue that the cognitive revolution was no revolution at all because it failed to adhere to certain hallmarks of revolution.[26] But by the dynamics that signify a paradigm shift, as defined by the late science philosopher Thomas Kuhn, the cognitive revolution not only occurred, but by Kuhnian measures, it effectively cleared the playing field. Topics previously considered unworthy of study, owing to their interiority and therefore (most egregiously for rigorous behaviorists) their inability to be directly observed and measured, were suddenly allowed entrée. Critically, those subjects comprise the very attributes that make us most human: emotion, empathy, memory, desire, imagination, reflection, projection, creativity—and music. A comprehensive study of the myriad causes that preceded and sustained these enormous omissions from modern psychology is outside the scope of this book, but the negative consequences of their exile are staggering when considered en masse, which is, admittedly, much easier to do now that they are in our collective rearview mirror.

Steven Pinker ascribes the omission of emotion at the start of the cognitive revolution to nothing more than plain geekiness. "These were nerdy guys interested in the nerdy aspects of cognition," he explains. "It's not that our emotions aren't interesting topics of study, but these weren't the topics that they were interested in."[27] This glib dismissal (Oh, those unemotional, rational scientists!) would be easy to buy but for our current cultural predicament, marooned in the quagmire of behaviorism, simultaneously dogged by the exaltation of rational thought as the pinnacle of human wisdom, yet haunted by the phantoms of banished emotion. And one can only stand astounded at the utter soullessness of this statement by B. F. Skinner: "My answer to Montaigne's question ["How to live?"] has shocked many people: I would bury my children rather than my books."[28] The true shock of this comment is its permanence, for it was not impulsively uttered in a live interview but penned by Skinner himself in his autobiography.

Pinker has complained that "much science journalism today is hostile to scientists," opining that "there is a presumption of guilt about scientists, that they are . . . experimenting on innocent victims, or tricked by drug companies into making drugs we don't need."[29] But we have reason to be wary of a science that disavowed emotion and to wonder at not only what was lost by its banishment but, more distressingly, at what damage was wrought by emotion's exile from mainstream psychology during most of the past century. It is a bitter irony that, along with Harvard's starring role at the start of the cognitive revolution, another of Harvard's most notable products during that same era was one Theodore John Kaczynski.

Between 1959 and 1962, Kaczynski, along with twenty-one other young undergraduates, volunteered for psychological experiments conducted at Harvard, whose ultimate purpose was far from clear. But the method was to create extreme conditions of intense psychological stress. Kaczynski's biographer, Alston Chase, contends that the ferocity of these experiments fractured Kaczynski's mind and engendered in him the seething hatred of science that erupted so terribly decades later within Kaczynski's alter ego, the "Unabomber."[30] Kaczynski's mail bombs, three of which were fatal, terrorized the United States over a period of seventeen long years before his brother David tipped off authorities, leading to Kaczynski's 1996 arrest in a Montana cabin.

Pinker grumbles that "the old notion of the scientist as hero has been replaced by the idea of scientists as amoral nerds at best," yet this characterization is not completely unfounded.[31] Psychologist Dr. Henry Murray (1893–1988) led the three-year-long study in which Kaczynski participated, which featured techniques described by Murray himself as "vehement, sweeping, and personally abusive."[32] Murray's motivation stemmed from his wartime experience as a lieutenant colonel in the Office of Strategic Services (the precursor to the Central Intelligence Agency). Murray was sobered by the effectiveness of the Nazi propaganda machine (methods he nevertheless studied) and aroused by irrefutable evidence that entire nations could be "brainwashed" to enact horrific acts of brutality. Thus Murray, like many psychologists of his era, was an enthusiastic participant in a concerted effort to bend biological, chemical, sociological, and psychological science to nothing less than the creation of a new "World Man."[33] So much of this effort was funded by the U.S. Department of Defense that, according to Ellen Herman, "between 1945 and the mid-1960s, the U.S. military was, by far, the country's major institutional sponsor of psychological research."[34]

As the new science of mind burgeons and beckons, we must view the shadier chapters in the history of psychology from the objective perspective of historical time and take care not to become (to borrow Brooks's word) "enchanted." That is, musicians can profitably experiment with the application of recent brain research to the business of music-making without chasing the chimera of absolute scientific truth. Besides, as Chase observes, "once you start quoting scientific data to support your position, you're immediately really only talking about half the truth."[35]

To allow oneself to be charmed by scientific half-truths is, at best, imprudent due to the simple fact that the new science of mind is still in its infancy. This new science, like any true science, is raising many more questions than can be answered. Ironically, some of these questions (How does emotion effect choice? What motivates desire?) are the same ones that behaviorism sought to address over one hundred years ago, though, regrettably, by exalting directly observable phenomena at the expense of the mind's mysteries.

At worst, fully embracing this "new enchantment" while discounting the playbook of psychology's dark arts does not allow us to defend the thing we love against its theft and debasement as a weapon for human torture.

MUSIC AS A WEAPON

"It is an important, irrefutable fact that Americans have theorized and deployed music and sound as weapons of interrogation for at least fifty years. It is not a phenomenon of the current administration or the current wars; it is not news. The only news is that in the last few years we have become increasingly aware of it; that, and perhaps the unnerving fact that our awareness of this practice has provoked no public outcry."—Suzanne Cusick[36]

The harsh interrogation techniques (like hypothermia and waterboarding) used by the CIA and approved by the Bush administration in the "global war on terror" included carefully crafted psychological methods. Investigative journalist Jane Mayer documented how techniques featured in the U.S. Department of Defense's SERE (Survival, Evasion, Resistance, Escape) program—techniques originally designed by trained psychologists to teach U.S. military personnel how to withstand torture—were actually reverse-engineered to torture suspected terrorists.[37] These techniques included the use of music as a weapon.

Suzanne Cusick, professor of music at New York University, was one of the first to investigate the "acoustic bombardment" protocols that were part of the torture playbook used by the U.S. military's Psychological Operations division. Chillingly nicknamed "The Music Program," it went well beyond simply hurling annoyingly loud rock music at prisoners.[38] Specific psychological methods were crafted to exploit what the late neurologist Oliver Sacks noted as music's peculiar ability to "cross a line and become, so to speak, pathological," referring to what are colloquially called "earworms." Sacks called them "brainworms," noting that one insidious symptom of what he called "sticky music" is that such music is almost always not to one's liking and is even odious, suggesting a "coercive process, that the music has entered and subverted a part of the brain, forcing it to fire repetitively and autonomously (as may happen with a tic or seizure)."[39]

Use of heavy metal, rap, and sexually suggestive music and, most grotesquely, songs such as "I Love You" from the children's television show *Barney, the Purple Dinosaur* were routinely employed to block a prisoner's ability to maintain his own thoughts (a necessity to keep from going mad), thus "softening him up" for interrogation.[40]

But music can be weaponized in a more brutally tactile way. After all, sound, at its most basic level, is the movement of air molecules within a medium. That medium can be air, wood, string, reed—or the human body. The acoustical properties of music can be inflicted upon detainees' bodies without leaving physical evidence, thus sparing the inflictors from criminal prosecution under the Geneva Convention. The high value of these and other psychological techniques is exposed by their rubric in CIA training manuals, filed under "No-Touch Torture." But one thing that the new science of mind has shown is that, while physical wounds heal, psychological ones can last a lifetime.[41]

What a macabre twist it is that empathy, imagination, creativity, music—the very attributes that were exiled from scientific consideration for much of the past century—have been hijacked and alchemized into weapons of psychological torture. The rendering of the very thing to which musicians' lives are devoted until it is, as Cusick says, "damaged beyond recognition as the thing it was" sparked outrage among many, especially those whose music was commandeered for harm. In 2009, a coalition of musicians (including members of R.E.M., Pearl Jam, Nine Inch Nails, and Rage Against the Machine) filed a freedom of information petition requesting the declassification of secret U.S. documents on "The Music Program" and its use as an interrogation device at Guantánamo Bay Prison.[42] In a statement, guitarist Tom Morello said,

> Guantánamo is known around the world as one of the places where human beings have been tortured—from waterboarding to stripping, hooding and forcing detainees into humiliating sexual acts—playing music for 72 hours in a row at volumes just below that to shatter the

eardrums. Guantánamo may be Dick Cheney's idea of America, but it's not mine. The fact that music I helped create was used in crimes against humanity sickens me.[43]

It is possible to cautiously embrace the new science of mind while at the same time stand firmly opposed to such debasement of our humanity. To do so necessitates grasping the vital role of the artist in relation to science's "half-truth." When science tackles a question, the tools are direct observation, and the result is empirical evidence. But elucidation is required in order to understand the meaning of such evidence, and at that juncture, even words may fail. The other half of science's "half-truth" lies with art.

SCIENCE AND ART

The fiftieth anniversary of C. P. Snow's famous and controversial 1959 Cambridge lecture and subsequent book *The Two Cultures and the Scientific Revolution* set off a wave of retrospective conferences, public symposia, and op-ed pieces on both sides of the Atlantic, all to reflect on what science historian D. Graham Burnett calls "the most frequently cited articulation of the relationship between science and society."[44]

In his book, Snow opines that, while among educated people ignorance of great literature was considered an abomination, ignorance of science was considered acceptable, even defensible. In turn, according to Snow, ignorance of science bred outright disdain for science, which halted its progress and its benefits for the greater good. Almost immediately, this schism was abbreviated in the media to simply "the two cultures controversy," and by the mid-1980s, both the thesis and Lord Snow had achieved the ultimate acknowledgment of cultural significance: the adjectival transformation of Snow's name—a "Snowvian disjuncture"—to describe the split.[45]

Despite the symmetry implied by the derivative version of Snow's two cultures, it was clear from Snow's original opening volley that, in his view, the fault for this "gulf of mutual incomprehension" was anything but mutual:[46]

A good many times I have been present at gatherings of people who, by the standards of the traditional culture, are thought highly educated and who have, with considerable gusto, been expressing their incredulity at the illiteracy of scientists. Once or twice I have been provoked and have asked the company, how many of them could describe the Second Law of Thermodynamics? The response was cold: it was also negative. Yet I was asking something which is the scientific equivalent of: *Have you read a work of Shakespeare's?*

I now believe that if I had asked an even simpler question—such as, What do you mean by mass, or acceleration, which is the scientific equivalent of saying, *Can you read?*—not more than one in ten of the highly educated would have felt that I was speaking the same language. So the great edifice of modern physics goes up, and the majority of the cleverest people in the Western world have about as much insight into it as their neolithic ancestors would have had.[47]

Both the affinity with which other Western cultures received Snow's *Two Cultures* and its extraordinary staying power are remarkable given that the original work was steeped in the British postwar culture in which it was born. Snow's "literary intellectuals" were largely men (notably not women) of high socioeconomic status who had received a classical education at either Oxford or Cambridge during an era in which literature was extolled but science was considered, at best, an expensive hobby for gentlemen scientists. But Snow's facile progression from identifying this social caste as a "traditional culture" to elevating them to "the dominant class" that, he pretentiously claimed, "manages the Western world," engendered harsh criticism yet may reveal more about Snow himself than any rift between science and art.[48] Snow had been born into humble circumstances and, through a science scholarship to Cambridge, had ascended to the upper classes through education alone. After a middling career in research science, he turned to writing novels. From this dual vantage point, he qualified himself to speak so knowingly of science and art.

Snow's *Two Cultures* included kudos to the Soviet Union for its science education and dark warnings about the risks of failing to include the world's poor in the riches of industrial progress. Thus in its original form, it surpassed its current reputation as simply a public outing of the dichotomy between science and art; as Burnett quips, there was much more to Snow's original lecture than "just an observation about how scientists and artists had difficulty chatting."[49] Yet it was precisely this disjunction that most resonated, literally around the world, and makes it still, as Burnett notes, a "touchstone for several generations of commentary."[50]

In 1964, Snow produced a second edition of *Two Cultures* in response to criticism that he had excluded the social sciences.[51] He optimistically prophesied that a third culture would rise in which humanists and scientists would communicate so effectively as to bridge the gap between them for the betterment of society. Throughout the ensuing decades, Snow's two- and three-cultures metaphors have been regularly trotted out to legitimize the perceived dichotomy between science and the humanities or, when it suits a particular agenda, science and "the arts."

But it was self-appointed intellectual impresario John Brockman who actually took up Snow's call and in the 1980s staked his claim to the third culture, writing a book of the same name. Brockman became the literary agent for a new tribe of science writers who sprang up in the last two decades of the twentieth century and who communicated their work in refreshingly comprehensible language. Many of his clients' books became surprising bestsellers, proof, he said, that there exists an educated readership who are willing to devote the time and brainpower to reading about scientific and technological ideas that "will affect the lives of everybody on the planet."[52]

When Brockman set out to consciously create this third culture, he, like Snow, felt that humanists not only displayed scientific ignorance but, perversely, seemed to revel in it. So Brockman decidedly ditched what he labeled the "quarrelsome mandarin class" of literary intellectuals in favor of people who belong to "the empirical world," defined as those science and technology intellectuals (nicknamed the "Digerati") whom Brockman deemed were "at the center of today's intellectual, technological, and scientific landscape."[53] Situated at the center of that landscape is his website, Edge.org, an online salon launched in 1996 and built on invitation-only submissions monitored by Brockman himself. Despite the claim that artists are included in the roster of invited Edge.org salon opinionaters, the scientists and the Digerati far outweigh Edge.org musings by artists. This may have less to do with any overt snubbing of artists and writers and more to do with the dearth of artists who have crossed the Snowvian juncture to join the Digerarti in Brockman's scientific landscape.

In this respect, Brockman's cultural creation resembles E. O. Wilson's "Consilience," the only other serious contender in the attempt to establish a third culture. Even though Wilson's 1998 book of the same name began with the need for the sciences and the humanities to "jump together," Wilson was criticized for suggesting not a mutual joining at all but a wholesale takeover of art by science.[54] So it is that only a handful of artists, thus far, have found their spiritual home in the third culture, and for those who have, it is digital technology that has provided the conduit for most of them, not the traditional sciences. Why is this so?

Perhaps artists are simply too consumed with the work of creation, too busy "out there doing it, rather than talking about and analyzing the people who are doing it" (this is somewhat ironic, considering that this quote comes from Brockman himself, describing his third-culture community).[55] Perhaps many artists lack enough scientific education to render science inspirational to their art—or maybe they simply do not find science artistically inspiring at all.

Among the many plausible reasons that artists spurn science, the most fundamental one may be the suspicion that scientific knowledge is more highly valued than artistic knowledge. The Western cultural milieu in which we live and work has, for much of the past century, supported a culture that values certain types of intelligence more highly than others. This premise formed the foundation of Howard Gardner's revolutionary *theory of multiple intelligences* and partially explains its enormous appeal to artists and creative thinkers as well as to their teachers and parents.

THE THEORY OF MULTIPLE INTELLIGENCES

Harvard psychologist Howard Gardner's theory of multiple intelligences, put forth in his 1983 book *Frames of Mind*, was greeted simultaneously with accolades from the public and hostility from the psychological establishment. The legacy of behaviorism, specifically its exaltation of measurable phenomena, partially explains both receptions. Multiple intelligences (MI) theory, in Gardner's words, can be summed up in a brisk sentence or two: Most people think that there is but a single intelligence; MI Theory holds that we each have eight or more intelligences, and we can use them to carry out all kinds of tasks.[56]

Despite—or perhaps precisely *because* of—MI theory's massive popular appeal, it was attacked in academic psychology circles.[57] The critics rounded on three cornerstones of Gardner's theory: his insistence on the word *intelligence* (as opposed to *ability* or *talent*) and his twin challenges to the notion of intelligence itself: that only math and language are reliable parameters of it and that intelligence testing can yield the single g, or *intellectual quotient* number of tested individuals.

As to the choice of the term *intelligence*, Gardner's initial defense was one of misapprehension: he hadn't fully appreciated the firestorm that this "seemingly minor lexical substitution" would ignite. He later admitted that, if he had used the term *talent* instead, his book would probably have received far less attention than it did.[58] Whether the choice was deliberate or random, Gardner's continuing steadfast defense of the term *intelligence* and his insistence that its conflation with the related terms *talent* and *ability* be free of rank have endeared him to legions of educators and parents:

> I am often asked whether an intelligence is the same thing as a talent or an ability. . . . I have no objection if one speaks about eight or nine talents or abilities, but I *do* object when an analyst calls some abilities (like language) "intelligences," and others (like music) "mere" talents. *All* should be called intelligences or talents; an unwarranted hierarchy among capacities must be avoided.[59]

Gardner often singles out music as an example of an intelligence that is all too often dismissed as "mere talent." This choice highlights the seminal bond between music and MI theory that is grounded in Gardner's own personal musical history; he was a serious enough pianist that he briefly considered pursuing it professionally. Instead, he landed at Harvard as a freshman in the fall of 1961 and was quickly drawn to the cognitive revolution, which was in full swing:

> I am often asked how I first got the idea of the theory of multiple intelligences. . . . As a young person, I was a serious pianist and enthusiastically involved with other arts as well. When I began to

study developmental and cognitive psychology, I was struck by the virtual absence of any mention of the arts. An early professional goal, then, was to find a place for the arts within academic psychology. I am still trying![60]

Gardner's rise to cultural prominence through MI theory was abetted by massive public support from individuals who displayed the very attributes that the psychological establishment of the time deemed outside the confines of g. Musicians, writers, performing and visual artists, inventors, and other creative thinkers found not a little of their own histories in statements such as this:

> In the heyday of the psychometric and behaviorist eras, it was generally believed that intelligence was a single entity that was inherited; and that human beings—initially a blank slate—could be trained to learn anything, provided that it was presented in an appropriate way. Nowadays an increasing number of researchers believe precisely the opposite; that there exists a multitude of intelligences, quite independent of each other; that each intelligence has its own strengths and constraints; that the mind is far from unencumbered at birth; and that it is unexpectedly difficult to teach things that go against early "naïve" theories or that challenge the natural lines of force within an intelligence and its matching domains.[61]

Even though MI theory corroborated what most educators had already observed through experience (i.e., that children learn differently from one another and that some children who do poorly in math or language may demonstrate brilliant abilities in other domains), the fact that a Harvard psychologist gave credence to these observations engendered a grassroots movement among teachers, parents, and learners that continues to this day despite the sheer difficulty of implementing MI principles in the classroom. The feasibility of teaching seven different intelligences in one classroom ranges from daunting to impossible for a public school classroom teacher in America, where the average class size is twenty-five students.[62]

But in a different setting, well known to musicians, implementation of MI principles can be regularly achieved. The standard music studio setup is based on one-on-one interaction so that music studio teachers provide pro forma what school districts call "individualized education plans," though it is hardly being labeled as such.

Nevertheless, at this moment in our national history, American music teachers inherit the products of the current standardized testing culture in their student clientele. Indeed, as children, they themselves were most likely tested by similar measures. Music teachers may find MI theory efficacious in predicting the training needs of those students who, for myriad reasons, score low on standardized tests, as well as those for whom such tests are easy. In both cases, because standard IQ tests measure knowledge gained at a particular moment in time, they can only provide a freeze-frame view of crystallized knowledge. They cannot assess or predict a person's ability to learn, to assimilate new information, or to solve new problems. Real learning takes place when students confront what cognitive psychologist Robert Bjork calls "desirable difficulties."[63] Conquering desirable difficulties demands a fluid response to instruction, not simply retrieval of prelearned information. On this basis alone, standardized and IQ tests are particularly useless when it comes to motor learning, the foundation upon which the acquisition of motor (or muscle) skill is built. Known by musicians as technique, this is the essential tool for singing or playing a musical instrument with expertise.

Although the cognitive revolution and the ensuing rejection of behaviorism was already two decades on by the time Gardner produced *Frames of Mind*, that schism had been cleaved within academe, so it was largely unfelt by average citizens. Conversely, Gardner's theory awoke potent qualms, particularly among members of the baby-boom generation, about how their own intelligences had been dichotomized, nurtured, or starved. Nagging doubts fed these parents' unease at watching their own children march through the seemingly unchanged behaviorist systems and psychometric testing procedures that had characterized their own schooling.

In the decades since the first publication of *Frames of Mind*, while the effects of the cognitive revolution continue to be felt, Gardner himself has since moved on to a number of other initiatives. He notes, with the calm distance of an elder statesman, that MI theory has so completely entered the culture that it has taken on a life of its own, perhaps outstripping its creator in name recognition. Even though *Frames of Mind* opened with this somewhat humble apologia, the idea of multiple intelligences is an old one, and I can scarcely claim any great originality for attempting to revive it once more. Even so, by featuring the word *idea* I want to underscore that the notion of multiple intelligences is hardly a proven scientific fact; it is, at most, an idea that has recently regained the right to be discussed seriously,[64]

the importance of Gardner's MI theory as a paradigm shift in the history of education in general, and in arts education in particular, cannot be overemphasized.

At about the same time that multiple intelligences were recognized as an idea whose time had come, another human trait, long shunned for most of the past century, was likewise restored to the panoply of human attributes worthy of scientific consideration. Brought in from the cold was banished emotion.

THE RESCUE OF EMOTION

"People did not think that after a century of rationalism, we needed to go from reason to emotion. And, of course, we do."—Antonio Damasio[65]

For much of the previous century, orthodox science had held that emotion was not only useless as a subject of research but downright seditious: emotion bewitched and muddled rational thought. Acclaimed neuroscientist Antonio Damasio led the charge to rescue emotion from exile and breached the wall of rationality with his landmark *Somatic Marker Hypothesis*, which proposed emotion as a central component in human decision-making. Far from a hero's welcome, however, Damasio recalled the mixture of consternation and utter disdain that greeted his theory in 1995: "I remember actually presenting my first paper on somatic marker hypothesis at the Society of Neuroscience. . . . There was one person in the first row that just shook his head and said, 'How can this poor guy be so wrong? You know, Why is he doing this?'"[66] and Damasio's colleagues worried that he had "gone off the deep end."[67] But the naysayers are now the poor guys who are so wrong, for emotion is now, as Damasio notes, "a huge field in neuroscience and everybody talks about it."[68]

Gardener's MI theory, most especially his personal intelligences component, was one harbinger of this change. Gardner made the case for the critical importance of intra- and interpersonal intelligences, not only toward the pursuit of life, liberty, and happiness, but because poor self-knowledge and lack of empathy can have such devastating consequences for the self and others. And while it may seem a kind of vindication for banished emotion that it has finally been deemed worthy of scientific scrutiny, we must acknowledge that science cannot wholly address our most meaningful questions. Science raises questions but cannot completely answer them—this is the "half-truth" of science. Where science falters, art begins.

THE OTHER HALF OF THE TRUTH

"The most exquisite stuff is what we can't explain. That's why we call it art."—Jonah Lehrer[69]

The third culture, as masterminded by Brockman, is not really the bridge of mutual comprehension between science and the humanities as envisioned by C. P. Snow but a one-way conduit of scientific information delivered by scientists themselves straight to an educated public. Wunderkind science writer Jonah Lehrer launched his meteoric career from this third culture platform, but noting the dearth of art, he posited the need for yet a fourth culture where science would concede that not everything can be known and would welcome a place at the table for the arts.[70] In his first book, Lehrer the provocateur even posited that certain artists (Proust, Cézanne, and others) actually "anticipated the discoveries of neuroscience" and, in doing so, "discovered truths about the human mind—real, tangible truths—that science is only now re-discovering. Their imaginations foretold the facts of the future."[71]

Before Lehrer was deposed for plagiarizing, he shared his third-culture perch with author Malcolm Gladwell.[72] Gladwell has made a lucrative career accessing science research and alchemizing it into such readable bestsellers as *The Tipping Point* (2000), *Blink* (2005), and *Outliers* (2008).[73] Similarly, author and inspirational speaker Daniel Pink enthusiastically declared "a seismic, though as yet undetected shift" away from "the age of left-brain dominance" and toward "creative and empathetic 'right-brain' thinkers," as explored in his bestselling book *A Whole New Mind* (originally subtitled *Moving from the Information Age to the Conceptual Age* and subsequently changed in paperback to *Why Right-Brainers Will Rule the Future*). If Pink is correct that we are poised at the dawn of a new "conceptual age," then people who can commandeer such distinctly human attributes as empathy and cooperation in service of problem-solving will soon eclipse those who are wedded to the kind of rational thinking that blocks creativity.[74] This optimistic viewpoint makes *A Whole New Mind*, in the words of one reviewer, "an encouraging graduation gift for liberal-arts graduates"— and, presumably, others who face similarly gloomy economic prospects, like musicians and visual artists.[75]

As optimistic as the projection for a rising creative age may be, as long as cultural and civic leaders remain (in Kohn's words) "marinated in behaviorism," it will take more time before we are no longer in thrall to science's "half truth," no longer chase rational thought as more highly evolved (and therefore more worthy) than emotion, and no longer spurn human capacities that are not expressed in mathematical equations or encapsulated in language. Performing artists who labor under these lagging cultural norms face double jeopardy, for they must also bear the legacy of dualistic thinking: the mind-body split.

THE MIND-BODY PROBLEM

If consciousness beckons researchers as the Holy Grail of brain science, the mind-body problem is its Rosetta stone. The ancient mind-body problem, the belief that the mind (or soul, depending upon one's perspective) is a entity separate from the body, was codified in modern Western thought most famously via seventeenth-century philosopher René Descartes's dictum "Ego cogito, ergo sum." This mind-body dualism was a bedrock of Western culture for centuries until it began to dissolve with the advent of neuroscience. Each new revelation about the biological bases for mental phenomena has added to the inexorable transformation of Descartes's dualistic "I think, therefore I am" paradigm to the new mantra of brain science: "The mind is what the brain does."[76]

As apparent as this new paradigm is to those on the forefront of brain science, performing artists and athletes who inhabit the realm of the body still await the full flowering of Pink's conceptual age, heirs as they are to the mind-body problem and its related prejudices, as Gardner notes:

> This divorce between the "mental" and the "physical" has not infrequently been coupled with a notion that what we do with our bodies is somehow less privileged, less special, than those problem-solving routines carried out chiefly through the use of language, logic, or some relatively abstract symbolic system.[77]

This "divorce" is a hallmark of Western culture, its corollary, the notion that the mind is a wise overlord, steeled by eternal principles to overrule the transitory passions to which the body is enslaved. Likewise, the devaluation of the body's output as "mere skill" versus the "noble" work of the mind has ancient roots in Western culture. The sixth-century Roman philosopher Boethius, in his treatise on music, likened the work of the performing musician to that of a mere artisan and thus a slave of the body. By contrast, the theoretician who considered music solely with his mind, without the taint of actually touching an instrument, was the true musician:

> Every art and discipline ought naturally to be considered of a more honorable character than a skill which is exercised with the hand and labor of a craftsman. For it is much better and nobler to know about what someone else is doing than to be doing that for which someone else is the authority. For the mere physical skill serves as a slave, while the reason governs all as sovereign. And unless the hand acts according to the will of reason, the thing is done in vain. Thus how much nobler is the study of music as a rational science than as a laborious skill of manufacturing sounds! It is nobler to the degree that the mind is nobler than the body.[78]

This attitude has seeped by cultural osmosis into the modern Western world. It explains, for example, the initial reluctance of some American Ivy-League colleges to introduce applied arts into their curricula, a move fought by some in academia long before the advent of such educational schemes as experiential learning and still periodically renewed to prevent encroachment on STEM and other supposedly practical subjects.[79] A defense of art for art's sake is perceived as weak when set against the potent argument of practicality, making art perennially vulnerable to the strange bedfellow of science as its paramour.

NEUROAESTHETICS

Perhaps we are no longer on the verge of a fourth culture, a unifying of science and art, but squarely in it, as evidenced by the rapidly rising new field of *neuroaesthetics*, defined as "the scientific study of the neural bases for the contemplation and creation of a work of art."[80]

The emergence of this field is no surprise, for, as Brooks notes, "there's 'neural' this and that, basically 'neural' everything."[81] As a more concrete and scientific rejoinder to Lehrer's assertion that "art got there first," this new discipline seeks to uncover why we create and enjoy art.[82] The field's inception in the visual realm has a simple explanation: much of our brain real estate is devoted to sight. But the emergence of a neuroaesthetic lens applied to all the arts, from poetry to dance to music, is underway. For example, the Society for Music Perception and Cognition, as its name suggests, is chiefly concerned with music perception (how we experience music) and what we do with those impressions—that is, how we cognitively process them.[83]

For those who view attempts to peer into the mind as it experiences our most sublime creations as either a heinous violation of the soul or an obtuse attempt to quantify the ineffable, Semir Zeki, a founder of neuroaesthetics, has this cautionary piece of advice: "It's a bit like the guys who said to Galileo, 'We'd rather not look through your telescope.'"[84]

If this admonition sounds familiar, it is simply a recapitulation of C. P. Snow's rebuke, Brockman's third culture initiative, and Wilson's one-sided consilience. And while all these initiatives were presented as invitations to a marriage between equals, in the final analysis, they were not propositions for fruitful cohabitation but rationales for the legitimization of art by science. In the witty words of D. Graham Burnett, artists should beware scientists who come a-courtin' and bearing bridges "for the message comes through clearly: Let us build a bridge . . . and take over your island."[85]

And lest we artists believe that, in such a scenario, all potential humanist conquests would fend off such advances virtuously, literary scholar Curtis D. Carbonell astutely observes (channeling Freud), "There are those in the humanities who suffer from science envy."[86] It should be acknowledged that Carbonell, like Zeki and Burnett, belongs to Brockman's "mandarin class," engaging in what academics do best: sparring with each other. Still the main achievement of the third culture has been to hurdle over the traditional gatekeepers of knowledge, an accomplishment almost unimaginable before the advent of the Internet. Third culture delivers knowledge straight to the people—albeit a public that, Zeki warns, "is getting more and more savvy about the brain."[87] Read: If artists want to remain relevant, just embrace science, already!

To be sure, there are scientists who are looking to art for the same reason. In a highly publicized experiment on jazz musicians, researchers at Johns Hopkins University sought to "investigate the neural substrates that underlie spontaneous musical performance" (although no one impugned *their* curiosity as music envy, except for a passing confession by the head researcher to the idolization of jazz saxophonist John Coltrane).[88] The researchers used fMRI imaging to discover that, during improvisation, brain regions typically associated with self-monitoring and self-evaluation calmed down, while brain areas associated with self-expression lit up. One wonders, Is this news? The researchers reported—apparently straight-faced—that

> in short, musical creativity vis-à-vis improvisation may be a result of the combination of intentional, internally generated self-expression . . . with the suspension of self-monitoring and related processes . . . that typically regulate conscious control of goal-directed, predictable, or planned actions.[89]

The researchers concluded that "creative intuition" springs forth when brain regions typically associated with self-monitoring quiet down, "allowing unfiltered, unconscious, or random thoughts and sensations to emerge."[90] This conclusion will surprise no one who regularly practices creativity, for such people understand that creativity is accessed through a fund of emotion and experience, unsifted by worries and what-ifs. As critic Russell Blackford summarily avers,

cognitive neuroscience [is] not about to put the humanities, in particular, out of business. At this stage, there is a banality in attempts to
produce illuminating comment about the arts based on evolutionary
considerations.[91]

Indeed, to many practicing musicians, scientific discoveries that periodically issue forth from cognitive neuroscience may be nothing more
than mildly amusing, while to others, it may be thrilling to view the
technicolor fMRI images that seem to verify phenomena already experienced. Either way, such discoveries should give artists pause because
art does not need science to validate or substantiate it. It would be-
hoove us all to restate this essential stance at the gathering edges of a
fourth culture, a culture in which, take note, the new science of mind
has already staked out a sizeable claim.

CAUTIOUS ENCHANTMENT

Science itself occupies a privileged position within our society as a ven-
erated fount of knowledge, and American psychology—whose modern
form owes its entire existence to "science envy"—is nothing less than
Herman's "veritable worldview."[92] If the recent past offers any admonition, it is that art must take its place as a stakeholder in the fourth
culture for while science pursues knowledge for its own sake, it is the
humanities that illuminate that knowledge with meaning. That the new
science of mind might provide an arena for an outright unification of
the arts and sciences is debatable. As Blackford notes,

> there are good reasons why the natural sciences cannot provide a
> substitute for humanistic explanation, even if we obtain a far deeper
> understanding of our own genetic and neurophysiological make-up.
> This is partly because reductive science is ill-equipped to deal with
> the particularity of complex events, partly because causal explanation
> may not be all that we want, anyway, when we try to interpret and
> clarify human experience.[93]

Scientists, as Gardner notes, are guided by "beliefs about how the universe must work, and basic convictions about how these principles are
best revealed."[94] By contrast, artists thrive in the gray area that enve-

lopes the black-and-white answers that scientists pursue. Artists, like scientists, are stimulated by mystery; both artists and scientists question and seek passionately to know. Yet, unlike scientists, the artist's role in society is to broach and explore profound questions, not to definitively answer them. As the great choreographer Agnes de Mille once said,

> Living is a form of not being sure, not knowing what next, or how. The moment you know how, you begin to die a little. The artist never entirely knows. We guess. We may be wrong, but we take leap after leap in the dark. [95]

To inhabit the realm of inquiry, whether scientist or artist, is to situate oneself in the midst of de Mille's dark yet dynamic place. Certainly this is the embarkation point for both scientist and artist. But the scientist's journey is dictated by the exacting choreography of the scientific five-step method, from initial impulse (hypothesis) to the finale (conclusion).

The artist's role by contrast is one of neither repose nor conclusion; the artist's role is fulfilled, at least in part, by simply operating within the realm of inquiry. In the words of esteemed neuroscientist Eric Kandel,

> It is important to be bold. One should tackle difficult problems, especially those that initially appear messy and unstructured. One should not fear trying new things, such as moving from one field to another or working at the boundaries of disciplines—where the most interesting problems often emerge. [96]

One need not be an expert to experiment between the boundaries of art and science. From any angle, it will take creative minds to engage the discoveries made there.

NOTES

1. Howard Gardner, *The Mind's New Science: A History of the Cognitive Revolution* (New York: Basic Books, 1985), 14.

2. Steven Pinker, "The Cognitive Revolution," *Harvard Gazette*, October 12, 2011, http://news.harvard.edu/gazette/story/multimedia/the-cognitive-revolution/. "The Cognitive Revolution, which took place at Harvard, was the start

of the modern scientific study of the mind. . . . [T]he school of behaviorism came to take over American psychology until the early 1950s when a number of scholars with ties to Harvard started to rethink that whole idea."

3. Jonah Lehrer, "Hearts & Minds," *Boston Globe*, April 29, 2007, www.boston.com/news/globe/ideas/articles/2007/04/29/hearts__minds.

4. George Mandler, "Origins of the Cognitive (R)Evolution," *Journal of History of the Behavioral Sciences* 38, no. 4 (Fall 2002): 339–53; see also Robert Proctor and Kim-Phuong L. Vu, "The Cognitive Revolution at Age 50: Has the Promise of the Human Information-Processing Approach Been Fulfilled?" *International Journal of Human Computer Interaction* 21, no. 3 (2006): 253–84.

5. George Miller, "The Cognitive Revolution: A Historical Perspective," *Trends in Cognitive Sciences* 7, no. 3 (March 2003): 142.

6. Thomas H. Leahey, "The Mythical Revolutions of American Psychology," *American Psychologist* 47, no. 2 (February 1992): 316.

7. Roddy Roediger, "What Happened to Behaviorism?" *Observer*, March 2004, www.psychologicalscience.org/observer/getArticle.cfm?id=1540.

8. Michel Legrand, "Du behaviorisme au cognitivisme," *L'annee psychologique* 90, no. 2 (1990): 248.

9. Ellen Herman, *The Romance of American Psychology* (Berkeley: University of California Press, 1995), 9.

10. Ibid., 1.

11. Daniel Robinson, *An Intellectual History of Psychology*, 3rd ed. (Madison: University of Wisconsin Press, 1995), 338.

12. Ibid., 342.

13. Kurt Koffka, *Principles of Gestalt Psychology* (New York: Harcourt Brace Jovanovich, 1935), 18.

14. Ibid., 8.

15. Robinson, *Intellectual History of Psychology*, 37.

16. See Penn Arts & Sciences, "Learned Helplessness Research," Positive Psychology Center, https://ppc.sas.upenn.edu/research/learned-helplessness.

17. Joseph LeDoux, *Synaptic Self: How Our Brains Become Who We Are* (New York: Penguin, 2002), 23.

18. Alfie Kohn, "Newt Gingrich's Reading Plan," *Education Week*, April 19, 1995, www.alfiekohn.org/article/newt-gingrichs-reading-plan/.

19. Po Bronson, "How Not to Talk to Your Kids: The Inverse Power of Praise," *New York Magazine*, February 11, 2007, http://nymag.com/news/features/27840/.

20. Jamie Cohen-Cole, "Instituting the Science of Mind: Intellectual Economies and Disciplinary Exchange at Harvard's Center for Cognitive Studies," *British Journal for the History of Science* 40, no. 4 (December 2007): 586.

21. Alfie Kohn, "Supernanny State," *The Nation*, May 23, 2005, www.thenation.com/article/supernanny-state.

22. See Gardner, *Mind's New Science*; and LeDoux, *Synaptic Self*, 23.

23. James S. Albus et al., "A Proposal for a Decade of the Mind Initiative," *Science* 317, no. 7 (September 2007): 1321.

24. David Brooks, "The Social Animal," TED Talk, March 2011, http://blog.ted.com/2011/03/14/the-social-animal-david-brooks-on-ted-com/.

25. Justin Barrett, "A Cognitive Revolution? Which Cognitive Revolution?" *The Immanent Frame*, July 18, 2008, http://blogs.ssrc.org/tif/2008/07/18/which-cognitive-revolution/.

26. Leahey, "Mythical Revolutions."

27. Quoted in Lehrer, "Hearts & Minds."

28. B. F. Skinner, *A Matter of Consequences: Part Three of an Autobiography* (New York: Knopf, 1983), 411.

29. Quoted in Robin Dougherty, "Between the Lines with Steven Pinker: Part of a Golden Age of Science Writing," *Boston Globe*, December 26, 2004.

30. Alston Chase, *Harvard and the Unabomber: The Education of an American Terrorist,* (New York: W. W. Norton, 2003).

31. Quoted in Dougherty, "Between the Lines."

32. Quoted in Alston Chase, "Harvard and the Making of the Unabomber," *Atlantic Monthly*, June 2000.

33. Chase, *Harvard and the Unabomber*, 257.

34. Herman, *Romance of American Psychology*, 126.

35. Sage Stossel, "The Disease of the Modern Era," interview with Alston Chase, *Atlantic Unbound*, May 20, 2003.

36. Suzanne Cusick, "'You Are in a Place That Is Out of the World . . .' Music in the Detention Camps of the 'Global War on Terror,'" *Journal of the Society for American Music* 2, no. 1 (2008): 3–4.

37. Jane Mayer, *The Dark Side: The Inside Story of How the War on Terror Turned into a War on American Ideals* (New York: Doubleday, 2008).

38. See Suzanne Cusick, "Music as Torture/Music as Weapon," *TRANS-Transcultural Music Review* 10, article 11 (2006), www.sibetrans.com/trans/trans10/ cusick_eng.htm.

39. Oliver Sacks, *Musicophilia: Tales of Music and the Brain* (New York: Alfred A. Knopf, 2007), 41.

40. BBC, "Sesame Street Breaks Iraqi POWs," May 20, 2003, http://news.bbc.co.uk/2/hi/middle_east/3042907.stm.

41. Grant Hilary Brenner, MD, "The Expected Psychiatric Impact of Detention in Guantánamo Bay, Cuba, and Related Considerations," *Journal of Trauma & Dissociation* 11, no. 4 (2010): 469–87; see also Vincent Iacopino and Stephen N. Demakis, "Neglect of Medical Evidence of Torture in

Guantánamo Bay: A Case Series," *PLoS Medicine* 8, no. 4 (2011), http://dx.doi.org/10.1371%2Fjournal.pmed.1001027.

42. "U.S. Bands Blast Use of Music in Guantánamo Interrogations," https://web.archive.org/web/20091025152431/http://news.yahoo.com/s/afp/usattack-sguantanamomusicprisoners.

43. See National Security Archive, "Musicians Seek Secret U.S. Documents on Music-Related Human Rights Abuses at Guantánamo," October 22, 2009, https://nsarchive2.gwu.edu//news/20091022/index.htm; Sam Stein, "Music Stars Demand Records on Bush Administration's Use of Music for Torture," Huffington Post, October 21, 2009, www.huffingtonpost.com/2009/10/21/music-stars-demand-record_n_329476.html; and Joe Heim, "Torture Songs Spur a Protest Most Vocal: Musicians Call for Records on Guantánamo Detainee Treatment," *Washington Post*, October 22, 2009, www.washingtonpost.com/wp-dyn/content/article/2009/10/21/AR2009102103743.html.

44. D. Graham Burnett, "A View from the Bridge: The Two Cultures Debate, Its Legacy, and the History of Science," *Daedalus* 128, no. 2 (Spring 1999):196.

45. Thomas Pynchon, "Is It O.K. to Be a Luddite?" *New York Times Book Review*, October 28, 1984, www.nytimes.com/books/97/05/18/reviews/pynchon-luddite.html.

46. C. P. Snow, *The Two Cultures and the Scientific Revolution* (Cambridge: Cambridge University Press, 1961), 4.

47. Ibid., 15–16.

48. Ibid., 12.

49. Burnett, "View from the Bridge," 199.

50. Ibid., 196.

51. Snow, *The Two Cultures: And a Second Look, An Expanded Version of the Two Cultures and the Scientific Revolution* (Cambridge: Cambridge University Press, 1964).

52. John Brockman, "The Third Culture," Edge.org, September 9, 1991, www.edge.org/conversation/john_brockman-the-third-culture.

53. John Brockman, "About Edge.org," Edge.org, http://edge.org/about-us.

54. E. O. Wilson, *Consilience: The Unity of Knowledge* (New York: Alfred A. Knopf, 1998).

55. Brockman, "About Edge.org."

56. Howard Gardner, *Multiple Intelligences: New Horizons in Theory and Practice* (New York: Basic Books, 2006), 26.

57. Jeffrey A. Schaler, ed., *Howard Gardner under Fire: The Rebel Psychologist Faces His Critics* (Peru, IL: Open Court, 2006).

58. Howard Gardner, *Frames of Mind: The Theory of Multiple Intelligences*, 20th-anniversary ed. (New York: Basic Books, 2004), xiv–xv.

59. Howard Gardner, *Intelligence Reframed* (New York: Basic Books, 1999), 83.

60. Gardner, *Frames of Mind*, xiii.

61. Ibid., xxxiii.

62. Sarah D. Sparks, "Class-Size Limits Targeted for Cuts," *Education Week* 30, no. 13 (December 2010): 1–16.

63. Robert A. Bjork, "Memory and Metamemory Considerations in the Training of Human Beings," in *Metacognition: Knowing about Knowing*, ed. Janet Metcalfe and Arthur Shimamura, 185–205 (Cambridge, MA: MIT Press, 1994).

64. Gardner, *Frames of Mind*, 11.

65. Antonio Damasio, "This Time with Feeling," YouTube, July 4, 2009, www.youtube.com/watch?v=IifXMd26gWE.

66. Ibid.

67. Ibid.

68. Ibid.

69. Jonah Lehrer, "Our Inner Artist," *Washington Post Book World*, January 11, 2009, T8.

70. Jonah Lehrer, *Proust Was a Neuroscientist* (New York: Houghton Mifflin, 2008), 196–97.

71. Ibid., vii.

72. Josh Levin, "Why Did Jonah Lehrer Plagiarize Himself?" Slate, June 19, 2012, www.slate.com/articles/life/culturebox/2012/06/jonah_lehrer_self_plagiarism_the_new_yorker_staffer_stopped_being_a_writer_and_became_an_idea_man_.html. Note that Lehrer's publisher, Houghton Mifflin Harcourt, publisher of all three of Lehrer's books, pulled the third (*Imagine*) from publication and offered refunds on the second (*How We Decide*) yet conducted a postpublication review of Lehrer's first book, *Proust Was a Neuroscientist* and, not uncovering any problems, decided to keep it in print. See Michael Moynihan, "Publisher Pulls Jonah Lehrer's 'How We Decide' from Stores," Daily Beast, updated July 12, 2017, www.thedailybeast.com/publisher-pulls-jonah-lehrers-how-we-decide-from-stores.

73. Malcolm Gladwell, *The Tipping Point: How Little Things Can Make a Big Difference* (New York: Little, Brown, 2000); Malcolm Gladwell, *Blink: The Power of Thinking without Thinking* (New York: Little, Brown, 2005); and Malcolm Gladwell, *Outliers: The Story of Success* (New York: Little, Brown, 2008).

74. Daniel Pink, *A Whole New Mind: Moving from the Information Age to the Conceptual Age* (New York: Penguin, 2005).

75. Daniel McGinn and Jennifer Barrett Ozols, "Quick Read," *Newsweek*, April 17, 2005, www.thedailybeast.com/newsweek/2005/04/17/quick-read.html.

76. Steven Pinker, *How the Mind Works* (New York: W. W. Norton, 1999), 24.

77. Gardner, *Frames of Mind*, 208.

78. Anicius Manlius Severinus Boethius, "What a Musician Is," *De institutione musica*, in *Music Theory Translation Series: Fundamentals of Music*, trans. Calvin M. Bower, ed. Claude V. Palisca (New Haven, CT: Yale University Press, 1989), 50–51.

79. Jacques Barzun, professor emeritus and former dean of the faculties and provost of Columbia University, in "Trim the College?—A Utopia!" (*Chronicle Review*, June 22, 2001), wrote,

> But what of the student whose interest lies in an area like film and theater, art and music, photography and television, and who wants to "qualify" for a job the day after graduation? Let there be a School of Applied Arts on campus or at the nearest university, similar to business and journalism schools. The applied arts are not college work; the very scheduling of long hours of practice makes for conflicts with other studies.

80. Suzanne Nalbantian, "Neuroaesthetics: Neuroscientific Theory and Illustration from the Arts," *Interdisciplinary Science Reviews* 33, no. 4 (December 2008): 357–68.

81. David Brooks, "The Best Books on Neuroscience: Recommended by David Brooks," Five Books, October 8, 2009, https://fivebooks.com/best-books/david-brooks-neuroscience/.

82. Jonah Lehrer, *Proust Was a Neuroscientist*, press release, www.houghtonmifflinbooks.com/booksellers/press_release/lehrer/.

83. Society for Music Perception and Cognition, 2019, www.musicperception.org/.

84. Quoted in Alexander C. Kafka, "Eric Kandel's Visions," *Chronicle Review*, March 11, 2012, http://chronicle.com/article/Eric-Kandels-Visions/131095/.

85. Burnett, "View from the Bridge," 214.

86. Curtis D. Carbonell, "The Third Culture," Institute for Ethics and Emerging Technologies, November 22, 2010, http://ieet.org/index.php/IEET/more/4334.

87. Quoted in Kafka, "Eric Kandel's Visions."

88. Charles Limb and Allen R. Braun, "Neural Substrates of Spontaneous Musical Performance: An fMRI Study of Jazz Improvisation," *PLoS ONE* 3, no. 2 (February 2008): 1–9, www.plosone.org/article/info:doi%2F10.1371%2Fjournal.pone.0001679.

89. Ibid., 5.

90. Ibid., 4.

91. Russell Blackford, "Will Science Put the Humanities Out of Business?" Institute for Ethics and Emerging Technologies, November 12, 2010, http://ieet.org/index.php/IEET/more/4315.

92. Herman, *Romance of American Psychology*, 4.

93. Blackford, "Will Science?"

94. Gardner, *Frames of Mind*, 150.

95. Jane Howard, "A Book and Show for Agnes de Mille, the Grande Dame of Dance," *Life*, November 15, 1963, 89–94.

96. Eric R. Kandel, "The New Science of Mind," *New York Times*, September 6, 2013, www.nytimes.com/2013/09/08/opinion/sunday/the-new-science-of-mind.html.

2

GROUNDWORK

At the Foothills

NEUROMYTHS AND BRAINSCAMS

Experts on the brain and cognition generally agree on the characterization of the brain as the most complex object in the known universe.[1] Neuroscientist and Nobel Prize winner Eric Kandel summarizes the journey ahead: "As we enter the 21st century, the new science of mind faces remarkable challenges. Researchers . . . are only standing at the foothills of a great mountain range."[2]

Yet these cautions have done little to quell the hyped-up neuromyths fueling so-called brainscams that boost the sale of questionable products, feeding outsize expectations about neuroscience while simultaneously obfuscating its marvelous revelations.[3] It just so happens that one of the most infamous neuromyths of all time involved one of the most famous musicians of all time: Wolfgang Amadeus Mozart.

The Mozart effect—the myth that merely listening to classical music makes you smarter—took off during the brain-obsessed 1990s, when poor Mozart was virtually exhumed, remixed, and exploited by savvy marketers peddling brainy-baby products (images of headphones strapped to pregnant bellies may come to mind). Even though the Mozart effect was eventually revealed to be a sham, this myth has exhibited remarkable staying power. As noted in the introduction to this book, 88 percent of American adults surveyed agreed with this statement: "Participating in school music corresponds with better grades/test scores."[4] Critically, the action here is *participating in*, not *listening to*, and indeed, some modest gains in cognitive development have been demonstrated in children who take music lessons and actually make music.

In this chapter, I explore some of the most exciting findings in recent research on music and cognitive development that promise benefits far more sustainable and profound than boosted test scores. But before I do, I must first consider how the myth of the Mozart effect yet haunts our culture and the effects of this haunting, which are not benign. It has corrupted how we value music, blinding us to its true worth while simultaneously tainting our understanding of how learning really works. Musicians should understand these ramifications and be properly prepared to champion our art both onstage and throughout our communities.

IN THE SHADOW OF THE MOZART EFFECT

The story of the Mozart effect begins in 1993, when researchers Francis Rauscher, Gordon Shaw, and Katherine Ky published a one-page paper in the journal *Nature*. They describe their experiment in which a small cohort of thirty-six college students showed a modest improvement in a spatial task after they listened to a Mozart piano sonata (as compared to silence or a "relaxation tape").[5] This modest improvement was not permanent or even long-lasting: it disappeared after fifteen minutes. Nevertheless, Rauscher and her colleagues submitted the paper for peer review. They were not prepared for what happened next:

> The first call came from the Associated Press before I even knew the paper was coming out. And then, all of a sudden, once it broke in the Associated Press, it was everywhere. I mean, we had people coming to our house and interviewing us for live television. I had to hire somebody to handle all the calls that were coming in.[6]

In the rush of media attention, Rauscher's findings were christened with the catchy headline "The Mozart Effect," a name neither Rauscher nor her team invented. Like the children's gossip game of telephone, key elements of the Rauscher team's study were transformed with each successive report. Their original results rapidly ballooned from a modest gain in one small parameter of brain function (the ability to mentally rotate images) to nothing less than overall intelligence, or g. The target group that supposedly benefitted from exposure to classical music morphed from a tiny collection of American college students to children, then infants, then even to the unborn. By 1998, even government officials had bought into the hype: Governor Zell Miller of Georgia successfully lobbied his state legislature to fund a giveaway program of classical music CDs to every newborn in the state of Georgia.[7] The state legislature of Florida mandated classical music be played daily in all childcare and early educational programs that received state funding.[8]

Entrepreneurs soon seized upon these ideas. Self-styled "author, lecturer, and musician" Don Campbell snatched the term *The Mozart Effect* and rushed to claim copyright. He published a book under the copyrighted name and developed CDs and other products that he claimed held music's "transformational power" to "heal the body" and "strengthen the mind," all "at the speed of sound."[9] (Note that Campbell's fortunes were largely made possible by snaffling copyright-free music from the public domain.)

The same year that Campbell's book appeared, the husband-and-wife team of William Clark and Julie Aigner-Clark shot a home video in their basement and from that humble beginning launched a line of CDs and videos with names like "Baby Mozart," furthering the notion that babies listening to this music—even in utero—could increase their g quotient. By the time the Clarks sold off "Baby Einstein" to the Walt Disney Company in 2001, sales had reached over $17 million.[10]

Despite the whiff of snake oil surrounding these ventures, we might wonder, what is the real harm here? Even if there is no scientifically proven cognitive benefit to hearing classical music, you may agree with Ms. Aigner-Clark's "lesser of two evils" reasoning when confronted with the evidence. "A child is better off listening to Beethoven while watching images of a puppet than seeing any reality show that I can think of," she bristled.[11] In other words, even if the kids are plugged into an electronic babysitter, at least that babysitter is regurgitating classical music and not Nine Inch Nails! But apparently even this kind of reasoning can get you into hot water, as Frances Rauscher discovered when she implied that rock music is toxic to cognitive development: "I started getting phone calls, literally death threats, from people that were so offended that I would say that rock music was bad for the brain. So I had to get an unlisted number. It was crazy."[12]

It is no wonder that researchers who study the cognitive effects of listening to music are wary of how reporters may misinterpret their findings and twist results into catchy headlines that bear little relation to the original studies: not only can such results be skewed for profit, they can also elicit death threats and even get you sued. In the case of the Clarks, two cognitive studies conducted at the University of Washington take direct aim at Baby Einstein:

> Despite marketing claims, parents who want to give their infants a boost in learning language probably should limit the amount of time they expose their children to DVDs and videos such as "Baby Einstein" and "Brainy Baby." Rather than helping babies, the over-use of such productions actually may slow down infants eight to 16 months of age when it comes to acquiring vocabulary.[13]

For good measure, the lead author on the study adds, "There is no clear evidence of a benefit coming from baby DVDs and videos and there is some suggestion of harm."[14]

Incensed, the Clarks sued the University of Washington to release details from the studies, claiming that the study denigrated their life's work (not to mention deflating "Baby Einstein" sales figures). Not only did the couple win, but the university had to cough up a portion of the Clarks' legal fees.[15] The Disney company, under threat of a class-action lawsuit charging that Baby Einstein products had been fraudulently marketed as educational, offered full refunds to customers.[16]

Meanwhile, back in the scientific community, the Mozart effect, which had met with immediate skepticism originally, was forthwith subject to intense scrutiny. A meta-analysis of many duplicate trials of the Mozart effect concluded that "any cognitive enhancement is small and does not reflect any change in IQ or reasoning ability in general."[17] The several studies that did manage to connect music to verifiably enhanced cognitive abilities concluded that any observable increase in spatial task performance was due to "arousal."[18] In other words, music made the test-takers feel good, so they performed better. This result has been replicated with many different genres of music so that Rauscher, when queried about the arousal effect, was able to throw a bone to the die-hard rock fans who had earlier wanted her head on a platter: "I think the key to it is, you have to enjoy the music. If you love Pearl Jam, you're going to find a Pearl Jam effect."[19]

So what if the Mozart effect was a sham? Is there harm, or even crime, in manipulating scientific research that later turns out to be untrue? Were Mr. Campbell, the Clarks, and others who profited from Rauscher's research just savvy entrepreneurs who nevertheless may have actually believed the hype? And regardless of whether pseudoscience is merely annoying or truly harmful, did we really need a psychology test to tell us that the music we like can move our emotions and put a spring in our step? Of course not. But all the hype, the marketing, and the flurry of counterresearch that surrounded the Mozart effect produced such a din that it effectively drowned out the most valuable finding revealed in the years shortly following Rauscher's original publication: there probably is some cognitive benefit to be gained from music instruction—from actually *making* music—as researchers like Schellenberg, Kraus, and others have endeavored to show.[20]

And here is where we must consider this myth's deepest harm: it falsely legitimized the notion of exposure. As demonstrated throughout this book, a fundamental tenet of all learning is that the learned thing must be actually experienced. Exposure is not learning. Given the reach and staying power of the Mozart effect myth, it is a very good bet that some portion of that 88 percent of parents referenced in the survey confused and conflated exposure with experience. You will revisit the damage to learning that this conflation causes and also consider its damage to policy-makers' decisions later in this chapter. But first, let us track this scientific legend so that we might understand its tenacity.

TRACKING A SCIENTIFIC LEGEND

Social science researchers Adrian Bangerter and Chip Heath define a "scientific legend" as "a widespread belief . . . that propagates in society, originally arising from scientific study, but that has been transformed to deviate in essential ways from the understanding of scientists."[21]

They tracked the evolution of the Mozart effect legend in three ways: first, they charted how the Mozart effect's fortunes rose and fell in the news media in close relation to similar topics like education and early childhood development. Second, they demonstrated that the Mozart effect was more widely propagated in states where primary education and childhood development were of grave concern. Finally, they demonstrated that the Mozart effect "mutated over time" and that the media "overextended the scientific findings to new, untested populations."[22] In other words, Bangerter and Heath showed how the original test subjects (college students) magically morphed in the press into babies and how spatial task performance was grossly inflated to include *all* intelligence.

Scientific legends are propagated by societal vectors and amplified by valid science. In the 1990s, the societal vectors that fed the Mozart effect included concern over the state of education in public schools and parental anxiety about raising children in an increasingly complex (and seemingly dangerous) world.

The science that fed the Mozart effect was the entwined discovery of neurogenesis and neuroplasticity, which overturned a century's worth of *fixed-brain theory*, the notion that the brain cells (*neurons*) with which we are born cannot regenerate. Unrelated scientific teams working around the globe almost simultaneously discovered that, not only is the human brain malleable (*plastic*), but it is capable of producing new brain cells right up to the moment of death.[23] Fixed-brain theory was laid to rest as we rolled into the new millennium, although that knowledge had not yet reached the general public in the 1990s. But the discovery of *synaptic pruning* had.

Groundbreaking neuroscience from the 1980s and 1990s had revealed that an infant's brain comes preinstalled with a bushy overgrowth of neuronal connections (*synapses*) and therefore develops by actually reducing, not growing more, connections. The popular press ran with this information, and soon fanciful renderings of babies' brains likened to overgrown trees appeared, appended with unsettling images of novice parents clumsily wielding gargantuan pruning shears.

At the same time, news of a so-called critical window or critical period of brain development broke into the popular consciousness, revealing that the first three years of an infant's life were crucial for brain development. Yet without the good news of neurogenesis and neuroplasticity, the combination of synaptic pruning and the critical window theory resulted in a frightening message: if pruning during this critical period were botched, it could hold permanent and disastrous consequences throughout the life of the child.

This barrage of scientific and pseudoscientific brain news coupled with arresting brain images and hyped-up parental anxiety all collided during the 1990s, inflaming media coverage of the Mozart effect and galvanizing child welfare activists, whose calls for early intervention garnered national attention. In the spring of 1997, First Lady Hillary Clinton hosted a White House conference on early childhood development and learning. The keynote speaker for this event, actor and child activist Rob Reiner, sounded the alarm for the "critical period" of development:

> If we want to have a real significant impact, not only on children's success in school and later on in life, healthy relationships, but also an impact on reduction in crime, teen pregnancy, drug abuse, child abuse, welfare, homelessness, and a variety of other social ills, we are going to have to address the first three years of life. There is no getting around it. All roads lead to Rome.[24]

The same year, Reiner created the I Am Your Child foundation and spearheaded the campaign to pass Proposition 10 in California (later named the California Children and Families First Act), which diverts a percentage of the sales tax on tobacco products toward early childhood programs based on the "determination" that "a child's first three years are the most critical in brain development."[25]

At the same time, another nonprofit organization, originally founded in 1977 and dedicated to child development, Zero to Three, gained traction. The current aims of Zero to Three are to "provide parents, professionals and policymakers the knowledge and the know-how to nurture early development" because, they claim, "neuroscientists have documented that the earliest days, weeks and months of life are a period of unparalleled growth when trillions of brain cell connections are made."[26]

As well-meaning as all these initiatives are, experts caution that, when the topic is the human brain, the issues are far more nuanced and complex than can be covered by journalists on a deadline or by activists and politicians who have little patience for verifying their beliefs through the slow work of science.

One of the more prominent critics of the first-three-years theory is John Bruer, a leading figure in the fields of cognitive neuroscience and education policy and author of *The Myth of the First Three Years*.[27]

Bruer convincingly argues that Proposition 10, Zero to Three, and the like all ironically evince a "strong formulation of the thesis of *infant determinism* [which is] the doctrine that early childhood experiences have irreversible, lifelong effects." Bruer cites evidence from an opposing viewpoint, *indeterminism*, which offers "a view of child development that emphasizes long-term complexity":

> The first steps on life's path are important, but still leave many routes open to diverse outcomes. This indeterminist thesis is relatively unpopular in policy, parenting, and even some academic circles. . . . [Indeterminist] research has indicated that children are highly resilient and show remarkable recovery from early privation, if their life circumstances improve.[28]

At its core, the indeterminist view promotes plasticity and is actually highly optimistic. Despite this, Bruer projects that it is "unlikely to turn the popular pro-determinism tidal wave."[29] And this helps explain why the myth of the Mozart effect is yet so enduring. Set against a sea of parental angst about getting the first three years "right," the idea that Mozart's music can be served up daily, right alongside the milk and gummy vitamins, is alluring because it is so easy. The Mozart effect is simply an inexpensive insurance policy even if it proves to be wrong, so what's the harm in trying? In this light, there is certainly no harm to supper served up with a savory side of Mozart's *Eine Kleine Nachtmusik*. And if this is all the child ever experiences of music, it is perhaps nothing more than a missed opportunity. Perhaps. The trouble comes when experience becomes confused with engagement. The enduring harm of the Mozart effect is that it spawned the neuromyth of exposure.

EXPOSURE IS NOT LEARNING

A buzzword that often connects music and childhood education is *exposure*. I play Mozart during mealtimes to expose my family to high art. If I allow my child to bring home a shiny trumpet from the school band program and he later loses interest, well, at least he was exposed—right?

A basic tenet of learning from the field of cognitive science holds that a thing is truly learned as evidenced by its repeatability. This is true for both facts and muscular movement. While exposure may be the necessary first step in the learning process, it must be followed by practice in order to encode it in memory and make it habitual. Just as musicians need not be convinced of the value of music instruction or advised that music arouses emotion, we need no convincing to agree that learning an instrument—any instrument—requires physical engagement; it is no wonder that many music schools have dubbed their performance studies curriculum "applied music." But the exposure account implies that, by simply allowing ourselves to be passive receptacles for tonal vibrations or letting our kids noodle around on a keyboard, some kind of cognitive benefit will occur.

Exposure is not learning because it lacks engagement, and engagement is a fundamental requirement of learning and, really, for understanding anything. Neural plasticity makes lifelong learning possible, but at its core, this potential cannot be realized through mere exposure. Motivation, attention, and effort are required. These are basic maxims of cognitive science, passed on as folk wisdom for millennia and recently confirmed at the cellular level by neuroscience. These basic maxims are very important for music teachers and learners to keep in mind. But they are utterly critical when a cash-strapped school board must choose between funding instrument repair or funding a field trip to the local symphony. The former represents a long-term investment in the future of music-making; the latter is a one-off experiment in exposure. Just imagine if all the infants born in the state of Georgia in 1998 had been gifted music engagement via enhanced funding for music instruction instead of a single CD in a cheap plastic case.

THE LEFT BRAIN–RIGHT BRAIN DICHOTOMY

The second exhibit in the neuromythology pantheon is the *left brain–right brain dichotomy*, which stands out both for its immense popularity and for its attractiveness to artists. The belief that humans possess right- or left-brain personalities or talents is almost as pervasive as the notion that the mind is wiser than the body—the classic *mind-body problem* of philosophy. While the latter springs from ancient roots in Western culture, the former is an artifact from the early history of modern neuroscience. Like most persistent myths, its staying power is rooted in the desire for it to be true and in the chunk of truth that feeds this desire. And like many stories about the brain, this one begins with damage.

Indeed, the annals of neuroscience are filled with tales of damage and loss because, up until very recently, the only way to study the brain was within those parameters. *Lesion-deficit analysis* is a method by which neurologists link the loss of an ability with a damaged area of the brain and then infer that the formerly healthy process must have resided there. The story of modern neuroscience begins in 1848 with just such a tale. Phineas Gage, an American railroad worker, suffered a shattered left frontal brain lobe when a three-foot-long metal tamping rod propelled by gunpowder shot through his jaw, traveled behind his left eye, and exited through the top of his skull. Remarkably, Gage eventually recovered (albeit with only his right eye intact), but his accident had produced a radical change in his temperament. After the accident he was given to such irascible fits of temper, indecision, and foul language that his friends and family pronounced him "no longer Gage."[30] Gage's ruined brain tissue dissolved the very core of what had once been Gage, a "capable and efficient foreman . . . with a well-balanced mind," and left behind an ornery stranger, raising the unsettling possibility that the brain, not the soul, is the seat of personality and behavior.

Gage's case advanced the theory of *functional specialization*, the observation that specific parts of the brain are responsible for specific functions and a theory that in turn paved the way for the left brain–right brain dichotomy. But unlike the stories of many brain-damaged individuals of the nineteenth century, Gage's story is one of hope, not despair. Gage went on to live another twelve years after his horrific accident, holding down the physically vigorous and (according to his biographer) mentally demanding job of stagecoach driving in South America. An observer who met him there reported him to have been "in the enjoyment of good health, with no impairment whatever of his mental faculties."[31] The last chapter of Gage's life story makes a compelling case for the brain's remarkable ability to heal itself.[32]

The stories of Gage and other brain-damaged patients are landmarks in the annals of brain science, though patients' identities came to be hidden, the patients identified only by their initials, their maladies subsumed under the names of their famous physicians. Such was the case with Paul Broca and Carl Wernicke, two nineteenth-century European physicians who advanced *functional specialization theory* (also called *brain localization theory*) by discovering the main locations in the brain for speech production and language comprehension. These brain areas were subsequently named for them, like provinces of a previously uncharted territory.[33] But Broca went down in neurohistory for yet another fundamental discovery.

Besides the location of speech, Broca's autopsies of speech-afflicted patients revealed that their deficits were located exclusively in the left hemisphere. But here was Broca's dilemma: to reveal these findings would be to challenge the reigning orthodoxy of absolute symmetry in the human body (such symmetry being seen as proof that humans descended from the divine). Thus Broca deemed his insight as dangerously "subversive," for evidence of asymmetry would surely disrupt this dogma. Eventually, however, his proof was too strong to deny, and Broca was moved to announce his findings in 1865 by the strength of his evidence—and also perhaps by a looming claim to the same knowledge by the disgruntled son of a deceased neurologist who is said to have made the speech-to-left-brain connection some twenty-five years earlier.[34] Nonetheless, Broca is largely credited with advancing the theory of *brain lateralization* (named after the brain's two largest lateral divisions, the left and right hemispheres), laying a solid foundation for the left-right dichotomy for decades.

Wernicke's lesion-deficit analyses, which revealed the left as the seat of language comprehension, soon followed in 1874, further elevating the status of the left brain as the seat of that most treasured of human abilities, language. By that time, it had long been known that the left-brain was also the location of right-handedness, and because over 90 percent of humans vastly prefer the use of their right hand for most tasks, it did not take long for scientists to equate the left-brain location of language and right-handedness with dominance. From there it was but a stone's throw to assert the left brain's superiority as the seat of reason and to disparage the right as vastly inferior, a stance maintained through the twentieth century. The late neuroscientist Roger Sperry acknowledged this state of affairs in his 1981 Nobel Prize lecture:

> Thus, with few exceptions, the bulk of the collected lesion evidence
> up through the 1950s into the early '60s converged to support the

picture of a leading, more highly evolved and intellectual left hemisphere and a relatively retarded right hemisphere that by contrast, in the typical righthander brain, is not only mute and agraphic but also dyslexic, word-deaf and apraxic, and lacking generally in higher cognitive function.[35]

Sperry won the Nobel Prize in 1981 for three decades of pioneering research on split-brain patients, so called because the dense plate of fibers that connects the two brain hemispheres (the corpus callosum), had been permanently severed in these people. That this severing, a procedure called corpus callosotomy, occurred by choice is evidence that the epileptics who underwent it viewed this extreme brain surgery as a last resort to combat their severe seizures.

Experiments in hemispheric specialization with these rare individuals demonstrated both the great degree to which the human brain is lateralized and the startling effects that occur when the two hemispheres cannot communicate.[36] Split-brain research confirmed the left hemisphere's dominance for many tasks, but perhaps more importantly, it also revealed that the right hemisphere, far from being "retarded," word-deaf, or word-blind, was actually quite the opposite. The right processes motor tasks, visual and spatial relations, and certain aspects of emotion. And where language is concerned, while the left is responsible for the mechanics of speech production and the literal meaning of words, the right hemisphere translates such parameters as pitch and timbre to effect a more nuanced understanding of language. Sperry reported that findings like these were so disruptive to the prevailing neuro-orthodoxy at the time that a coauthor of one of his early studies "felt obliged in good conscience to withdraw his name."[37]

This split-brain news did not stay confined to the lab. In 1967, Michael Gazzaniga (who had joined Sperry's lab in the 1960s as a PhD student) published an article in *Scientific American* titled "The Split Brain in Man," its header proclaiming, "The human brain is actually two brains, each capable of advanced mental functions."[38] Similar articles in mainstream print media soon followed, sparking a rush of imaginative interpretations.[39] As tartly noted by a prominent debunker of neuromythology, "demonstration of the specializations of the two halves of the brain brought a well-deserved Nobel Prize to Roger Sperry and much unearned income to a swarm of hemispheric 'educators.'"[40]

One of those educators was art instructor Betty Edwards. In the mid-1970s, curiosity about why her students experienced random successes in her drawing classes compelled her to seek "an organizing principle that would pull it all together."[41] Edwards found her way to the accounts of the split-brain studies, which, she said,

> provided me with the sudden illumination that an individual's ability to draw was perhaps mainly controlled by the ability to shift to a different-from-ordinary way of processing visual information—to shift from verbal, analytic processing (in this book called "left-mode or "L-mode") to spatial, global processing (which I have called "right-mode or "R-mode").[42]

Edwards's illumination was purveyed in her best-selling 1978 book *Drawing on the Right Side of the Brain.* Now in its fourth edition, it has been translated into seventeen languages and has sold over three million copies worldwide. Quoting Richard Bergland, she bases her method on the claim that

> you have two brains: a left and a right. Modern brain scientists now know that your left brain is your verbal and rational brain; it thinks serially and reduces its thoughts to numbers, letters and words. . . . Your right brain is your nonverbal and intuitive brain; it thinks in patterns, or pictures, composed of "whole things," and does not comprehend reductions, either numbers, letters, or words.[43]

Edwards claims that learning to draw requires staying in one "processing mode" (the right brain) "without significant interference from the other" (the left brain).[44] As such, she is a member of that "swarm" derided by academics as a neuromythmaker, although such derision has not dampened enthusiasm for her method, as promulgated by the many thousands of satisfied art students over the past couple decades who have testified to its success. At best, critics say, hers and others' similar claims about left- and right-brain processing oversimplify complex cognitive processes. So what does it look like when a neuroscientist investigates these processes in a creative brain?

Neuroscientist Charles Limb investigated this question through that most creative of musical enterprises, jazz improvisation. After rolling a jazz pianist into an fMRI scanner and observing his brain while he played, Limb hypothesized that creativity flourishes when portions of the right hemisphere are allowed to ramble freely, unfettered by the self-evaluation of the left hemisphere.[45] As Limb explained in a TED Talk,

> we have this combination of an area that's thought to be involved in self-monitoring, turning off, and this [other] area that's thought to be autobiographical, or self-expressive, turning on. . . . A reasonable hypothesis is that, to be creative, you should have this weird dissociation in your frontal lobe. One area turns on, and a big area shuts off, so that you're not inhibited, you're willing to make mistakes, so that you're not constantly shutting down all of these new generative impulses.[46]

This echoes Edwards's claims. Yet the notable difference between Limb and Edwards is Limb's science credentials. Limb's lab coat seems to add a cloak of respectability to such subjects as creativity, just as his fMRI images make what Edwards had already observed over decades of experience seem more "real," thus adding more proof to what multiple studies have shown: we are more likely to believe experts when they possess degrees, dress in uniforms, and display tools of the trade, like stethoscopes. Psychologists call this "stage-setting," and it is used to display "expert power."[47] It seems we are even more likely to believe accounts that are accompanied by florid pictures of the brain—what critics have derisively labeled "brainporn."[48]

Similarly, the credibility of Jill Bolte Taylor, a Harvard researcher who suffered a cerebral hemorrhage and lived to tell the tale, was arguably enhanced by her previous career as a neuroscientist (which she considered a "cool" perk because in the midst of her brain trauma it offered "the opportunity to study [my] own brain from the inside out"). Taylor, in one of the five most-viewed TED Talks of all time, claims that our "two hemispheres are completely separate. Because they process information differently, each of our hemispheres think about different things, they care about different things, and, dare I say, they have very different personalities."[49]

In tone and words more comparable to those of a preacher than a scientist, Taylor has described the months she spent consigned by her brain trauma to the domain of her right hemisphere variously as "euphoric," a "nirvana," and "la la land." She says that her motivation for healing was borne from the desire to lead others to this land if they could but "choose to step to the right of their left hemispheres."[50]

Another neuro-expert and advocate for the right hemisphere is psychiatrist Iain McGilchrist, whose highly acclaimed masterwork *The Master and His Emissary: The Divided Brain and the Making of the Western World* promotes a view similar to Taylor's. Like her, McGilchrist assigns personalities to each hemisphere (the "master" and the "emissary" of the title, after a tale by Nietzsche), asserting that "the left hemisphere manipulates the world, the right hemisphere *understands* the world."[51] McGilchrist holds that the left brain's habit of deconstructing and categorizing our experiences in ordered, manageable bits has spawned a mechanical, uninspired view of the world because we never return these component shards to the right brain for synthesis, interpretation, and nuance; instead, we allow the left hemisphere's penchant for processing experiences in a one-dimensional way to define and validate reality for us. In other words, we practice one-sided thinking—and as I will show, practice is powerful. McGilchrist maintains that this left-biased state of affairs, begun during the Industrial Revolution, has since gathered steam in Western culture to the detriment of practically everything since, from individual happiness to world peace. McGilchrist's book, twenty years in the making, has inspired a string of laudatory reviews and prominent champions (including British actor John Cleese), the obligatory TED Talk, a documentary film, and a pilgrimage to spread his message throughout the world.

Into the left-right fray has stepped yet another neuro-expert, positing a division in a different direction. Cognitive neuroscientist Stephen Kosslyn (with cowriter Wayne Miller) has put forward the *theory of cognitive modes*, which posits that the brain is best understood from top to bottom, challenging the left-right dichotomy as "the dominant mainstream brain story of the last half century" that, while "broadly embraced by the popular culture," is nevertheless "scientifically unsound." Their theory, they say, is the "first time that these findings have been systematically brought to a mainstream audience."[52] Perhaps, but Roger Sperry hinted at this difference in directionality back in 1981: "The left-right dichotomy in cognitive mode is an idea with which it is very easy to run wild. Qualitative shifts in mental control may involve up-down, front-back, or various other organizational changes as well as left-right differences."[53]

Sperry's remarks presaged the current, prevailing view of how the brain actually works, which is that brain functions are best understood as interrelated systems. In the healthy brain, these systems, located in both hemispheres, communicate with each other while doing practically everything but especially during complex cognitive processes. Yet no matter which direction these processes run, there *are* observable physical differences in the two brain hemispheres as well as in their processes—which is precisely the basis of McGilchrist's argument and why he holds that "the old story deserves to be buried, but the real left brain/ right brain story is one we are only just beginning to understand."[54] That new story is a unified theory of *network connectivity*, and like all things involving that most complex object in the known universe, it is an interwoven and constantly evolving tale.

BRAIN PERSONALITIES AND LEARNING STYLES

Despite the current understanding of the brain as an interconnected network of subsystems, the notion that the left brain is rational and the right brain is creative persists in popular culture. Similarly persistent are related beliefs about right-brain versus left-brain personalities and learning styles. Against this backdrop, a team of neuroscientists at the University of Utah in 2013 made headlines with a two-year study that investigated the neural substrates of the left brain–right brain theory of personality. Their host institution did not mince words when it announced in a press release, "Researchers Debunk Myth of 'Right-Brain' and 'Left-Brain' Personality Traits." The researchers themselves are a bit more circumspect; they note that "lateralization of brain connections appears to be a local rather than global property of brain networks, and our data are not consistent with a whole-brain phenotype of greater 'left-brained' or greater 'right-brained' network strength across individuals."[55] In other words, while it is true that certain functions can be seen to occur in only one hemisphere of the brain or the other ("a local rather than global property"), according to the lead researcher, "people don't tend to have a stronger left- or right-sided brain network."

Equally spurious is the theory of learning styles, the belief that people evince a specific aptitude for receiving information (a "visual" rather than a "verbal" learner, for example). A recent review of the scientific literature reveals virtually no compelling evidence to support this hypothesis. In fact, related research has made a compelling case against the theory of learning styles despite the fact that it remains enormously popular and, as one research team notes, has spawned a "thriving industry" of resources for parents and teachers.[56]

Again we must ask if there is some detriment to maintaining these scientifically invalid notions. The simple answer is yes, for at least several reasons. First, these notions do not mesh with what is currently known about how learning actually works and, by extension, how best to boost it. A major finding from cognitive science is that learning of any sort involves effort. So while the existence of learning styles has not been proven to be demonstrably true, it is true that most of us have particular abilities and preferences—things we are good at and things we prefer. But absent any frank learning disorder, preferences are not styles—they are just preferences.

Another reason we should eschew the linked neuromyths of brain personalities and learning styles is because these myths are actually quite limiting to learners. This is ironic because many of these ideas were first promoted within a rigid educational system meant to free students (particularly children) from strictures that were thought to restrict learning. So if these are truly myths and hold no validity, why are they both appealing and persistent? One answer is that the urge to label others or oneself is natural because humans generally seek order. Neat categorizations of personality types are appealing, particularly in occupations that require us to assess and manage large groups of people, like classroom teaching or coaching athletics.

Labeling oneself may also be attractive, for we would all like to believe that we are unique. Self-labeling can therefore be seductive, especially if we wish to project a certain air: that of the freewheeling artist, the down-to-earth rational thinker, or the creative genius, for example. Such labeling can be a get-out-of-jail-free card when we behave impulsively, unemotionally, or forgetfully—neglecting the anniversary bouquet is perhaps more easily excused when committed by an unapologetic "left-brainer," as is the rash countercultural behavior of the family's artsy black sheep. It is more appealing to pass off such lapses as part of who we believe ourselves to be, especially since doing so guards against any expectation that we will change these behaviors in the future.

Labels may be seemingly harmless, but they have long-term negative consequences when children are taught that their right-brain learning style excuses poor math grades or that their left-brain personality may shield them from learning social graces, like how to engage in conversation. As I explain in chapter 5, these labels are symptoms of what psychologist Carol Dweck dubs the *fixed mindset*, and, instead of providing freedom and psychic healing balm, such mindsets stunt growth and constrain potential and possibility.

In the arena of music, imagine how limiting it is for the baritone who harbors the notion that, as a rational left-brainer, he has a talent for sight-reading but just isn't cut out for acting, or the budding percussionist who excuses her musical mistakes as those of a right-brain learner who has never been any good at rhythm. There exist talented musicians who play their instruments reasonably well by ear but refuse to learn to read music because they have an "aural learning style." Perhaps. But in the absence of a diagnosed learning disorder like dyslexia, such a self-affixed label is ultimately a barrier to learning, not a door to freedom.

When we limit ourselves and our children with labels that restrict and restrain, it is time to replace these neuromyths with the more wholistic view of network connectivity and to embrace the new findings of neurogenesis, or how the brain can change. Who wants to make music—or do anything for that matter—with half a brain? Besides, real findings from neuroscience about the brain and music are actually far more intriguing than the neuromyths.

REAL BRAIN GAINS

The research field called the *cognitive neuroscience of music* is primarily devoted to music perception, or what happens in the brain when we listen to music. More noteworthy (but less studied) is what happens in the brain when we *do* music. One researcher who has pursued this question is Gottfried Schlaug, director of the Music and Neuroimaging Lab at Harvard Medical School.

Schlaug calls musicians "auditory-motor athletes" and was initially intrigued by the related question of whether accomplished musicians show any brain differences as compared to nonmusicians and whether they show any brain changes due to training, which typically begins in early childhood. His seminal studies showed that, not only are the brains of accomplished adult musicians generally larger in areas of the brain that serve musical functions, but the corpus callosum (the main band of fibers that connects both left and right hemispheres of the brain) is both larger and more fibrous in musicians than nonmusicians.[57] This was very exciting news for musicians, but thanks in part to wariness over the Mozart effect, a skeptical view of this research held that perhaps these asymmetries and size differences were there all along due to inborn aptitude or talent.

To investigate this nature-versus-nurture question, Schlaug and a team of researchers were able to demonstrate structural differences in the motor and auditory brain regions of young children after only fifteen months of keyboard instruction.[58] The fact that these differences actually correlate with improvements in movement and hearing skills is notable. The takeaway message from this landmark study is that music training actually induced brain plasticity, which is a necessary precursor to cognitive enhancement. In other words, while music training didn't make these children "smarter," it made their brains more receptive to learning. This is a theme we see repeated again and again in music and learning: there is no easy musical potion that makes us instantly smarter, but music engagement seems to rev up the brain and make it fertile territory for learning.

Schlaug's lab has gone on to research another aspect of brain plasticity, not in the developing brains of children, but in people who have experienced brain damage through stroke or other brain trauma. Because the mechanics of speech reside in the left hemisphere, when damage occurs there, a typical impairment is aphasia, characterized by damaged speech and comprehension. This disorder affects about 2 million Americans, with over 180,000 new cases added each year.[59] *Melodic intonation therapy* (MIT) was developed for such patients in the early 1970s based on the observation that some speech impairments seemed to improve with singing. But it was only recently that neuroscience could confirm the effects at a cellular level.

MIT essentially hacks into the undamaged right side of the brain (which is responsible for certain aspects of speech, like motor control and emotion) and hitches it to speech through singing. Patients are taught to elongate common words in a singsong style while simultaneously tapping the rhythm with their left hands. This tapping links to motor neurons in the right hemisphere that then charge the organs of speech. With persistent work over time, Schlaug's lab has shown that, as the right side of the brain takes over for the damaged abilities of the left, it actually grows and strengthens with practice. This is truly a remarkable finding.

Schlaug notes that, as a therapy, music is an "ideal" stimulus because it is a "multisensory motor experience," stimulating movement and emotion by engaging the pleasure and reward systems, which encourages perseverance. Remarkable stories of such persistence—such as that of Laurel Fontaine, an American woman who suffered a stroke at the age of eleven that left her barely able to speak but for whom MIT restored that function to almost 100 percent—demonstrate how effective MIT can be with disciplined practice.[60] Even though Fontaine's remarkable recovery was owed in part to her youth, older patients have shown dramatic improvements with MIT—it just takes a bit longer with an older brain.

Indeed, neuroscientist Nina Kraus, who has spent decades researching how music training transforms sound processing in the brain, has boldly stated that "a lifetime of playing an instrument protects musicians from age-related neural declines." Kraus calls musicians "auditory experts" who, through practice, are "constantly mapping sound to meaning."[61] She has linked this auditory expertise to such critical cognitive skills as attention and memory. As I explain in the next chapter, attention and memory bookend learning, not only the act of learning but in the entire human lifespan of learning, from attention as learning's prerequisite (and thus of primary importance to the development of young brains) to the age-related neural decline that is most cruelly visited upon memory, as seen in Alzheimer's disease.

Attention is part of the *executive function system* in the brain, an umbrella term for the cognitive processes located in the frontal lobe that govern such critical and related attributes as planning and impulse control—the very components that are undeveloped in children. Indeed, we might say that a large percentage of parents' and teachers' jobs is devoted to nurturing and refining these attributes in young children. So the initial results of an ongoing longitudinal study overseen by Antonio Damasio at the University of Southern California are noteworthy, for they demonstrate significant structural brain changes in school-age children who receive music instruction in comparison with

two age-matched control groups. Tests performed on children who began training at age six showed that two years of music training accelerat-
ed growth in areas of their brains responsible for, among other things,
executive function. Earlier tests in the study showed that music instruction boosted areas in the brain responsible for sound processing, language development, speech perception, and reading skills.[62]

That the test group was comprised of students from a low-income
area of Los Angeles marked by "extreme poverty levels, gang violence,
and drug trafficking" adds to the urgency of exorcising the ghost of the
Mozart effect once and for all. Exposure does not equal learning, yet
engagement does. The evidence of the negative effects of poverty and
violence on the minds of children is mounting, but so is evidence of the
positive effects of music training as, in the words of the researchers, "a
powerful intervention that may facilitate regional brain maturation during childhood."[63]

The hyped-up claims that music per se somehow makes people
vaguely smarter has overshadowed deeper and more significant research, such as that produced by Schlaug, Kraus, Damasio, and others.
The question of whether we will ever be able to claim that music makes
us smarter is perhaps an open one, but what is now clear is that music
engagement feeds brain plasticity and molds the vital building blocks of
cognition (such as attention, memory, motor movement, and emotion)
upon which learning is built. The question of *why* humans pursue music is an even deeper question.

WHAT IS THE USE OF MUSIC?

The cognitive revolution has permeated ancient intellectual pursuits
like philosophy, but it has also spawned new fields like *evolutionary
psychology*, which traces the development of the human brain over
evolutionary time by posing the ultimate questions of Darwin's theory
of natural selection: Why did a certain human trait or ability survive (or
"persist," in the parlance of evolutionary theorists)? What is its use? As
cognitive psychologist Steven Pinker points out, to most evolutionary
theorists, music is a mystery in this regard: "Music is an enigma. . . .
What benefit could there be to diverting time and energy to the making
of plinking noises, or to feeling sad when no one has died?"[64] Good

questions. But Pinker goes on to pronounce this enigma a "pure pleasure technology, a cocktail of recreational drugs that we ingest through the ear" with no adaptive function. Thus they are only so much "auditory cheesecake." "Music," Pinker infamously declared, "is useless."[65]

Pinker's musings resonate with another similarly dismissive evolutionary theory that regards music as a purely hedonistic invention that sprouted by hitching onto the developing language ability in primitive humans' brains, offering its ability to both auditorily parse chunks of information and provide meaning by way of pitch and rhythm. This theory holds that, over evolutionary time, as the human vocal tract developed and once language was up and running, these acoustic properties of speech (pitch and rhythm) were no longer needed but hung around anyway as a "parasitic" leftover that eventually morphed into music.[66]

Esteemed psychologist Howard Gardner, writing years before Pinker's now-infamous valuation of music, proffers a profound assessment of music and the human condition that makes the cheesecake and parasite explanations seem positively churlish and suggests that it is music's very "uselessness" that ought to set anthropologists on fire to figure it out:

> Precisely because [music] is not used for explicit communication, or for other evident survival purposes, its continuing centrality in human experience constitutes a challenging puzzle. The anthropologist Lévi-Strauss is scarcely alone among scientists in claiming that if we can explain music, we may find the key for all human thought—or in implying that failure to take music seriously weakens any account of the human condition.[67]

One who did take up the challenging puzzle of music's persistence was Steven Mithen, a pioneer of yet another new field borne from the cognitive revolution, *cognitive archaeology*. Mithen acknowledges music's evolutionary survival as warranting a full-on evolutionary history of music:

> We can only explain the human propensity to make and listen to music by recognizing that it has been encoded into the human genome during the evolutionary history of our species. . . . While several other attributes of the human mind have recently been examined

and debated at length . . . music has been sorely neglected. Accordingly, a fundamental aspect of the human condition has been ignored and we have gained no more than a partial understanding of what it means to be human. [68]

Mithen wields his considerable cognitive archaeological might against the vexing question of music by investigating how and why music has endured throughout evolution by marshaling evidence from the archaeological record and combining it with research in child development and brain science. The result is his provocative book, *The Singing Neanderthals*. Mithen and others argue that, on the evolutionary timeline, our first utterances were a kind of blended "musilanguage" that conveyed both information and emotion. [69]

Several other theories on why music has persisted for millennia have been posited by anthropologists and evolutionary theorists. One is that music may have functioned as a type of mating call among early humans. Another is that the voice of the mother crooning her baby to sleep, which morphed into the lullaby, in a small yet significant way may have helped ensure the survival of the species. Another theory notes music's social bonding power: those who sing together stick together and defend each other.

Evolutionary theories necessarily consider adaptive function and therefore only serve as evidence to explain music's persistence. But what evidence could ever prove music's ultimate worth? Perhaps musicians already know, in which case, we need no proof of music's worth.

Yet many of us would still like to know why. Most musicians have at least paused to wonder, Why am I doing this? Musicians who play in bands with friends likely have a ready social answer. But what about instrumentalists who endure seven-hour practice sessions alone in windowless practice rooms? Or musicians who experience debilitating stage fright and yet persist? Or singing actors who trudge from one cattle-call audition to another, only to be rejected (by the laws of supply and demand) a majority of the time?

Of what use is music, and why are so many musicians compelled to make it? As Gardner and Mithen note, if we can definitively answer this, we can perhaps explain the human condition—a tall order indeed, one that at present anyway is unanswerable. But one thing about music and utility is certain: juxtaposed against these existential questions, Pinker's cheeky analogy to cheesecake is silly at best. At worst, it is deeply insulting to musicians who have made music their lifework, not to mention music-lovers for whom utility is the last thing they seek from music.

THE BIG ONE

With rapid advances in neuroscience, the gulf that once separated mind and body is rapidly eroding, as evidenced by Descartes's famous insight "I think, therefore I am," now challenged by Pinker's neurocreed "The mind is not the brain but what the brain does."[70] Neuroscience is confronting some of the most confounding questions of human existence, and one of the most fundamental of those is the very nature of consciousness itself.

An easily grasped definition of consciousness is to say it is a kind of self-consciousness; that is, I am not only aware, but I am aware that I am aware. This state of mind—awareness of awareness—is also called *sentience*, or even *subjectivity*. Psychologist Daniel Robinson describes consciousness as that thing which "every man, woman and child know to be true during every waking hour of daily life."[71] Australian philosopher and cognitive scientist David Chalmers calls the question of consciousness "the hard problem of consciousness."[72] Neuroscientist Joseph LeDoux labels the question simply "the Big One."[73]

LeDoux recounts how, until recently, this question was primarily the province of elderly scientists facing their own mortality while younger researchers avoided the Big One altogether for fear that confronting it would give budding scientists a "bad reputation."[74] Yet the question is now at the forefront of scientific research, abetted in part by the pairing of philosophy with neuroscience.

At first glance, this pairing might seem a strange combination, yet philosophy has been concerned with the workings of the human mind as far back as the ancient Greek philosophers. The most recent union of philosophy with neuroscience began in the 1970s, when cognitive psychology (the science of how the mind works) started marching toward its inevitable merger with neuroscience (the science of the brain), eventually producing the new field of cognitive neuroscience. Experiments, such as those with split-brain patients, proved so enthralling that age-old existential questions were reignited. Did splitting the brain split the soul? The soul was supposed to be indivisible, but split-brain research showed that, if the brain's hemispheres are disconnected, mental states are disconnected. And this was powerful support for the hypothesis that mental states are states of the physical brain itself, not states of the nonphysical soul. Into this breech stepped the neurophilosophers, who have given us the *theory of embodied cognition* as a step toward repairing the mind-body split by "developing cognitive explanations that capture the manner in which mind, body, and world mutually interact and influence one another."[75]

The merger of such disparate fields as philosophy and artificial intelligence into cognitive neuroscience also secured a central place for biology in the study of mental processes. Nobel laureate and pioneer in neurobiology Eric Kandel writes that "the new biology posits that consciousness is a biological process that will eventually be explained in terms of molecular signaling pathways used by interacting populations of nerve cells."[76]

But LeDoux opines that the quest to explain consciousness is "being overemphasized" and asks us to imagine a scenario in which, somehow, "an indefatigable neuroscientist finally has solved the consciousness problem. Would that really tell us what makes people tick?" LeDoux's answer is "No!"[77] LeDoux contends that "the mystery of personality crucially depends on figuring out the unconscious functions of the brain," among which are

> the many things that the brain does that are not available to consciousness . . . from standard body maintenance like regulating heart rate, breathing rhythm, stomach contractions and posture, to controlling many aspects of seeing, smelling, behaving, feeling, speaking, thinking, evaluating, judging, believing and imagining.[78]

The fact that scientists are even discussing the Big One, let alone musing on consciousness as grounded in the body, is revolutionary. Until now, the ancient binary of *know-that* (facts) and *know-how* (movements) has ruled the way we comprehend being human. The new science of mind reveals that thought is a far more integrated process than this simple binary can capture. What is coming into view is the ultimate resolution of the ancient mind-body problem.

KNOW-THAT AND KNOW-HOW

With the advent of psychology as a formal discipline in the nineteenth century, many learning theories sprang forth, but the majority of the mainstream ones reflected a fundamental division between the mind and the body. The terminology still in use reflects this split: *explicit learning* versus *implicit learning*; *declarative* versus *procedural*; *propositional knowledge* versus *tacit knowledge*. Whatever terms are chosen, at their base level, they all share an assumed division between the purely mental and the purely physical. Yet the big news from neuroscience is the steady erosion of this historic dichotomy.

This dichotomy has its roots in the ancient world, when Greek philosophers used the word *epistêmê* to mean "knowledge" and the term *technê* to signify "craft" or "general know-how." They understood knowledge as a product of the mind and craft as a product of the body via activities. This ancient distinction is known in academic philosophy as *knowledge-that* and *knowledge-how*, or simply *know-that* and *know-how*. As such, we are not born with knowledge-that; rather, we must be taught in order to receive it. Know-that is why we go to school (as in "I know that 2 plus 3 equals 5"). Thus a hallmark of know-that is learning that is dependent upon knowledge of facts. Since that is the case, know-that requires many important prerequisites, and at the top of the list are motivation and attention. We have to want to learn, to pay attention. This very fact is embedded in the use of the word *pay*, which reflects our fund of attention and implies that learning costs us something. Knowledge of this sort (learning to read musical notation, for example) may not come easily, and it is often distinguished by layers of difficulty. Once one has mastered the first layer, one must persevere ever outward, in a concentric ring of challenge. Knowledge-that is seemingly limitless and requires a dogged commitment to repetition and practice when the going gets tough. Knowledge-that is unmoved by petitions regarding learning styles.

Conversely, know-how is bound to the body. It is often linked to the tacit knowledge that is one's birthright, as in knowing how to walk. Thus know-how is described as a kind of learning that occurs automatically and outside one's conscious attempts to learn. But this description immediately raises questions: Does this mean that *all* types of know-how never first require attention? What about learning to ride a bicycle, which first requires learning certain things (facts, perhaps?) and yet later is conducted automatically, outside our conscious awareness? And what about fine-motor activities, like playing the piano? How do descriptions of know-how work in the realm of higher-order muscular activities like fine singing or dancing or playing an instrument? Surely these activities require learning facts before we can execute them, do they not?

Thus the title of a 2013 neurophilosophy paper is a provocative one; "Motor Skill Depends on Knowledge of Facts" is a deliberate mash-up of these divided ways of thinking about thinking.[79] The two authors, Jason Stanley and John Krakauer (a philosopher and a neuroscientist, respectively), take issue with the ancient assumption that the mind is wiser than the body. Or, as they put it in a later opinion piece, "It is hard, and perhaps not possible, to forge a theoretically significant distinction between working with one's hands and working with one's mind."[80]

Howard Gardner accounts for the privileged place of knowledge in his theory of multiple intelligences (MI theory) and also acknowledges that "body intelligence may have been taken for granted or minimized in importance by many researchers [because] motor activity has been considered as a less 'high' cortical function than functions subserving 'pure' thought."[81]

In just a matter of a few decades since the debut of MI theory, results from neuroscience research have radically shifted our notion of how the mind works from a top-down processing model (the idea of a wise superbrain controlling the dumb body) to an integrative, bottom-up model, revealing that emotions and physical actions are more fundamental to the way we make decisions and take action than was previously understood. Taking recent research into account, it is no longer plausible to talk of the muscular movements of the body as always (to borrow Gardner's terminology) "subserving high cortical function."

Stanley and Krakauer translate this idea in colloquial terms in an opinion piece with the catchy headline "Is the Dumb Jock Really a Nerd?" They hold that any motor skill presupposes that some kind of direction is given and that the skill has to be practiced until it is mastered. This, they conclude, shows that "motor skill, like any other cognitive task, requires knowledge."[82]

To musicians, this conclusion is not exactly earth-shattering or particularly revelatory. Of course, singing and playing instruments are motor skills that involve both gross- and fine-motor coordination. Of course this kind of coordination is a higher-order function than, say, brushing one's teeth. And of course, fine playing and singing require knowledge. Depending upon the musical style, learning to make music at a professional level requires particular and special knowledge of the sort that can only be gotten from an experienced guide: knowledge of repertoire, of technique, of language, of historic style periods, of literature and dramatic conventions. So why then should performing artists care about philosophy or neuroscience—or its hybrid, neurophilosophy? Because, in the words of Stanley and Krakauer, "We are not supposed to call LeBron James a 'genius' because cultural biases have infected science without the moderating input of the humanities."[83]

We care because athletes and musicians who inhabit the realm of the body are heirs to these cultural biases and because, despite the erosion of the mind-body dichotomy, like the left brain–right brain theory of personality, this division yet remains alive in the culture. Just take a look at what is emphasized in school curricula and even the notion of intelligence itself. The products of the mind are still privileged over the products of the body—and not just any mind. Gardner calls this mind "the law professor mind—somebody who's very linguistic and logical."[84]

In performance art and high-level athletics, the boundary line between the declarative and the procedural is blurred. We must have knowledge of facts before we can effect that knowledge in a procedural, physical form. Singers, instrumentalists, dancers, and athletes must first know-that in order to know-how.

But this is only an initial step. Know-how has to quickly progress to encoding deep in our memory so that later retrieval of know-how is automatic. LeDoux asserts that "cognitive processes are not dependent upon consciousness."[85] In fact, he says, there is so much activity that occurs outside our awareness that "actually, consciousness depends upon *unconscious* cognitive processes."[86] For athletes, dancers, and musicians, it is the *unconscious* bits of cognitive processes that concern us. While the Holy Grail for neurophilosophers is the question of consciousness, a perpetual quest for musicians is the automaticity of learned actions—that is, how reliably can we access our technique without consciously thinking about it?

Stanley and Krakauer state that, "in the enterprise of uncovering truth, the paths of the scientist and the humanist must often intersect."[87] Agreed. At that intersection, let us imagine a kind of performance art where the neuroscientists set to examining the biological processes of consciousness, the neurophilosophers exercise their minds over their "hard problem," and we musicians simply do music.

Experienced musicians have known all along that the ancient mind-body problem is no problem at all because, for us, the division between body and mind is recognized through experience as false. When we sing, whether through our throats or through our instruments, we are all in, as the song goes, body and soul.

HOW THE THING WORKS

The date was April 14, 2005, and the setting was the Vanuxem Public Lecture Series at Princeton University. An enthusiastic audience had gathered to hear the famous neuroscientist Michael Gazzaniga give a speech titled "Personal Identity, Neuroethics and the Human Brain":

> Bingo! Modern neuroscience! So we're moving down this path, and everybody is being told that we are coming to a greater and greater understanding of the mechanistic nature of the human brain and we are; that's just the deal, we are. Someday, somewhere, somehow, someone is going to figure out how the damn thing works![88]

Audience reaction to this public declaration by such an esteemed neuroscientist as Gazzaniga ranged from delight to bemusement to consternation.[89] Given his outsize history as a pioneer of the field, Gazzaniga's zeal is understandable, but the quest to understand the mechanistic nature of any system, be it the human brain, the human hand, or the human voice, is only part of the question. We must also ask what revealing the mechanism might tell us about how we learn, remember, create, feel, and communicate—the essence of what makes us human—and in doing so, help us do those things better. The final, related existential question—*why* what we do matters at all—is left to the poet, the painter, and the musician to answer simply by plying their art.

The human brain functions as both artist and scientist by producing abilities and then comprehending them—by bringing forth actions and interpreting them. It takes two hemispheres in constant communication with one another to experience and interpret the world, just as it takes a whole brain to bring forth and perceive compelling music.

NOTES

1. Christof Koch, "Decoding 'the Most Complex Object in the Universe,'" NPR, June 14, 2013, www.npr.org/2013/06/14/191614360/decodingthe-most-complex-object-in-the-universe.

2. Eric Kandel, "The New Science of Mind," *Scientific American Mind* (April/May 2006): 65.

3. See B. L. Beyerstein, "Brainscams: Neuromythologies of the New Age," *International Journal of Mental Health* 19, no. 3 (1990): 27–36; S. Della Salla, ed., *Mind Myths: Exploring Popular Assumptions about the Mind and Brain* (New York: John Wiley & Sons, 1999); and S. Della Salla, ed., *Tall Tales about the Mind and Brain: Separating Fact from Fiction* (New York: Oxford University Press, 2007).

4. See UPI, "Poll: Music Education Is Important," April 21, 2003, www.upi.com/Top_News/2003/04/21/Poll-Music-education-is-important/UPI-99891050959298/#ixzz35CK0oZUx; and NAMM, "New Gallup Survey by NAMM Reflects Majority of Americans Agree with Many Benefits of Playing Musical Instruments," April 29, 2009, www.namm.org/news/press-releases/new-gallup-survey-namm-reflects-majority-americans.

5. Francis Rauscher, Gordon Shaw, and Katherine Ky, "Music and Spatial Task Performance," *Nature* 365 (October 1993): 611.

6. Quoted in Alix Spiegel, "Mozart Effect, Schmozart Effect: Science Misinterpreted," NPR, June 26, 2010, www.npr.org/templates/story/story.php?storyId=128104580.

7. "Governor Wants Babies to Hear Classical Music," *Augusta Chronicle*, http://chronicle.augusta.com/stories/1998/01/14/met_220543.shtml.

8. State of Florida Senate Bill 660, May 21, 1998.

9. The Mozart Effect Resource Centre, 2016, www.mozarteffect.com.

10. Karen Auge, "Baby Einstein DVD Creators Find Redemption in Documents Suggesting Negative Study Was Flawed," *Denver Post*, June 30, 2011, www.denverpost.com/ci_18381772.

11. Tamar Lewin, "'Baby Einstein' Founder Goes to Court," *New York Times*, January 13, 2010, www.nytimes.com/2010/01/13/education/13einstein.html.

12. Spiegel, "Mozart Effect, Schmozart Effect."

13. Joel Schwarz, "Baby DVDs, Videos May Hinder, Not Help, Infants' Language Development," UW News, August 7, 2007, www.washington.edu/news/2007/08/07/baby-dvds-videos-may-hinder-not-help-infants-language-development/.

14. Ibid.

15. Auge, "Baby Einstein DVD Creators."

16. Tamar Lewin, "No Einstein in Your Crib? Get a Refund," *New York Times*, October 24, 2009, www.nytimes.com/2009/10/24/education/24baby.html.

17. Christopher Chabris, "Prelude or Requiem for the 'Mozart Effect'?" *Nature* 400 (August 26, 1999): 826–27.

18. See Pippa McKelvie and Jason Low, "Listening to Mozart Does Not Improve Children's Spatial Ability: Final Curtains for the Mozart Effect," *British Journal of Developmental Psychology* 20, no. 2 (2002): 241–58.

19. Spiegel, "Mozart Effect, Schmozart Effect."

20. E. Glenn Schellenberg, "Music Lessons Enhance IQ," *Psychological Science* 15, no. 8 (2004): 511–14.

21. Adrian Bangerter and Chip Heath, "The Mozart Effect: Tracking the Evolution of a Scientific Legend," *British Journal of Social Psychology* 43, no. 4 (December 2004): 608.

22. Ibid., 619.

23. See Norman Doidge, *The Brain That Changes Itself* (New York: Viking Penguin, 2007).

24. Quoted in Sarah Moughty, "The Zero to Three Debate: A Cautionary Look at Turning Science into Policy," PBS, January 31, 2012, www.pbs.org/wgbh/pages/frontline/shows/teenbrain/science/zero.html.

25. Ibid.

26. Zero to Three, "Our Work," 2019, www.zerotothree.org/our-work .

27. John T. Bruer, *The Myth of the First Three Years* (New York: Free Press, 1999).

28. John T. Bruer, "A Path Not Taken," 2002, James S. McDonnell Foundation, www.jsmf.org/about/j/path_not_taken.htm.

29. Ibid.

30. Malcolm Macmillan, "The Phineas Gage Story," Cummings Center for the History of Psychology, University of Akron, www.uakron.edu/gage/story.dot .

31. Ibid.

32. Malcolm Macmillan and Matthew Lena, "Rehabilitating Phineas Gage," *Neuropsychological Rehabilitation* 20, no. 5 (2010): 641–58, doi:10.1080/09602011003760527.

33. While Broca's area is designated for speech production, Wernicke's contribution was the location of the place for language processing. This area, named after him, is far, in "brain measurements," from Broca's area. Thus Broca's aphasics typically cannot utter much beyond a few syllables but comprehend what is being said to them, while Wernicke aphasics can speak perfectly well but make little sense.

34. See Sam Kean, *The Tale of the Dueling Neurosurgeons* (New York: Little, Brown, 2014); and Hugh W. Buckingham, "The Marc Dax (1770–1837)/Paul Broca (1824–1880) Controversy over Priority in Science: Left Hemisphere Specificity for Seat of Articulate Language and for Lesions That Cause Aphemia," *Clinical Linguistics & Phonetics* 20, nos. 7–8 (2006): 613–19.

35. Roger W. Sperry, "Some Effects of Disconnecting the Cerebral Hemispheres," Nobel Prize, www.nobelprize.org/prizes/medicine/1981/sperry/25059-roger-w-sperry-nobel-lecture-1981/.

36. For information on split-brain patients, see Michael S. Gazzaniga, "Spheres of Influence," *Scientific American Mind* (June/July 2008); and Emily Esfahani Smith, "One Head, Two Brains," *Atlantic*, July 27, 2015.

37. Sperry, "Some Effects of Disconnecting."

38. Michael Gazzaniga, "The Split Brain in Man," *Scientific American* 217, no. 2 (1967): 24–29.

39. For an excellent overview, see Stephen M. Kosslyn and G. Wayne Miller, *Top Brain, Bottom Brain: Surprising Insights into How You Think* (New York: Simon & Schuster, 2013), ch. 5.

40. Barry L. Beyerstein, "Brainscams: Neuromythologies of the New Age," *International Journal of Mental Health* 19, no. 3 (Fall 1990): 32.

41. Betty Edwards, *Drawing on the Right Side of the Brain* (Los Angeles: J. P. Tarcher, 1979), vii.

42. Ibid.

43. Richard Bergland, *The Fabric of the Mind* (New York: Viking Penguin, 1985). Dr. Bergland served as a neuro-expert for art teacher Betty Edwards. According to Bergland's son, his father later regretted abetting this popular account of the creative right brain; see Christopher Bergland, "The Split-Brain: An Ever-Changing Hypothesis," *Psychology Today*, March 30, 2017, www.psychologytoday.com/blog/the-athletes-way/201703/the-split-brain-ever-changing-hypothesis.

44. Edward, *Drawing on the Right Side of the Brain*.

45. Charles Limb and Allen R. Braun, "Neural Substrates of Spontaneous Musical Performance: An fMRI Study of Jazz Improvisation," *PLoS ONE* 3, no. 2 (February 2008).

46. Charles Limb, "Your Brain on Improv," TED Talk, November 2010, www.ted.com/talks/charles_limb_your_brain_on_improv.

47. Bertram Raven, "The Bases of Power: Origins and Recent Developments," *Journal of Social Issues* 49, no. 4 (Winter 1993): 237–38.

48. Christopher Chabris and Daniel Simons, *The Invisible Gorilla: How Our Intuitions Deceive Us* (New York: Crown, 2010), 142.

49. Jill Bolte Taylor, "My Stroke of Insight," TED Talk, February 2008, www.ted.com/talks/jill_bolte_taylor_s_powerful_stroke_of_insight/transcript.

50. Ibid. I met Taylor as she was writing the first, self-published version of what would later become her best-selling memoir, *My Stroke of Insight*. A subsequent invitation to accompany her on a late-night guided visit to the cadaver lab at Indiana University revealed a person who truly believed in these two brain "personalities" and was unequivocal about which side—the right—held the promise of a "deep inner peace," both interpersonally and globally.

51. Iain McGilchrist, "Of Two Minds: The Origins of Our Mental Malaise," YouTube, March 7, 2012, www.youtube.com/watch?v=6JbImYfRaZ8.

52. Kosslyn and Miller, *Top Brain, Bottom Brain*, xii.

53. Sperry, "Some Effects of Disconnecting."

54. Iain McGilchrist, "Echange of Views: Top Brain, Bottom Brain: A Reply to Stephen Kosslyn and Wayne Miller," http://178.62.31.128/exchange-of-views/.

55. Melinda Rogers, "Researchers Debunk Myth of 'Right-Brain' and 'Left-Brain' Personality Traits," University of Utah Health Care, August 14, 2013, https://healthcare.utah.edu/publicaffairs/news/2013/08/08-14-2013_brain_personality_traits.php.

56. Harold Pashler, Mark McDaniel, Doug Rohrer, and Robert Bjork, "Learning Styles: Concepts and Evidence," *Psychological Science in the Public Interest* 9, no 3 (2008): 105–19. See also Polly R. Husmann and Valerie Dean O'Loughlin, "Another Nail in the Coffin for Learning Styles? Disparities among Undergraduate Anatomy Students' Study Strategies, Class Performance, and Reported VARK Learning Styles," *Anatomical Sciences Education* 12, no. 1 (2019): 6–19.

57. Christian Gaser and Gottfried Schlaug, "Brain Structures Differ between Musicians and Non-Musicians," *Journal of Neuroscience* 23, no. 27 (2003): 9240–45. See also Gottfried Schlaug, Lutz Jäncke, Y. X. Huang, and H. Steinmetz, "In Vivo Evidence of Structural Brain Asymmetry in Musicians," *Science* 3 (1995): 267.

58. Krista L. Hyde, Jason Lerch, Andrea Norton, Marie Forgeard, Ellen Winner, Alan C. Evans, and Gottfried Schlaug, "The Effects of Musical Training on Structural Brain Development: A Longitudinal Study," *Annals of the New York Academy of Sciences* 1169 (2009): 182–86.

59. National Aphasia Assocation, "Aphasia FAQs," www.aphasia.org/aphasia-faqs/.

60. Richard Knox, "Singing Therapy Helps Stroke Patients Speak Again," NPR, December 26, 2011, www.npr.org/sections/health-shots/2011/12/26/144152193/singing-therapy-helps-stroke-patients-speak-again.

61. See Northwestern University, "Auditory Neuroscience Laboratory," 2019, Brainvolts, www.soc.northwestern.edu/brainvolts/.

62. Emily Gersema, "Music Training Can Change Children's Brain Structure and Boost the Decision-Making Network," USCDornsife, November 28, 2017, https://dornsife.usc.edu/news/stories/2711/music-training-can-change-childrens-brain-structure-and-boost-th/.

63. Assal Habibi, Antonio Damasio, Beatriz Ilari, Ryan Veiga, Anand A. Joshi, Richard M. Leahy, Justin P. Haldar, Divya Varadarajan, Chitresh Bhushan, and Hanna Damasio, "Childhood Music Training Induces Change in Micro- and Macroscopic Brain Structure: Results from a Longitudinal Study," *Cerebral Cortex* 28, no. 12 (2017): 4336–47.

64. Steven Pinker, *How the Mind Works* (New York: W. W. Norton, 1997), 534.

65. Ibid.

66. See Dan Sperber, "The Modularity of Thought and the Epidemiology of Representations," in *Mapping the Mind: Domain Specificity in Cognition and Culture*, ed. Lawrence A. Hirschfeld and Susan A. Gelman (Cambridge: Cambridge University Press, 1994), 56. See also Dan Sperber, *Explaining Culture: A Naturalistic Approach* (Cambridge, MA: Blackwell, 1996).

67. Howard Gardner, *Frames of Mind: The Theory of Multiple Intelligences* (New York: Basic Books, 1983), 123.

68. Steven Mithen, *The Singing Neanderthals* (Cambridge, MA: Harvard University Press, 2007), 1.

69. For an overview of the many hypotheses about the importance and use of music that both pre- and postdate Pinker's infamous "cheesecake" dismissal of it, see Mithen, *Singing Neanderthals*, 5, where he cites the work of Ian Cross, Elizabeth Tolbert, Nicholas Bannon, Robin Dunbar, John Blacking, and Alison Wray.

70. Pinker, *How the Mind Works*, 24.

71. Daniel Robinson, *An Intellectual History of Psychology*, 3rd ed. (Madison: University of Wisconsin Press, 1995), 338.

72. David Chalmers, "Facing up to the Problem of Consciousness," *Journal of Consciousness Studies* 2, no. 3 (March 1995): 200–19.

73. Joseph LeDoux, *Synaptic Self: How Our Brains Become Who We Are* (New York: Penguin, 2002), 10.

74. Ibid.

75. Monica Cowart, "Embodied Cognition," Internet Encyclopedia of Philosophy, www.iep.utm.edu/embodcog/#H2.

76. Eric Kandel, *In Search of Memory: The Emergence of a New Science of Mind* (New York: W. W. Norton, 2006), 9.

77. LeDoux, *Synaptic Self*, 10.

78. Ibid., 11.

79. Jason Stanley and John W. Krakauer, "Motor Skill Depends on Knowledge of Facts," *Frontiers of Human Neuroscience* 7, no. 503 (August 2013): 1–11.

80. Jason Stanley and John W. Krakauer, "Is the Dumb Jock Really a Nerd?" *New York Times*, October 27, 2013, http://opinionator.blogs.nytimes.com/2013/10/27/is-the-dumb-jock-really-a-nerd/.

81. Howard Gardner, *Intelligence Reframed* (New York: Basic Books, 1999), 22.

82. Stanley and Krakauer, "Dumb Jock."

83. Ibid.

84. Howard Gardner, "Big Thinkers: Howard Gardner on Multiple Intelligences," Edutopia, April 1, 2009, www.edutopia.org/multiple-intelligences-howard-gardner-video.

85. LeDoux, *Synaptic Self*, 23.

86. Ibid.

87. Stanley and Krakauer, "Dumb Jock."

88. Michael Gazzaniga, "Personal Identity, Neuroethics and the Human Brain," Media Central, April 14, 2005, https://mediacentral.princeton.edu/media/Personal+Idenity%2C+Neuroethics+and+the+Human+Brain/1_3mogkeqb.

89. My personal account, as I was in attendance. Reaction can be heard in Gazzaniga, "Personal Identity," starting with Gazzaniga's statement at 15:47.

3

HOW LEARNING WORKS

What is learning? This is the vital question of cognitive science. Certainly learning is a fundamental—some say *the* fundamental—human enterprise. Given that the relatively new field of cognitive neuroscience is investigating the most complex system in the known universe, it should not be terribly surprising that exactly how humans learn is still not completely understood, yet the dogged quest to do so continues.

The most widely accepted working theory is that learning is not one discrete process but rather a complex, three-step process of attention, learning itself, and memory. Let's consider these related processes within the binary system encountered in chapter 2 (know-that and know-how) but only because this binary system and its vocabulary are still very much in use in psychology. As noted in chapter 2, this binary view was deeply rooted in the ancient world, so it will take some time for the eroding boundaries between body and brain to produce a new concept, and a new vocabulary, for understanding ourselves as a unified whole.

TWO BASIC MODES OF INFORMATION PROCESSING

Our construct of human knowledge presently rests on two pillars: knowledge that is gained by exercising the human attribute of reason, or *rational knowledge*, and knowledge gained through sensory experience, known as *empirical knowledge*. This dichotomy is still reflected in standard modern learning theories, despite the many terms used to describe them. Two of the most accepted are *declarative learning* and *procedural learning*.

Declarative learning (know-that) is information that one can speak about, or "declare." The construction know-that refers to knowledge of facts, as in "I know that a formant is a resonance of the vocal tract." This kind of knowledge is not innate; it has to be declared to the learner and is best elucidated with an expert teacher as a guide. Declarative learning typically takes place over a time period of days, weeks, or months. Memory for words and life episodes also falls under the category of declarative learning.

Procedural learning (know-how) refers to learning physical skills (procedures) by doing and is inclusive of both those innate movements with which we are born, like crawling, and advanced skills like learning to ride a bicycle or play a musical instrument. The field of study dedicated to research in procedural learning is called *motor learning*, wherein *motor* refers both to motion and to the *motor* neurons (brain cells) that create movement.

Procedural learning in humans begins almost from birth. We are, one might say, preprogrammed to learn to grasp and crawl and then walk all on our own as toddlers, which we do by trying, falling, and trying again—no teacher is necessary. Acquisition of the physical movements needed for survival advance relatively quickly, usually in a matter of hours. Thus a crucial difference between declarative learning and procedural learning is the speed with which each adheres.

However, advanced muscular skills (also called *higher-order* muscular tasks), like those on display in a concert pianist, do not come preinstalled in humans and must be learned via a combination of declarative and procedural learning. Singing displays this dual nature: we explore the range and extent of our own voices by wailing, giggling, and cooing as babies. As we mature, we can easily find our own singing voice, particularly if our surrounding culture provides for it and supports it: family sing-alongs and community singing in religious services provide just these opportunities. Many singers of popular styles report these experiences as formative and rightfully claim to be self-taught.

However, those wishing to learn the Western, classical tradition of singing—which is distinguished by a large pitch range, sustained breathing, natural amplification, seamless register shifts, and agile execution of rapid scale passages—must first be led by a master teacher as a guide and then must practice with regularity and discipline. Due to these requirements, this style of singing is anything but natural; indeed, it could be called "supranatural." Singers of contemporary commercial styles may experience a great deal of success on their own, but those who wish to extend their vocal range, stamina, and control find that working with a voice coach typically advances these aims further than going solo.

Regardless of the instrument, working with a music teacher involves learning high-order tasks that are more complex and refined than generic strumming or voicing. High-order and complex muscular tasks all have one attribute in common: they require practice over time. High-order muscular tasks are situated at the nexus of declarative and procedural learning: as described by Stanley and Krakauer in chapter 2, we must first *know that* in order to *know how*. Table 3.1 illustrates the standard synonyms in use for declarative and procedural learning and their attributes.

LEARNING DEFINED

From the inception of the field of psychology in the early nineteenth century, learning has been its most assiduously studied topic. Schools of thought and their resultant vocabularies arose in both Europe and America, yet in the face of the subject's enormity and without the connective power of the Internet, the creation of a commonly accepted definition of learning was nearly impossible. In the twenty-first century, our ability to view the brain's inner workings in real time via fMRI and the rapid dissemination of digital information have generated much more information yet not necessarily more clarity toward a definition of learning.

Nevertheless, a definition of learning is needed in order to understand some fundamental properties of learning and then apply those properties to music teaching, learning, and performance. Therefore two simple definitions for each of the modes of learning are offered here, condensed from the most common elements found in accepted learning theories.

Table 3.1. The Two Basic Modes of Human Information Processing and Their Attributes

Declarative Learning (also called Declarative Memory)	Procedural Learning (also called Procedural Memory)
propositional	tacit
explicit	implicit
controlled	automatic
learned	inherent
slow	fast
demands attention	can multitask
avoidable	unavoidable
volitional	not volitional
know-that	know-how
top-down (via the executive control center of the brain)	bottom-up (via the autonomic nervous system)

—⟐⟐⟐—

The Classic Two Modes of Learning

Declarative Learning. A process that results in a permanent change in behavior as a result of *experience*.

Procedural Learning. A process that results in a permanent change in behavior as a result of *practice*.

—⟐⟐⟐—

Notice that both definitions are exactly the same except for the crucial factor that causes each type of learning to adhere, or "cause a permanent change in behavior." These factors are experience and practice.

In the case of declarative learning, if the information presented is easily understood and there is a desire to learn it, it is often enough to simply be introduced to a topic to be able to claim it later as learned. More challenging types of declarative information (such as note names and key signatures) must be studied in order to be learned. As any student knows, studying facts to the extent that they can be successfully recalled for an exam requires motivation and diligence. Thus another key attribute of declarative learning that distinguishes it from procedural learning is *volition*—the learner must want to learn, as captured in this canny bit of folk wisdom: You can lead a horse to water, but you can't make it drink.

Motivation, desire, and volition are all components of our inner emotional landscape and undergird *episodic memory* (life experiences), which, as already noted, are a subset of declarative learning. Typically these experiences must contain enough emotion to be remembered, like the joy of one's wedding day or the excruciating grief experienced by the loss of a loved one. These events do not require practice to embed them in memory; they are seared there by strong feelings. This explains why not all things that are experienced are necessarily remembered, like where you parked at the grocery store, an unarguably unremarkable event—unless you are at the same time rear-ended by a distracted driver. The addition of strong emotion (shock, anger, humiliation) rockets an event from routine to remarkable in an instant.

Conversely, procedural learning requires doing. No substitutions are viable. Procedural learning of basic human skills occurs concurrently with the development of *proprioception*, which is the body's own sense of its movements, positions, balance, and *spatial orientation* (where it is in relation to other people and objects). Learning these most fundamental human physical skills is largely *nonvolitional*; we learn them by experiencing the world, thus the learning will occur whether we wish it to or not, as a matter of survival.

Thus procedural learning and declarative learning exhibit significant differences regarding speed of acquisition and volition. But both types of learning share certain common processes, which I will address before returning to their differences in chapter 4.

THE TRIUMVIRATE OF LEARNING

The three-step process of attention, learning itself, and memory functions much like the ancient Roman triumvirate, a political alliance of three separate but equally powerful players who worked together toward a common goal. And like those ancient Roman politicians, these three phases are complex and display their own distinct attributes. Yet they also overlap within a connected neural network and attend both declarative and procedural learning. A very simplified scheme of these three phases is provided here as I explain both the psychological and the neurobiological processes that support learning.

———◦◦◦———

How Learning Works

Step One: Attention. This is the prerequisite condition for learning. Learning cannot happen until and unless one first pays attention. Note: Attention has a limited capacity in the human brain.

Brain Activity—Biochemical changes, specifically the release of chemical messengers called *neurotransmitters*. In the early stages of learning, the *synapses* (the gaps between brain cells where chemical messages are exchanged) are temporarily destabilized.

Step Two: Learning Itself. This is the dynamic process whereby new information is first absorbed (called *short-term memory*), sorted and manipulated (called *working memory*), and then combined with what we already know (called *constructive memory*).

Brain Activity—More release of neurotransmitters. With repetition, the number of synaptic connections in the brain begins to stabilize. This process is called *memory consolidation*.

Step Three: Long-Term Memory. Once a thing has been learned, it has exited the realm of learning (short-term and working memory) and exists in the realm of *long-term memory*. Long-term memory is like a treasure chest where things of value are stored and from which they can be retrieved. The evidence that a thing is learned is its repeatability. In the motor realm, this is called *automaticity*.

Brain Activity—Anatomical changes in brain tissue are observed. The brain has reorganized itself.

———◦◦◦———

Step One: Attention

Attention is the first and arguably the most powerful player in the triumvirate of learning. As such, it is the subject of much current scientific research and even the star of its own academic journal. Given its prominence, attention is a player you will encounter repeatedly throughout this book.

Perhaps the most important attribute of attention is that it is not a solo entity but a complex neurological system distributed throughout the brain via a connected neural network. Scientists' current understanding of attention is that this network is made up of four components, the first two being our primary ways of paying attention: first, a state exemplified by its name, the *default mode*, and second, a state called *executive attention*, which governs conscious control of attention for staying on task. The third component of attention acts an *attentional switch*, directing the brain's resources among the previous two primary two modes of attention. The fourth component is an *attentional filter*, constantly patrolling the perimeter outside our conscious awareness like a sentry poised to alert us to the presence of danger or some other compelling distraction.[1] Let us consider the first three components (I will revisit the fourth in chapter 6 for its role in performance anxiety).

Default mode is the place to which the brain returns when not engaged in a cognitive task or hijacked by some other arousal.[2] One of the default mode's discoverers, Marcus Raichle, notes that it was discovered almost by accident. When people whose brains were being scanned during cognitive tasks were given a rest, their brain activity actually increased instead of decreasing as expected. In fact, in subsequent experiments, Raichle and his team discovered that "the cost of intrinsic [brain] activity far exceeds that of evoked activity"; in other words, the great majority of the brain's energy budget—estimated to be an amazing 60–80 percent—is given over to fuel this interior default mode instead of tasks that come at us from the outside.[3] This is an enormously important finding. Raichle nicknamed this brain energy "dark energy" to describe forces as yet "unaccounted for."[4]

Two nicknames for the default mode, "daydreaming mode" and "mind-wandering mode," further enlighten us as to its function. Unfortunately, these labels conjure images of laziness and lethargy, which obfuscate not only the intrinsic brainwork that happens in this state (as evidenced by its energy consumption) but also the deep worth of this mode to our cognitive function. Far from being a slothful state, the default mode is where we go to plan, project, and envision our lives. Because of this, the default mode is also credited with being an arena where connections occur and creativity happens. This explains the sudden insight that can attend such mind-wandering activities as a short doze or a walk in nature—even a bout of mindless housekeeping chores can help our brains reset.

This research is both exciting and even vindicating for composers, writers, and other creative thinkers who have historically been exhorted to get their head out of the clouds and stop daydreaming. Now it appears that the cloud of the mind (not the Internet) may be the most fertile place for a brain to be.

By contrast, executive attention pushes out distractions when "evoked activities" necessitate it, sharpening the mental focus necessary for staying on task and the mental acuity needed for jobs that require a high degree of accuracy. An important point about these first two, primary ways of paying attention is that, when one system is operational, the other is down. Thus we can trust that a trained surgeon who operates on us is herself operating strictly in executive attention and not daydreaming (or default-moding) her way through our procedure.

Attention Aids: Emotion and Desire

So far, a few points about attention are clear. First, attention is the prerequisite condition for learning; a person simply cannot learn until he first attends. In fact, it is generally agreed that all high-order cognitive tasks depend on attention as regulated by executive attention (the central executive network). But it is equally clear that refreshment in the daydreaming state is not only pleasant but essential to our mental health and our humanity and similarly essential to becoming and being a musician. With such importance attached to attention, we might well wonder what assists attention and what is toxic to it. We will now consider the former and return to the latter in chapter 7.

People with normally ordered brains can choose to switch on executive attention by exerting the human parameter of free will but only when inspired to do so by desire; learners must first want to pay attention before they truly can. Furthermore, our brains are receptive to new information relative to how much we care about that information. Therefore, the measure of desire is a particularly significant component of voluntary attention. But what sparks desire in the first place? The simple answer is emotion. But like everything else having to do with the human condition, emotion is far from simple. Emotion is a vast and complex subject as well as an age-old conundrum. Emotion has bedeviled human beings for as long as we have been sentient.

Aristotle's (384–322 BCE) term for emotion was *pathé*, variously translated as "desire" or "appetite." During the seventeenth century, René Descartes recognized the physiological upheavals generated by these appetites as "passions of the soul" and attributed this agitation to the pineal gland in the brain, which he believed to be home base for the human soul.

Eighteenth-century beliefs about emotion were rocked by romantic thought, which regarded emotion as a natural and raw human attribute that, enchained by propriety, longed to escape its restraining fetters. This take on emotion persisted through the nineteenth and early twentieth centuries, and in some sense it is still present in popular culture, particularly among artists.

As noted in chapter 1, in the early twentieth century, emotion experienced a banishment at the hands of behaviorist psychologists, who eschewed emotion as far too frivolous for serious scientific study. And even though the cognitive revolution overturned behaviorism at mid-century, the pioneers of cognitivism had as much interest in emotion as had their predecessors, which is to say, almost none.

Yet new research on emotion from neuroscience reveals that emotion, rather than being rationality's silly and polar opposite, is fundamentally entwined with human reason. Neuroscientists like Antonio Damasio, Jaak Panksepp, and Joseph LeDoux have worked to repair the mind-body split proposed by Descartes by plucking emotion from the ephemeral realm of the spirit and grounding it within the physical functions of the body. Emotions, according to LeDoux, are solidly defined as "biological functions of the nervous system." Damasio, through his now-famous somatic marker hypothesis, has advanced emotion as a critical component of human decision-making and thus an assistant to reason—a far cry from its centuries-old characterization as a fickle temptress who leads us astray from reason. And as already noted, unless a person cares enough to expend some effort, he will not learn because he will not have "attended." So emotion sparks desire, which in turn ignites attention.

Emotion plays an equally critical role in *memory consolidation*, which is the cognitive term for learning. Emotion helps encode our experiences into long-term memory, all the more so if the emotions are strong ones. It is perhaps for this reason that extreme technical breakthroughs in a music lesson, or superlative performance experiences, are deeply remembered.

On the other end of the emotion spectrum, extremely frightening or humiliating events can become so encoded in memory that certain stimuli, especially smells and sounds, can activate the so-called alerting network of our attentional filter. Harmless sounds like fireworks can recall a returning war veteran's memories of enemy fire with devastating consequences for mental health, as is seen in post-traumatic stress disorder (PTSD). Even the scent of a certain aftershave or a special sound (the personal ringtone on a cell phone), if they are entangled with memories of particularly brutal or humiliating events, can engender symptoms of PTSD. Please note, however, that emotion's role in the triumvirate of attention, learning, and memory has been qualified as needing to be intense in order to persist. Tripping during a stage entrance or enduring the snarky comments of a nasty colleague, as unpleasant or unwarranted as such events might be, should not deeply encode themselves in the long-term memories of most people or to such a degree as to cause long-term damage. An outsize reaction to such slights may be a component of music performance anxiety, an affliction I will consider separately in chapter 6.

Attention Aids: Motivation and Rewards

Desire is the ignition system of attention. Most musicians can recall an event or series of experiences that first sparked their desire to learn to play an instrument or sing. The early learning experiences that followed may have been marked by joyful exploration. But how do musicians keep desire alive during the long slog to mastery? How do they stay motivated to commit to a practice regimen? Admittedly, desire and motivation are among the most elusive conditions to sustain, as anyone who has tried to commit to a study schedule, exercise routine, or diet can attest. Still, there are a few things known to ignite desire and to support continued motivation for staying on course.

Before considering them, let us quickly dispense with a popular yet ultimately counterproductive method for boosting desire and motivation: the use of rewards, such as candy, praise, or money, all of which come straight from the behaviorist playbook. As noted in chapter 1, researcher Alfie Kohn has shown that such incentives are not only ineffective but can actually contribute to a damaging spiral of regression into stasis. Readers are strongly encouraged to read Kohn's persuasive writing on this issue, but some of his most essential findings are summarized here. Note that these findings apply to all people who operate within a reward system, whether as children in a family, students in school, or adults in the workplace.[5]

- Rewards are dispensed by a giver who is in a more powerful position than the doer, who is the receiver of the reward. Therefore, rewards are ultimately about power and manipulation. In this configuration, there is little space for the doer to develop their own intrinsic motivation. These are very shallow roots upon which to build moral behavior, strong learning, or a fulfilling career. Shallow-rooted trees blow over in a strong wind.
- People who operate within a reward system tend to hyperfocus on the end goal (the reward) and rush toward it, to the detriment of quality. Similarly, people who rush toward the reward do so to the detriment of creativity. Quality and creativity take time to achieve.
- People who operate within a reward system, whether children, students, or adults, may respond in the short term to rewards, but since the reward itself is the goal and not improved behavior, stronger learning, or higher-quality work, these attributes do not survive once the reward is removed. Treats and financial incentives are quick fixes but do not cultivate long-term habits.

So if rewards are not the primary forces that stimulate human endeavor and creativity, what are? It seems that most humans are more stimulated by intrinsic rewards—for example, joy in pursuing the endeavor itself, the excitement of discovery, a deep sense of meaning and contribution to a cause, or the freedom of charting one's own course. Indeed, autonomy has proven to be one of the most prized characteristics cited by employees on ratings of job satisfaction.[6]

Kohn has often noted that, in his research on this topic, he is continually reminded that punishments and rewards are ultimately about power and manipulation. When motivation and desire become mixed up with power and manipulation, the propensity for coercion always crouches close by. Yet there is this deep truth: no one person can tempt, bribe, or force another to sincerely feel desire for learning or experience motivation for staying on a focused path. Even in the most extreme cases of coercion, no one can be forced to feel a false emotion. Children pushed to take music lessons may go through the motions (like practice) to please a coach or receive parental rewards, but there is no way around this essential truth. The extremely abusive childhood of internationally renowned Chinese pianist Lang Lang bears this out.

In an interview, Lang Lang recounted a litany of abuse by his father, Lang Guoren, who quit his job as a policeman in their industrial home-town, left his wife (and Lang Lang's mother) behind, and moved with his nine-year-old son to the city of Beijing so he could oversee a brutal practice regimen meant to ready Lang Lang for audition at the Central Conservatory of Music. Lang Lang's father's creed was "pressure always turns into motivation." But Lang Lang reports that, even as a child, "I found the pressure unnecessary because I was a workaholic from the very beginning. I could understand if I was lazy and didn't care, but I didn't need that kind of push, because I knew what I wanted."

Despite his motivation, the nine-year-old was kicked out of his Beij-ing music teacher's studio (she said he had no talent), causing his father to go, in Lang Lang's account, "totally nuts." Lang Guoren actually demanded that the boy kill himself for shame, handing him a bottle of pills to do the deed. Lang Lang ran to the balcony of their small apart-ment, but his father followed, screaming, "Then jump off and die." Obviously, Lang Lang did not comply, and today he is one of the world's reigning concert pianists. But he recalls beating his hands vio-lently against the wall in order to ruin them and make practicing impos-sible, an embargo that lasted for months. It was only when he found his own joy in playing that he returned to his practice routine, motivated by an inner desire to reaudition for the conservatory, which he accom-plished at the tender age of ten, receiving a full scholarship.[7]

This admittedly extreme example of coercion demonstrates that if attention is completely voluntary, so too is the deployment of its aids, desire and motivation. When these systems are firing at full speed, there are several procedures that can also assist attention.

Attention Aid: Goal-Setting

One of the best techniques shown to sustain motivation and keep atten-tion on track is *goal-setting*, the conscious act of listing one or several goals that one wishes to reach. Goal-setting has been shown in the short run to stimulate motivation and in the long run to actually increase achievement. Goal-setting works in part by concretizing vague notions of achievement.

It also promotes focus, cultivates self-regulation by aiding impulse control, and helps calibrate efficient use of time and financial resources. These various benefits accrue to promote positive feelings, which in turn feed more motivation. In order for these benefits to occur, several factors must be taken into consideration.

Who is the goal-setter? Given the high degree of independence needed in mastering an instrument, the goal-setter must be the student musician himself, not his teacher, parents, or friends. This correlates with similar findings that self-motivation is the most effective type of motivation. In this case, mastering one's destiny can be an extremely powerful motivator. Interestingly, the best learners are those who demonstrate both greater persistence and willingness to fail—both of which are necessary conditions for learning.

Goals must be valued by the goal-setter. Aspirations that are not one's own are doomed from the outset. In addition, dreams so freighted with the wishes of others (parents, for example) can severely compromise the mental health of the learner who takes on another's vision, as the biographies of wunderkinds in music and sports have sadly attested.

Goals must be specific. Goals that are specific ("I want to develop a more efficient fingering strategy") are more likely to be attained than goals that are vague ("I want to become a better musician"). Similarly, goals that are written down, shared with a teacher, or posted on the bathroom mirror are more likely to be heeded than those that exist simply in the learner's mind.

Goals must be realistic and realizable. Learners can follow the old adage "Don't bite off more than you can chew," but teachers are enormously influential in this category and can set learning parameters that are both challenging and achievable.

There must be both short-term and long-term goals. Learners will likely stay more motivated if they can experience success relatively quickly with a short-term goal while keeping their eyes on the prize of a long-term goal. Teachers can construct lessons that guarantee early accomplishment, gradually moving the goals outward in concentric rings of success.

Goal-setters must answer the question "How?" One study reported that students who were required to not only state their goals but also write exactly how they intended to achieve them were more likely to succeed. Rather than saying "I will practice a lot," which is vague, a developing musician should assess how much practice time they can devote to their instrument per week, draft a schedule, then commit to it.

A note to teachers: You can require your students to share these goals with you in writing at the outset of your relationship. If musicians in your studio are failing to achieve at their predicted rate, it can be very enlightening for both parties to return to this document for an assessment.

Musicians can use these tools to refashion their practice routines to ensure higher rates of success. As noted, the desire to pay attention—what some researchers have termed the *arousal*, or *preattentional*, phase of learning—is key. Once hooked, we must apply effort to our learning, a certain doggedness known as grit, which mainlines strong emotion to fuel perseverance. Without emotion, desire, and motivation, our experiences are ephemeral; nothing sticks. Exposure is not learning.

Attention Aid: Sleep

Besides emotion, desire, motivation, and goal-setting, one final parameter that is known to boost attention is sleep. Lack of sleep damages attention. The eye-popping news from neuroscience, however, is that sleep is actually a critical phase of the learning process itself.

Like so many other brain states under review, sleep is now understood as a complex set of brain processes and not a single state of being. It is known that lack of adequate sleep impairs brain function overall, damages learning, weakens performance in cognitive tests, and slows reaction time for tasks that require alertness, like driving and operating heavy machinery. Yet the underlying biological reasons for why sleep deprivation is so damaging and conversely why abundant sleep is so restorative are still something of a mystery. Several studies offer some clues.

An important sleep study in 2013 revealed that sleep may be critical for what amounts to brain cleaning. According to these researchers, the brain lacks a conventional version of the *lymphatic system* (which clears cellular debris out of the body), so it evolved its own metabolic system, dubbed the *glymphatic system*, which operates during sleep to flush away waste products accumulated during wakefulness. This waste is not benign but actually toxic to brain cells. According to this theory, the uncluttered and detoxified brain should rise from sleep refreshed and more able to pay attention.

A second theory holds that sleep and attention may have coevolved as brain states that serve to regulate each other, albeit in different ways. This theory is based on the observation that sleep and executive attention share two common traits essential for normal brain function: suppression and plasticity.

Regarding suppression, this theory starts with the observation that the sentry-like qualities of the attentional filter—agility, vigilance, and the suppression of trivia—come at a cost: this vigilance tires the body and requires sleep to reenergize it. During sleep, a type of suppression different from the one that is active during the day seems to come on duty. We might think of this as a changing of the guard: while one sentry sleeps, the other is actively blocking external stimuli in order that we might fall asleep and stay asleep. Recent research suggests that the difference between these two sentries is the degree to which their efforts affect the entire brain. The sentry on "wakefulness watch" duty must operate alongside the other three components of the attentional system, and so its efforts are somewhat shared and thus attenuated. But during sleep, the "nighttime" suppression sentry has been observed (in studies of humans and other mammals) to completely overtake the brain, allowing us to enjoy a deep, refreshing sleep.

The second of the two common traits of sleep and executive attention is neuroplasticity. Note that *neuro-* refers to neurons, the nerve cells that make up the brain, and *-plasticity* in this case refers to the malleable nature of the brain, which undergoes physiological changes due to experience. This is important: Neuroplasticity is nothing less than the biological basis of learning. As such (and as you might imagine), neuroplasticity is certainly at work during our waking hours, but what has been discovered is that neuroplasticity is also active during sleep. We might say we are learning twenty-four hours a day, even during sleep! How is this possible?

It starts with the theory of *synaptic pruning*, the processes by which synapses (connections between neurons) that are weak (due to lack of attention or practice) wither away, leaving behind those synaptic connections that are strongest. It is believed that sleep is the state most conducive to this pruning process because the brain is least subject to interference from incoming stimuli (recall our suppression sentry).

Finally, a related theory is that one cognitive purpose of sleeping and dreaming is to replay short-term memories gathered throughout the previous day and in so doing strengthen the neural pathways of those memories and send them along their journey to long-term *memory consolidation*—the cognitive term for learning itself.

Step Two: Learning

"If you are learning, you have not at the same time learned."
—Aristotle

Aristotle's profound observation perfectly captures two important facets of learning. The first is its essence, which is its dynamic nature. That is, learning is marked by change, even instability. Learning is messy. If approached with a no-holds-barred spirit of adventure, learning can be fun. But learning can also be challenging to the point of joylessness, distress, or even humiliation. Nevertheless, we cannot take a pass on learning; it is a fundamental—some say *the* fundamental—human endeavor.

Yet given learning's dynamic nature, we cannot always be in a state of upheaval and transition. Learned items must be stowed in order to make way for new experiences and ideas and also for later retrieval. Thus, once learning has progressed from the transitive to the past tense ("I have learned"), we are no longer actively learning. The second facet of Aristotle's astute observation is then realized: the learned thing is a fait accompli and is now stored in long-term memory.

This process—from "learning" to "have learned"—is memory consolidation. Much research has been devoted to this process, which leads from the moment new information is first absorbed and held in the mind for a period of seconds (short-term memory) to the sorting and manipulation of this information while we are actively learning (working memory) to the final result, long-term memory.

In order to comprehend this process, see the next section, "Working Memory and Manipulation." Picture short-term memory as a brainpad of sticky notes—a place to temporarily jot down impressions, facts, or sensations—but just like a real wad of sticky notes, short-term memories are easily misplaced if we are not attentive to them.

Working memory is the heart of the learning process in which we manipulate our sticky notes, toss them about with facts we already know, and recombine them with experiences we have already had in order to make sense of them. Researchers refer to this part of the learning process as *maintenance* or *maintenance plus manipulation.* An attribute of working memory that is just as important as this juggling act is its ability to keep irrelevant information from entering our attentional field. What follows is a restatement of this process in condensed form so as to incorporate one new and vital piece of information.

———《〆/〆/〆》———

Working Memory and Manipulation

Learning is the process whereby we hold about seven bits, or four chunks, of information in mind, manipulate those bits or chunks, and recombine them with facts or experiences we already know.

———《〆/〆/〆》———

Working memory, or learning, is a process that starts by considering a few bits or scraps (or sticky notes, if you prefer) of information. The number of bits is "seven (plus or minus two)," the compound number famously posited in 1956 by George Miller, a founder of cognitive psychology (and one of those early revolutionaries introduced in chapter 1). More recently, these bits are now understood as chunks of information, of which we seem to be able to manage around four. Let us consider how this works.

Chunking

Working memory is what is allowing you to read this chapter and hopefully learn from it. As your reading progresses, your success is partly dependent upon your ability to maintain the information from the previous paragraphs in your mind; each successive paragraph can build on the next only by your retention of the former. For example, if you have been reading with concentration, you know that we are now considering step 2 of the learning process, learning itself. Step 1 is the topic of attention, with side trips featuring bits of information about emotion, desire, and sleep that nevertheless were all related to the main topic of attention. As such, we may call the topic of attention a chunk made up of the mini-components (bits, scraps, or sticky notes) of emotion, desire, sleep, and so forth. Researchers have invented a new verb—*chunking*—to describe this amalgamation of bits. Chunking itself is the subject of much research; for example, people with superior memories seem to be able to manipulate greater numbers of chunks than the average person, plus the chunks themselves contain many more bits than the average person can juggle. Yet evidence is mounting that all of us can learn to use chunking to improve learning and develop better memory capabilities. It just takes practice.

Constructed Memories

One final component of learning deserves mention: the notion of *recombination*. As I have already shown, learning begins with attention, followed by absorbing new bits information into our short-term memory, then using working attention to manipulate those bits, and finally storing those bits in long-term memory. But no learner is a blank slate, and our individual slates become more populated with ideas and experiences as we navigate our lives. We call these ideas and experiences *memories*.

Any process of absorbing new information will necessarily collide with our previous memories, so in order to calm the collision and make sense of it all, we recombine the new information with the memories we already own. This dynamic moment in the learning process is called *constructive memory*, and its product we may call a "constructed memory," which we may loosely liken to a dairy treat in which the vanilla ice cream is like the foundation of our memories and the chocolate chips, nuts, and multi-colored sprinkles mixed in are bits of accumulated new information.

The main benefit of constructive memory is its cumulative quality: we use past experiences to change our actions in the present and also to imagine the future. We learn from our mistakes and build on our little victories. But detriments due to constructive memory abound, chief among them being memory's fallibility. It is known that human memory is enormously prone to distortion and outright error. Because the information we absorb (the chocolate) is always mixed in with what we already know—or think we know—(the vanilla ice cream base), our memories are constantly in flux and never completely pure or stable. This is the dynamic core of learning itself. As our memories pile up, our minds create frameworks to keep them organized. These frameworks are called *schemas* (or *schemata*) and are defined as a cognitive structure for representing, organizing, and retrieving related information. As you shall see in chapter 4, schemas are particularly important in motor learning.

Step Three: Memory

The complex neurobiological process of learning itself is encoded in a maxim called Hebb's rule: "Neurons that fire together wire together."[8] Learning begins when the synapses (the gaps between neurons) are excited by a thought or a sensation. With the addition of attention, emotion, and desire, short-term memory rapidly progresses to working memory—otherwise known as learning. Repeated reactivation of the same neurons (through repetition or practice) is what creates a *neural pathway*—a memory. The process of encoding working memory to long-term memory is called memory consolidation. As elegantly phrased by cognitive scientist Gary Marcus, "the ability to learn starts with the ability to remember. An organism can learn from experience only if it can rewire its nervous system in a lasting way; there can be no learning without memory."[9] For our purposes in this book (understanding how humans learn), the word *memory* may be considered synonymous with *have learned*.

Neuroscientist Eric Kandel was awarded a Nobel Prize in 2000 for his groundbreaking discoveries about the biological bases of memory.[10] By studying the lowly sea slug (a simple animal with relatively large neurons), Kandel discovered that short-term memory is not a diminutive version of long-term memory, as was previously believed, but is altogether biologically distinct. Short-term memories cause biochemical changes in the brain by the release of neurotransmitters, but long-term memories cause anatomical changes in brain tissue by growing new synaptic connections. In other words, learning stuff excites the brain, but storing stuff changes its structure.

Kandel's discoveries coincided with those of other researchers around the same time and led to the astounding realization that the brain continually remodels itself. This revelation of neural plasticity and the related discovery that the brain continually makes new brain cells cannot be overstressed, superimposed as they were on centuries of fixed-brain theory. Kandel's excitement—"We could see for the first time that the number of synapses in the brain is not fixed—it changes with learning!"—is palpable in his memoir tracing the process, *In Search of Memory*, a book that is also a deeply personal journey into his own past. When Kandel was a boy living in Nazi-occupied Vienna, his family was evicted, his father arrested without charge, and his home ransacked during the infamous Kristallnacht of 1938, the night of broken glass, in which Jewish homes, shops, and synagogues were ransacked throughout Germany and Austria. Kandel's haunting memories of that night and the exhortation to "never forget" is what led him to "investigate the biological basis of that motto: the processes in the brain that enable us to remember."[11]

Personal quests to understand have historically characterized scientific investigation, and brain science is no exception. Psychiatrist and author Norman Doidge (after first encountering Kandel at Columbia University as a resident) set off on a personal quest of his own to identify and interview researchers working in the vanguard of neuroscience. The result was his phenomenal bestseller *The Brain That Changes Itself*, one of the best popular-science books to date about neural plasticity.

Doidge calls neuroplasticity nothing short of a "revolution"—remember that word from chapter 1? Be alert when public intellectuals speak of revolution for at least two reasons, the first being its aftermath: is it over? Second, bear in mind the entity against which the revolution is pushing. In the case of the cognitive revolution, the antagonist is behaviorism. In the case of neuroplasticity and neurogenesis, the antagonist is fixed-brain theory.

NEUROGENESIS AND NEURAL PLASTICITY

For much of the past several centuries, it was believed that the adult brain did not change much past childhood and was, by all accounts, rather fixed. But thanks to the work of intrepid neuroscientists who plowed ahead with their research against the dogma of the time, that previous model of the brain as a mechanistic, ultrarational supercomputer that houses the ephemeral mind (Ryle's "ghost in the machine") has been deposed, replaced by a mutable, fizzing, biological mass of tissue that continually changes in response to all thought and experiences in the act of living. It is now accepted wisdom that brain cells (neurons) can regenerate (neurogenesis) and that the brain changes continually in response to experience (neuroplasticity). This is truly revolutionary.

Yet, according to Doidge, this excellent news has yet to sift its way into the general population. Many of us are still unwitting subscribers to fixed-brain theory (recall the paranoia that fueled the first-three-years movement in child development discussed in chapter 2). Doidge calls this "neurological nihilism," an outlook that has poisoned our belief in the possibility for change.[12] The tenacity of this outdated view is revealed when people speak of abilities as "hardwired" or refuse to apply themselves to a task on the grounds that they lack the talent or that it does not fit their "learning style."

The late renowned neuroscientist Oliver Sacks used the occasion of New Year resolutions for 2011 to combat neurological nihilism and campaign for brain change. In an essay titled "This Year, Change Your Mind," Sacks laments that most people still "do not realize that they can strengthen their brains" and exhorts readers to think again about "cognitive fitness" in light of the doctrine of neuroplasticity:

> Whether it is by learning a new language, traveling to a new place, developing a passion for beekeeping or simply thinking about an old problem in a new way, all of us can find ways to stimulate our brains to grow, in the coming year and those to follow. Just as physical activity is essential to maintaining a healthy body, challenging one's brain, keeping it active, engaged, flexible and playful, is not only fun. It is essential to cognitive fitness.[13]

Indeed, just as a bicep is enlarged or a waist whittled by sessions at the gym, the brain actually changes its structure in response to how it is used. Except in cases of frank brain disease, it does this continually, retaining a measure of this ability well into old age; in fact, studies of the brains of recently deceased people reveal that older adults produce just as many new brain cells as young people do, even up to the moment of death.[14] The old saw "You cannot teach an old dog new tricks" is no longer valid.

But neural pathways aren't simply constructed. They can also disintegrate when we deliberately stop or change our thoughts, for example (a technique used in anger management therapy), or through disuse from inactivity, injury, or disease. Hence an aphorism popular in many rehabilitative therapies, including those for stroke and dementia, has taken on new urgency due to current research in neural plasticity: "Use it or lose it." This aphorism applies to the physical components of technique (see chapter 4) as well as to the intellectual abilities needed in certain musical genres.

Singers who have studied foreign languages may especially appreciate this observation. When preparing an opera role or a song cycle in a foreign language, for example, the rate at which that language is acquired accelerates dramatically if the singer is living, working, and performing in a country in which that language is spoken. Unfortunately, when the curtain falls for the last time, if that same level of practice is not maintained, most people find that their newly acquired foreign language abilities atrophy significantly.

Practice may not make our music-making completely perfect, but at least it aims us in that direction by keeping us fit and in the game. In this age of brain science, our notion of fitness should updated to include the cognitive fitness that Sacks urges us to consider. Yet due to the complexity of the human brain, there is a flipside to cognitive fitness of which musicians must be aware.

THE PLASTIC PARADOX

New neural pathways can be startlingly quick to emerge and can, once constructed, become more established with use. The new twist on an old saw is, therefore, "You certainly can teach an old dog new tricks." But this old saw is a double-edged sword, for, while old dogs can continually learn new tricks, the older the dog, the more ingrained the habit (or trick). This is fine for habits you want to nurture. But if the habit is a chain you want to cast off, the more robust the neural pathway, the harder it is to break free. Doidge has called this rigidity "the plastic paradox."[15]

So is change from rigid habit even possible? Apparently yes; it is just difficult. Think of habit change as the most intense form of declarative learning; thus, it demands focused attention plus a heavy dose of I-want-to-ness (volition), and a dash of goal-setting would not hurt either. Yet even these attributes may not be strong enough to break up a strongly entrenched neural pathway. What is needed then is a stronger, more visceral approach.

Doidge likens this type of approach to going around a roadblock: just as when we are driving in heavy traffic and we encounter a roadblock, we find a way to go around. A growing body of brain research shows that the brain can do the same thing. This phenomenon has been observed in blind individuals (either from birth or blind because their visual cortex has been temporarily disabled) and also in deaf individuals. In these cases, other sensory systems are recruited to help, notably touch and sound for the blind and touch and sight for the deaf.

Perhaps even more astonishing than the recruitment itself is the speed with which it apparently happens. In early studies in which test subjects' vision was temporarily disabled, in only two days' time, their hobbled visual cortices took up the task of processing touch and sound sensations as evidenced by brain scans. And when the study was over, the subjects' usual brain functions returned to normal in just half that time.[16] In neuroscience, this has come to be called *cross-modal plasticity*, or the ability of a brain system to hack into a nearby system to take up the load for a damaged one.[17]

From this evidence, we may surmise that musicians, dancers, and others who depend upon a high level of motor skill could create roadblocks for themselves in order to heighten other senses. Certainly roadblocking is what a musician does when she closes her eyes in order to hear more acutely or wishes to sense her physical responses with more awareness.

Given Doidge's use of the term *roadblock* as a diverting of one's attention away from deeply ingrained and harmful habits in order to develop new and healthy ones, this might be a particularly potent tool for good in the music studio that nevertheless goes vastly underutilized, especially if it causes psychic discomfort in the learner.

The twin discoveries of neurogenesis and neural plasticity offer solid evidence for the promise of remodeling our habits of mind at any stage in life, just as we can remake our physical selves by dieting or embarking on an exercise regimen. Indeed, brain-training has long been championed by Michael Merzenich, a pioneer in brain plasticity research, who challenges us to act upon these revelations:

> Your issue, as it relates to this science [of brain plasticity], is how to maintain your own high-functioning learning machine. And of course, a well-ordered life in which learning is a continuous part of it is key. But also in your future is brain aerobics. Get ready for it. It's going to be a part of every life not too far in the future, just like physical exercise is a part of every well-organized life in the contemporary period. [18]

The fact that change is possible does not, of course, imply that change is easy. The fickle imps of motivation and desire must first be brought to heel. Merzenich acknowledged as much in a TED Talk on brain plasticity:

> Now that you know, now that science is telling us that you are in charge, that it's under your control, that your happiness, your well-being, your abilities, your capacities are capable of continuous modification, continuous improvement, and you're the responsible agent and party . . . of course a lot of people will ignore this advice. . . . Now that's another issue, and not my fault! [19]

Nevertheless, this news that has been anointed "the most important discovery in neuroscience in four centuries" overturns a deterministic and ultimately pessimistic view of learning and, by extension, of life itself, making plasticity one of the brightest sectors of brain science research. [20]

BACK TO THE BODY

Now that we have considered the cognitive processes common to both declarative (know-that) and procedural (know-how) learning, we can move on to spotlight the latter and two of its most significant differences: speed and volition. In the next chapter, I turn to a branch of psychology called *motor learning research*, wherein *motor* refers to muscle. Vestiges of the binary vocabulary encountered in chapters 2 and 3 are again evident in chapter 4 because they are still in use in psychology. Yet as you move through the chapter, note that the false boundaries between body and brain increasingly evaporate because the mind-body split, at least from the perspective of cognitive neuroscience, has resolved to a concept of embodied cognition.

NOTES

1. See Daniel Leviton, *The Organized Mind: Thinking Straight in the Age of Information Overload* (New York: Dutton, 2015), 37–74.

2. Marcus E. Raichle, Ann Mary MacLeod, Abraham Z. Snyder, William J. Powers, Debra A. Gusnard, and Gordon L. Shulman, "A Default Mode of Brain Function," *Proceedings of the National Academy of Sciences* 98, no. 2 (2001): 676–82.

3. Marcus E. Raichle and Abraham Z. Snyder, "A Default Mode of Brain Function: A Brief History of an Evolving Idea," *Neuroimage* 37, no. 4 (2007): 1087.

4. Marcus E. Raichle, "The Brain's Dark Energy," *Science* 314, no. 5803 (2006): 1249–50.

5. See Alfie Kohn, *Punished by Rewards: The Trouble with Gold Stars, Incentive Plans, A's, Praise, and Other Bribes* (Boston: Houghton Mifflin, 1993); and Alfie Kohn, "Rewards Are Still Bad News (25 Years Later)," October 28, 2018, www.alfiekohn.org/article/rewards-25-years-later/:

6. University of Birmingham, "Autonomy in the Workplace Has Positive Effects on Well-Being and Job Satisfaction, Study Finds," April 24, 2017, *ScienceDaily*, www.sciencedaily.com/releases/2017/04/170424215501.htm.

7. Rosanna Greenstreet, "Lang Lang: 'I'd Play the Piano at 5 a.m.,'" *Guardian*, May 13, 2011, www.theguardian.com/lifeandstyle/2011/may/14/lang-lang-piano-china-father.

8. Attributed to psychologist Donald Hebb in his 1949 book *The Organization of Behavior: A Neuropsychological Theory* (New York: Wiley, 1949).

9. Gary Marcus, *The Birth of the Mind: How a Tiny Number of Genes Creates the Complexities of Human Thought* (New York: Basic Books, 2004), 99.

10. John H. Byrne, "How Neuroscience Captured the Twenty--First Century's First Nobel Prize," *Cerebrum*, April 1, 2001. https://www.dana.org/article/how-neuroscience-captured-the-twenty-first-centurys-first-nobel-prize/.

11. Eric Kandel, *In Search of Memory: The Emergence of a New Science of Mind* (New York: W. W. Norton, 2006), 5.

12. Norman Doidge, *The Brain That Changes Itself* (New York: Viking Penguin, 2007), xviii.

13. Oliver Sacks, "This Year, Change Your Mind," *New York Times*, December 31, 2010, www.nytimes. com/2011/01/01/opinion/01sacks.html.

14. Cell Press, "Older Adults Grow Just as Many New Brain Cells as Young People," *Science Daily*, April 5, 2018, www.sciencedaily.com/releases/2018/04/180405223413.htm.

15. Doidge, *Brain That Changes*, 242–43.

16. Alvaro Pascual-Leone and Roy Hamilton, "The Metamodal Organization of the Brain," *Progress in Brain Research* 134 (2001): 427–45.

17. Daphne Bavelier and Helen J. Neville, "Cross-Modal Plasticity: Where and How?" *Nature Reviews Neuroscience* 3 (2002): 443–52; see also Doidge, *Brain That Changes*.

18. Michael Merzenich, "Growing Evidence of Brain Plasticity," TED Talk, February 2004, www.ted.com/talks/michael_merzenich_on_the_elastic_brain?language=en.

19. Ibid.

20. Doidge, *Brain That Changes*.

4

LEARNED MOVEMENT
Motor Learning

In chapter 3, I explained the cognitive processes that all learning shares in common (attention, learning, and memory) as well as what the learner must possess in order to be successful; namely, a desire to pay attention, willingness to expend some effort to do so, and ready submission to the brain cleaning that occurs during sleep. Given that music learning almost always involves a partnership, the following questions arise: If these are the necessary traits in a learner, what are their counterparts in teachers? What must the music teacher possess in order to be successful?

The traditional emphasis in teacher training is on content, that is, what the teacher knows. Institutions looking to hire faculty typically confine their parameters to a teacher's knowledge and the quality of that knowledge, as demonstrated by her output. Famous universities hire faculty whose vast knowledge is reflected in their career output, as evidenced by Nobel Prizes, Pulitzer Prizes, and Grammy Awards. From these glittering and visible signs of accomplishment, prospective college students are meant to infer great teaching prowess. But an open secret in higher education is that these accomplishments do not, in themselves, guarantee the best teaching. The reasons are as variable as are human beings themselves, but this open secret is based on one essential truth of teaching: *what* you know matters far less than *how* you impart what you know. This insight certainly does not mean that possessing knowledge in the first place is not an absolute prerequisite (it is, and yes, generally speaking, the more knowledge the better), nor should it be inferred that professionals do not deserve accolades for their accomplishments. Nevertheless, there is a stark truth embedded in this essential one: a teacher's knowledge has little value to a learner if the teacher cannot find a way into the learner's mind. As education professor Deborah Loewenberg Ball puts it, "teaching depends on what other people think, not what you think."[1] This epiphany was revealed to Ball early in her teaching career as she struggled to discover effective ways of teaching a declarative learning subject (math) to children. This truth is equally apparent in teaching motor skills, albeit in uniquely challenging ways.

THE QUESTION IS HOW, NOT WHAT

The successful transference of any physical technique from teacher to student, be it in the realm of athletics, dance, or music, ultimately hinges on the ability to impart a motor skill from teacher to student. But what teachers know of fingering, bowing, and breathing techniques does not guarantee that they will be able to successfully give it to their students. Indeed, the more expert motor performers become at their craft, the worse they can become at passing it on. This inverse relationship is known in psychology as the "curse of knowledge" or the "curse of expertise," catchy monickers that describe the testy relationship between knowing *what* versus knowing *how*. A beginning musician in the early phase of this relationship may vaguely understand what needs to be done, yet he does not know how. A master musician understands exactly how to play her instrument, but unless she can empathize with the beginner and put herself in the beginner's mindset, she will struggle to teach the how. And if she struggles to teach, her student will fail to learn. Yet the power dynamics inherent in the teacher-to-student relationship typically mask this failing as the teacher's, and instead failure to thrive is ascribed to the student's shortcomings or lack of talent.

The good news is that recent research in cognitive science can be employed to break this dispiriting cycle by answering the question "How?" in motor training. Yet in order to do so, a fundamental change of emphasis is in order, from how much teachers know (the what) to how well they impart their knowledge (the how). This necessitates a priority shift in pedagogy from the content of the teacher's brain to the landscape of the learner's mind. Since teachers are also lifelong learners, this shift is an ever-evolving negotiation between accumulating knowledge for oneself (learning) and translating it for consumption (teaching). This is an apt working model for traversing this chapter on recent research in motor performance and learning and realizing its potential to enrich musicians' teaching, learning, and performance.

MOTOR LEARNING AND PERFORMANCE

The field dedicated to understanding how movement is learned is variously called *motor learning, motor control and learning,* or *motor learning and performance.* For ease, throughout this chapter *ML* denotes all three (although, as you will see, by cognitive measures, there is a profound difference between learning and performance). The field of ML research is a fascinating one, and musicians stand to gain much from its findings. However, musicians should approach this large and multifaceted field with at least one caveat in mind: the majority of ML studies have been carried out on athletes. Far fewer studies have involved musicians. Correspondingly, discrete athletic tasks, specifically called *limb tasks*, such as ball throwing, dart sticking, and keyboard tapping, form the bulk of ML experiments. Nevertheless, expert ML researcher Gabriele Wulf and others have stated that there is no reason to think that most of the findings from ML research cannot be effectively applied to music training.[2] This is a valid stance that is explored in this chapter.

As noted in chapter 3, procedural learning is a process that results in a permanent change in behavior as a result of practice, with practice (rather than experience) being the crucial factor that distinguishes declarative from procedural learning. Exposure is not learning, and in the motor realm, neither is simple experience. In essence, motor learning must be learned by doing, through trial and error, and can only be declared as definitively learned—note the past tense—with practice. A more complex definition of motor learning than that used in chapter 3 encapsulates this progression.

Motor Learning Defined

Motor learning is a **process** that is **inferred** rather than directly observed that leads to **permanent changes** in habit as the result of **practice**.

—————⚬⚬⚬—————

Many variations of this definition exist in ML research literature, but the most prominent ones contain the components emphasized in this definition. In order, these are:

The term *process* underscores the dimension of time. The acquisition and retention of physical skills occurs along a continuum. Temporary breakthroughs notwithstanding, progress does not happen all at once but over a period of time measured in hours, days, weeks, months, academic semesters, and years. The dimension of time in this definition underscores the complexity of motor learning, for while the entire definition of motor learning is shared with declarative learning—minus the crucial swap of practice for experience—what is being built is not only a neural pathway in the brain but the robustness and flexibility of muscles, too; we are training strength and flexibility into our muscle tissue along with habits of mind. This is what makes motor learning and performance a kind of total body sport and why there is no substitution for just doing it (a sentiment efficiently captured in the Nike company's Zen-like ad campaign "Just Do It"),

That this process is *inferred* refers to learning's dynamism for learning itself cannot be directly observed; we can only assume it is happening and wait for proof that the learned thing has adhered. This proof shows up in two guises: relatively *permanent changes* in movement and the stability of these changes to the extent that they can be called physical habits that bear up repeatedly even under variable conditions. Finally, these changes in habit are the result of *practice*—of actually doing and not thinking about doing.

Now that I have made one pass through the complex definition of motor learning, it is time to dig a bit deeper into each of its parameters. Doing so, it is so vital to continually bear in mind the essential differences between learning and performance that it is worth pausing to inspect these common words whose use is ubiquitous. In fact, they are often used practically interchangeably. But phrases like "lesson performance" and "invited dress rehearsal" are, from a cognitive perspective, a contradiction in terms.

DIFFERENCES BETWEEN LEARNING AND PERFORMANCE

Learning is the process by which one acquires skill or knowledge. Performance refers to the manner in or quality with which someone functions. Remember: learning is dynamic, unstable, and messy. Performance, on the other hand, is like the freeze-frame button on a video projector—it captures where the learner stands at a certain point in time along the learning continuum. Because of this frozen quality, most of us want our performances to be as polished as we can manage—the opposite of unstable and messy. This is particularly true for musicians whose art is captured by recording and may explain both why it is so difficult to capture a live vibe or feeling of spontaneity in a recording session and, conversely, why it is so easy for the pall of permanence to infect a recording session. The goals of learning and performance are—and *should* be—not just different but diametrically opposed. When this is not well understood, the goals of learning and performance are conflated, and both typically suffer.

Learning suffers when we are not willing to seem silly, uncoordinated, or unmusical. In a music lesson, this may unfold as singing out of tune, messing up a scale passage, or feeling restricted when learning to add vibrato (and here I must acknowledge that such unwillingness may not emanate from the student himself but could stem from his teacher). True learning is effortful, and effort is often as messy (and as fun) as messing with mud pies! Yet most of us would certainly avoid presenting our mud-splattered, exploratory selves to an audience. We would rather clean up for a performance. This is all beautifully reflected in a saying credited as one of Chinese leader Deng Xiaoping's favorites: "If you open the window for fresh air, a few flies will blow in." Assuming that flies are undesirable, we nevertheless may wager that they are a small price to pay for the cool air. Learning is like the opening of this window; performance is what happens after we shoo the flies out, close the window on learning, and operate within the newly refreshed space.

Momentary flat singing or playing or klutzy movements are a small—and critically necessary—price to pay on the path to mastery.

Indeed, without the willingness to pay this price (on both the part of the student and the teacher), learning can be harmed if the learner operates under performance conditions. This outcome is particularly dire in the early stages of learning. Willingness to pay this cheapest price of learning (with the currency of a bruised ego) is perfectly captured in a featured term within the lexicon of ML research: *trials*. ML experiments typically feature many tries, or trials, of the same task, repeated under the same or variable conditions. Much ML research is therefore concerned with what influences performance outcomes over repeated trials, both positively and negatively, and why. Data gleaned from ML trials informs the construction and refinement of athletic training regimens. This is a near-perfect model for training musicians.

But what if operating under performance conditions is, paradoxically, the learning aim? It must be acknowledged that there are certainly times when this is warranted, yet a complete acknowledgment would have to admit that the aim, in this case, is performance and not learning. For example, if an invited dress rehearsal is literally just a rehearsal, there should be ample room for the singing actors onstage to make mistakes (i.e., engage in learning). Not so because you are two days out from opening night and the performers need a dose of reality and a jolt of adrenaline? Then a more accurate description would be "invited dress performance."

In summary, for teachers: scale your interventions depending upon which mode your student is using. If in learning mode, encourage exploration and freedom; if in performance mode, the advice is simple: stop teaching! Starting from a few days to even some weeks out from a major performance, scale back your instruction to zero. Why is this? Because learning, at its core, is wobbly and unstable, and in order for students to regain their balance, they must find that balance on their own by processing all of the feedback they have garnered at that point in time. They must, to use the previous metaphor, push their own freeze-frame button. Besides, as you will see a bit further on in this chapter, feedback from the teacher at this stage is not just unnecessary; it can intrude on the student's own processing and actually harm learning.

For learners: as you enter a music-making situation, know which mode you are in, learning or performance. If in the latter mode, give it your best shot!—and don't devolve into a spiral of self-blame if perfection is not attained, for it rarely is. If in learning mode, like Charles Limb's jazz musicians in chapter 2, do not allow the cognitive processes that stifle and constrain to come to the fore. How is this done? Here are two possible answers: practice (yes, messiness can actually be practiced—just ask any improvisor) and understanding the cognitive substrates of *performance shifts.*

PERFORMANCE SHIFTS: UPSIDES AND DOWNSIDES

The evidence that a motor skill is truly learned is its repeatability—and repeatability under many different conditions. These two parameters are called *retention* and *transfer*, respectively. Without proof that the learning has been retained, we can only say that the learner was merely exposed to the information. So what about changes observed during training that are not permanent? ML researchers call these changes during repeated trials *performance shifts*, and they can be both positive and negative. Motor learners can absorb powerful lessons from both flavors. Let us begin with positive performance shifts.

Most musicians are familiar with the phenomenon of instant success upon a first or second trial—which may occur in the midst of instruction or a solo practice session—that then vaporizes moments later. This may occur in weekly lessons, especially if the student feels that she never sings or plays as well in her own practice or performance as she does in her lessons. This experience is particularly common in a one-time masterclass setting in which a guest master teacher is able to evoke a positive response from the student on display but only in that moment; the student is at a loss to recapture that magical moment later in his own practice. I have dubbed this phenomenon "masterclass syndrome."[3]

Masterclass syndrome begins as a prime example of a positive performance shift, yet while such an experience may have been positive or significant for the student, lacking the proof of retrievable, permanent change, real learning cannot be said to have occurred. How is this possible? As is typical in this situation, while our masterclass musician might register disappointment, he may still reflect afterward, "Oh well, at least I learned something." More accurately, he *experienced* something. But exposure is not learning. All is not lost for our masterclass musician, however; if what was experienced was positive and desired, there is some evidence that the student's practice session immediately following may commit the gesture to memory. The only caveat here is that the effectiveness of this strategy is going to be relative to the student's ability at that time. Beginners with little previous experience will have no prior memories with which to recombine any new input from a masterclass. Conversely, more advanced musicians can expect some transference from the masterclass to their own increased performance, provided that they run, not walk, to the practice room immediately following a positive masterclass experience.

Other stunning examples of short-term positive performance shifts can be seen in interventions involving equipment or manipulation with a pair of human hands. For example, gadgets to help keep the pinky finger of the bow hand of young string players curved range from specially produced "pinky nests" to the use of bunion stickers (available from the drugstore) as a cheaper option. A popular gadget among piano teachers to teach proper hand position is a curved squeeze toy in the shape of a ladybug. Such manipulations may feel almost magical to the student musician due to their immediate positive effect, and indeed, these manipulations can help learners use proprioception (feeling) rather than verbal cues to get the knack of unfamiliar physical positions.

These and other short-term performance gains may be worthwhile, and indeed, positive performance shifts are, at their most basic level, what students (and their parents) probably expect as a return on their investment in lessons. At first glance, we might also think that positive performance shifts are what teachers proffer (and upon which they stake their reputations and pay their mortgages). In whatever manner short-term performance gains are accomplished (through manipulations, equipment, or even heaps of verbal praise), the goal of achieving them by any means necessary comes with several cautions. The first has to do with the hallmark of motor learning: repeatability. Unless the learner can repeatedly perform at the same level with the manipulation removed, by herself, and under changing conditions, the task cannot be said to have been learned by her.

More shocking, perhaps, is this news: in certain scenarios, teaching that improves performance in the short term can actually *harm* long-term learning. In other words, intervention by a teacher that helps a student play or sing well in the moment may cause a regression in the student's actual learning over time.[4] Consider the following examples, taken from an online discussion group of string teachers who instruct young children.[5] The topic was the use of "bow helpers." An initial string of comments like this one testified to their benefit:

> I started using the bow hold "buddies" a few weeks ago, and I am so relieved, I don't have to nag anymore, any of my students to keep a right bow hold. Now we can concentrate on other things, and progress faster. I highly recommend it, especially for beginners, or as remedial work for poor bow holds. I will use it with all new student also. It saves months of work on bow hold. And kids just love it.

But one teacher posted a caution about immediate gain and urged patience:

> I personally do not like to use any external "helpers" for my students' bow holds. Each hand is different and each student may need a different explanation, or seven, of how to make a reliable and satisfactory bow hold. Fine motor coordination is needed and sometimes it just takes time to develop the bow hold.

Another answered:

> I agree. I don't like using any helpers on the bows to teach my students the proper bow holds.

Most interesting and insightful was this teacher's reasoning as to why he eschews the use of gadgets:

> The more dependent [that] students get on any external helpers, the harder it will be for them to learn to play without them. Just taking the tapes off the fingerboards is something they find heartbreaking and makes them unsure they'll ever be able to play in tune without them.

These posts illustrate a few key points. First, manipulations can be powerful learning tools. Teachers and students alike express passionate "love" for them. Alternatively, however, they can create dependencies that not only harm learning but when removed can create a cascade of humiliation, discouragement, and fear. This is the essence of a well-known hypothesis in ML theory called the *guidance hypothesis*, which holds that feedback in which the learner is physically guided (i.e., hands-on manipulation) or that strongly blocks error from occurring can actually harm learning if it makes learning too easy.[6] Why is this? Part of the answer is related to *proprioceptive feedback*, which I will explain later in this chapter. The other part of the answer lies inside a factor you have already encountered for its role in attention and learning: effort.

Research into the biochemistry of the brain reveals that the more difficult the task, the more neuronal firing from our brains is required; in essence, we must dig deeper for more complicated tasks. In related findings, researchers have concluded that the solutions learners work out for themselves, through effort, are truly learned and are thus retained and retrievable. Taken together, repeated firing of the neurons creates a neural pathway that becomes stronger each time it is activated during learning. As you have seen, this is the explanation of what happens in working memory, and not incidentally, this is the neuroscientific definition of *practice*.

With enough practice, difficult tasks become easier and eventually, if mastered, are stored in long-term memory. Our memory bank is not limitless, however; we must constantly update our motor memories through practice and boot out previous motor trials to make way for new (and hopefully improved) ones. This is one parameter of the late ML researcher Richard Schmidt's *schema theory*, which helps us understand how performers are able to constantly improve and why learning is fastest for beginners and curiously slows as mastery is gained.[7]

Cognitive psychologist Robert Bjork poetically labeled the hurdles we encounter and master through effort "desirable difficulties."[8] In effect, teachers are in charge of creating an obstacle course of desirable difficulties because obstacles must form the foundation of any viable teaching method—that is, if the goal is deep learning that adheres over time and not simply improved short-term performance. The latter is the downside of positive performance shifts; positive does not always mean good. In fact, it can even be claimed that withholding desirable difficulties can actually damage learning. And here it must be emphatically stated that dishing up desirable difficulties must always be accomplished with care and empathy and compassion. The concept of desirable difficulties sanctions no space for abusive behavior.

Admittedly, serving up desirable difficulties is a difficult enterprise itself, fraught as it can be with any combination of balky students, demanding parents, high expectations, and short timelines. Teachers withhold desirable difficulties for a myriad of reasons, ranging from misguided attempts to be nice to job burnout to lack of will due to depression. To be sure, with particularly resistant students, it can simply be too dispiriting to hold the bar high and encourage that student to reach for it. An old saw says that teaching is the only product for which customers do not demand their money's worth!

Indeed, learning and performance are so synonymous in the public mind that music students who do not regularly and tangibly improve often infer that they are not actually learning. At best, they blame themselves for lack of effort or talent. At worst, they blame the teacher for not advancing them. There are certainly situations in which all these could be accurate, but that can be easily remedied by simple solutions (work harder, practice more, bring your concerns forward, or change teachers). But there is one scenario in which the propensity to infer disaster is so massively in error that it deserves special mention: when a negative performance shift coincides with the theory of *unlearning*.

NEGATIVE PERFORMANCE SHIFTS AND UNLEARNING

As previously stated, performance shifts can be both positive and negative. But it is important not to define these terms colloquially or emotionally. Recall that *positive* does not necessarily mean good. As you have just seen, increases in ability are called positive performance shifts only because performance improves in the short term; it is a plus sign on the data chart and thus positive. In fact, learning may not have occurred at all, or worse, it may actually have been harmed. Within this topsy-turvy inversion, let us now consider negative performance shifts.

Negative performance shifts are situations in which performance shows short-term decrements. This is not necessarily *bad*, although it can sure feel that way if brought on by illness, depression, or injury. But negative performance shifts can sometimes be truly *good* events. The reason is that a downturn in performance may signal that unlearning is occurring.[9] This theory holds that, when someone is attempting to learn a new motor skill, there may be a simultaneous destabilization of a previous, habitual motor pattern. Sometimes just knowing this theory can help the motor learner through this bumpy transition phase.

In some learners, though, unlearning may cause psychological distress. For example, a baritone who transitions to tenor may wager he has nothing to lose in the attempt; he assumes the familiar voice will always be there, just like a piece of comfortable clothing. Such singers may be distressed to find that, after a time, the old habit no longer "fits"—like when you return from vacation to find your reliable pair of jeans cannot be zipped over your expanded waistline. Yet the new technique does not fit either, for it has not yet stabilized. So this particular juncture in motor skill learning—the unlearning phase—appears particularly porous and unstable, and thus the learner is probably vulnerable. Therefore, musicians in this phase would do well to ban distraction from the practice room and pay total and complete attention to the task before them.

On the whole, if the learner has faith in his teacher's pedagogy, negative performance shifts can be seen as positive signs that a new, learned skill is actively destabilizing an old, ingrained habit. A student's worst lesson by this measure may actually be his best in terms of learning gains. If the learner can hang in there and apply effort to the cause, he may end up with exactly what he had hoped for: a new and better technique with which to make music.

Exactly how the destabilized habit becomes a stable new skill occurs via the last component of our complex definition of motor learning: practice.

THE PATH TO CARNEGIE HALL

"How do I get to Carnegie Hall?" the hapless New York City tourist asks. "Practice!" goes the punch line. This is the foundational premise of what is known in ML research as the *power law of practice*.[10] Simply put, practice is recognized as the number one, most important variable in motor learning. As such, practice is a hot topic in current ML and expertise studies research, as are the related topics of practice quantity and practice quality, known in the expertise literature as *deliberate practice*. In this chapter, I will start by assaying three essential findings, or rules, from ML research regarding the most effective kinds of practice.

———◦◦◦———

The Three Rules of Practice

1. Distributed practice is more effective than massed practice.

This rule of practice concerns timing. Translated for musicians, it means that practicing every day for one hour per session will prove much more beneficial than practicing twice a week for three and a half hours per session, even though the total number of hours per week are the same. This is because cognitive development is nurtured by rest, not just by doing. People whose regular practice sessions alternate with periods of rest retain more than when they pile on information all at once in megapractice, or *massed practice*, sessions. Even more compelling is the finding that the longer the rest session between practice sessions, the better the learning, as evidenced by both retention and transfer in later performance. This is likely due to the cognitive benefits of sleep, as noted in the previous chapter. Note, however, that in order for these benefits to accrue, the spaced time between practice sessions should not be *too* long—think hours instead of days. Otherwise, the neural trace that was experienced in practice will not establish itself in long-term memory.

An added benefit of distributed, or spaced, practice is protection from injury. Athletes studied in ML research are more at risk for injury during massed practice. Why is this? The answer is quite simple: massed practice without rest leads to muscle fatigue, and tired muscles are more vulnerable to injury.

Conversely, too little practice makes musicians and athletes vulnerable to injury due to lack of fitness. Musician guilt over lack of preparation may feed prerehearsal panic, which fuels the desire for massed practice, which in turn can lead to injury. Therefore, distributed practice is not only cognitively beneficial for learning; it is a sensible strategy for developing a safe and healthy training regimen and has an added potential for keeping anxiety levels in check.

2. Varied practice is more effective than constant practice.

This rule of practice concerns conditions of practice and is somewhat dependent on whether the skill one is practicing already displays an inherent amount of variability (called an *open-skill task*) or is one that does not (a *closed-skill task*). Examples in athletics are downhill skiing, in which conditions are constantly varied, versus bowling, in which the setting is fairly predictable. We find these variabilities among types of musical genres and the musicians who play them. Classical music parameters may be more stable (less varied) than those of jazz, for example.

Trained singing, especially when paired with acting, is an inherently open skill task; variability is built in to the endeavor. Consider the trajectory involved with learning an operatic role from the very beginning to opening night: there are vocal technique lessons with a teacher, coaching sessions with a pianist for style and diction, staging rehearsals with a director, and dress rehearsals with a conductor and an orchestra. All of these carefully rehearsed parameters may yet be varied again by costumes, makeup, and jitters in front of a live audience. Clearly, honing one's craft as a singing actor involves navigating quite a lot of variable conditions. So how does variability make for effective practice?

Recall that the evidence that a thing is learned is its repeatability and that a goal of motor learning is that the task remain repeatable even under the challenge of variable conditions. So the second rule of practice means that variation in practice, while potentially unnerving, is actually quite good for learning—so good, in fact, that it not only strengthens the very specific task at hand but has been shown to positively boost other, related skills. This latter effect is called *generalizability* in ML research. So instrumentalists who feel thrown off by a change in venue or singers unnerved by the new timbres encountered with orchestral rather than piano accompaniment might embrace these variations as vitamin packs for learning that boost both the target skill itself as well as the many related skills needed for performance.

Variety is the spice of life as well as the spice of practice. Experienced musicians can add variation to their practice via some rather obvious strategies, such as practicing several different pieces of repertoire per session. Varied repertoire will presumably also feature enough variations in tempo and articulation that many different skills will be tested. This is simple enough. Yet this rule of practice challenges teachers who believe that no new repertoire must be assigned to students until and unless their current repertoire is mastered, as if to do so would be to reward sloth, accede to sloppiness, or accept low-quality music-making. Yet by the rule of varied practice and its codicil, generalizability, allowing students to add on or even move past their current repertoire may paradoxically strengthen it.

3. Randomly ordered practice is more effective than blocked practice.

This rule of practice concerns practice modules. *Blocked practice* focuses on training one discrete movement over and over again until mastery is gained. The use of blocked practice is a popular method for inculcating specific skills that make up complex activities, particularly when training beginners. For example, wind players may be required to practice tone onset exercises over and over again until coordination improves, while pianists may practice the onset of a difficult hand position dozens of times in a row. While these methods may seem to make common sense, *randomly ordered practice*—that is, not repeating the same task over and over again—has been shown over decades of ML research to be more effective for long-term learning than blocked practice.

Note my use of the phrase "long-term learning," which highlights an interesting twist regarding this rule of practice: blocked practice actually boosts performance in the short term, that is, during the skill-acquisition phase. This explains the one situation in which blocked practice is probably preferred, and that is for rank beginners. But if testing the viability of such boosts in real-world performance venues is delayed or avoided altogether, blocked practice can eventually lead to a false sense of accomplishment, for both student and trainer. In that scenario, such musicians make excellent "practicers" but fall apart in performance.

The salient point here is that both randomly ordered practice and practice under varied conditions may degrade immediate performance but boost long-term learning, as evidenced by superior retention and transfer, because they hold up in many different situations. This rule of practice highlights another maxim from ML research that you have already encountered: learning and performance are two different, indeed opposite, endeavors. What boosts one may likely degrade the other.

—⟨᷍᷍⟩—

These three rules of practice are like a basic recipe upon which variations can be made according to the instrument and the level of the
learner. The binding agent in this recipe is *planning*, which allows all
musicians (both teachers and students) to maximize two of their most
precious resources: time and attention. The switch from aimless to organized practice can exert profound effects on musicians' progress at
any stage.[11] But planning for practice also commands a fascinating aspect of motor movement that occurs at the cellular level in our brains
and that issues an initial "go" command before our bodies respond. In
essence, our brains move before our bodies do. This, and related findings about the neural mechanisms for motor control and learning, are
enormously important for all performers in the physical realm.

The first consideration here is *reaction time*, the interval between
the impulse to move and the movement itself. In ML research, a fine
distinction is therefore made between *action* (which begins life as a
cognitive command) and *movement* (that command's result).[12] As might
be imagined, reaction time is rapid—it is measured in milliseconds.[13]
An essential distinction between reaction time and reflexes is that the
latter is involuntary while the former is not. A person does not choose to
blink his eyelids when dust flies up into his face, but he does choose to
reach up with his mitt and catch a baseball hurtling toward him (or, if
the speed of the ball is too unnerving, to jump out of the way). Voluntary reaction time therefore requires decisions based upon a preexisting
motor pattern (also called *motor program* or *motor plan*). The term
preexisting is significant here; our baseball catcher must have some
experience with snagging a ball in a mitt to be successful. For musicians, our preexisting motor patterns have been constructed through
the hours of practice that have installed the necessary neural pathways
in our brains.

Speed regarding reaction time has critical, real-world consequences
for everyone—when braking a car that's sliding on an icy highway, for
example. But quick reaction time can be cashed in for rewards in athletics, performance art, and music. Narrowing the gap between choice and
movement results in assured and facile body movement versus late
entrances, flubbed fingerings, and mallet malfunctions. So we musicians will want to know that, besides just doing it, there is a special type

of practice that can strengthen our motor program and improve reaction time, all without lifting a finger.

MOTOR IMAGERY: THINKING ABOUT DOING

An important kind of practice—one that surely belongs in a book about music and the brain—is mental practice, which also goes by many other names, including *visualization*; *mental simulation*; and, most commonly in cognitive science, *motor imagery*.[14] A basic description of this technique, as all these names imply, is that the musician imagines the movements of playing or singing without actually doing them. Musicians and athletes have been practicing mental simulation for decades, particularly as a way to conjure success, with results confirmed by anecdotal evidence (i.e., self-reports by the performers themselves) as well as objective evidence such as coach and audience approval, and in sports—winning![15] And even though visualization is not a new concept, it has largely been passed down from master to student rather than developed in a systemized way in music pedagogy.

Similarly, for much of the previous century, while research on mental practice was conducted, many ML researchers were skeptical that actual learning could occur through mental practice due to the (understandable) belief that the only way to truly learn an action was to actually perform it.[16] In a way this belief holds true: the essential fact of motor learning is that actions must be learned by doing. Still, the cognitive substrate of motor learning, the motor plan that is constructed while the learning happens, must also be taken into account. So what is the thinking that accompanies the doing? This question has hovered over ML research for over a century. Yet without the means to investigate what was going on inside the mind, early researchers were confined to external investigations of the body, like the series of seminal experiments conducted in the early 1930s by Edmund Jacobson, who sought to investigate "what takes place in the nervous or neuromuscular system during a particular mental activity, [and] to measure the process in physical terms."[17] In other words, do muscle cells fire if we simply imagine their use? Jacobson discovered that they do and noted that the only measurable difference in the imagined versus the actuated movement was the degree of voltage. He surmised that his results might lead to "a branch of study analogous with physical chemistry, and which may appropriately be called physical psychology."[18] Galvanic experiments on muscles continued, and research later in the century revealed that, along with muscle cells firing through imagination, heart rate, blood pressure, and respiration also increased. But what was happening behind the scenes, inside the brain, had to wait until the imaging tools of modern neuroscience could investigate this question toward the twentieth century's end.

The explosion of neuroscience research in the 1990s brought forth one amazing revelation after another about the inner workings of the brain. In ML research, on the question of mental practice, brain imaging showed that merely thinking about an action actually causes the related motor program in the brain to activate.[19] This hugely important finding was called *motor simulation theory*, also known as the *functional equivalence hypothesis*.[20] In a shout-out to Team Music, note that one of the earliest fMRI studies successfully tested the functional equivalence hypothesis in pianists.[21]

Another discovery related to the functional equivalence hypothesis arose during the same decade, in which a similar behavior in monkeys was observed. But in this case, the animals' motor programs fired when watching other animals eat (the "other animals" were human scientists on lunch break in the lab!).[22] The neurons that fired in the monkey's brains were christened *mirror neurons* for their ability to mirror others' actions. Although the initial discovery received little attention, as the decade progressed and turned into a new millennium, this discovery got a huge boost when the famous and charismatic neuroscientist V. S. Ramachandran, writing for John Brockman's Edge.com, declared mirror neurons and their ability to mimic as "the driving force behind the great leap forward in human evolution":

> The discovery of mirror neurons in the frontal lobes of monkeys, and their potential relevance to human brain evolution . . . is the single most important "unreported" (or at least, unpublicized) story of the decade. I predict that mirror neurons will do for psychology what DNA did for biology: they will provide a unifying framework and help explain a host of mental abilities that have hitherto remained mysterious and inaccessible to experiments.[23]

This was big news. Like so many other brain stories during the intoxicating, early days of brain imaging, the mirror neuron story quickly gathered steam and (helped along by a much sexier name than *functional equivalence*) burst into the national consciousness, perhaps most captivatingly through the use of the *broken mirror hypothesis* as a possible explanation for the mystery of autism. As the news spread, what began as the ability of lab monkeys' brain cells to imitate observed actions morphed into something far more complex and profound. Imitation mutated into understanding, and from there it was but a short leap to posit mirror neurons as the key to empathy, the quality that allows us to feel the emotions of others, making empathy nothing less than the bedrock of human civilization. This was heady stuff.

Fortunately the hyperbolic reportage of mirror neurons cooled to the objective distance needed for science to ascertain if such neurons, proven to exist in macaque monkeys, actually do exist in humans. While much had been inferred, up until 2010 only one study had uncovered "*direct* electrophysiological evidence" of mirror neurons in humans.[24] This phrase, and the emphasis on the word *direct*, is noteworthy for a reason that many outside the neurocommunity are unaware of, to wit: most scientific conclusions reached in brain science imaging are inferred rather than directly observed. For example, using fMRI, scientists make theoretical conclusions (inferences) about what the brain is doing via information derived through a multistep process that assesses the ratio of oxygenated blood and deoxygenated blood within the brain. And here we must stop; if this process sounds complicated, it is. In the words of neuroscientist Nikos Logothetis, "the beautiful graphics MRI and fMRI produce, and the excitement about what they imply, often mask the immense complexity of the physical, biophysical and engineering procedures generating them."[25] So why is fMRI used? The biggest reason is safety: as a noninvasive procedure, there is virtually no risk. Conversely, in order to achieve directly observable results, highly invasive brain techniques must be used, such as inserting thin wire electrodes directly into the brain through a small hole drilled into the skull, as is done to diagnose epilepsy. Thus it was that researchers at UCLA were able to use this procedure, already being used with epileptics, to find the elusive mirror neuron in humans.[26]

With the discovery of human mirror neurons, motor simulation theory and the functional equivalence hypothesis were back in the news, and the news was truly big. Even one of the most ardent and early mirror neuron skeptics now believes that human mirror neurons do exist.[27] So we shall proceed to explore both the functional equivalence hypothesis and the human mirror neuron system as neatly summed up by a team of researchers this way: "Whether one moves, or one is planning to move, or thinking about someone else moving, overlapping neural networks are activated."[28] These actions involve both the planning and the actual production of action, and, critically, they are "a direct consequence of the stored memories of information necessary to anticipate and interpret the behaviors of others." In other words, our motor imagery only works if we have done the activity enough ourselves to have developed our own motor memories (or motor program) of the action. Remember our baseball catcher.

Many athletes, dancers, and musicians have found mental practice to be not only viable but powerful. It is the no-practice-practice routine that can be utilized in a variety of situations to stand in for the real thing, most valuably during recovery from injury. As far as your brain is concerned, you took your instrument for a spin, yet with no wear and tear on your body. The no-practice-practice routine holds great promise not only as insurance against atrophy during short-term leaves of absence but as an adjunct to rehabilitative therapies after surgery or serious injury.

Another asset to mental practice is its utility when making musical noise is just not possible. (Traveling musicians, take note: you need not disturb hotel guests when practicing for your big audition!) These are some practical uses of mental practice. Richer, perhaps, are the cognitive benefits of mental practice.

It is theorized that mental practice (thinking of an action) strengthens the cognitive substrates of movement. This is Merzenich's "brain aerobics" in action. Indeed, one tantalizing finding from a recent study on mental imagery found that "you can increase muscle strength solely by sending a larger signal to motor neurons from the brain."[29] Researchers demonstrated this by tasking volunteers with performing "mental contractions" of their little finger or elbow. The volunteers were instructed to mentally "push maximally" (i.e., as hard as they could) against an imaginary force (one that they had already encountered for real in pretrials). The researchers noted that

this mental exercise was not simply a visualization of oneself performing the task; rather, the performers were instructed to adopt a
kinesthetic imagery approach, in which they urged the muscles to
contract maximally, and this was accompanied by significantly elevated physiological responses.[30]

In other words, volunteers did not just lie about, dreaming vaguely
about moving their muscles, nor did they merely envision themselves
performing these actions from afar; rather, they were to feel the movements in their minds. This is an important point: later studies have
shown that, in order for motor imagery to work well, practitioners must
use *internal imagery* (also known as *kinesthetic imagery* or *first-person
imagery*) rather than *external imagery* (also known as *third-person* or
visual imagery).

Volunteers in this study practiced internal imagery five times a week
for twelve weeks, and training sessions were fifteen minutes each. The
results were rather astonishing: the little-finger group increased their
finger abduction strength by 35 percent and the elbow group by 13.5
percent. The human mind is truly remarkable.

In the words of a group of motor imagery researchers, "mental imagery research has a long past but only a short history of robust empirical findings, so that many questions remain and new pathways for discovery are emerging."[31] While we await those discoveries, we musicians
can certainly apply what is known thus far about motor imagery to
develop a robust mental practice routine. The following is a suggested
mental practice regimen. The scenario is a musician preparing for a
same-day solo musical performance. The worth of this practice regimen
lies in its ability to sharpen the mind without tiring the body.

A Mental Practice Regimen

1. Sit or lie down in a quiet room, then close your eyes to shut out
   all extraneous stimuli (this is the roadblocking technique described in chapter 3).
2. Use internal imagery. Aim to actually feel the movements yourself rather than observe yourself doing them.

3. Take yourself through each phase of your performance. Aim to stay on top of each of your movements (also known as staying "in the moment") until you can feel your instrument in your hands, the touch of the keys on your fingers, the air blowing thorough your lips, or the text being formed in your mouth.

4. Take yourself through each phase of your performance in real time. This is important; do not skip around or ahead. Mentally manage each phase of the movement.

5. Make no actual movements or sounds but take yourself to the edge of your imagination. Likewise, practice with maximal effort. If any technique or portion of your program is physically difficult, go deep into this difficulty (mentally) rather than imagining yourself cruising past it. Know that you are accessing the motor program for the real deal. This should be a real workout for your brain cells.

―――《◇◇◇》―――

If musicians are to benefit from the cognitive revolution and neuroscience, music teachers should be teaching us not merely what to do but how to think. Mental practice is a technique that can be taught right alongside bowing, fingering, and breathing technique.

CONTROLLED VERSUS AUTOMATIC PROCESSES

An ancient distinction has existed between things we do with conscious attention and those things we do automatically. In motor learning, these two modes are called *controlled processing* and *automatic processing*, respectively, and they have received quite a lot of attention in ML research. Two reasons for this are that *automaticity* is a vaunted goal of motor training (we expect our motor programs to run automatically), and automaticity is an attribute often reverently assigned to expert performers: "Her movements appear so effortless as to be automatic." Recent research on automaticity has painted a mixed picture, with strongly held views on both sides. A similarly mixed picture, with equally strongly held opinions, can be seen in the varied pedagogical approaches used by music teachers, with some who promote a technical or even a science-based approach and others who prefer more intuitive methods.

Teaching methods that employ specific, frank instructions, such as "lift your soft palate as you ascend in pitch" or "engage your abdominal muscles as you move more air for a crescendo," are examples of directives that require controlled processing of the learner. In contrast, automatic processing does not call attention to these mechanics. Teachers who use a combination of emotion (for example, a stifled sob), imagery ("spaghetti fingers"), or allusion to common physical gestures ("inhale through the gesture of a yawn") invoke automatic processing.

Many music teachers use a combination of controlled and automatic directives on the way to achieving automaticity. Controlled processing is helpful with beginners and when frank technical adjustments need to be made, but, with intermediate and advanced musicians, automatic directives may be more fruitful, especially when considered through the lens of *attentional focus*, which you will read about later in this chapter.

Regardless of whether controlled or automatic directives are used in a music lesson, student musicians are being showered with feedback, which is an essential part of motor learning. In fact, ML researchers regard feedback as so essential to motor learning that it is bested only by practice in importance.[32] Therefore, a detailed look at the many researched aspects of feedback is in order.

FEEDBACK

An unsubtle definition of feedback is this: any and all information available to the learner. But feedback is divided into many different subclasses, as can be seen in figure 4.1. What is apparent at first glance in this illustration is the sheer amount of information coming at the learning musician as he plays his instrument. This raises many questions: How much of this information can be processed at one time? Are there different kinds of information, and if so, is there a hierarchy of importance? What about differing cognitive processing speeds; how much can the brain handle? And is more information better information?

The first step in answering these questions begins with the important division between feedback felt and feedback given. That is, *inherent feedback* (what the learner him- or herself perceives and feels) and

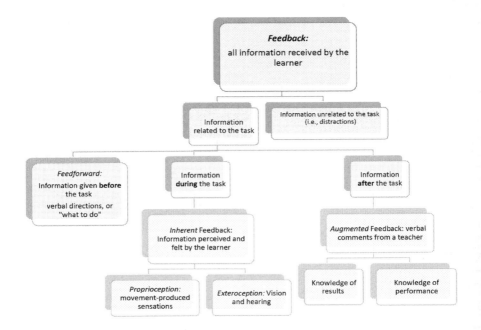

Figure 4.1.   Divisions of feedback. Adapted from Lynn Maxfield, "Improve Your Students' Learning by Improving Your Feedback," *Journal of Singing* **69, no. 4 (March/April 2013): 472.**

augmented feedback, which is information delivered by an external source like a coach or teacher. Let us begin with the type of feedback that all motor learners experience naturally.

Inherent Feedback

All musicians guide their own performance through inherent feedback (also called intrinsic feedback.) Refer to figure 4.1 and note that inherent feedback is comprised of information that is generated within the body through sense receptors (proprioception) and information that is relayed back to us from outside (exteroception), especially through vision and hearing. These two "buckets"—proprioception and exteroception—contain huge scoops of information, even before we account for the instructor's directives.

Imagine a musician who is practicing alone (we'll name her Irena) without guidance from a coach. In this scenario, we must further stipulate that Irena is an instrumentalist and not a singer (the reason for this will soon become clear). She is a guitarist. As she practices, her proprioception delivers sensory information to her, for example, the press of her fingertips on the strings and the vibration of the guitar body on the tops of her thighs. For exteroceptive feedback, she can look down to ensure accurate placement of her fingers upon her fretboard, but, like most musicians, Irena relies most heavily on hearing to monitor her performance. This acoustic information is composed of

1. *airborne sound* (also called *direct airborne sound* or *sidetone* in some studies)
2. *room-reflected sound* (also called *indirect airborne sound*)

Airborne sound, as the term implies, arrives direct and unimpeded to Irena's ear. Conversely, room-reflected sound arrives indirectly. Its alternative name, indirect airborne sound, indicates that this sound is altered by its encounter with obstacles (like plaster walls or padded seat cushions). If Irena were in a lesson with a coach, from a purely physical standpoint, what Irena heard through these two sound conduction pathways and what her coach heard would be identical. (Arguably, a master teacher will hear artistic differences that a young musician may miss, but for the purposes of understanding feedback, let us agree that the sound sources for Irena and her coach are perceived as similar.)

Now let us conjure a singer called Sanjay. Like Irena, Sanjay is receiving proprioceptive information—quite a lot of it. For while all instruments share an *actuator* (something that makes it go), a *vibrator* (something that wiggles and generates sound energy), and a *resonator* (an open space that gathers sound energy and molds it into enhanced musical tone), all three of these components are contained within Sanjay's own body.

Like Irena, Sanjay also receives exteroceptive information: through vision if he is monitoring his body movements with a mirror during practice and through hearing via both airborne and room-reflected sound. But here the similarities between Irena and Sanjay stop. Since a singer's instrument is located entirely within his or her own body, Sanjay is also receiving a third type of auditory feedback: *body-conducted* (or *bone-conducted*) *sound*. And therein lies the source of the special challenge for singers: they experience all three sound conduction pathways simultaneously—all these facts and "alternative facts."[33]

This phenomenon explains why the way we perceive our own speaking or singing voice and the way others do differs enormously. In body-conducted sound, the vibrations emanating from our vocal folds interacts with our bones, tissues, and cerebrospinal fluid (the clear liquid that circulates in the space around the brain and spinal cord), which dampen certain frequencies while boosting others.

Meanwhile, airborne sounds and room-reflected sounds travel as their names imply, boosting and dampening an assortment of frequencies—creating distinctly different *sound prints* than what is heard internally via body-conducted sound.[34] If these three sound systems are in conflict for singers during learning (and they often are), this conflict

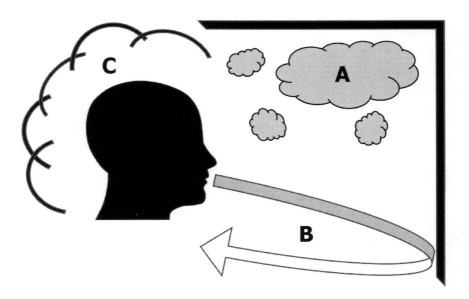

The three sound conduction pathways of singers' perception:
A) airborne sound, B) room-reflected sound, C) body-conducted sound.

Figure 4.2.   The three sound conduction pathways of a singer's perception: (a) airborne sound, (b) room-reflected sound, and (c) bone-conducted sound. Image by the author based on information in Manuj Yadav and Densil Cabrera, "Autophonic Loudness of Singers in Simulated Room Acoustic Environments," *Journal of Voice* 31, no. 3 (May 2017): 388.

creates a cognitive dissonance that is particular to singers. In the words of one researcher, "this fact poses enormous problems in learning to sing."[35] Yes, indeed it does, and we will consider this problem and some remedies for it at the end of this section on feedback.

Vision

So far I have discussed only one form of exteroception, namely hearing, which is unquestionably crucial to musicians. The second most common form of exteroception is seeing, though the importance of sight is somewhat dependent upon its centrality to the task; for example, vision is arguably more important to a baseball pitcher than it is to a musician. But vision is an important exteroceptive feedback system in the early stages of learning an instrument, since it can guide the proper grip of a mallet or bow or the instrument itself. In later learning, sight can be an aid for corrective measures, either directly or via a mirror or film to analyze deficiencies.

Yet examples of such blind and successful musicians as Andrea Bocelli, Ray Charles, Diane Schuur, and Stevie Wonder also attest to the amazing ability of other senses (notably hearing and touch) to make up for vision loss. Besides, vision per se is not always a bonus, especially when the plight of performers who must face audiences straight on and contend with visual distractions is considered. Chatting ushers or patrons who text, kiss, or fall asleep can cause reactions in the performer that range from mildly unsettling to so completely unnerving as to cause choking. In ML research, choking is defined as a marked decrease in motor performance under pressure (a subject I will turn to in chapter 6). Without the exteroceptive feedback of sight, performers might be spared choking in these cases, and indeed, the performance setup for certain types of performances (classical pianists, for example) actually shields the player from this kind of feedback. For singers, however, this is not an option; they must not only face the audience but show emotion through facial expression and even interact directly with the audience. When sight is considered as part of the barrage of feedback that musicians receive while performing, it becomes clear why using variable practice conditions are so important: one never knows what will happen in a live performance, so planning change in the practice routine can help instill needed focus.

Before we move on to consider what happens to musicians when they dip into bucket 2 (proprioception), let us circle back to Sanjay and delve deeper into singers' particular challenges processing inherent feedback.

Singers' Alternative Facts: Cognitive Dissonance

Within the world of musicians, singers occupy a category of their own for this one, fundamental reason: the instrument they play is within their own bodies. Why is it that this fact "poses enormous problems for learning to sing"?[36] The answer lies in two competing parameters: inherent feedback and augmented feedback. To understand this conflict, let us first consider the following philosophical riddle that is often used to engage learners in a lesson about the physics of sound.

The riddle is "If a tree falls in a forest and no one is around to hear it, does it make a sound?" The answer is that it depends on which definition of sound is used. If it is this definition, "Sound is a disturbance of air molecules that impinges upon the eardrum," then the answer is no. There is no one in the forest, so there is no set of eardrums around to receive sound waves generated by the crashing tree. The sound did not occur. (Of course, the discussion can sidetrack here to nonhumans: what about a rabbit who happens to be in the vicinity? A bunny is a sentient being! So let us agree that no creature, human or otherwise, is present in our fictional forest to hear the crash of the tree.)

If another definition of sound is used, "Sound is the compression and rarefaction of air molecules within the medium of air," then the answer is yes. In this scenario, the scrunching up (*compression*) and elongation (*rarefaction*) of air particles does occur, regardless of whether any eardrums were there to perceive it—human or otherwise.

It is clear that the impediment to definitively solving this riddle is perception. With perception on the table as a necessary component to sound, then the answer will always be no. Remove perception, and the answer will always be yes. So it is with learning to sing: the impediment is perception. What the teacher (as audience) hears and what the singer hears are two different entities. Indeed, they are two different voices. Neither of the two voices is any less real than the other, yet in the classic teaching paradigm, the teacher's interpretation of what is heard takes primacy over the student's.

If you are a teacher who protests that this just is not so because you have developed a method whereby you always honor your student's experience, then bravo. There are excellent pedagogical reasons to prime your feedback in this way. However, the primary reason that all musicians take lessons is because they want to sound better, thus the tacit understanding upon a student entering a teacher's studio is that the teacher can guide the student to that goal. Ultimately it is the teacher who will utilize both his perception and his interpretation of his student's vocal sounds to improve them. The student's task is having the willingness to follow the teacher's lead—and to do that, she must agree with the teacher's perception of her sound. And therein lies the catch: the perception and the interpretation of the two voices differ, often dramatically so, particularly among young singers and their teachers or within a new teacher-student partnership. Thus a significant impediment to student singers' learning is the way in which they perceive their own sound. They must hold two impressions in mind—impressions that are often contradictory—as they struggle to reconcile the teacher's facts with their own "alternative facts." This struggle can create a whole host of problems for student singers ranging from psychic discomfort to outright disbelief and a burgeoning distrust of the teacher. This struggle is the very definition of *cognitive dissonance*, a theory originated in 1957 by social psychologist Leon Festinger, who explains it this way:

> Two items of information that psychologically do not fit together are said to be in a dissonant relation to each other. The items of information may be about behavior, feelings, opinions, things in the environment and so on.[37]

Festinger holds that, if this dissonance were uncomfortable enough, people will attempt, in a variety of ways, to reconcile the conflict. In a happy coincidence of music and psychology, musicians understand this in musical terms as resolving dissonance to consonance.

While the *what* may be easy enough to comprehend, the conundrum here is in the *how*, as in, how might this particular cognitive dissonance be resolved? Here is a step-by-step scheme to resolve the problem.

──────◦◦◦──────

Resolving Cognitive Dissonance for Singers

1. State the problem (the what). Tell the student clearly, from day one, this basic fact: Singers perceive their own sound differently from everyone else in an audience. Most singers intuitively understand this, but if examples are needed, ask them what their impressions were the first time they heard a recording of their own speaking voice, and relate that back to the singing voice. Ask, "In a contest between singer and audience, whose opinion wins?" Performers understand this: "The people who paid for the ticket."

2. Explain the problem (expand on the what). Here is the space for facts and an opportunity for teaching about vocal resonance.[38] Explain the difference between *forced resonance* and *free resonance*—singers produce both, but forced resonance gets stuck in the body and many of the vibrations that we produce are quickly dampened by our own body tissues. Free resonance is produced within the open spaces in our heads (mostly within the pharynx and oral cavity, with a bit within the larynx), and it is this resonance that audiences hear. Free resonance is what we want to nurture and cultivate.

3. Agree on the challenge (of the what). The challenge is that singers perceive both free and forced resonance *simultaneously*. While they are producing tone, their ears are receiving three versions of auditory information: (bucket 1) along with the *pallesthetic* (vibratory) and *kinesthetic* (muscular) sensations (bucket 2) that their body senses: facts and alternative facts. In this scenario, cognitive dissonance often ensues. The challenge is, students must decide which set of facts to believe.

4. Agree on the goal. Teacher and learner must approach the challenge and the goal as partners; therefore, agreement on both points is crucial. The student's challenge is "I am receiving conflicting feedback information." The goal is to resolve the cognitive dissonance. Stated more frankly, the singer's goal should be this: "My goal is to train my motor program to match what you and I have agreed is the optimal tone." Of course, this requires at least two components: aesthetic agreement on what constitutes beautiful tone and trust. The former is generally easy; student singers should know who their vocal role models are. The latter requires time and empathy.

5. Plant trust with empathy. It is well known in medical literature that the main reasons, above all others, that patients comply with their physician's recommendations is "physician warmth and empathy," that is, how much a patient feels his doctor cares about him.[39] There are many ways to cultivate empathy, and they can be practiced. In the music studio, teachers can cultivate empathy by talking with their students about their own artistic journeys. To pursue art is to struggle, so teachers can share their struggles with their students (without sharing overly personal details). This sharing can plant the seeds of empathy, which in turn inculcates trust.

6. Require objective listening. Require students to record their voice lessons and listen to them afterward; ditto for rehearsals and practice sessions, if warranted. Note: high-quality listening is a must, especially if the singer has not resolved her cognitive dissonance regarding perception of her own voice. Many student singers are amazed at the difference between built-in laptop speakers and high-quality headphones.

7. Require a written weekly practice journal. Students should summarize their listening and practice week in a short but dense journal entry. Both listening to and writing about practice, if done thoughtfully, engages motor imagery and the mirror neuron system, which, as you have seen, can cause the motor program that guides singing to fire.[40]

8. Create a community of learners. An aid to objective listening as a learning tool can be found within the student members of the studio. Holding regular studio performance classes allows studio mates to share their journeys, provided that a spirit of camaraderie rather than competition has been instilled and nurtured. Require those not singing to be active participants by offering helpful feedback. Feedback coming from a peer rather than a teacher can be very powerful. Another note: it is worth a teacher's time to instruct the entire studio in how to both give and take criticism. An effective rule of thumb about giving a critique is to always begin with something positive. Never allow students to shame each other in this setting. Equally taboo in a learning situation are comments about personal appearance or comments that are overtly sexual (e.g., "You look hot in that outfit"). Not only are

these types of comments nonproductive (they typically invoke a flight-or-flight response), they are also unethical in a learning setting.

9. Use peer feedback. If peer feedback gets to the heart of the cognitive dissonance within the student, refer back to these in-class comments in private lessons to wean the student from external auditory feedback.

10. Expect a nonlinear trajectory. Learning itself is nonlinear. The path to learning is both circuitous and circular; it twists and turns and doubles back on itself. Learners often have to learn the same lessons over and over again, which is why teachers find themselves repeating the same nostrums. Teaching requires practicing patience, which begins with empathy. Teachers: Circle back to step 5 and remember the struggle.

—≈≈≈≈—

Proprioception

In ML literature, proprioception is defined as "movement-produced sensations," that is, what our bodies are feeling while making music. How does this inherent feedback system operate? Let us check in on our instrumentalist Irena, remembering that she is a guitarist. We know she is receiving the inherent (extero-) feedback of hearing and seeing while practicing. Also, the feeling of the fingers of her left hand pressing on the fretboard and those of her right hand strumming the guitar strings produce proprioception, which can be defined simply as "the feeling of what happens." In the next practice room over, Sanjay is also receiving proprioception, only not through his fingers (as for Irena) but in his throat and mouth. If Sanjay is an opera singer, he may be feeling strong sensations in his entire thorax.

Pause for a moment and silently imagine playing your own instrument. Chances are, you cued into the memory of proprioception. If you are a keyboard player, you imagined the familiar touch of your fingertips on the keys—perhaps your right foot on a pedal came to mind. Wind players probably imagine their lips, while string players may call up the sensations in hands and arms as they nestle their bodies around their instruments.

Whatever you play, the way you feel your instrument guides your music-making and also guides adjustments to your schema, or interior motor plan. This is why practice is the most important variable in motor learning: our bodies must sense, then adjust, in a continuous, "open loop" of learning. But this very flexibility is both the power and the danger of proprioceptive learning. Just because it feels good does not mean it produces a desirable sound or a healthy use of the body. Motor learners who struggle to undo entrenched and harmful muscular patterns are up against this paradox and generally cannot guide themselves out of a movement rut but must seek objective help from a teacher.

Very gifted teachers are usually those who have vivid and eloquent descriptions for exactly how hard the fingers should press, how lightly the weight of the arm should rest, how relaxed the jaw should be. Many of us remember our teachers by their unique sayings, especially if they were particularly imaginative and helpful. But verbal instructions can also be negative, either by simply being ineffective or, worse, physiologically incorrect, thus sparking maladjustments. An infamous canard in the world of cultivated singing is the directive to "breathe from the diaphragm." At best, this is ill-informed because it is not physiologically possible to do so. At worst, it may summon in singers the vocal faults of extreme belly distention, collapsed ribcage, and inattention to the pharynx, all of which contribute to poor breath management.

Assuming that teachers know the basic physiology required to play their instrument, they then need to invent a range of metaphors to describe the technical requirements that must be met to play until they find those that resonate just right with their learners. Indeed, the development of refined proprioception comprises a significant percentage of overall music instruction. But the number-one tool that teachers use to guide the student's proprioception is language. This guidance is called augmented feedback.

Augmented Feedback

As the term implies, augmented feedback is extra information beyond the learner's own fund of inherent information. Augmented feedback is typically verbal feedback proffered by a teacher, although information delivered by any external source (such as a video recorder) also gives augmented feedback. ML researchers Schmidt and Lee note, "Most importantly, this feedback is information over which the instructor has control; thus, it can be given or not given, given at different times, and given in different forms to influence learning."[41] This description portrays augmented feedback rather capriciously, like a tool with many interchangeable parts that is wielded at the whim of the instructor. This is somewhat alarming considering what is known about augmented feedback, namely, that it is considered by most ML researchers to be "the single most important variable (except, of course, practice itself) for motor learning."[42] Given augmented feedback's powerful influence on learning and the many different varieties available, it is of paramount importance that music teachers understand the augmented feedback choices available and the ramifications of those they actually choose when training musicians.

The first consideration is the parameter of time: how often to give feedback and when to give it. As noted in figure 4.1, the divisions before, during, and after a task are available. Each carries specific benefits and hazards.

Concurrent Augmented Feedback

Let us now imagine that a music student, Bo, has arrived for his weekly piano lesson with Professor Steinway. After initial pleasantries have been exchanged, a discussion ensues between them about a difficulty that Bo encountered in the previous lesson and the relative success of three different practice strategies suggested by Professor Steinway. Bo reports "strategy number 2" as somewhat successful, so Professor Steinway directs Bo to give it a go with the strategy discussed, albeit at a slower tempo than he reported using in practice. This common feedback strategy—simple instructions given before launching—is generally efficient and effective, mostly by focusing the student's mind on the task at hand. (I will return to this very important aspect of motor learning, attentional focus, later in the chapter.)

However, if the teacher had given Bo a moment to imagine his desired finger movements before launching and then given her verbal directions, Professor Steinway would have set up what is known as a *feedforward* scenario in ML research.[43] This very powerful motor-learning teaching technique is linked to motor imagery and mental practice, as previously described. Using a feedforward scenario in a lesson is like a microversion of the mental practice regimen reviewed earlier. In this scenario, Bo closes his eyes (roadblocking other stimuli) while Professor Steinway describes for Bo what he should optimally attempt to feel. This entire microversion of mental practice should last far less than a minute. A vivid directive to capture this process is "Feel first, then go!"

Bo "goes," and at this juncture in the lesson—Bo is playing and Professor Steinway is observing critically—choices must be made by Professor Steinway about the most effective time to give Bo her augmented feedback. Should she wait until Bo is finished or deliver it in the moment while Bo is actually playing? *Concurrent augmented feedback* is typically a stream of verbal coaching delivered in real time while the student is playing or singing, but frequent gestures—such as facial signs of approval or disapproval (smiles or frowns) or hand signals (thumbs up or thumbs down)—are also forms of concurrent augmented feedback. Whichever it might be, ML research is pretty clear that concurrent augmented feedback should be used sparingly for at least five reasons.

Problems with Concurrent Feedback

1. If Professor Steinway uses verbal concurrent feedback, her words cannot adequately describe sensations; they offer a poor substitute for feeling.
2. Professor Steinway's language is cognitively processed in Bo's brain quite differently from his own proprioception. For one thing, language is translated more slowly than sensation. For this reason and reason number 1, verbal directives get "lost in translation."
3. A third problem (related to the first two) is that Professor Steinway's stream of verbal concurrent feedback could effectively block Bo from receiving and processing his own sensory information (proprioception); this is the central argument of the guidance hypothesis. Further, if Professor Steinway's verbiage contradicts what Bo himself is sensing, cognitive overload in Bo's brain could ensue.

4. Let us imagine that that Professor Steinway's feedback is not verbal but a continuous range of highly emotive facial expressions; her face reflects a beatific glow when she is pleased with Bo's playing and a stormy gloom when he errs. A fourth concern is that the student in this scenario subconsciously focuses on gaining the beatific smile reward. What this means is that learners who are focused on pleasing their teachers are therefore unable to focus on what they should actually be doing: learning. (Important note: learners at all ages and stages are vulnerable to this influence, especially those who rate high on measures of empathy and compassion.)

5. Finally, concurrent augmented feedback displays the troublesome characteristics of the guidance hypothesis, which boosts short-term performance but depresses long-term learning.

Speaking of the guidance hypothesis: another form of concurrent augmented feedback is physical guidance in the form of a device (the aforementioned squeeze toy) or direct physical contact in the form of the instructor's hands. Let us lay aside the ethical and legal considerations of laying on of hands for a moment and consider what the evidence suggests about manipulative correction. It usually leads to the same outcome as all other forms of concurrent augmented feedback: such solutions may temporarily boost performance, but ultimately that boost may not take root in the student's long-term memory. Nevertheless, anecdotal evidence does suggest that the immediate benefit from manipulation techniques may be retained if they are not used routinely or for very long. The trick is the removal of such training wheels earlier rather than later in the learning process before a dependency is developed, forcing the learner to encode the desired sensations in his own memory banks. I will explain the ethical ramifications of manipulation later in this chapter.

Terminal Feedback

Let us now imagine a different scenario for Professor Steinway. In this scenario, she has learned about the pitfalls of concurrent augmented feedback and never uses it. Instead, she relies on *terminal feedback*—that is, information given after the student has concluded playing or singing. Indeed, most music teachers likely use some form of terminal feedback, but which one is best? This is an excellent question, for ML research has atomized terminal feedback into discrete segments: *instantaneous*, *immediate*, and *delayed*. The results from research on these parameters of feedback timing have yielded varied results on the question of timing, and new research has challenged some old orthodoxies. Let us inspect them in order.

The most rapid response is instantaneous feedback, which is verbal commentary given with no time lapse between trial and instruction. Some instructors will even interrupt the student while he is playing to give instantaneous feedback. Even though this kind of feedback is not quite the same as concurrent, the effect of instantaneous feedback on learning appears to be similar to that of concurrent. That is, instantaneous feedback offers no quiet space in which the learner can pause, reflect, and process what he just did. It scripts for the learner what he *should* have felt instead of allowing him to work out for himself what he *did* feel. It is fascinating how often findings from ML theory validate Bjork's theory of desirable difficulties.

On the other end of the time spectrum is delayed feedback. Elements that must be taken into consideration with this type of feedback are length of time and what happens during the delay. Regarding the former, common sense indicates that a student will gain very little, perhaps even zero, if a lesson occurs on a Monday but the student receives no feedback until Tuesday. So let us look at what happens when very brief delays (as measured in seconds) are used in teaching.

Immediate feedback appears to be the most effective. This is verbal feedback provided during the lesson but after a short time delay (*short*, meaning a few seconds). The efficacy of delay has been one of the most surprising findings in recent ML research, in part because lab animals typically demonstrate learning decrements relative to time elapsed between trial and feedback. But (surprise!) humans are not lab animals. In studies using feedback delays ranging from seconds to several minutes, no degradation in learning has been noted in motor learning. But one important variable must be mentioned here: the delays studied were "empty"; that is, nothing happened in the interim to distract the learner. It appears critical that the learner's own feedback systems (inherent) be allowed to fill this empty space before the teacher rushes in with verbal commentary. In the words of Schmidt and Lee, "learning is enhanced when processing of the inherent feedback occurs *before* augmented feedback is provided."[44] In studio settings, we see this when music teachers ask a student at the conclusion of a passage, "How did that feel?"

Conversely, *filled feedback-delay intervals* are those pauses in which another activity intervenes. If this interruption is not related to the music lesson—Look! A squirrel!—learning generally suffers. Teachers should consider this when they allow chatting off topic, a knock at the door, or a phone call to interrupt lessons. We teachers must ourselves eschew distractions, no matter how attractive, in order to prevent damaged learning.

Feedback Frequency

A final parameter of time in regard to feedback is feedback frequency, that is, how often a teacher should provide augmented feedback. A commonsense approach, backed up by ML research, is for the teacher to provide frequent feedback in the early stages of music study and then fade out the feedback as mastery increases. Recall that, while frequent feedback in the early stages of learning generally boosts performance, it can also create dependencies in the learner and distract the student from processing her own inherent feedback. Obviously the question of when to begin the fade is paramount. ML theory might answer, "The sooner, the better."

An alternate method to faded feedback is *bandwidth feedback*, in which the learner and teacher basically agree ahead of time that as long as certain parameters are met, the teacher will give no feedback. In practicing bandwidth feedback, no feedback equals good feedback; the learner can infer that her task was correct and therefore "good enough." Note to teachers: you may encounter students who have been reared on frequent praise (whether by parents or former teachers) and who will feel puzzled or even bereft at the loss of it. A commonsense solution is to first ascertain if this is the case and, if confirmed, solicit the student's assent to a new form of confirmation. Be sure to avail yourself of this research so that your student (and, in the case of children and teens, her parents) understands that you are not mean. *Au contraire*, you are operating your studio by the *au courant* laws of ML theory! How lucky your student is to be in such a modern learning environment! (You will revisit the topic of excess praise in chapter 5.)

Finally, *summary feedback* allows the learner to attempt a task several times in a row before feedback is given. This can be a particularly effective teaching and learning method with advanced musicians who wish to try several different ways to reach the same goal and assess what was most effective afterward. Besides, advanced students should not need (or even want) augmented feedback after each and every try. But all students should want to know about the *types* of augmented feedback they receive. Therefore, now that I have described the parameter of feedback timing, the next consideration is feedback quality. What, exactly, is the stuff of augmented feedback?

Knowledge of Performance and Knowledge of Results

Augmented feedback typically breaks down into two main categories according to ML research: *knowledge of performance* and *knowledge of results*. (This nomenclature is somewhat bedeviled by the important distinction between learning and performance covered earlier in this chapter.)

Knowledge of results (KR), as the name implies, is information about the outcome of what the student just did. As such, it is very applicable in some domains while possibly rather useless in others. For example, a coach may need to give KR to a swimmer who, due to the solitary, rather sightless nature of competitive swimming, otherwise has no idea where he placed in time trials until told. Similarly, track and field athletes fidget nervously on the sidelines while awaiting KR.

But KR should be used sparingly in most music lessons, depending on the pursuit. Most instrumentalists do not need a teacher to state the obvious: "Your hand slipped, and you bungled that scale passage." However, singers' special hearing challenges (as previously described) may necessitate frank and immediate KR. But results like "Sasha, your ultimate high C was flat" are always best delivered with a dose of empathy: "I know this is disappointing to hear, since you have been working so hard on intonation, but your ultimate high C was flat. Let's see what you can do to correct it."

Conversely, knowledge of performance (KP) is information about the movement or technique that led to the performance outcome. Using Sasha as an example, KP in a lesson might be scripted like this: "Sasha, your jaw was dropped too low, which wiped out the higher harmonics in that high C, and so it was perceived as flat."

KP is the most common type of augmented feedback given in music lessons, and most teachers use a variety of two kinds: *descriptive* and *prescriptive*. As the names imply, teachers may describe what happened ("You did not move your thumb under quickly enough") and then prescribe a remedy: "Try that scale passage again at a slower tempo, and anticipate the movement of your thumb a bit earlier."

Too Much Information?

For much of the past century, a common opinion concerning the optimal amount of feedback that learners should receive was essentially "the more, the better." And "more" applied to just about every parameter of feedback: more immediate, more precise, more frequent, more informationally rich, and as well more generally useful—this was supposedly all good.[45] Interestingly, this viewpoint harkens back to the beginning of this chapter, with the traditional teacher-student paradigm emphasizing what the teacher knows and not how best the student should receive that knowledge. Cognitive science is concerned with the latter question, and because so much more is now known about the way that humans process information, a shift in emphasis is called for in the pedagogy of just about every discipline imaginable. How much better could teaching and learning go if the focus were switched from the content of the teacher's brain to the landscape of the learner's mind? When the lens is refocused in this way, it becomes much easier to see that the "More is better" approach harms learning in at least four ways.

First, lots of feedback can create a dependency within the learner. This is the aforementioned guidance hypothesis, which holds that student dependency distracts from student effort, a necessary component to learning. This is especially toxic when gobs of feedback are exceptionally positive, for, when that positive feedback is withdrawn, the student can feel set adrift, rebuffed, and lost.

A second and related theory about the negative effect of too much feedback holds that learners can become so addicted to praise that they pursue the task to earn the praise reward and not to learn the task itself. This is particularly damaging to the learning habits of children, as you will see in chapter 5.

A third case against the "More is better" approach is that too much feedback may evoke the same responses that concurrent and instantaneous feedback do: when the student focuses on her teacher's feedback, it blocks her from processing her own.

A fourth theory as to why more feedback is not better feedback is the truth behind the popular complaint "That's just too much information," or TMI for short. Even though urban American slang usually reserves *TMI* for news that is overly and embarrassingly personal, the term captures the theory of *cognitive overload* beautifully. Recall that, by our most recent estimates, most normal humans can juggle only about four items at a time in working memory (i.e., in the act of learning). Now refer to figure 4.1, and allow yourself to be astonished and humbled, both as teacher and as learner, by the sheer amount of feedback a student musician must process and the variety of sources from whence it springs in the quest to learn. TMI syndrome is real.

And if reading all the information in this chapter about feedback is itself TMI, then here is a good rule of thumb: augmented feedback is best when it is simple, delivered in one lump sum after several trials and, at that, after a short delay. One final observation about feedback is certain: if you prioritize a concern for how your student learns over how much you yourself know, your feedback is bound to be more nuanced and fruitful.

Hands Off

Before leaving this section on feedback, take a look at the ethical considerations of the physical feedback known as *manipulation*. This is literally a hands-on teaching approach in which the teacher touches the student's body in order to elicit a physical or tonal response. Even though there can be some remarkable benefits to hands-on guidance, both student and teacher should think soberly about the risks of touching: the potential for misunderstanding, misuse, or outright abuse is high, particularly if there are no witnesses present, which is very often the case in one-on-one studio teaching, where student and teacher are alone, behind closed doors.

Teachers should be aware that simply asking permission to touch a student is not sufficiently comprehensive. Due to the asymmetrical power dynamic inherent in the teacher-student relationship, the student may not feel free to say no. Indeed, very young students or introverted personality types may simply be unable to refuse, even if that is exactly what they wish to do. Students should know that they have the fundamental human right to forbid touching—even if doing so creates awkwardness or anxiety. A coping mechanism for students is to write their teacher an e-mail clearly stating their preferences regarding touching during lessons.

Despite these significant concerns, physical guidance or manipulation remains a very useful tool for motor learning. Therefore, a simple and sensible solution to this dilemma is for the teacher to demonstrate upon her own body, never directly touching the student but guiding the student to act in mirror imitation upon his own. Another solution is for the teacher to give written instructions for manipulation as homework, being sure to detail and describe the sensations the learner should seek ("Notice when your spine is aligned that your jaw tends to relax"). Adding together the ethical and legal hazards that attend touching, plus the cognitive benefits for learners who discover the right sensations for themselves, hands-off guided manipulation seems the best approach for both parties.

THE THEORY OF ATTENTIONAL FOCUS

Across all ML domains, the central goals of skilled performance are *movement effectiveness* and *movement efficiency*. The former encompasses the goals of accuracy, fluidity, speed, and consistency; the latter (also known as *muscular efficiency*) concerns the ability to enact complex muscular movement with a minimum amount of energy.[46] Exactly how to usher the performer to a place of maximum effectiveness with an economy of effort is a question for both performer and trainer, so the issue of attention—specifically, where the learner should place it in both learning and performance—is of primary concern. Much ML research is devoted to a fundamental question: Where should performers aim their attention while learning and performing muscular tasks? Should they focus internally, on the various body parts and micro-

movements involved (the mechanics), or should they place their awareness externally on the end goal of the movement (the target)?

This question—known as the *theory of attentional focus*—has inspired so many studies in ML research that prominent ML researcher
Gabriele Wulf, a leading expert on attentional focus, was invited to
conduct a comprehensive review of the literature on it. According to
Wulf, the jury is no longer out on attentional focus:

> Over the past 15 years, research on focus of attention has consistent-
> ly demonstrated that an external focus (i.e., on the movement effect)
> enhances motor performance and learning relative to an internal
> focus (i.e., on body movements).[47]

The efficacy of *external focus* is perhaps best illustrated through anec-
dote, and Wulf offers her own lesson in windsurfing, a sport in which
the primary attribute needed is balance. Wulf found that, when she
focused her attention internally on the position of her feet and the
location of her hands (the mechanics), she repeatedly fell into the water. However, when she shifted her attention to the tilt of the board as
she turned, she stayed afloat. In other words, when she focused on the
goal of the movement rather than the mechanics of her movements, she
experienced "instantaneous success."[48]

I recall a similar experience learning to play darts at a local bar. A
friend instructed me in the most minute details of throwing a dart: the
grip of my fingers around the shaft, the cock of my elbow, the snap of
my wrist, and the exact point at which I should release the dart. After
many frustrating trials and added damage to the pockmarked wall behind the dartboard, an amused bystander suggested that I should simply "Be the dart" and decide where I wanted my dart-like self to land.
As I intoned that mantra, like Wulf on her sailboard, I experienced
instantaneous success (and a lot of congratulatory beer).

The principle of external focus goes by many mottos in popular
culture: "Go with the flow" and "Be in the moment" encourage a Zen-
like oneness with the experience, while exhortations like "Get out of
your head" and "Don't overthink" imply an anti-intellectualism that
some find appealing when working in the physical realm. Remedies
offered for difficult musical tasks include "Don't fight it," "Just let it
happen," and "Throw your voice to the balcony!" These sayings are
appealing because they offer simple solutions to difficult challenges,

and they are popular because they so often seem to work. Indeed, the principle of nonattention to mechanics is so ubiquitous that philosopher (and former ballet dancer) Barbara Montero dubbed it "the Maxim":

> Both in the ivory tower and on the football field, it is widely thought that focusing on highly skilled movements while performing them hinders their execution. Once you have developed the ability to tee off in golf, play an arpeggio on the piano, or perform a pirouette in ballet, attention to your bodily movement is thought to lead to inaccuracies, blunders, and sometimes even utter paralysis. At the pinnacle of achievement, such skills, it is urged, should proceed without conscious interference. In the oft-spoken words of the great choreographer George Balanchine, "Don't think, dear; just do." Let me call the view that bodily awareness tends to hinder highly accomplished bodily skills "the Maxim."[49]

Montero is an erudite opponent of the Maxim, which she later renamed the *just-do-it principle*.[50] I will return to consider Montero's and others' challenges to the Maxim, but let us begin by looking at the current, prevailing view in ML research: "In almost all situations, an *external focus of attention* results in more skilled performance than an *internal focus of attention*."[51]

Several theories have been developed by various researchers in support of the Maxim. Wulf's own is her *constrained action hypothesis*, which holds that an internal focus of attention interferes with automatic control processes based on the premise that automatic responses are accomplished much more rapidly than are consciously controlled ones. Refer to table 3.1 in chapter 3 and note that declarative learning is generally slow, while procedural learning is relatively fast. Since processing speed has been positively correlated with motor learning goals, the constrained action hypothesis holds that all of these goals (fluidity, accuracy, speed, etc.) are harmed when performers slow down their own motor systems by, in popular parlance, "thinking too much." In other words, when rapid, bottom-up brain-processing speed clashes with top-down, cognitively measured processing speed, we mess up.

Other robust hypotheses in support of the Maxim suggest that directing attention to mechanical movement while learning ironically causes existing (poor) muscular patterns to stabilize, thus working in opposition to the positive benefits of unlearning. Another theory related to this "ironic effect" involves the degree of freedom with which the body operates most efficiently and posits that an internal focus of attention seems to exert a freezing effect on the joints.[52]

Finally, the limitations of language have been noted as a barrier to motor learning because of the difficulty in describing physical sensations in words. It is reasoned that poorly described sensations are tracked into the nonmotor regions of the brain, where they are essentially lost in translation.[53]

A vote in favor of external focus (or any ML research finding, for that matter) is its so-called generalizability to other domains. Wulf states that the worth of external focus is "now well established," as evidenced by its "generalizability to different skills, levels of expertise, and populations, as well as its impact on both the effectiveness and efficiency of performance,"[54] and she suggests that the case is closed regarding the veracity of the Maxim:

> In my review I found no exception to the rule that external-focus instructions or feedback result in more effective and efficient performance or learning than those inducing an internal focus.[55]

ATTENTIONAL FOCUS IN MUSIC

Wulf steps out of the boundaries of her own field of expertise (sports) and flatly declares, "I am convinced that the enhanced movement effectiveness and efficiency seen when individuals focus externally *applies to all human beings*," implying that the external focus "rule" can be applied across virtually every skilled motor pursuit.[56] In her book *Attention and Motor Skill Learning*, Wulf includes guest chapters from practitioners across the ML spectrum. Adina Mornell, concert pianist and professor of instrumental pedagogy at the University of Music and the Dramatic Arts in Graz, Austria, testifies for music:

> In performance, musicians' most valuable assets can become their worst enemies. The same finely tuned ear that enables musicians to weave intricate musical lines can suddenly pick up a disturbing sound in the hall. The same emotional sensitivity that generates beauty in their playing exposes musicians to vulnerability and self-doubt. In the moment concentration becomes interrupted, for what-

ever reason, self-consciousness is created. A sudden shift in attentional focus—towards what Gabriele Wulf defines as "internal focus"—throws the brain engine into a lower gear with a loud roar and pulls the hand brake, disrupting a fluid glide through the musical composition. In short, nothing is worse for a musician than the sudden urge to deliberately manage movement, a departure from external focus.[57]

Indeed, many musicians can likely recall a moment in which *nonattention* to mechanics was the magic wand that allowed their musicianship to blossom. This observation was the seed of tennis pro Timothy Gallwey's 1974 best-selling book, *The Inner Game of Tennis*. Gallwey describes his teaching method as based on "establishing harmony between mind and body" and learning to "get out of your own way so that you can learn and perform closer to your potential."[58] Gallwey's book with coauthor bassist Barry Green, *The Inner Game of Music*, generated a veritable inner-game mini-industry on the topics of golf, skiing, and general work. Inner-game themes have been promulgated by many who train instrumentalists and singers, like voice scientist Katherine Verdolini-Abbott, who has written and lectured extensively on principles of ML theory as they relate to voice training.[59] In an article intended for choral directors, Verdolini-Abbott invokes the Maxim by implying the efficacy of such popular directives as "Stop trying" and "Don't judge":

> **Principle #5: Motor Learning Does Not Involve Trying.** Now we come to an interesting contradiction. Although motor learning appears to require cognitive effort, intentional trying may be harmful. What we mean here by "trying" refers to conscious cognitive effort to identify, use, and judge specific information, rather than letting the non-conscious mind solve the motor problems. In motor learning, conscious "trying" not only has a high likelihood of introducing unwanted muscular tension; it probably invokes the "declarative" or "explicit" memory processes which are probably largely irrelevant to motor learning.[60]

These ideas are appealing in part because they resonate with the current zeitgeist and also because they are backed up by anecdotal accounts of musicians' "unwanted muscular tension" melting under the soothing directive to leave off trying. But how do we know that muscular tension is caused by "overthinking"? How do we know for sure that, in Mornell's words, "nothing is worse for a musician than the sudden urge to deliberately manage movement"?

Ironically, Mornell's unequivocal statement in Wulf's book is immediately followed by her equally unequivocal concession that, "as logical and obvious as this sounds, there has been almost no empirical research done to date on this phenomenon."[61] Given that the scientific method is still the best mechanism we have for validating a claim, Mornell's acknowledgment of the dearth of hard evidence regarding the efficacy of external focus in music should at least give musicians pause.

Before investigating this issue further, let's take a short side trip to the one arena in which at least some ML theorists—even those who espouse the benefits of external focus—allow that there may be some advantages to an internal focus.

NOVICE LEARNERS AND INTERNAL FOCUS

Despite both anecdotal and research evidence that testifies to the success of external focus, it is not unreasonable to wonder about its efficacy for beginners, not to mention its very availability. After all, a beginner in the motor learning realm is a beginner precisely because he has no baseline of efficient function; therefore, the training of beginners is all about establishing a foundation of physical skills. So it ranges from ineffective to irresponsible to exhort beginners who are struggling to just "go with the flow" because it ignores their basic reality: there is, as yet, no flow with which to go.

Sian Beilock, a leading ML researcher on the question of choking in motor performance, concludes that, for this reason, an internal focus is beneficial in the early stages of learning motor skills:[62]

> Different teaching styles are required at various stages of learning to address the changing attentional mechanisms of the performer. . . . It may be beneficial to direct performers' attention to step-by-step components of a skill in the early stages of acquisition.[63]

Beginners accounted for, the question of where advanced and expert performers place their attention yet remains. These people possess an established foundation of physical gestures from which to draw—colloquially, we call these *habits*. Using inner-game speak, we might call it "a flow with which to go." Yet even with established physical habits, is "go with the flow" really the best strategy in motor learning and performance? Or are there better tactics that actually usher the performer to the heart of learning and performance challenges instead of away from them? Researchers besides Wulf who study expert populations are offering some alternatives to external focus and "go with the flow."

CHALLENGES TO THE MAXIM AND JUST DO IT

Psychological research on skill acquisition throughout the previous century established theories that largely account for today's popular view of experts in the motor realm. The buzzword that accompanies adoring fans' assessment of superstar athletes is *automatic*. As Montero drily notes, "in the Psychology literature, the stand-in for divine inspiration is automaticity."[64] The idolatry of automaticity has certainly helped bolster the theory of external attentional focus, popularized as "getting out of your own way." This veneration has spawned the interrelated views that (1) experts operate "automatically," outside their own awareness, and therefore (2) motor training toward a goal of automaticity is paramount, while (3) thinking or verbalization during motor performance spoils automaticity.[65]

To account for these interwoven accounts, Montero redubbed the Maxim the just-do-it principle, defined as follows:

> For experts, when all is going well, optimal or near performance proceeds without any of the following mental processes: self-reflective thinking, planning, predicting, deliberation, attention to or monitoring of their actions, conceptualizing their actions, conscious control, trying, effort, having a sense of the self, or acting for a reason. Moreover, when all is going well, such processes interfere with expert performance and such mental processes should be avoided.[66]

Montero wrote a book-length argument against the just-do-it principle, in which she challenges "whether thinking interfere[s] with doing" and counters with a principle of her own about how human thought works when human bodies are in action,[67] called the "cognition-in-action" principle:

For experts, when everything is optimal or near optimal, performance frequently involves some of the following conscious mental processes: self-reflective thinking, planning, predicting, deliberating, attending to or monitoring actions, conceptualizing actions, controlling movement, trying, making an effort, having a sense of the self, and acting for a reason. Moreover, such mental processes do not necessarily or even generally interfere wth expert performance and should not be avoided.[68]

Other significant challenges to the just-do-it principle have been mounted by researchers John Toner, Aiden Moran, and John Sutton, among others. The following five key criticisms are the most salient for musicians:

Key Criticisms of the Just-Do-It Principle

1. Most ML research subjects are not experts.
2. ML lab studies do not study complex motor skills.
3. Studies conducted in a lab rather than on a court or on a mountainside—let alone in a concert hall—are not "ecologically valid."[69]
4. Elite performers in some domains actually *reject* automaticity, either for artistic reasons (jazz) or because ever-changing conditions do not allow it (skiing and stand-up comedy).
5. Experts seek continually to improve, and improvement demands practically all of the attributes eschewed by the just-do-it principle (e.g., self-reflective thinking and making changes based on variable conditions).

Musicians should carefully consider each of these points before swallowing the just-do-it principle whole. Let us consider each one of them here. The first, the fact that most ML research is conducted on nonexpert subjects, highlights a central challenge in research across disciplines: there is an overabundance of so-called naive subjects. Why is this? There are two basic reasons. Most research in the United States is conducted at research universities that by their very nature house an abundance of naive subjects (students). Conversely, experts become expert by pursuing what they do with a laser-like intensity that brooks few interruptions. This zeal is precisely what psychologist Mihaly Csikszentmihalyi found while developing his famous theory of "optimal experience," or "flow."[70] Many of the experts whom Csikszentmihalyi contacted flatly refused his invitation to interview them because they viewed participation as a distraction from their work. Several experts politely explained that they became expert precisely by refusing invitations like Csikszentmihalyi's. Expert test subjects are difficult to snare.

On the second point, ML lab studies are generally confined to simple, so-called limb tasks such as ball throwing, dart sticking, and keyboard tapping. Yet music making is a complex activity. A related concern is that most ML research is based on studies in athletics and not the performing arts. While performing artists have much in common with athletes, performance goals for artists are different than those for athletes, often wildly so. Without getting into the weeds over whether Olympic-worthy gymnastics are more or less cognitively complex than the musical skills on display at the Cliburn International Piano Competition (not to mention the relative artistry between the two), no one would argue that both are decidedly more complex than, say, balance-boarding (an oft-studied skill in ML research). When expression and artistry are added to the fundamental ML goal of muscular efficiency, cognitive load must surely increase. Classical singers have the added cognitive burden of language and must appear emotionally convincing and fluent in a language that is often not their own.

Comparing simple physical-sports tasks with expert-level musical technique seems, at best, careless. At one time Wulf herself (a lead researcher and champion of external focus) coauthored a study bluntly titled "Principles Derived from the Study of Simple Skills Do Not Generalize to Complex Skill Learning." The study calls "into question the adequacy of utilizing primarily simple tasks in the study of motor learning and control" and concludes that research on simple skills should stick to its simple lane.[71] Expert music-making, in any genre, is not a simple skill.

On the third point, musicians well know that the environment in which they play has a strong effect (for good or for ill) on performance, and a laboratory environment may be uninspiring or worse. One wonders just how spontaneous and, frankly, capable those jazz pianists of Dr. Limb's were able to be while placed inside an fMRI scanner, using a custom-built keyboard that was

> placed on the subjects lap in supine position, while the knees were elevated with a bolster. A mirror placed above the subjects' eyes allowed visualization of the keys during performance. Subjects were instructed to move only their right-hand during the scanning and were monitored visually to ensure that they did not move their head, trunk, or other extremities during performance. The subjects lay supine in the scanner without mechanical restraint.[72]

This awkward setup elicited giggles from the TED audience to which Limb presented his experiment, as did an interview with one of the subjects, a jazz pianist, who gamely reported on what it was like to play as normally as possible in an exceedingly abnormal (not to mention claustrophobic) environment:

> The hardest thing for me was the kinesthetic thing, you know, of just looking at my hands through two mirrors, laying on my back, and not able to move at all, except for my hand, that was challenging . . . but again, you know . . . there were moments, for sure . . . you know, I mean, there were moments of real honest-to-god musical interplay, for sure.[73]

In the audiotape of this interview, the listener can hear this musician trying to rationalize the disparity between the highly unnatural setup and his ability to improvise. Limb himself later coauthored a paper, allowing that

> if a creator is placed in an abnormal, constraining environment during the course of a scientific study, the creative process itself is threatened, calling into question the validity of any observations made thereafter.[74]

Indeed, and seconded. Outside the laboratory setting, there remains a world of difference separating practice and performance or between a rehearsal and the real deal. In research, this problem is known as *ecological validity*. This, along with other challenges when conducting psychological research, have upended the entire field and ignited a full-on "reproducibility crisis."[75] We should keep in mind that fMRI studies can only reveal brain activity during an experiment—not how performers actually think in performance, much less how they mentally prepare for them.

These questions are posed by research psychologist Roger Chaffin in his longitudinal case studies of expert musicians, which offer a treasure trove of information for musicians in training and those who teach them. Chaffin's partnerships with expert pianists, cellists, and singers have revealed that these musicians develop and access "memory retrieval cues," which he has called *performance cues*:

> Performance cues are the landmarks of the piece that an experienced musician attends to during performance, carefully selected and rehearsed during practice so that they come to mind automatically and effortlessly as the piece unfolds, eliciting the highly practiced movements of fingers, hands, and arms. Performance cues become an integral part of the performance and provide a means of consciously monitoring and controlling the rapid, automatic actions of the hands.[76]

Note that Chaffin's performance cues "provide a means" of conscious monitoring and control. This is the opposite of external focus, or "nonattention" to mechanics. Research on attentional focus has suffered due to a lack of expert subjects generally and a lack of performing artists as subjects specifically. If this state of affairs could somehow be rectified, Chaffin's studies offer a refreshing and egalitarian model for how research partnerships between art and science might proceed most fruitfully. His

> studies combine the third-person perspective of the scientist, which provides objectivity and rigor, with the first-person perspective of the musician, which provides a rich understanding of the musical judgments that shaped the performance. Often the studies confirm the musicians' understanding of their experience of performance, providing objective support for their intuitions. Sometimes the musicians are surprised and then everybody learns something new.[77]

Let us now consider a fourth criticism of the vaunted goal of automaticity, namely, that automaticity is actually scorned in some domains even though the ability to execute skilled movement "without thinking" has been lionized in ML theory as a hallmark of expertise, with "automaticity" revered as the Holy Grail of expert performance across multiple pursuits:

> With talent and a great deal of involved experience, the beginner develops into an expert who sees intuitively what to do without applying rules and making judgments at all. . . . Normally an expert does not deliberate. He or she neither reasons nor acts deliberately. He or she simply spontaneously does what has normally worked and, naturally, it normally works.[78]

This account is hardly new, owing much to romantic-era notions of genius in which inspiration supposedly gushes forth as long as the rational mind does not staunch it (ironically, much popular writing has sought to take Limb's fMRI discoveries as scientific proof of this romantic account). To those outside the border of expertise, revered players within the magic circle of talent appear to issue forth their gifts effortlessly. Is it any wonder, then, that lack of effort is inferred to be the reason for their success? Yet a deeper look at the work habits and opinions of actual experts across many domains reveals common threads of effort, discipline, and pointed disdain for the "no effort" myth. The late Sam Snead (anointed by former USGA president William Campbell "the best natural player ever") got at the heart of how insulted many experts feel when their abilities are ascribed to mere talent:

> People always said I had a natural swing. They thought I wasn't a hard worker. But when I was young, I'd play and practice all day, then practice more at night by my car's headlights. My hands bled. Nobody worked harder at golf than I did.[79]

While athletes and musicians may view the intersection of talent and effort similarly, they may part ways at attitudes toward risk. Risk-taking in sports can carry significant consequences, as when a star pitcher's throw or golfer's stroke goes awry, while the sportscaster's phrase "off his game" is an admonition against straying from the path of automaticity. Athletes' risk-taking can result in even graver consequences, like torn ligaments and broken bones. So while automaticity may be a desirable trait in some athletic pursuits, in music performance it is, at best, confined to its role in fluidity and dependability. At worst, musicians risk criticism for wooden or uninspired performances when they are judged as being too automatic. In fact, risk-taking in music (particularly in jazz) is highly valued and even considered a badge of honor among elite musicians.

So how might musicians find the sweet spot between cultivating enough automaticity to withstand the rigors of performance (and the adrenaline rush that attends it) while resisting uninspiring performances? The solution, according to Chaffin and colleagues, is to "interweave thought and action" by practicing automaticity and performance cues at the same time, enfolding both technique and expression in one gesture.[80] That is, practice the emotional response along with the physical one, and tuck them away in the mind as one unified cue, available for retrieval at will.

A final critique of the just-do-it principle rests on the clear-eyed observation that experts seek continually to improve; that is why they are expert. And improvement demands practically all of the attributes eschewed by just-do-it (self-reflective thinking, planning, predicting, deliberation, attention to and monitoring of actions, and so forth). If this is true of the expert, it necessarily follows that this *should* be true of the students of expertise. The cognitive skills needed for improvement should be taught to expertise seekers.

Given the robust arguments against it, then, why does the veneration of automaticity persist? The vision of someone like musical titan Itzhak Perlman mindlessly practicing his violin while watching television certainly helps, endearing him to fans as a regular guy:

> "Actually, the best show to practice on is baseball," Perlman said. "It's terrific, because you can turn off the sound, and you know what's going on, and you practice your technique. I'm not talking about practicing thinking or anything like this," he said. "That's a totally different thing. I did some of my greatest practicing when I was in London watching cricket. It's a very, very low game. That's when you practice."[81]

Even though in this and other interviews Perlman is always careful to explain that, when he puts himself "on automatic pilot," he is working on "technique, as opposed to musical content," that nuance may be lost on learners who emulate him.[82] We may assume that Perlman (a child prodigy who made his Carnegie Hall debut at age eighteen) has logged well over ten thousand practice hours and so possesses a motor program that runs on track like a well-oiled machine. Apparently all he has to do is push the "on" button. But for lesser musicians and for student musicians in training, the possibility of practicing mistakes while on autopilot—and thereby encoding them into memory—is probably fairly high. This is yet one more argument against automaticity.

So if automaticity is so bad (toxic to creativity and an intoxicant for damaged learning), why is it so popular? Is there anything good about playing on automatic pilot? The answer is a qualified yes. For one thing, it would be cognitively impossible to consciously process each and every mundane motor task we do every day. Imagine issuing commands to yourself to twist a doorknob with just the right amount of wrist flexion, and you get the idea. Musicians ply their craft with similarly mundane tasks: once we know how to flip our thumbs under on a keyboard to achieve velocity on a scale passage, hours of practice seal it up in the vault of long-term memory, and we never have to think about it again—unless, due to injury, we have to retrain that habit in a new way.

Absent the latter scenario, the most cogent argument for automaticity is the former: routine tasks can be marked "done," shelved, and stocked in the vault of the mind for retrieval at will. This stockpiling of simple tasks, it is thought, reduces cognitive load, leaving more mental real estate available for other cognitive tasks, like expressivity. This is the upside of automaticity. Yet this very advantage (more room in the brain) is also the Achilles's heel of automaticity, which I will discuss in chapter 6.

FLEXIBLE ATTENTION

Now that I have explained the just-do-it principle, questions remain: Are musicians to focus internally or externally? Should we chase automaticity? Foreswear overt self-commands? They beg an essential one for musicians: Are these either-or propositions? Must musicians make a definitive choice between an internal or an external focus of attention (as Wulf's opinion clearly implies), or might we toggle between them in the midst of our music-making as training and performance conditions demand? If automaticity reduces cognitive load, might we access a dash of automaticity and use our cognitive balance in the service of art? To answer these questions, let us look to a team of Australian researchers who have proposed a "flexible attention" approach they call "applying intelligence to the reflexes," or AIR:

> By the notion of "applying intelligence to the reflexes," then, we mean that certain patterns of behaviour which might appear stably chunked, automated, and thus inflexible are in skilled performance already and continually open to current contingency and mood, past meanings, and changing goals. Experts have opened their "reflexes" up into acquired adaptive patterns, and constructed, over time . . . dynamic repertoires of potential action sequences which can be accessed, redeployed, and transformed appropriately.[83]

In other words, experts exhibit the ability to rapidly switch their technique. They do this by employing what appear at first glance to be rather fixed (automatic) gestures. But a closer look at very skilled performers (like musicians) offers a completely different interpretation. Sutton's team proposes that these "patterns of behaviour" are actually "chunked" abilities that the researchers say operate like "Lego blocks . . . scattered around a musician" as he begins to play. These blocks remain handy to deploy or leave on the table—performers' choice. How might we deploy these blocks? ML researchers John Toner and Aidan Moran note that performers use executive control (also called *cognitive control*) to deliberately deploy these chunks in all three phases of motor learning and performance (training, preperformance strategizing, and the performance itself).[84]

The reasons that performers might choose to alter their techniques vary, but they all spring from the aforementioned characteristic of expert performers: experts seek continually to improve.[85] Sometimes this quest to improve is within our control; at other times, it is sought by necessity.

PLANNING FOR DISRUPTIONS: TRAINING HOW TO THINK

In the ongoing search for excellence, many trainers and expertise seekers will deliberately alter practice conditions in order to challenge themselves. Musicians may do this by changing their practice space or holding an invited dress rehearsal. This is the "varied rule of practice" in action.

At other times, altered performance conditions are not of our choosing. They are visited upon us either by injury or by the conditions of the activity. For example, musicians recovering from repetitive strain injuries may have to alter finger or bowing patterns, and singers recovering from abdominal surgery have reported having to relearn how to breathe. Executive control must be used by these musicians to intentionally attend to their previously automated abilities.

Similarly, Toner and Moran note that experts who perform under challenging situations do so by accessing their executive control in order to heighten their technique or retrain their motor programs. This effect has been studied in expert skiers, who must continually adapt to changing weather patterns that affect snow conditions, both in the preplanning stage and in real time as they speed down the slope.

Musicians cope with rapidly changing situations just like downhill skiers do. Any number of surprises can happen during a live performance, all of which require quick thinking and flexibility. Common challenges include unfamiliar acoustics in a new performing space or adjusting to the feel and touch of a new instrument, a recurring professional hazard for pianists, who cannot pack their instruments with them. Singing actors are equally familiar with challenging scenarios. Singing through an upper respiratory infection or dealing with an ill-fitting costume are only a few obstacles that require quick thinking and expert technical adjustments, not automaticity. And let us recall that there are also positive reasons why a performer may wish to avoid automaticity and suddenly change their interpretation "in the moment" for artistic reasons.

Indeed, Toner and Moran note that "disruptions" are a fact of the motor-performing life, and thus we are probably better off devising "creative solutions in order to address these disruptions" proactively.[86] While a just-let-it-go directive may be successful when performance conditions are excellent, if this is attempted during disrupted performance conditions, the move is, at best, a gamble. In this light, planning for disruptions ahead of the game seems more sensible, and in order to do that, we must integrate this flexibility in our training. As Sutton, McIlwain, Christensen, and Geeves note, the pursuit of excellence in action involves "training up of the right indirect links *between* thought and action, not the evacuation of thought from action."[87] Ergo, musicians should practice how to think, not just what to do.

TRAINING-EMBODIED COGNITION

Even though musicians are often showered with best wishes before a performance, as actor Dennis Hopper scolded in a popular ad campaign about retirement preparation, wishes don't cut it: "You need a plan," he intoned. But how to create a musicians' performance plan? You might start by considering how motor-skill learning really works, and you could encrust it with details. Sutton and colleagues' description of "building and accessing flexible links between knowing and doing" is an accurate and elegantly concise description of motor learning for music.[88]

At the beginning of motor learning, these links between thought and action are first bequeathed to the student as directives from his teacher, who uses her tools (usually verbal) to inculcate her own, ultimately ineffable sensations within the student's body. But this transference is incomplete; it depends on the learner to finish it. A musician's performance plan can only be built by the musician himself by creating the links between knowing and doing, within his own mind and body, through deliberate practice.

Indeed, distinct directives, flexible links, mental Lego blocks—the stuff of any musician's performance plan—are all just ideas until and unless they are literally made incarnate, made flesh, through doing. This is, in essence, a description of embodied cognition, the philosophy that challenges the dualistic mind-body split.[89]

Once established, these links must be at the beck and call of the musician. They must be automatic, yes, to a degree, but they must also be consciously retrievable. In highly skilled performance art, in both practice and performance, musicians continually traverse between top-down and bottom-up processes, plying these flexible links in service of their art—changing, and being changed by, the constantly shifting interactions.

NOTES

1. Quoted in Elizabeth Green, "Building a Better Teacher," *New York Times*, March 7, 2010, www.nytimes.com/2010/03/07/magazine/07Teachers-t.html.

2. See Gabriele Wulf, *Attention and Motor Skill Learning* (Champaign, IL: Human Kinetics, 2007); and Ingo Titze and Katherine Verdolini-Abbott, *Vocology: The Science and Practice of Voice Habilitation* (Salt Lake City, UT: National Center for Voice and Speech, 2012), ch. 7.

3. Lynn Helding, "Master Class Syndrome," *Journal of Singing* 67, no. 1 (2010): 73–78.

4. Robert Bjork, "Memory and Metamemory Considerations in the Training of Human Beings," in *Metacognition: Knowing about Knowing*, ed. Janet Metcalfe and Arthur Shimamura, 185–205 (Cambridge, MA: MIT Press, 1994).

5. Suzuki Association of the Americas, "Bowhold Training Aids," June 24, 2011, to May 5, 2014, https://suzukiassociation.org/discuss/6730/.

6. A. W. Salmoni, R. A. Schmidt, and C. B. Walter, "Knowledge of Results and Motor Learning: A Review and Critical Reappraisal," *Psychological Bulletin* 95 (1984): 355–86. See also Richard Schmidt and Timothy Lee, *Motor Control and Learning: A Behavioral Emphasis*, 4th ed. (Champaign, IL: Human Kinetics, 2005), 359–60.

7. R. A. Schmidt, "A Schema Theory of Discrete Motor Skill Learning," *Psychological Review* 82 (1975): 225–60. See also R. A. Schmidt, "Motor Schema Theory after 27 Years: Reflections and Implications for a New Theory," *Research Quarterly for Exercise and Sport* 74 (2003): 366–75.

8. Bjork, "Memory and Metamemory."

9. See Schmidt and Lee, *Motor Control and Learning*, 428.

10. Ibid., 322.

11. See performance psychologist and musician's Noa Kageyama's website for more researched practice tips: "Turn Your Practice Up to 11," Bulletproof Musician, https://bulletproofmusician.com/resources/.

12. Tadhg E. MacIntyre, Christopher R. Madan, Aidan P. Moran, Christian Collet, and Aymeric Guillot, "Motor Imagery, Performance and Motor Rehabilitation," *Progress in Brain Research* 240 (2018): 145.

13. The average reaction time for humans is 0.25 seconds for a visual stimulus, 0.17 seconds for an audio stimulus, and 0.15 seconds for a touch stimulus. Daisy Yuhas, "Speedy Science: How Fast Can You React?" *Scientific American*, May 24, 2012, www.scientificamerican.com/article/bring-science-home-reaction-time/; Backyard Brains, "Experiment: How Fast Your Brain

Reacts to Stimuli," 2017, https://backyardbrains.com/experiments/reaction-time.

14. Aidan Moran, Aymeric Guillot, Tadhg MacIntyre, and Christian Collet, "Re-imagining Motor Imagery: Building Bridges between Cognitive Neuroscience and Sport Psychology," *British Journal of Psychology* 103, no. 2 (2012): 225.

15. See Alvaro Pascual-Leone, "The Brain That Plays Music and Is Changed by It," *Annals of the New York Academy of Sciences* 930, no. 1 (2001): 315–29.

16. Schmidt and Lee, *Motor Control and Learning*, 353–55.

17. Edmund Jacobson, "Electrical Measurements of Neuromuscular States during Mental Activities: I. Imagination of Movement Involving Skeletal Muscle," *American Journal of Physiology—Legacy Content* 91, no. 2 (1930): 569.

18. Ibid., 607. According to his obituary in the *New York Times*, Dr. Jacobson came to be known as the "father of progressive muscle relaxation" and maintained clinics in both Chicago and Manhattan, where he taught this technique to patients. He authored over one hundred articles as well as thirteen books, including *How to Relax and Have Your Baby: Scientific Relaxation in Childbirth* (New York: McGraw-Hill, 1959), which joined the rising "natural birth" movement.

19. For an extensive overview of this research, see A. Guillot, M. Louis, and C. Collet, "Neurophysiological Substrates of Motor Imagery Ability," in *The Neurophysiological Foundations of Mental and Motor Imagery*, ed. A. Guillot and C. Collet, 109–24 (Oxford: Oxford University Press, 2010). See also S. L. Beilock and I. M. Lyons, "Expertise and the Mental Simulation of Action," in *The Handbook of Imagination and Mental Simulation*, ed. K. Markman, B. Klein, and J. Suhr, 21–34 (Hove, UK: Psychology Press, 2009).

20. M. Jeannerod, "The Representing Brain: Neural Correlates of Motor Intention and Imagery," *Behavioral and Brain Sciences* 17 (1994): 187–202; and M. Jeannerod, "Neural Simulation of Action: A Unifying Mechanism for Motor Cognition," *Neuroimage* 14 (2001): S103–S109, https://doi.org/10.1006/nimg.2001.0832.

21. Ingo G. Meister, Timo Krings, Henrik Foltys, Babak Boroojerdi, M. Müller, R. Töpper, and A. Thron, "Playing Piano in the Mind—An fMRI Study on Music Imagery and Performance in Pianists," *Cognitive Brain Research* 19, no. 3 (2004): 219–28. See also Pascual-Leone, "Brain That Plays Music."

22. G. Rizzolatti, L. Fogassi, and V. Gallese, "Neurophysiological Mechanisms Underlying the Understanding and Imitation of Action," *Nature Reviews Neuroscience* 2, no. 9 (2001): 661–70, https://doi.org/10.1038/35090060.

23. Vilayanur S. Ramachandran, "Mirror Neurons and Imitation Learning as the Driving Force behind the Great Leap Forward in Human Evolution,"

Edge.org, May 31, 2000, www.edge.org/conversation/mirror-neurons-and-imitation-learning-as-the-driving-force-behind-the-great-leap-forward-in-human-evolution.

24. Roy Mukamel, Arne D. Ekstrom, Jonas Kaplan, Marco Iacoboni, and Itzhak Fried, "Single-Neuron Responses in Humans during Execution and Observation of Actions," *Current Biology* 20, no. 8 (2010): 750–56. See also Christian Keysers and Valeria Gazzola, "Social Neuroscience: Mirror Neurons Recorded in Humans," *Current Biology* 20, no. 8 (2010): R353–54.

25. Nikos Logothetis, "What We Can Do and What We Cannot Do with fMRI," *Nature* 453, no. 7197 (2008): 870.

26. American Association for the Advancement of Science, "UCLA Researchers Make First Direct Recording of Mirror Neurons in Human Brain," EurekAlert! April 12, 2010, www.eurekalert.org/pub_releases/2010-04/uoc--urm041210.php.

27. Raleigh Mcelvery, "How the Brain Links Gestures, Perception and Meaning," *Quanta*, March 25, 2019, www.quantamagazine.org/how-the-brain-links-gestures-perception-and-meaning-20190325.

28. Gerry Leisman, Ahmed A. Moustafa, and Tal Shafir, "Thinking, Walking, Talking: Integratory Motor and Cognitive Brain Function," *Frontiers in Public Health* 4 (2016): 94.

29. Phillip Cohen, "Mental Gymnastics Increase Bicep Strength," New Scientist, November 21, 2001, www.newscientist.com/article/dn1591-mental-gymnastics-increase-bicep-strength/.

30. Vinoth K. Ranganathan, Vlodek Siemionow, Jing Z. Liu, Vinod Sahgal, and Guang H. Yue, "From Mental Power to Muscle Power—Gaining Strength by Using the Mind," *Neuropsychologia* 42, no. 7 (2004): 945.

31. MacIntyre et al., "Motor Imagery, Performance and Motor Rehabilitation," 142.

32. Schmidt and Lee, *Motor Learning and Performance*, 258.

33. Lynn Helding, "Cognitive Dissonance: Facts versus Alternative Facts," *Journal of Singing* 74, no. 1 (September/October 2017): 89–93.

34. See Manuj Yadav and Densil Cabrera, "Autophonic Loudness of Singers in Simulated Room Acoustic Environments," *Journal of Voice* 31, no. 3 (May 2017): 13–15.

35. N. Scotto Di Carlo, "Internal Voice Sensitivities in Opera Singers," *Folia Phoniatrica et Logopaedica* 46 (1994): 79–85.

36. Ibid.

37. Leon Festinger, "Cognitive Dissonance," *Scientific American* 207, no. 4 (October 1962): 93.

38. See Scott McCoy, *Your Voice: An Inside View*, 3rd ed. (Delaware, OH: Inside View Press, 2012).

39. World Health Organization, *Adherence to Long-Term Therapies: Evidence for Action* (Geneva, Switzerland: World Health Organization, 2003), 137.

40. See Lynn Helding, "Mindful Voice: Teaching Voice with the Brain in Mind," *Journal of Singing* 70, no. 3 (January/February 2014): 349–54.

41. Schmidt and Lee, *Motor Learning and Performance*, 258.

42. Ibid.

43. Ibid., 68.

44. Ibid., 282 (emphasis mine).

45. Ibid., 262.

46. Gabriele Wulf, "Attentional Focus and Motor Learning: A Review of 15 Years," *International Review of Sport and Exercise Psychology* 6, no. 1 (January 2013): 78.

47. Ibid., 77.

48. Ibid., 78–79.

49. Barbara Montero, "Does Bodily Awareness Interfere with Highly Skilled Movement?" *Inquiry* 53, no. 2 (March 2010): 105–6.

50. Barbara Gail Montero, *Thought in Action: Expertise and the Conscious Mind* (Oxford: Oxford University Press, 2016).

51. Schmidt and Lee, *Motor Learning and Performance*, 56.

52. Wulf, "Attentional Focus," 89.

53. See R. A. Poldrack, J. Clark, E. J. Paré-Blagoev, D. Shohamy, J. Creso Moyano, C. Myers, and M. A. Gluck, "Interactive Memory Systems in the Human Brain," *Nature* 414 (2001): 546–50; and R. A. Poldrack and M. G. Packard, "Competition among Multiple Memory Systems: Converging Evidence from Animal and Human Brain Studies," *Neuropsychologia* 41 (2003): 245–51.

54. Wulf, "Attentional Focus," 99.

55. Quoted in Cary Groner, "Internal vs. External Focus: Effects on Motor Learning," *Lower Extremity Review Magazine*, September 2014, 2.

56. Gabriele Wulf, "Why Did Tiger Woods Shoot 82? A Commentary on Toner and Moran," *Psychology of Sport and Exercise* 22 (January 2016): 337–38 (emphasis mine).

57. Adina Mornell, in Gabriele Wulf, *Attention and Motor Learning*, 140–41.

58. W. Timothy Gallwey, *The Inner Game of Tennis*, rev. ed. (New York: Random House, 1974), xii–xiv.

59. See Katherine Verdolini-Abbott, "Perceptual-Motor Learning Principles: How to Train," in *Vocology: The Science and Practice of Voice Habilitation* (Salt Lake City, UT: National Center for Voice and Speech, 2012), ch. 7.

60. Katherine Verdolini, "On the Voice: Learning Science Applied to Voice Training: The Value of Being 'In the Moment,'" *Choral Journal* 42, no. 7 (February 2002): 49–50.

61. Adina Mornell, in Wulf, *Attention and Motor Skill Learning*, 141.

62. Wulf, "Attentional Focus," 91; Sian Beilock, Thomas Carr, Clare Mac-Mahon, and Janet Starkes, "When Paying Attention Becomes Counterproductive: Impact of Divided versus Skill-Focused Attention on Novice and Experienced Performance of Sensorimotor Skills," *Journal of Experimental Psychology: Applied* 8, no. 1 (March 2002): 6–16; and Sian Beilock, Bennett Bertenthal, Annette McCoy, and Thomas Carr, "Haste Does Not Always Make Waste: Expertise, Direction of Attention, and Speed versus Accuracy in Performing Sensorimotor Skills," *Psychonomic Bulletin and Review* 11, no. 2 (April 2004): 373–79.

63. Beilock, Carr, MacMahon, and Starkes, "When Paying Attention," 15.

64. Montero, *Thought in Action*, 25.

65. See H. Dreyfus and S. Dreyfus, *Mind over Machine* (New York: Free Press, 1986); and P. M. Fitts and M. I. Posner, *Human Performance* (Monterey, CA: Brooks/Cole, 1967).

66. Montero, *Thought in Action*, 237.

67. Ibid., 77.

68. Ibid., 237–38.

69. P. W. Burgess, N. Alderman, C. Forbes, A. Costello, L. M. Coates, D. R. Lawson, N. D. Anderson, S. J. Gilbert, I. Dumontheil, and S. Channon, "The Case for the Development and Use of 'Ecologically Valid' Measures of Executive Function in Experimental and Clinical Neuropsychology," *Journal of the International Neuropsychological Society* 12 (2006): 194–209.

70. Mihaly Csikszentmihalyi, *Flow: The Psychology of Optimal Experience* (New York: Harper & Row, 1990).

71. Gabriele Wulf and Charles H. Shea, "Principles Derived from the Study of Simple Skills Do Not Generalize to Complex Skill Learning," *Psychonomic Bulletin and Review* 9, no. 2 (2002): 185–211.

72. Charles Limb and A. Braun, "Neural Substrates of Spontaneous Musical Performance: An fMRI Study of Jazz Improvisation," *PLOS One* 3, no. 2 (2008): e1679.

73. Charles Limb, "Your Brain on Improve," TED Talk, November 2010, www.ted.com/talks/charles_limb_your_brain_on_improv.

74. Malinda McPherson and Charles J. Limb, "Difficulties in the Neuroscience of Creativity: Jazz Improvisation and the Scientific Method," *Annals of the New York Academy of Sciences* 1303 (November 2013): 80.

75. For a succinct overview, including links, see Benedict Carey, "Many Psychology Findings Not as Strong as Claimed, Study Says," *New York Times*,

August 27, 2015, www.nytimes.com/2015/08/28/science/many-social-science-findings-not-as-strong-as-claimed-study-says.html.

76. Roger Chaffin and Topher Logan, "Practicing Perfection: How Concert Soloists Prepare for Performance," *Advances in Cognitive Psychology* 2 (2006): 115.

77. University of Connecticut, "Roger Chaffin, Professor: Biography," https://musiclab.uconn.edu/roger-chaffin/#.

78. Hubert Dreyfus and Stuart E. Dreyfus, "The Ethical Implications of the Five-Stage Skill-Acquisition Model," *Bulletin of Science, Technology & Society* 24, no. 3 (2004): 251–64.

79. Guy Yocom, "My Shot: Sam Snead," *Golf Digest*, August 12, 2010, www.golfdigest.com/magazine/myshot_gd0204?currentPage=1.

80. Tânia Lisboa, Alexander P. Demos, and Roger Chaffin, "Training Thought and Action for Virtuoso Performance," *Musicae Scientiae* 22, no. 4 (2018): 527.

81. CBSNews.com staff, "Revisiting the Violinist: Itzhak Perlman, Virtuoso, Now Conductor, Too," *60 Minutes*, January 17, 2000, www.cbsnews.com/news/revisiting-the-violinist/#1995.

82. Ira Berkow, "A Musician Connects with Baseball," *New York Times*, October 14, 1981, www.nytimes.com/1981/10/14/sports/a-musician-connects-with-baseball.html.

83. J. Sutton, D. McIlwain, W. Christensen, and A. Geeves, "Applying Intelligence to the Reflexes: Embodied Skills and Habits between Dreyfus and Descartes," *Journal of the British Society for Phenomenology* 42 (2011): 96. See also Andrew Geeves, Doris J. F. McIlwain, John Sutton, and Wayne Christensen, "To Think or Not to Think: The Apparent Paradox of Expert Skill in Music Performance," *Educational Philosophy and Theory* 46, no. 6 (2014): 674–91. One fact that makes this research particularly appealing to musicians is that they studied musicians, and one of their members (Geeves) is a music performance coach for Opera Australia ("Andrew Geeves," Academia, 2019, https://mq.academia.edu/AndrewGeeves).

84. See John Toner, Barbara Gail Montero, and Aidan Moran, "Considering the Role of Cognitive Control in Expert Performance," *Phenomenology and the Cognitive Sciences* 14, no. 4 (December 2015): 1127–44.

85. See K. Anders Ericsson, "The Influence of Experience and Deliberate Practice on the Development of Superior Expert Performance," in *The Cambridge Handbook of Expertise and Expert Performance*, ed. K. A. Ericsson, N. Charness, P. Feltovich, and R. R. Hoffman, 685–706 (Cambridge: Cambridge University Press, 2006).

86. John Toner and Aidan Moran, "Enhancing Performance Proficiency at the Expert Level: Considering the Role of 'Somaesthetic Awareness,'" *Psychology of Sport and Exercise* 16, no. 1 (January 2015): 115.

87. Sutton, McIlwain, Christensen, and Geeves, "Applying Intelligence," 93.

88. Ibid., 95.

89. For an excellent description of this complex topic, see Monica Cowart, "Embodied Cognition," Internet Encyclopedia of Philosophy, www.iep.utm.edu/embodcog/#H2 .

5

PERFORMANCE STUDIES

Chapters 3 and 4 on learning have at their core the twin suppositions that there is something to instill (on the part of the trainer) and something to learn (on the part of the student). That something is skill. But just as attention exhibits a preattentional phase, the pursuit of musical skill displays a similar prelude—let us call it a demonstrated ability—as well as the shared spark of desire. Yet are ability and desire enough? Or is the pursuit of musical skill altogether impossible without that special kind of ability known as *talent*?

As Mama Rose intones in the musical *Gypsy*, "Ya either got it, or ya ain't!" The "it" of which Mama sings is talent. Mama observes, "Some people got it, and make it pay" while others (the poor losers) "can't even give it away." If "you ain't got it," according to Mama, "you've had it!"

Whether the severity of this judgment is true or not, the majority of people who pursue musical training, either for themselves or on behalf of their progeny, do so inspired by the belief that there are at least some embers of musical talent glowing in the center of the soul. But just what is talent, exactly? Psychologists Michael Howe, Jane Davidson, and John Sloboda observe,

> It is widely believed that the likelihood of becoming exceptionally competent in certain fields depends on the presence or absence of inborn attributes variously labeled "talents" or "gifts" or, less often, "natural aptitudes."[1]

This totally uncontroversial opinion, published in their landmark 1998 paper "Innate Talents: Reality or Myth?" nevertheless concludes with this bombshell: "Innate talents are, we think, a fiction, not a fact."[2] By throwing down this gauntlet, Howe, Davidson, and Sloboda go far beyond the equally uncontroversial observation that it is training, not talent, that ultimately transforms inborn gifts into accomplishment. They set out to debunk the entire notion of inborn gifts, an agenda they brand "the talent account," claiming that "even people who are not believed to have any special talent can, *purely as a result of training*, reach levels of achievement previously thought to be attainable only by innately gifted individuals."[3]

"Innate Talents: Reality or Myth?" aroused strong reactions among the reigning luminaries in psychology at the time of its publication. Thirty opinion pieces were published as peer commentary along with the target article, taking a variety of stances against the extreme *environmentalist* views of Howe, Davidson, and Sloboda. (Note that, in this case, an environmentalist is not a tree-hugger but a person who sides with nature in the historic nature-versus-nurture debate, holding that environment trumps heredity in the development of humans. Translate this into modern inspirational speak, and you get a popular aphorism: "Try hard enough and anything is possible!")

Esteemed psychologist and *Flow* author Mihaly Csikszentmihalyi grumps that Howe and others are "flogging the dead horse of the nature versus nurture controversy," an exercise "particularly useless in the context of talent" due to recent research in the heritability of certain traits (or gifts).[4] Of gifts and heritable characteristics, there is much disagreement. However, there is one parameter about which most experts agree: body or body part size. In activities like basketball, where height is crucial, this must be deemed an inborn gift given the fact that nothing can be done to effect a change after childhood growth is complete. Arguably the same could be said of the attributes needed for success in certain instruments, most obviously the human voice. The big, hardy voices required for certain opera roles are simply born and not made (though training is absolutely required to bring this gift to full fruition). Likewise, the span of one's hand plays a role in one's success at tackling a keyboard or a large stringed instrument.

Apart from body or body part size, though, many critics of Howe, Davidson, and Sloboda simply cite a highbrow version of Mama Rose's opinion: regardless of what you call it, some people got it, and some people ain't, and we know it when we see it. After all, one critic reasons, the lookouts that professional sports teams send on reconnaissance are "talent scouts, not practice scouts."[5] Cognitive psychologist Robert J. Sternberg follows with a comment, the snarky title of which presages his opinion: "If the Key's Not There, the Light Won't Help."[6]

Even Howe and his coauthors admit that, while they think talent is a myth, they still "do not claim to have a full or precise answer to the question 'If talents do not exist, how can one explain the phenomena attributed to them?'" Phenomena like the spectacular talents of extraordinary people and the curious cases of musical savants are perennially listed as exhibit A in the evidence for giftedness:[7]

> If anyone can prove that the works of these individuals can be explained without recourse to a construct like natural talent, we will concede that talent does not exist: Mozart, Picasso, Shakespeare, Martina Hingis, Baryshnikov, Pavarotti, Ramanujan, Judit Polgar, Michael Jordan, and Robin Williams. Practice, indeed.[8]

Another researcher allows that, even though Howe, Davidson, and Sloboda's article demonstrates scant evidence to support the talent account, he still isn't buying training and exposure as the only factors that might account for individual achievement. This critic's plaintive plea "Might we adopt the learning-related account instead of the talent account?" and his subsequent suggestion that there are "problematic social implications" in stressing hard work alone, "especially in cultures in which effort is emphasized," reveal his own biases: the late Giyoo Hatano was a professor of cognitive science at Keio University in Tokyo, Japan, a country that suffers one of the highest suicide rates among industrialized nations.[9] The causes for suicide are varied and complex, but most experts attribute Japan's epidemic suicide problem to the toxic result of personal failure within a culture that values extreme effort.

Several critics stress the importance of "industriousness," sidestepping the talent question entirely with the observation that, by emphasizing talent, Howe, Davidson, and Sloboda vastly underrate the importance of hard work.

DELIBERATE PRACTICE

Hard work has been the focus of psychology professor K. Anders Ericsson's research career. Ericsson, widely recognized as one of the world's foremost authorities on expertise and human performance, has studied both the quality and the quantity of hard work that it takes to become an expert at anything. Ericsson coined the term *deliberate practice*, which he defines in a seminal 1993 study of violin students as "an effortful activity designed to optimize improvement."[10]

This research is also the original source of the vaunted number 10,000, the number of practice hours that it supposedly takes for anyone to attain a level of mastery at just about anything. Ericsson suggests this number in a 1996 academic publication with the subheading *The 10-Year Rule of Necessary Preparation*, in which he acknowledges the many studies previous to his that, spanning almost a century, demonstrate this conclusion, along with the related observation (in yet another denomination of 10) that it seems to take about decade of dedicated practice to become an expert.[11]

Despite the availability of this information, it wasn't until author and inspirational speaker Malcolm Gladwell christened it the "10,000-Hour Rule" in his best-selling popular psychology book that the idea was planted in the public consciousness. It is now Gladwell's name that is most associated with this popular concept, not Ericsson's, nor any of the other eleven researchers whose own deliberate practice provided the data for the theory.

"Ten thousand hours is the magic number of greatness," Gladwell states, a glib interpretation that misses some crucial nuances detailed by Ericsson himself in a popular science book published over a decade later.[12] Under the brusque subheading "No, the Ten-Thousand-Hour Rule Isn't Really a Rule," Ericsson takes Gladwell to task for the several ways in which Gladwell gets it wrong about practice—and acknowledges the one way in which he gets it right.[13]

The wrongs include the number 10,000 itself. Some domains require far fewer than 10,000 hours for mastery, while some actually require far *more*. For example, Ericsson notes that most elite concert pianists (the type who win prestigious international piano competitions) tend to do so when they are around thirty years of age, and by that time, he estimates they would have logged 20,000–25,000 hours of practice.

Gladwell also lumps together practice, performance, and generic playing—what musicians might call "noodling"—conflating all the Beatles' musical activity during their formative years as an ensemble in the early 1960s. But in failing to distinguish playing from practice, Gladwell misses a crucial detail. As you saw in chapter 4, learning and performance are diametrically opposed. Practice is learning, and learning is messy. Performance, conversely, is all about best impressions, and therefore it is anything but messy. This conflation echoes Gladwell's most fatal translation error: it is not the sheer number of hours played or practiced that matters most but the *quality* of those hours. Quality is the defining characteristic of Ericsson's deliberate practice. And quality of practice can be measured by at least one main attribute you have already encountered in this book: effort.

This crucial component of practice is typically ignored by young students in training in favor of sheer repetition. Consider the average music teacher's standard query at the beginning of each weekly lesson: "Did you practice your assigned repertoire this week?" The desultory response "I ran over it every day" calls to mind the sad, splattered carcasses of animals left for dead on the highway. Music practiced effortlessly profits about as much as those unlucky little beasts.

Besides, mindlessly "running over" repertoire yields more than just stagnancy; it causes learning to actually regress. Unless effort is expended toward intentionally correcting parts that are difficult, mindless practice just digs the rut of error deeper. Seasoned musicians will recognize this as practicing one's mistakes.

Deliberate practice is an altogether different animal, distinguished by a number of traits with which Ericsson has since enhanced his original definition of deliberate practice. These enhancements carry important implications for both teachers and learners. For teachers, Ericsson's enhancements include knowledge of the history of the field, of fads and traditions, and of what works and what does not work based on experience with various training regimens. At first glance this may seem a rather quotidian addition, yet it should not go without notice that some of the best teachers are those who have experimented with a variety of approaches and have selected the best components of all they sampled. In contrast, and for this very reason, some of the best performers in the motor realm who hew to one technique may not make the best teachers. Related knowledge includes the importance of foundational skills, an admittedly unsexy yet essential topic and one that is beset by the curse of expertise noted in chapter 4.

For students, Ericsson's enhancements of the qualities needed for deliberate practice include accepting discomfort, complete attention, feedback (to self), and constructing mental representations of what to do. Common to both teachers and students are goal-setting; feedback; and that ubiquitous parameter, effort. For music teachers, a condensed job description according to the new tenets of deliberate practice might read as follows:

> Wanted: Music teacher of deliberate practice. Must be well-versed in the efficacies (or lack thereof) in training regimens for the instrument over the length of its history through his or her own performance experience. Must design regimens of effortful activities, starting with building fundamental skills and modifying these to suit the individual student's developing abilities and needs over time. Must meet with student to craft well-defined goals in advance, then meet periodically thereafter for lessons to proffer honest yet empathetic augmented feedback.

This job description may seem simple, yet a variety of pitfalls can lead teachers away from the essential responsibilities of directing deliberate practice, responsibilities that echo Bjork's desirable difficulties encountered in chapter 4. Withholding desirable difficulties, while perhaps well intentioned, does not square with the number-one requirement of deliberate practice, which is effort. Trainers who err on the side of being "nice" do so at the expense of effective training. At the same time, it must be stated unequivocally that psychologically abusive training should never be construed as firm and stringent teaching. Rigor must never be confused with cruelty. The story of pianist Lang Lang should be chilling enough, but those trainers who swear by a tough love approach to teaching should be sure to read in chapter 6 about the cascade of physical symptoms that attends perceived threat. Psychologically abusive teaching is not only morally reprehensible; it is ultimately ineffective.

Related to the pitfall of being too nice is a propensity for some trainers to skip training fundamentals altogether. Admittedly, this part of training can be rather dull for both trainer and trainee, but akin to skipping the veggies and heading straight for dessert, a student trained in this way may find himself flabbergasted to learn in later years that his training has failed to nourish him by failing to build and sustain an identifiable and secure technique. Retooling one's fundamental skills midcareer is a humbling process and one with no guarantee of success.

Another common pitfall for teachers involves the phenomenon known as *inattentional blindness*, a condition whereby (barring any physical problem with vision, of course) people fail to see what is right in front of them. This phenomenon was hilariously demonstrated in the now-infamous gorilla experiment, in which subjects who watch a video of others engaged in a ball-throwing task and are asked to count passes of the ball often fail to see an actor in a gorilla suit who waltzes through the midst of the game.[14] The auditory equivalent of inattentional blindness can infect the music studio so that teachers evince a tendency to hear the same faults in each and every student or to harbor the same timbral goals for all of them.[15] The result is undifferentiated template teaching, insensitive to the unique needs and abilities of each student. Teachers should design individual practice regimens for each student based on that student's unique needs and well-defined goals. As already noted in chapter 3, goal-setting is known to boost learning generally, since it ignites motivation. But goal-setting is also a particularly crucial component of motor learning, since attempting a specific action has been shown in ML research to be a far more effective learning tool than a vague directive to "do better."[16] Ericsson includes goal-setting in his definition of deliberate practice to distinguish it from what he called "purposeful practice"—though well-intentioned, it is just deliberate practice without the sting of effort.[17]

Even though deliberate practice relies on the expertise of teachers who by job description must design effortful practice regimens, it must be emphasized that the success of deliberate practice is a two-way street: learners must meet training demands with an eager willingness to fully participate. A fantasy job description for student musicians bound by the tenets of deliberate practice might read as follows:

> Wanted: Music student who is seeking teacher of deliberate practice. Must craft agreed-upon, written-out goals with teacher before embarking on commitment to daily regimen of effortful activities with complete attention. Practice regimen includes building fundamental skills and self-reflection activities with repertoire to advance in difficulty as skills improve. Expect occasional feelings of psychic discom-

fort and empathy from teacher during these learning moments. Joint celebrations of joy to occur during occasions of superior accomplishment.

A deliberate practice regimen, as designed by the teacher and followed by the student, targets specific movements, notes successes, scrutinizes flaws, and—by analysis—continually redesigns the regimen. There is nothing vague about this type of practice. The requirements for the learner—an ability to work alone, to confront one's weaknesses, and to pay focused attention for a set amount of time each day—all highlight the fact that the kind of effort demanded of motor learners engaged in deliberate practice is not purely physical but also requires building and accessing emotional and cognitive resources.

THE COGNITIVE DEMANDS OF DELIBERATE PRACTICE

All humans use mental pictures to navigate everyday life, as reflected in such phrases as "Call to mind" and "Picture if you will." These visualizations even define the word *imagine*. Expertise researchers in the 1970s noted that experts—specifically, chess grandmasters—turn this human trait to their advantage through hours of deliberate practice. They do not merely picture the board in their mind but are able to push the fast-forward button and predict the most advantageous moves several steps in advance. Whereas a novice might simply visualize random pieces, experts chunk individual pieces into groups based on their relationships. From there, they are able to manipulate those chunks and move them around in their imagination. As discussed in chapter 3, chunking is a critical component of working memory (otherwise known as learning).

The same phenomenon is at work with language. A string of random words like this one: *woke our who noisy the long barked all angry then dog night and became neighbors* is much harder to recall than the same words rearranged: *the noisy dog barked all night long and woke our neighbors who then became angry*. Individual words gain resonance only when they carry meaning.

Motor experts do much the same thing by forming a mental picture of what to do. Ericsson calls these "mental representations" of the task at hand. Like verbal memory, motor pictures carry meaning. Yet motor performers' mental pictures differ from the mental pictures of chess players in several important ways.

First, what the motor performer imagines are her own bodily actions rather than an external, objective setup like a chessboard. This is a bit like the difference between a video and a photograph: one is moving, and one is static. And even though chess masters mentally move their pieces forward in time, it is not the movement per se that is the focus of this mental manipulation. But for motor performers, movement is entirely the point. Mental plans do not just offer a helpful little jolt to motor learning; they are, in fact, integral to success in the motor realm. This point is most easily seen through an extreme example: the high-risk sport of ski jumping.

Moments before our jumper takes flight, she calls to mind her most advantageous movements, picturing them in her mind and feeling them within her body. Not only will this imagery ensure a better chance of success, but it will also lessen the chance of injury. We might call this the "look (inside) before you leap" rule.

But there is a crucial catch: mental representations cannot exist without our first actually experiencing the movements upon which they are based. This is the quandary of flow, as noted in chapter 4: beginners have no flow with which to go—they have not yet mounted and affixed their mental videos in the screening room of their mind, so how can they possibly just go with it?

This chicken-or-the-egg dilemma must be progressively overcome, albeit with giant heaps of perseverance on the part of the learner. If he sticks with it, each time he experiences the necessary movements through trial and error (in the case of high-risk sports like skiing, a few bruises and broken bones), his mental representation of the skill grows. In turn, the more complete the mental representation, or schema, the more effectively he can practice, which in turn increases the mental representation, and so on. Ericsson nicknames this symbiosis the "virtuous circle of deliberate practice."[18]

Another catch of mental representations is that, in order to be effective, they must be what researchers call *domain-specific*. In other words, while both skiers and musicians may accurately be labeled "athletes"—both train their bodies in highly skilled ways—the actions specific to their calling and therefore their mental representations are radically different from each other. Therefore, neither will achieve excellence (or even above-averageness) without practice devoted to targeted movements specific to their disciplines. A string player profits little by learning how to shift her weight like a skier.

Skier and musician represent two different genera in the taxonomy of athletics: genus/skier and genus/musician. The genus/musician can be further subdivided, resulting in two distinctly different species: *instrumentalist* and *singer*. You can reasonably expect that each species will follow the domain-specific rule insofar as it applies to developing specific mental representations: singers have little need of mapping the movements of their fingers, and string players need not consider the shape of their lips. And even though wind players and singers share the same actuator (breath energy), the specifics of how that breath is applied is very particular to each instrument.

This domain-specific rule seems rather obvious, and yet some music curricula in American universities, particularly those with strong music education schools, favor the cultivation of limited proficiency in a broad number of different instruments over what is viewed as a narrow (and, by inference, restricted) course of study. We might call this a *wide-versus-deep* approach to musical skill. The opposite approach (*deep-versus-wide*) characterizes the ethos at many music conservatories and preprofessional programs.

Certainly by the laws of practice as outlined in chapter 4, there are cognitive benefits to breaking up the intensity of deep, vertical practice with variation. Indeed, the development of Schmidt's schema theory spawned later evidence regarding the value of variation in practice versus the monotony of repetition. This evidence may seem to support a wide-versus-deep approach to music learning. Yet the domain-specific rule cannot be ignored, and in light of new evidence regarding the erosion of attention due to the lure of digital media (the topic of chapter 7), it is wise to reassert its truth to aspiring musicians. At this cultural moment, most novice musicians are not in danger of cognitively diving too deeply into practice.

The cognitive demands of deliberate practice—Ericsson's mental representations—are similar to those concepts encountered in chapter 4: Schmidt's schema theory, Sutton's patterns of behavior, and Chaffin's performance cues. As the motor learner becomes more expert, these mental structures coalesce into what athletes, dancers, and musicians call *technique*. And as already noted, fluidity of movement is a major objective of motor learning. Within this parameter, musicians have much in common with athletes, particularly those who transform fluid movement into art, like figure skaters and dancers. But here we musicians part ways with our artist-athlete colleagues, for musicians are not just visualizing what a movement looks like. While we are imagining the feel of our movement (our proprioception), our ultimate objective is translating that feeling into sound. This last point is a critical distinction between musicians and all other motor performers.

Musicians spend an extraordinary amount of time experimenting with the many ways that differences in movement will alchemize to musical tone. The weight of the wrist over a keyboard, the handgrip on a mallet, the crispness with which a string is plucked, and the degree of glottal closure within the larynx are all subject to a variety of choices. So how do musicians create these choices? The answer is through deliberate practice that builds mental representations of movement to sound. Yet, as fully fledged musical artists, exactly how have we acquired these mental representations to mix and match at will? The simple answer is *more* deliberate practice—this is Ericsson's virtuous circle. I will return to these elemental questions later in this chapter, but let us first consider a question that ML researchers, as nonmusicians, have largely failed to explore, and that is the question of artistic expression. After all, compelling musicians with ardent followers are not successful because they are awesome practicers. Musicians' fans adore them because they spark emotion in their listeners. And in order to do that, the first requirement is that musicians must feel emotion deeply themselves.

THE EMOTIONAL DEMANDS OF DELIBERATE PRACTICE

How do musicians create technical choices that are so unshakably trained that they are available on command yet still result in fresh and emotionally compelling performances? The answer (at least according to Chaffin and colleagues) is a composite type of deliberate practice, one that involves targeted effort over time, like regular deliberate practice, yet adds the element of expressive intention. Cellist Tânia Lisboa teamed up with Chaffin and fellow researcher Alexander Demos to describe this process in great detail.

   Lisboa first created a set of performance cues (PCs) strategically placed at transition points in the score to aid memorization of a Bach prelude and serve double duty as guideposts to rescue her from potential memory lapses in performance. Along the way, she found that the PCs she developed were not merely safety nets; they helped her play more expressively, too:

> My PCs at these musical transitions reminded me of my musical goals, for example, to bring out the "singing" qualities of the melody, ensuring that I remained fully engaged with the music. When a performance is going well, I experience the sound flowing from my cello out into the auditorium as I listen for musical qualities that I have worked to create in my performance. Musical thoughts are in the foreground, technical options in the background, available when needed.[19]

Lisboa's account is a beautiful example of the worth of practicing how to think, not just what to do. In practicing how to think, musicians can also practice how to emote. Some musicians may reject this suggestion, citing the risk of an emotionally stale performance. But if that were the case, then virtually every successful actor could be slapped with a charge of emotional fakery. What do actors do except rehearse a scene over and over again, practicing not just what to do but how to feel?

   An actor's job is to absorb another's emotional state to such an extent that the audience, for a time, inhabits the portrayed character's soul. This is most tangible in actors who play known or historical characters such as Meryl Streep as Julia Child, Olivia Colman as Queen Anne, or Ben Kingsley as Mahatma Gandhi. These actors are lauded for their ability to transcend mere mimicry and inhabit the soul of a fellow human being. And while it is perhaps easier to elicit sympathy from an audience for likeable characters, the ability to do so while playing a detestable one deserves especially high honors, which Frank Langella earned for his portrayal of American president Richard Nixon, who left office in disgrace.

   In postproduction interviews, Langella stressed that the secret to his eerie likeness of Nixon was his ability to link Nixon's vulnerabilities to common traits in all of us:

His pain, and the obviousness of his pain, stays with you. It's not a sentiment that's new to any of us—you could see it on him at all times, his discomfort in public—but I discovered he could be equally funny and charming. He just wasn't a relaxed man, and was forever churning away, trying to achieve greatness.[20]

Exactly how these actors achieve this emotional depth is by practicing the emotion, both on and off the set, even if it means staying in character throughout the entire production period. This acting method was first developed by the great nineteenth-century Russian director and teacher Konstantin Stanislavski, whose Method of Physical Action was later promoted in the United States by actors Lee Strasberg, Stella Adler, and Sanford Meisner, where it came to be known as simply "the Method." A core principle of the Method entails complete sublimation of oneself in the character being played and staying in character even while backstage, even if it makes fellow actors squirm. Anne Hathaway described being Meryl Streep's costar in the movie *The Devil Wears Prada* this way:

When I met her she gave me a huge hug, and I'm like, "Oh my god, we are going to have the best time on this movie," and then she's like, "Ah sweetie, that's the last time I'm nice to you." She then went into her trailer and came out the ice queen, and that was really the last I saw of "Meryl" for months, until we promoted the film.[21]

Frank Langella's description of his own total character immersion while on the film set of *Frost/Nixon* is a perfect description of the Method at work and the spell it casts over an entire artistic enterprise:

Richard Nixon was so pervasive in my thoughts and my mind that I asked if once I put him on, [once] we had created him and I was finished in my trailer, when I stepped out of the trailer I tried and maintained it really for ninety-five per cent of the film. When I left my trailer, I was Nixon and I stayed Nixon on the set, sat quietly— and I love to knock it around with actors, I love to make jokes and have fun between takes; I think the more relaxed you can be, the better your work is. But I thought, if I let down, if I showed myself too much to the company, it wouldn't be as good for them. So when I walked on the set, everybody said, "Good morning Mr. President, how are you Mr. President," and it created a wonderful separateness for Nixon so that I could maintain his feeling of isolation. . . . I wanted that sense that this was the President of the United States, both for them and for me. And it worked.[22]

The virtuous circle of deliberate practice that begets embodied cognition for athletes must be widened for musicians, actors, and other performance artists to include emotion. This enriched version of the virtuous circle is essential to developing a comprehensive musician's practice plan, for it creates a space for the emotional demands of deliberate practice. And while a musician's virtuous circle is not fraught with the physical peril that attends high-risk sports, it can be fraught with emotional peril, the most extreme form of which is *performance anxiety* (also called *stage fright*). This serious affliction must be considered apart from the emotional demands of deliberate practice primarily because the topic itself is many-layered and deserves its own chapter (see chapter 6). As unsettling as performance anxiety is, it does not alter the fact that much music practice requires emotional stamina. Almost all music performance requires emotional courage. Let us now consider a concept that claims to roll these and similar virtues into one monosyllabic construct, a compound virtue that can be taught.

GRIT

Much has been made recently of a quality known as *grit*, which is defined by sociologist Angela Duckworth as "the tendency to sustain interest in and effort toward very long-term goals."[23] Duckworth's research netted her a MacArthur Genius Grant as well as one of the most viewed TED Talks of all time. The concept of grit (and Duckworth's best-selling book of the same name) struck a chord in the public consciousness for several reasons: it codified folk wisdom (Grandpa was right! Hard work pays off!); reified a historic and particularly American brand of work ethic; and, most tantalizingly, following the playbook of deliberate practice, suggested that grit is a skill that can be trained by teachers and acquired by learners. Grit has been championed by proponents of the latest iteration of an educational movement, known as *character education*.[24]

But grit has also attracted its share of detractors in proportion to its extraordinary success. Critic David Denby acknowledges grit as "a pop-psych smash," yet fears that its zealous application by education reformers could have the unintended consequence of knocking the stuffing out of what makes us human (qualities like empathy, honesty, kindness, exploration) and, worse, does so during childhood, our most absorbent age.[25] Alfie Kohn dismisses grit as just the latest "social science craze" while worrying that there is a sell-by date for persistence, past which it begins to smell and eventually curdle into a full-on psychological disorder called "nonproductive persistence."[26] Which is to say, there is an upside to quitting (mental health) that the grit narrative completely ignores.

Among academics, a research team headed by Marcus Credé at Iowa State University conducted a meta-analysis of the grit literature, charging Duckworth with exaggerating her effect sizes and making outsize claims about grit's effectiveness, both of which were judged as expected outcomes for a study whose subjects were confined to already high achievers.[27] This defect dogs expertise research in general: studying a homogenous group of subjects begets homogenous results.

The Iowa State University group also convincingly argues that grit is just part of a suite of strongly heritable personality traits long identified in academic psychology as the Big Five: *conscientiousness, agreeableness, extroversion, neuroticism,* and *openness.* Grit, according to its detractors, is just conscientiousness in new clothing.

But grit's most ardent criticism centers on social justice. Children who are hungry, sleep-deprived, or anxious stand little chance of achieving academic success if their basic needs for food, shelter, and a loving adult go routinely unmet. Now, in the age of brain science, there is corroborating neuroscientific evidence of poverty's toxicity to brain development.[28] In short, grit's detractors cry, how dare educational reformers fly the flag of grittiness above the heads of disadvantaged children! And how dare they unwittingly hand social services budget-cutters yet more ammunition to pursue their austere agendas.

Even Duckworth herself is now somewhat chastened by grit's rapid rise and vehement rebuke. In a recent interview, when asked about grit's "misapplication," she replied, "I think the more I know, the more I worry":[29]

Sometimes, I think people believe that I, or others, see grit as the only thing kids need to be successful and happy. In fact, I think character is [on] a very long list of things that kids need to be happy and productive. It's not just grit. It's also curiosity. It's not just curiosity. It's also gratitude and kindness. It's not just that. It's emotional and social intelligence. It's not just that. It's open-mindedness. It's not just that. It's honesty. It's not just that. It's humility.

I think when we are talking about what kids need to grow up to live lives that are happy and healthy and good for other people, it's a long list of things. Grit is on that list, but it is not the *only* thing on the list. I'll tell you, as a mother, but also as a scientist and as a former teacher, that it's not the first thing on the list either.[30]

Above grit's fray, beyond grit's hype, and besides the social-justice argument against weaponizing grit, there yet remains this implacable reality: performers in the motor realm need resilience in order to commit to all the requirements of deliberate practice and to withstand the rigors of performance. There is no way around this requirement. The obstinacy of this truth is charmingly captured in a children's book about family members who go on a journey to hunt a scary beast, bravely chanting,

> We're going on a bear hunt.
> We're going to catch a big one.
> What a beautiful day!
> We're not scared!

As they encounter a series of obstacles (a tall gate, a muddy bog), they stop and reckon with their predicament:

> We can't go over it.
> We can't go under it.
> Oh no!
> We've got to go through it![31]

So it is with pursuit of excellence. There is no way around hard work. Duckworth echoes this obstinacy:

I don't think we're born knowing how to work hard. I don't think it's automatic that we know how to work on our weaknesses with a certain discipline and to accept feedback on what we could do better. I think those are hard things to learn.[32]

For all motor performers, daily practice and its attendant daily dose of feedback is a stark reality. For musicians, an added fact of professional life is the audition, an exercise almost no musician enjoys yet all serious performers know is necessary. Nevertheless, for many musicians, rejection after audition ranks as the number one soul-crusher—even worse than flubbing in performance. Perhaps this is because responsibility for the latter rests solely with ourselves (which means we can improve with more practice) yet in the former scenario, our fate rests partly in the hands (and ears) of others. Either way, the choice of responses ranges wildly between smashing your instrument to pieces and reverently placing its shards on the altar of what is left of your ego or accepting your audition results (which are, after all, just another form of feedback) and—sigh—returning to deliberate practice.

And yet, is quality practice the *only* requirement for achieving excellence? Just like grit, deliberate practice has had its Warholian fifteen minutes of fame. Its legitimacy as the one factor that transforms ability to mastery is now being questioned.

BEYOND DELIBERATE PRACTICE

In 2014, the journal *Intelligence* published a special issue, "Acquiring Expertise: Ability, Practice, and Other Influences," entirely devoted to challenging Ericsson's conclusions about the efficacy of deliberate practice. "Ericsson," the editor writes, "argues that anybody can be good at anything" and introduces the eight papers in the issue written by expertise researchers who are "in general disagreement with the suggestion that abilities do not influence the development of expertise."[33] (Note the choice of the word *abilities* as opposed to *talent*.) Authors of one of these papers proclaim deliberate practice as "not even close to sufficient" as an explanation for why some people become experts and others do not.[34]

So what factors fill the gap between rigorous training and accomplishment? There are several significant ones that have been well known in expertise literature for quite some time. They are (listed here in no particular order of importance) IQ, working memory capacity, early starting age, caring adult mentors, and supportive family structures.

All these factors involve a complex interplay between genes and environment, and so they are challenging to tease apart. Take, for example, IQ and working memory capacity (i.e., the ability to learn). The former is somewhat heritable, and the latter grows with challenge and use, but inherited intellectual ability will not fully bloom until and unless it is stimulated and challenged. If this sounds circuitous, it is. While studies suggest that genetic factors underlie intelligence, researchers caution that genetics account for differences in intelligence among individuals only about 50 percent of the time; the rest is up to the environment.[35] This cautionary analysis can be read in an opposite manner, depending upon the agenda of the researcher. Authors of a recent article in *Scientific American* who are known critics of the deliberate-practice explanation take the same figure and, in a glass-half-full interpretation, declare both working memory and music aptitude as "*substantially* heritable."[36] Regardless of the heritability of these factors, the environment in which budding musicians are raised is the other half of the story of whether inborn gifts will bloom or wither.

EARLY STARTS AND CARING MENTORS

It has long been known that an early starting age and, by extension, early intervention by adults in the form of parents and teachers cause defining differences between superior and average performers in almost every domain of accomplishment: academic, athletic, and musical. One of the seminal studies on this subject was the Development of Talent Research Project, conducted by educational psychologist Benjamin Bloom in the early 1980s at the University of Chicago. Bloom's team examines the role of giftedness "as necessary prerequisites of talent development" by closely examining the underlying structures—specifically, parents and teachers—that helped accomplished concert pianists, sculptors, Olympic swimmers, tennis champions, research mathematicians, and research neurologists actually develop whatever inborn gifts they might have possessed as children.[37]

Bloom identifies three phases of development that eventually result in adult expertise: an early "fun" stage (noodling around with an instrument); a second stage of middle development, where parents typically decide to find a teacher for the child; and a third stage, where the child (usually a teenager) takes over his own disciplined practice. Ericsson and colleagues have proposed a fourth stage to account for the arrived expert, or master.[38] In the musical realm, we would anoint such a person a fully fledged artist, one who not only demonstrates technical ability but actually has something unique and compelling to express and, in one of the hallmarks of an expert, seeks continually to improve.

Yet it is the second stage of talent development that matters here, for this is a critical stage of learning not only for children but for parents, who must insist on a certain amount of regular practice for the child if he is to progress to mastery. Some parents of young musicians (especially those who are not musicians themselves) are repelled by this idea for fear of wringing the fun out of music-making. Yet a reliance on fun versus nurturance is equivalent to the difference between exposure and learning. Recall from chapter 2 that exposure is not learning. Likewise, noodling is not practicing. A commonsense approach is informed by the child's age and the first rule of practice from chapter 4: Distributed practice is more effective than massed practice. For very young children, this translates to a daily practice regimen of about twenty minutes per session, perhaps five times per week. As children grow, these increments can be increased.

Does this mean that parents must suck the joy out of music in order for their child to succeed at it? Hardly. There is a certain joy in mastery, and even the smallest victories can bring celebration. Nevertheless, Bloom's conclusion stands as an unambiguous rejoinder to the talent account:

> No matter what the initial characteristics (or gifts) of the individuals, unless there is a long and intensive process of encouragement, nurturance, education and training, the individuals will not attain extreme levels of capabilities in these particular fields.[39]

A similar study to Bloom's, yet larger in scale, was conducted in England in the mid-1990s by Jane Davidson, Michael Howe, Derek Moore, and John Sloboda, nicknamed the "Leverhulme Project" after the UK grant-making foundation the Leverhulme Trust, which supported it.[40] The team tracked five diverse groups of musically active children whose musical engagement ranged widely from "outstandingly able" to "tried an instrument but gave it up."[41] While the team learned that the similarities between the five disparate groups of young people far outweighed their differences, one significant difference stood out as a defining factor in the acquisition of musical expertise: parents.[42] The top two groups of musicians had been the beneficiaries of "early parent-initiated activity," a fancy euphemism for soccer moms, hockey dads, and helicopter parents.

Indeed, the parents of future elite performers in many domains (sports, dance, music) devote considerable resources of money and time for coaches' fees, equipment, and ferrying their children between lessons, masterclasses, clinics, and competitions. In some cases, performers and their families even relocate to be closer to a chosen teacher, training facility, or competitions.[43]

So it appears that the concern of parents who care deeply enough about their children's development to pay for lessons, drive them to rehearsals, supervise their practice, and make instrument repairs when necessary is so integral to their children's success that it virtually wipes out any essential benefit attributable to natural gifts in all but perhaps the most gifted. Such children possess a "rage to master," a memorable characterization conceived by psychologist Ellen Winner, an expert on gifted children.[44] Still, it is difficult to imagine how that rage might find a musical outlet if there is no instrument in the house (sing-alongs to the radio notwithstanding). Environment matters quite a lot, since it functions as a petri dish for talent development.

Canadian psychologist Françoys Gagné developed a theory to describe this development process. His *differentiating model of giftedness and talent* clearly separates gifts from talents by describing the former as natural abilities with which we are born and the latter as what develops "systematically."[45] In other words, giftedness is a biological potential that may or may not grow into full-blown achievement—*talent*. How this happens depends on the gifted one's desire (and, Duckworth would add, grit) as well as his environment. Does his environment feature opportunities for his gifts to grow? Do his adult caregivers function as curators or blockers of this child's natural gifts?

Yet even in the face of such tangible and obvious gifts as body (and body part) size, we must immediately account for the fact that such gifts never bloom outside the fertile ground of opportunity. This caveat adds weight to Gagné's differentiation between giftedness and talent, and because these two terms are often used synonymously, Gagné's construct becomes all the more valuable in disentangling the effects of genetics from the effects of environment. Still, while Gagné's model establishes a clear and linear trajectory from gift to ability, by taking giftedness as its starting point, his model evades tackling Howe, Davidson, and Sloboda's outright refutation of talent.[46]

Indeed, people who regularly train gifted individuals agree with Mama Rose's frank assessment of talent, and, what is more, they claim they can spot it instantly. Violinist Pinchas Zukerman recalls hearing the violin prodigy Midori play when she was a ten-year-old student at the Aspen Music Festival and School:

> Out comes this tiny little thing, not even 10 at the time. I was sitting on a chair, and I was as tall as she was standing. She tuned, she bowed to the audience, she bowed to me, she bowed to the pianist— and then she played the Bartok concerto, and I went bananas. I sat there and tears started coming down my cheeks. I said, "Do you play something else?" And through an interpreter she said, "Yes, the Sauret cadenza of the Paganini concerto." Ten years old, and she already played the Sauret cadenza like only a few people in the entire universe can do any time! I'm talking about forever. And she had a tiny little half-size violin, but the sound that came out—it was ridiculous. I was absolutely stunned. I turned to the audience and said, "Ladies and gentlemen, I don't know about you, but I've just witnessed a miracle."[47]

Early starts and parental support feature prominently in the biographies of musical prodigies, and when combined with deliberate practice (which the parents of prodigies almost always seem to insist upon), the results are predictable, as echoed in the title of Howe's book *Genius Explained*. Midori's biography as it appeared in the *New York Times* might therefore be renamed *Miracle Explained*:

> Born in 1971 in Osaka, Midori grew up to the sound of her mother's violin. Setsu Goto, now in her early 40s, was active in Japan as a teacher, chamber-music player and orchestral concertmistress. . . . In a 1987 interview she recalled that when Midori "was 2, she often slept by the front row of the auditorium when I rehearsed. One day I heard her humming a Bach concerto—the very piece I'd been practicing two days before." On Midori's third birthday, she was presented with a one-sixteenth-size violin, and her lessons began.[48]

Another parent-and-child duo from the annals of musicology (and a more famous one) is Wolfgang Amadeus Mozart and his father, Leopold. By historic accounts, the toddler Wolfgang started playing the clavier around the age of three—a very early start. That there was music in the home is undisputed, since Leopold was a master musician, composer, and violin pedagogue. He was also the teacher of Mozart's sister Nannerl, five years Wolfgang's senior and a piano prodigy to boot. According to Nannerl, little Wolfgang so loved to sit in on his sister's lessons that, by age four, Papa began his son's formal instruction. Despite the evocation of little Wolfgang's middle name ("Beloved by God"), by all accounts Leopold took no chances on the development of his son's reportedly God-given gifts.

If Mozart practiced an average of three hours a day, by the time Leopold Mozart packed off his children on the first of many performance tours in June 1763, seven-year-old Wolfgang would have already completed around 3,300 practice hours—a third of the requisite 10,000.

—⟳⟳⟳—

Mozart and the 10,000-Hour Practice Rule

- 1760: Mozart (age 4) begins regular, deliberate practice. He practices 3 hours a day, 7 days a week, which equals 21 hours per week times 52 weeks, which equals approximately 1,100 hours per year times 3 years, which equals 3,300 practice hours by age 7.
- 1763: The start of the Mozart family's first European grand tour, for a total of 6,600 practice hours by age 10 and 9,900 practice hours by age 13.

—⟳⟳⟳—

At this pace, by the time Wolfgang was thirteen, he would have more or less reached the requisite 10,000-hour milestone—that is, if he stuck to three hours per day, but there is every reason to surmise that Leopold would have required more than three hours per day in order to ready the children for their performances in the royal courts of Europe, ventures upon which he had staked the family's fortune.

That Leopold Mozart completely gave up his own career to invest all of his resources in his children is not in dispute, but historians disagree on whether Leopold was a demanding oppressor, exploiting his children's talents for his own gain, or whether he was simply a committed parent trying to secure his childrens' future. Leopold remained deeply entwined in his adult children's lives, vexed by his impulsive son's decisions and tasked with raising Nannerl's first-born child. We might say that Leopold was one of the original helicopter parents, a demanding musical manager whose own fame as a taskmaster far outshone the musical talents of his daughters.

TIGER MOMS AND HELICOPTER PARENTS

> This is a story about a mother, two daughters, and two dogs. It's also about Mozart and Mendelssohn, the piano and the violin, and how we made it to Carnegie Hall.[49]

So begins Amy Chua's now-infamous 2011 memoir *Battle Hymn of the Tiger Mother*, which was preceded by an excerpt released in the *Wall Street Journal* under the provocative headline "Why Chinese Mothers Are Superior."[50] The barrage of *Tiger Mother* responses on the *Wall Street Journal* blog took Chua to task for resuscitating the cliché of the overachieving Asian American "automaton," stoking the fires of parental anxiety over the college admissions process, and feeding Americans' growing unease about China's emerging economy. And those were just about the article. Her book's opening gambit is now infamous:

> A lot of people wonder how Chinese parents raise such stereotypically successful kids. They wonder what these parents do to produce so many math whizzes and music prodigies, what it's like inside the family, and whether they could do it too. Well, I can tell them, because I've done it.[51]

The book rocketed to berths on best-seller lists around the world, instantly igniting a media firestorm with Chua at its center, where she just as quickly became a reviled target of condemnation. Child psychologists, pediatricians, and parents assailed her harsh child-rearing practices. Grown children of other tiger parents posted heartbreaking testimonies of damaged lives and ruined parent-child relationships. Sociologists cited high suicide rates among Asian American women. Calls for her arrest on child abuse charges were legitimized by law professor Chua's weird confession in the book itself that her tactics might seem "legally actionable to Westerners."[52] She received death threats and had to hire bodyguards.

Whether Chua's account is representative of a common parenting style that shepherds all musical prodigies from childhood to mastery is both debatable and unknowable. Nevertheless, as a counterweight to the talent account, it offers a rare, firsthand chronicle of what could be called a "deliberate practice account." Musicians—and their parents—should take a contemporary look at the tiger mom (and her now-adult cubs), for, despite this newspaper headline at the time, "Musicians Debate the Merit of Tiger Mother's Parenting Methods," and its writer's assertion that the book is "about as controversial in the classical music world as it is in parenting circles," only two musicians were consulted for the article and were interviewed separately, so there was no debate.[53] As for controversy "in the classical music world," no such controversy erupted onto the national scene (unless you count the parents of musical tots fuming on Suzuki parent blogs). Besides, no controversy among musicians could ever equal the international uproar among parents around the globe over Chua's severe parenting.

"Early parent-initiated activity," Chua-style, was her insistence that her two daughters play the instruments of Mother's choice (piano for Sophia, violin for Lulu) while renouncing a long list of common modern American childhood pastimes (TV, video games, and sleepovers). Even being in the school play was deemed a thief of precious music practice time.

And how did the Chuas make it to Carnegie Hall? Yes, practice was the ticket to a solo performance for her daughter, but Chua wasn't kidding when she used the *we* word. Despite the fact that it was thirteen-year-old Sophia Chua-Rubenfeld who took the stage alone in her charcoal-tinted, satin, floor-length gown, it was Tiger Mother Chua who supervised practically every minute of the practice hours required to get there. Why? Chua's blunt explanation: "Children on their own never want to work."[54] Enter the helicopter–tiger parent. Despite marketing her book as a general "parenting memoir," detailed descriptions of her daughters' music training formed its core, with entire pages devoted to the unedited daily practice directives that Chua wrote up by the dozens. These were measure-by-measure practice instructions, not the sticky love notes of encouragement—You can do it!—so popular by today's parenting norms.

Chua, a professor at Yale Law School and, we may presume, a pretty busy person on any given day, describes regularly dashing from her office at mid-afternoon in order to retrieve her daughters early from school for mega-practice sessions at home. Chua insists that her kids practice more than the measly thirty minutes accepted by soft, "Western" parents, bragging, "For a Chinese mother, the first hour is the easy part. It's hours two and three that get tough," an account she vivifies by documenting the·screaming and shaming that occurred during practice sessions, particularly with the recalcitrant Lulu, who did not share her older sister's penchant for quiet obedience.[55]

Indeed, much of Amy Chua's public condemnation had to do with her liberal use of such epithets as "garbage" slung at her kids, though a few of Chua's defenders cite her "brutal honesty" and "willingness to share her struggles."[56] But it was just this brutal honesty that elicits accusations of child abuse, with exhibit A being the tale "The Little White Donkey," in which seven-year-old Lulu explodes in frustration over a piano piece of the same name. Tiger Mom orders a return to the bench and a threat to cease being "lazy, cowardly, self-indulgent and pathetic," and she says she will haul the child's dollhouse to the Salvation Army if the piece is anything less than "perfect" by the next day. Tiger Mom is briefly rebuked by Dad, who is immediately batted away for his spinelessness. Tiger Mom forces the seven-year-old to practice piano "right through dinner into the night, and I wouldn't let Lulu get up, not for water, not even to go to the bathroom."[57] As one critic archly notes, "I know a lot of social workers who would be very interested to learn of a 7-year-old forced, as Lulu once was, to sit at the piano, apparently for hours, without water or even a bathroom break."[58]

Whether severe practice regimens like this one constituted child abuse or not, one characteristic of the Chua-Rubenfeld household comes through loud and clear in this memoir: this is one high-stakes, high-stress family. Stress is as ubiquitous in Chua's tale as are music and yelling. Missing is any account of the musical desires and motivations of her daughters, except when Lulu turns thirteen and begins a concerted campaign of defiance.

With all due respect to the accomplishments of Sophia Chua-Rubenfeld (who was tagged as a prodigy by—guess who!) and despite Mother Chua's demure protestations that she "can't take any credit" for Sophia's college acceptance to both Harvard and Yale, her claim "I don't think my parenting had anything to do with it—I think Sophia did it 100% herself" rings completely false when compared with the evidence for "early parent-initiated activity."[59] Behind every prodigy, it seems, is a helicopter parent. And elite performers themselves know this. One study found that they rated at least one of their parents as "the most influential person in their career."[60]

Whether that influence was overwhelmingly positive or negative is an individual story in every case. The mother of Olympic swimmer Michael Phelps believed in her son's abilities even after frustrated grade school teachers pronounced him incapable of focusing. In consultation with her young son, they mutually agreed to replace his ADHD medication with hours of stringent swimming practice. However, Debbie Phelps was no tiger mother:

> I've been there not to dictate or guide. I'm there to listen to what he wants to do and try to help him problem solve and make a wise decision, . . . Every time Michael gets on the blocks, he has a goal for himself, and he knows what he wants to do. . . . I don't set those goals, and I'm a very strong advocate of [the idea that] I'm the parent, not the coach or the agent or whatever there is to be.[61]

Ms. Phelps's hands-off creed is in stark contrast to the famously pushy parents of such sports stars as Tiger Woods, Jennifer Capriati, and Andre Agassi or the emotionally abusive father of pianist Lang Lang.

And what of Amy Chua? Her comparison of herself to her daughter's eventual piano master, Wei-Yi Yang, gives the reader the impression that the Tiger Mother was at last tamed to the backseat: "All I could think was, This man is a genius. I am a barbarian. Prokofiev is a genius. I am a cretin. Wei-Yi and Prokofiev are great. I am a cannibal."[62]

However, such humility dissolved on the eve of fourteen-year-old Sophia's Carnegie Hall debut. Like so many stage parents before her, Chua's own need to "make sure Sophia's performance was flawless" trumped Master Wei-Yi's sage advice to allow the girl to remain calm and focused and not tire her fingers: "Contrary to everyone's advice, we practiced until almost 1 a.m."[63] Who was in charge in this scenario? Certainly not the girl or by extension the genius Wei-Yi Yang. Tiger Mom's self-professed barbarian instincts won out.

The negative consequences of overbearing parents are easy to predict: anxiety disorders and repetitive strain injuries top the list. But permissive parents who refuse to enforce practice rules create problems of a different kind for their children. For those who fear that deliberate practice takes all the fun out of music-making, consider this maxim from expertise expert Ericsson:

> The requirement for concentration sets deliberate practice apart from both mindless, routine performance and playful engagement, as the latter two types of activities would merely strengthen the current mediating cognitive mechanisms, rather than modify them to allow increases in the level of performance.[64]

In other words, fun is play, but it is not deep practice. And worse, if the child diddles on the fiddle or mindlessly "runs over" a song, he actually fortifies his poor habits by stewing in his own abilities. And when those abilities are weak to begin with, as they are for young people at the beginning of training, a downward spiral of failure is created. It is not for lack of fun that so many eager elementary school musicians are barely playing their rental instruments by their first year's end; it is most likely for lack of deliberate practice. For those who still insist that music should be always about fun, Chua has a rejoinder:

> Nothing is fun until you're good at it. To become good at anything, you have to work, and children on their own never want to work, which is why it is crucial to override their preferences.[65]

This pronouncement is multifaceted, contradictory, and fascinating to dissect. First, it appears repeatedly in negative opinion pieces about Chua, as if the final clause is a gotcha moment, the smoking gun behind Chua's domineering proclivities. But the book is full of much juicier evidence than this. More importantly, it implies that there is some arrival point past which practicing becomes fun. But honestly, deliberate practice is rarely fun at any stage of development. Better descriptors for effortful practice are *engaging, enlightening,* and *challenging.* Given that the vast majority of most musicians' time is spent practicing, chasing the chimera of fun is wrongheaded if mastery is the endgame. And it is this attitude toward fun that reveals a major difference between the parents of Mozart or Midori and Amy Chua: the former were themselves musicians. Ms. Chua is not. And besides, her statement is also somewhat disingenuous given that fun as a goal for her children was nowhere apparent in her account. Her aims for her children—in any and every endeavor—were to simply be "the #1 in every subject."[66] Amid the perpetual quest for perfection, the lack of joy was just one of the troubling deficiencies in Chua's musical goals for her kids. The others were expression, communal music-making, and sharing one's talents for the good of the whole, like the school plays in which her kids were never allowed to participate.

Despite these contradictions, Chua nevertheless encapsulates a basic, core truth: to become good at anything, you have to work. And by the accounts of her now-adult daughters, she appears to have bequeathed to them the invaluable gift of what social psychologist Carol Dweck dubbed a *growth mindset*.

THE INVERSE POWER OF PRAISE

Carol Dweck has recast the nature-versus-nurture debate as it applies to human self-regard with two catchy labels: *fixed mindset* (my nature is due to heredity and the talent account) and *growth mindset* (through nurture in my environment and my own effort, I can grow and change).[67] These labels describe how these two conflicting self-perceptions arise through childhood and influence peoples' life trajectories. They also illuminate the dark side of such dogmatic fixtures in the parental toolkit as limitless praise.

Dweck has found that emphasizing a child's innate abilities (the talent account) promulgates a fixed mindset that virtually positions a child for eventual failure. Children who have been stoked by tales of their natural talent and fed big dollops of praise tend to clutch that talent as a talisman, which wards off both effort (unnecessary anyway, due to the magic of their natural gifts) as well as failure. Nothing ventured, nothing gained—and neither pride nor face is lost.

This kind of behavior leads to a double whammy for the fixed-mindset kid: unexposed to failure, he neither progresses very much nor develops any strategies to respond to inevitable failures in the future. And it seems that those who have been stroked the most often fall the hardest, even to the point of complete psychological collapse. This vicious cycle has been fittingly dubbed "the inverse power of praise."[68]

If a talented protégé enters a music teacher's studio with Dweck's fixed mindset, then the reasons for his puzzlingly unremarkable output are at least more clear: the inverse power of praise doomed him from the outset and relegated him to the gallery of those who woulda'/coulda'/shoulda' been contenders. Dweck's mindset theory helps explain why, all too often, precocious children labeled prodigy, genius, or wunderkind do not successfully transition to adulthood. Adult life is filled with trial and failure—except for those who are pathologically averse to effort. In that case, the path of least resistance is truly no effort at all.

It appears that Tiger Mom conferred a growth mindset on at least one of her cubs. According to the grownup Lulu,

> people assume that tiger parenting would beget low self-esteem because there isn't that constant praise, but I think I'm exiting with a lot more confidence than some others, because my confidence is earned. [My mom] gave me the tools to drive my own confidence.[69]

BUILDING MOTIVATION

Chua's tale of tough love leaves at least one question unanswered, and that is one of motivation. We may well wonder what would cause a six-year-old to want to sit still long enough to practice the piano. Is there such a thing as inherent motivation, something one is simply born with? Or is it egged on by an external force, like sibling rivalry? Is it the product of incessant browbeating by an overbearing parent, in which case the motivator is simply a desire to avoid punishment? And in the latter case, do some children possess an inner strength to absorb that negative energy (like Sophia, who states, "Early on, I decided to be an easy child to raise"), while other children crumple under the pressure, like Lulu?

There are many theories about motivation, including the *arousal levels* that favor learning. It appears that an intermediate arousal level is best, a sort of Goldilocks approach that falls midway between "make music or die!" and "I think I might want to, maybe." Teachers and parents can stoke arousal levels by eliciting exactly what students are capable of producing at any time along their learning path. This teaching-learning philosophy is beautifully captured by Robert Bjork's doctrine of desirable difficulties. Bjork says that learning difficulties are obstacles that slow down the rate at which the learner absorbs information. This process has been shown to enhance long-term retention—in other words, learning itself. But Bjork also stresses the importance of the desirability factor, noting that difficulties can quickly become *undesirable* if thrown in the path of the learner too soon or too late. Too little arousal, and nothing is accomplished. Boring. But too much arousal can make learners so anxious that the so-called fight-or-flight defense response is stoked. Panic ensues! Selecting the just-right amount of arousal and instilling motivation itself constitute the art part of teaching.

But teachers should not delude themselves into thinking that motivation can be instilled. Once kids progress past their natural curiosity, the motivation to practice must be sustained by the child himself as he progresses through adolescence to adulthood. There is no standard formula for this, but Dweck's research on the growth mindset offers some intriguing considerations. Dweck posits that, when teachers and parents instill the belief in a child that ability and intelligence are flexible rather than fixed, this inculcates a sense of control in the youngster, which in turn can seed a love of learning for its own sake. This is neurogenesis in action. It is already known that practice causes changes in the brain. Ericsson posits that a reasonable research question for the future is whether the skill-building effects of practice "may also produce changes in the brain structures that regulate motivation and enjoyment."[70] This adds heft to Chua's declaration that nothing is fun until you are good at it. And what she has to say about the sustainability of motivation is also spot on.

As a parent, one of the worst things you can do for your child's self-esteem is to let them give up. On the flip side, there's nothing better for building confidence than learning you can do something you thought you couldn't.[71]

Ever the iconoclast, Chua's take on the fundament of self-esteem (more work!) is likely not shared by a majority of Americans, who bought wholesale into a very different interpretation of it during the self-esteem fad of the previous century.

SELF-ESTEEM THEORY

The rewards of self-love and its corollary, the harm of self-loathing, began to circulate in the communal psyche in the freewheeling 1960s, until, two decades later, the benefits of instilling high self-esteem were practically unquestioned. *Self-esteem theory* got a huge public relations boost from the California state legislature when in 1986 the legislature funded a Task Force on Self-Esteem and Personal and Social Responsibility, convinced by a state assemblyman (whose own psychological therapy had spurred him to find a political outlet for his self-actualization) that boosting each citizen's self-esteem could significantly ameliorate chronic social ills like drug abuse, teen pregnancy, and crime.[72] Throughout the remainder of that decade and into the 1990s, the mantras of self-esteem theory ("Believe in yourself!" and "I am special because I am me!") seeped into the zeitgeist and were unquestioningly adopted in school curricula and social policies across the United States. Parenting books published in the last two decades of the twentieth century stress self-esteem as the bedrock upon which all other values are built, touting giant doses of praise as a psychological vitamin pack for the developing child. These doses are to be administered without any connection to output or accomplishment, for it is enough to simply be.

The problem is there is little evidence and no science behind self-esteem theory. In due time, cracks appeared in its facade for the simple reason that it did not deliver on its promise. In 2003, a team of four psychologists from the United States and Canada were commissioned by the American Psychological Society to conduct a meta-analysis of the extant self-esteem literature. The results were a bombshell to self-esteem proponents, including some of the study's authors:

> We have not found evidence that boosting self-esteem (by therapeutic interventions or school programs) causes benefits. Our findings do not support continued widespread efforts to boost self-esteem in the hope that it will, by itself, foster improved outcomes. In view of the heterogeneity of high self-esteem, indiscriminate praise might just as easily promote narcissism, with its less desirable consequences.[73]

One of the study's authors, Roy Baumeister, has gone beyond punctur-ing the high-flying claims of self-esteem theory to demonstrating that very high levels of it may be the underlying culprit for such socially aberrant behavior as aggression, bullying, and violence.[74] It turns out that the corollary view (bullies are just sad folks with a soft core and low levels of self-worth) is therefore also probably false. Baumeister's re-search has shown that bullies are tyrants with such preternaturally high self-regard that they become enraged when they are not treated with the deference they feel they are due.

Even though research like Baumeister's is slowly dismantling self-esteem theory, it took root in the culture long enough to have spawned what psychologists Jean Twenge and W. Keith Campbell call a full-on societal *narcissism epidemic*, which is also the title of their 2009 book. According to these authors, overdoses of self-esteem administered to many Americans born after 1970 poisoned them with narcissism, simply defined as an inflated view of the self. Yet narcissism, Twenge and Campbell say, is neither healthy self-worth nor confidence but the over-weening sense that one is "special" and therefore better than everyone else.

By Twenge and Campbell's measures, one of the many pieces of collateral damage of the narcissism epidemic are legions of people who have been inoculated against criticism even when it is proffered in two of its most benevolent packages: parenting and teaching. Given that one of the most important components of learning is feedback, the narcis-sism epidemic has damaged some people's ability to learn. And while musicians must nourish a healthy sense of self-worth if they are to feel confident enough to take the stage and command an audience's atten-tion, becoming an artist entails going beyond the cult of self to speak to our common humanity.

Twenge and Campbell end their book with a treatment plan for slowing the epidemic enough to starve it out of the culture, aiming high and wide by using a public health model to take on narcissism in televi-sion, movies, and politics and aiming locally by encouraging readers to examine their parenting and teaching styles. In both cases, the message is clear: narcissism isn't genetic. It is behavior learned through the environment, and with enough mindfulness of the problem, this behav-ior can be changed.

NATURE VERSUS NURTURE

The environmentalist stance within the classic nature-versus-nurture debate holds that a person's environment in which she is nurtured largely determines her outcome. This *nurture assumption* is precisely what author Judith Rich Harris assails in her notable book of the same name[75] in which she argues that the complex mix of heritable traits played out within the larger social world of peers has the greatest effect on the way children turn out rather than the effects of genes. Even though Harris updates the nature-versus-nurture lexicon to the more accurate and less emotionally loaded terms *heredity* and *environment*, her related thesis, captured in the book's subtitle, *Why Children Turn Out the Way They Do: Parents Matter Less than You Think and Peers Matter More*, set off a firestorm of indignation.[76]

Nevertheless, independent scholar Harris attracted the support of Steven Pinker, who himself confronts the nature-versus-nurture conundrum in one of the most erudite and provocative books on the subject yet written, *The Blank Slate: The Modern Denial of Human Nature*.[77] In his book, Pinker takes on three doctrines as both fundamental and dogmatic within Western culture: "the blank slate" (the belief that we are born pure, with no innate traits coded within our DNA); "the ghost in the machine" (the notion that the mind is the seat of the soul and is free from its biological moorings); and "the noble savage" (the romantic belief in an Eden-like innocence and goodness among primitives that was only corrupted by modern culture). All of these precepts, Pinker argues, combine to impede the benefits of modern science from reaching society. Of the three, the blank-slate myth is of concern here for its contradiction of the talent account most resonant in the staunchly environmentalist view espoused by Howe, Davidson, and Sloboda.

As I have shown, current science tells us that human traits like intelligence and music aptitude are somewhat heritable, but the rest is up to the environment. This complex interplay is, at present, impossible to tease apart, so an either-its-genes-or-its-nurture proposition is a false dichotomy when applied to humans. As psychologist Gary Marcus puts it, there is

a misconception people harbor about genetics: that it will be possible one day to determine, once and for all, whether nature or nurture is "more important." Genes are useless without an environment, and

no organism could make any use of the environment at all if it were
not for its genes. Asking which one is more important is like asking
which gender, male or female, is more important.[78]

There is no recipe or blueprint for how genetic information is realized
in a living human being. Rather, the ways in which heritable traits play
out in one's environment are as complex, unique, and difficult to predict as individuals themselves. So why are the conjoined theories of the
blank slate and environmentalism so compelling? Perhaps it is because
we all wish to believe that our potential is limitless. Most of us believe
that our achievements are the just results of our own honest toil and not
a genetic gift we did nothing to deserve. And these wishes and beliefs
are not solely confined to learners. Teachers and parents can be equally
in thrall to these theories in proportion to their sense of mission and
power. Because the environment is the one variable that is seemingly
under parental control (especially when children are young), it is tempt-
ing to believe this control to be all-powerful. As in the case of Tiger
Mom, she wielded that power absolutely, but if Rich Harris's theories
are accounted for, Chua was successful in part by largely quarantining
her cubs, ensuring little peer interaction and influence.

But what happens when a child or protégé does not fulfill the promise of environmental ministrations? The blank slate, the nurture assumption, and environmentalism are all of a piece, and if one espouses
them, whether as learner or teacher, then one assumes full and equal
responsibility for defeats as well as victories—the flip side of pure environmentalism can resemble blaming the victim, which can produce a
tremendous amount of pressure on parent-child, teacher-student, and
coach-trainee relationships. Nevertheless, belief in valiant effort as the
only determiner of success persists, instilled early in the young through
inspirational books like *The Little Engine That Could*. If you missed it
as a child, the story tells of a tiny, anthropomorphized engine that
volunteers to haul a string of stranded boxcars over a steep mountain
pass. Against all odds, it perseveres by incessantly chanting, "I think I
can, I think I can, I think I can," a mantra that little children learn to
intone with motorized rhythm, gleefully increasing the tempo as the
little train gathers momentum.

Stories like these pursue us into adulthood by way of inspirational
posters—"If you can dream it, you can do it!"—posted ubiquitously on

bulletin boards in breakrooms and cafeterias, trumpeting the benefits of hard work and perseverance. Even the peace of the office toilet no longer offers refuge from institutional messaging, with this cluelessly plastered inside a bathroom stall: "If you aren't going all the way, why go at all?"

Adults understand that, in the real world of cause and effect, effort is necessary for achievement, and the worth of that effort is conjoined to its quality. The message of the iconic little blue train is simpler: effort is rewarded by success. Yet no matter how that simple idea is expanded as children mature and are capable of a more nuanced understanding, adding riders ("If you really want it") and caveats ("But you have to work really hard") has not inoculated this simple maxim against mutation into its more virulent strain: Any and *all* effort *should be* rewarded by success. When things don't work out the way the Little Engine script foretells they should, psychologists like Jennifer Crocker note an alarming tendency for certain types of learners to simply give up. Crocker has discovered a noxious kind of perfectionism among students who, while believing they can work harder and improve, harbor a deep connection between self-worth and superior performance. In experiments, these students tended to behave in ways disturbingly similar to those of Dweck's fixed-mindset people. When given the opportunity, they avoided practicing or allowed distractions to interrupt them (both of which could later be blamed for poor performance). Thus, just like fixed mindset students, they were self-handicapped.[79] The researchers conclude that a "growth mindset" may be fairly worthless to learners who cannot divest themselves of the linkages between effort, perfection, and worth. Crocker has some advice for how to break these harmful snares:

> A glib way of putting it is to say "Get over yourself." . . . If you want to stop acting in self-defeating ways, then think about how your schoolwork will help people outside of yourself.[80]

Crocker's advice is notable as much for what it contains—stepping outside oneself, thinking of others, the communal good—as what it does not: believing in the self or, in the words of one of those ubiquitous inspirational posters, working "on being in love with the person in the mirror."

THE TALENT ACCOUNT: SO WHAT?

The nagging question of talent persists. Some experts attempt to settle it by outright dismissal of ardent environmentalists as earnest but deluded zealots. Such is the aim of expertise researchers of an op-ed piece in the *New York Times*, "Sorry, Strivers, Talent Matters."[81] So there.

Meanwhile, outside research labs, music teachers and coaches weigh in with tales from the front, instances in which extreme effort, excellent training, supportive benefactors, and generous financial support were just not enough for significant achievement. Lack of talent is usually proffered as an explanation for failure. If it is proffered directly to the failed one, it is seen by some as a kind of euthanasia, a mercy offered to end the striver's exertions. But to a musician on the receiving end of this verdict, it feels stingingly like the popular insult "When the talent was passed out, you must have been standing behind the door." The damaging effects of such black humor are what set Howe and colleagues on a mission to explode the talent myth and are also what sparked the self-esteem movement.

Yet even if talent as a construct is real, Carol Dweck's research has ably demonstrated the curse of the talent myth on those judged to possess it most, while Baumeister, Twenge, and Campbell's research shows the damaging effects of overly inflated views of talent. To growth-minded high achievers in the motor realm, the intimation of talent as an explanation for their success is frankly insulting, as described by golfer Sam Snead in chapter 4, and echoed more stridently by NBA basketball star Ray Allen:

> When people say God blessed me with a beautiful jump shot, it really pisses me off. I tell those people, "Don't undermine the work I've put in every day." Not some days. Every day.[82]

The critical question for musicians is not whether talent exists per se but this: How damaging are the effects of the talent account both to those who secretly fear they don't have it and to those who believe they possess it the most?

TOXIC TALENT AND SOCIAL JUSTICE

By the code of the talent account, "gifts," including intellect, are inherited. If the ministrations of a parent are added as fertilizer to the stew of biological potential brewing within the child, this creates a positive feedback loop: smart parents stand a 50-50 chance of begetting intellectually gifted kids. These kids will probably get an early start (due to the inclinations of their smart parents), thereby increasing their ability to learn, thereby increasing their actual abilities (talents). This loop is sometimes called the *Matthew effect*, a term coined to describe a virtuous cycle of "cumulative advantage." Named after the biblical gospel of Matthew, it describes the phenomenon of how the rich get richer.[83] But play this virtuous cycle in reverse, and the outcome is the vicious cycle of poverty that bankrupts opportunity and learning.[84] A similar impoverishment occurs when decisions are made regarding the allocation of precious resources.

The same studies that have revealed the strong connections between parental support and expertise have also noted that even the most supportive families must make choices along with their sacrifices. Institutions behave in much the same way. What guides these choices? There is a propensity for both parents and schools to heap scarce resources on those deemed most talented, reasoning that the truly gifted will benefit the most and therefore maximize the investment. While this reasoning may make some superficial fiscal sense, it also reveals the toxicity of the talent account. And if only a tiny percentage of the population is deemed gifted, that means a vast majority are marooned without the resources to unlock their nascent abilities. In the absence of adult support, be it parental or institutional, any inborn talent for music stands little chance of growing. It is no wonder that so many educational researchers conclude, as Bloom does, that there must be an enormous potential pool of talent in the United States. It is likely that some combination of home, teachers, schools, and society may in large part determine what portions of this potential pool of talent become developed. It is also likely that these same forces may, in part, be responsible for much of the great waste of human potentiality.[85]

THE GOOD-ENOUGH MUSICIAN

Whether one believes outright in the talent account or not, the bald truth for many in the teaching profession is that they simply do not have the luxury to entertain the highfalutin notion of talent. With the exception of an elite corps of teachers who maintain studios in cosmopolitan cities or music conservatories, many music instructors must teach those very folks Mama Rose claims "can't even give it away." But even this raw state may not preclude the joy of the pursuit (at least on the part of the learner). People study music for a myriad of reasons, many of which are nonprofessional, and these reasons should be valued for the intrinsic worth of the pursuit of beauty—even if that pursuit never results in the full flower of flawless performance. Memoirs of adults who have taken up music attest to this value even if this noble pursuit is brought low by their own ineptitude. Author Jennifer Weiner describes her own tussle with Rachmaninoff, who was said to play the piece she was rehearsing "as if all the hounds of hell were chasing him":

> Right now, I play it as if all the hounds of hell are dozing in the sun as I stroll toward an idling bus that's going to take me to get a root canal. Instead of a delicate, rippling flow of notes, I produce a muddy tumble, a kicked sack of potatoes thudding discordantly down the stairs.[86]

Weiner recalls reading about how changing your brain can change your life and follows Oliver Sacks's advice to try a completely new activity. So she embarks on her humiliating piano adventure in order to conquer a noxious entanglement of competitiveness, disappointment, and insomnia. It works:

> I have come to believe in the value of doing something where I know I will never be better than OK. . . . I will embrace the joy of making music (loosely defined) only for myself. I will invite failure into my life and play without the expectation of being the best, or even mediocre, until failing isn't a terrifying unknown but just another possibility, and one I can survive.[87]

Gary Marcus, a renowned cognitive scientist, decided to become his own guinea pig and learn the guitar at the age of forty. His journey is documented in *Guitar Zero*, a hilarious and humbling investigation of the nature-versus-nurture debate and a process he boils down to this: "It's not nature versus nurture; it's nature working together with nurture":[88]

> There is good scientific reason to believe that talent matters in a wide variety domains, from sports to chess to writing to music. Cognitive activities are a product of the mind, and the mind is a product of genes working together with the environment. To dismiss talent is to ignore all evidence from biology.[89]

So it seems clear that certain traits—or gifts or talents—do separate eventual experts from wannabes. But—so what? In the absence of the situation necessary to reveal it, the mentorship necessary to nourish it, the expertise necessary to train it, and the effort necessary to sustain it, talent as a construct within music is virtually worthless—except for the critical exception of one arena: social justice. Society will surely never be touched by the gifts of its potential musical artists until and unless all children have equal access to musical education and musical nourishment. But by the measures of some scientists in the field of expertise science, even that impossible scenario would still separate the talented from the merely able. As expertise researchers Hambrick and Meinz conclude in their article "Sorry, Strivers, Talent Matters," "sometimes the story that science tells us isn't the story we want to hear." The particular science story to which they refer can indeed seem devastating—but only if one wantss to become an expert and only if science is the only voice we heed. If it takes 10,000 hours of practice to become an expert, it probably takes 7,000 to become pretty good, and 5,000 to become passably okay—and that may be all we desire anyway.

Musicians striving for betterment anywhere along the continuum of achievement have much to learn from the practice and performance habits of experts, but no musician—beginner, novice, or master—should sacrifice the pure pleasure of music-making on the high altar of the talent account.

NOTES

1. Michael Howe, Jane Davidson, and John Sloboda, "Innate Talents: Reality or Myth?" *Behavioral and Brain Sciences* 21, no. 3 (1998): 399.

2. Ibid., 437.

3. Ibid., 407 (emphasis mine).

4. Mihaly Csikszentmihalyi, in Howe, Davidson, and Sloboda, "Innate Talents," 411.

5. Robert J. Sternberg in Howe, Davidson, and Sloboda, "Innate Talents," 425.

6. Ibid., 425.

7. Howe, Davidson, and Sloboda, "Innate Talents," 407.

8. Ibid., 414.

9. Ibid., 416–17.

10. K. Anders Ericsson, Ralf Th. Krampe, and Clemens Tesch-Römer, "The Role of Deliberate Practice in the Acquisition of Expert Performance," *Psychological Review* 100, no. 3 (1993): 363–406.

11. K. Anders Ericsson, ed., *The Road to Excellence: The Acquisition of Expert Performance in the Arts and Sciences, Sports, and Games* (Mahwah, NJ: Erlbaum, 1996), 10–11.

12. Malcolm Gladwell, *Outliers: The Story of Success* (New York: Little, Brown, 2008), 41.

13. K. Anders Ericsson and Robert Pool, *Peak: Secrets from the New Science of Expertise* (Boston: Houghton Mifflin Harcourt, 2016), 109.

14. Christopher Chabris and Daniel Simons, The Invisible Gorilla, 2010, www.theinvisiblegorilla.com/videos.html.

15. See Arien Mack and Irvin Rock, *Inattentional Blindness* (Cambridge, MA: MIT Press, 1998).

16. Richard Schmidt and Timothy Lee, *Motor Learning and Performance: From Principles to Application*, 5th ed. (Champaign, IL: Human Kinetics, 2005), 229.

17. Ericsson and Pool, *Peak*, 98.

18. Ibid., 79–80.

19. Tânia Lisboa, Alexander P. Demos, and Roger Chaffin, "Training Thought and Action for Virtuoso Performance," *Musicae Scientiae* 22, no. 4 (2018): 535.

20. Quoted in Michelle Kung, "From Dracula to Nixon," *Wall Street Journal*, November 28, 2008, www.wsj.com/articles/SB122780196170361765.

21. Julie Miller, "Anne Hathaway Remembers Meryl Streep Icing Her Out on *The Devil Wears Prada* Set," *Vanity Fair*, November 3, 2014, www.vanityfair.com/hollywood/2014/11/anne-hathaway-meryl-streep-the-devil-wears-prada.

22. ArtisanNewsService, "Frank Langella Is Richard Nixon in *Frost Nixon*," November 25, 2008, www.youtube.com/watch?v=nSzkUSsUscA.

23. A. L. Duckworth, C. Peterson, M. D. Matthews, and D. R. Kelly, "Grit: Perseverance and Passion for Long-Term Goals," *Journal of Personality and Social Psychology* 92, no. 6 (2007).

24. See Character.org, "Who We Are," www.character.org/who-we-are/.

25. David Denby, "The Limits of 'Grit'," *New Yorker Magazine*, June 21, 2016.

26. Alfie Kohn, "The Downside of 'Grit,'" *Washington Post*, April 6, 2014.

27. Marcus Credé, Michael C. Tynan, and Peter D. Harms, "Much Ado about Grit: A Meta-analytic Synthesis of the Grit Literature," *Journal of Personality and Social Psychology* 113, no. 3 (2017): 492–511.

28. Kimberly G. Noble et al., "Family Income, Parental Education and Brain Structure in Children and Adolescents," *Nature Neuroscience* 18, no. 5 (2015): 773–78.

29. Jeffrey R. Young, "Angela Duckworth Says Grit Is Not Enough: She's Building Tools to Boost Student Character," EdSurge, April 20, 2018, www.edsurge.com/news/2018-04-20-angela-duckworth-says-grit-is-not-enough-she-s-building-tools-to-boost-student-character.

30. Ibid.

31. Michael Rosen and Helen Oxenbury, *We're Going on a Bear Hunt* (New York: Margaret K. McElderry Books, 1989).

32. Young, "Angela Duckworth Says."

33. Douglas K. Detterman, "Introduction," in "Acquiring Expertise: Ability, Practice, and Other Influences," *Intelligence* 45 (July–August 2014): 1.

34. David Z. Hambrick, Frederick L. Oswald, Erik M. Altmann, Elizabeth J. Meinz, Fernand Gobet, and Guillermo Campitelli, "Deliberate Practice: Is That All It Takes to Become an Expert?" *Intelligence* 45 (July–August 2014): 41.

35. U.S. Department of Health & Human Services, "Is Intelligence Determined by Genetics?" October 15, 2019, https://ghr.nlm.nih.gov/primer/traits/intelligence.

36. David Z. Hambrick, Fredrik Ullén, and Miriam Mosing, "Is Innate Talent a Myth?" *Scientific American*, September 20, 2016 (emphasis mine).

37. Benjamin Bloom, ed., *Developing Talent in Young People* (New York: Ballantine Books, 1985), 3.

38. Ericsson, Krampe, and Tesch-Römer, "Role of Deliberate Practice," 369.

39. Bloom, *Developing Talent*, 3.

40. John Sloboda, "Acquisition of Musical Performance Expertise," in *The Road to Excellence: The Acquisition of Expert Performance in the Arts and Sciences, Sports, and Games*, ed. K. Anders Ericsson (New York: Lawrence Erlbaum, 1996), 109–10.

41. Ibid.

42. Jane Davidson, Michael J. A. Howe, Derek G. Moore, and John A. Sloboda, "The Role of Parental Influences in the Development of Musical Performance," *British Journal of Developmental Psychology* 14, no. 4 (1996), 399–412. See also John Sloboda, *Exploring the Musical Mind* (Oxford: Oxford University Press, 2005): 276–79.

43. See K. Anders Ericsson, Neil Charness, Paul J. Feltovich, and Robert R. Hoffman, eds., *The Cambridge Handbook of Expertise and Expert Performance* (Cambridge: Cambridge University Press, 2006), 693; and Robert Lipsyte and Lois B. Morris, "Teenagers Playing Music, Not Tennis," *New York Times*, June 27, 2002, https://archive.nytimes.com/www.nytimes.com/learning/students/pop/20020628snapfriday.html.

44. Sam Whalen, "Sustaining 'The Rage to Master': A Conversation with Ellen Winner," *Journal of Secondary Gifted Education* 11, no. 3 (2000): 109–14.

45. Françoys Gagné, "Building Gifts into Talents: Brief Overview of the DMGT 2.0," 2012, http://gagnefrancoys.wixsite.com/dmgt-mddt/dmgtenglish.

46. Howe, Davidson, and Sloboda, "Innate Talents."

47. Quoted in K. Robert Schwarz, "Glissando," *New York Times*, March 24, 1991, www.nytimes.com/1991/03/24/magazine/glissando.html.

48. Ibid.

49. Amy Chua, *Battle Hymn of the Tiger Mother* (New York: Penguin Press, 2011).

50. Amy Chua, "Why Chinese Mothers Are Superior," *Wall Street Journal*, January 8, 2011, www.wsj.com/articles/SB10001424052748704111504576059713528698754.

51. Chua, *Battle Hymn*, 3.

52. Chua, "Chinese Mothers."

53. Colin Eatock, "Musicians Debate the Merit of Tiger Mother's Parenting Methods," *Houston Chronicle*, February 13, 2011, www.chron.com/life/article/Musicians-debate-the-merit-of-Tiger-Mother-s-1691798.php.

54. Chua, *Battle Hymn*, 29.

55. Ibid.

56. Sheryl Sandberg, "Amy Chua: Tough-Love Mother," *Time*, April 21, 2011, www.time.com/time/specials/packages/article/0,28804,2066367_2066369_2066449,00.html.

57. Chua, *Battle Hymn*, 62.

58. Caitlin Flanagan, "The Ivy Delusion: The Real Reason the Good Mothers Are So Rattled by Amy Chua," *Atlantic*, April 2011, www.theatlantic.com/magazine/archive/2011/04/the-ivy-delusion/8397/.

59. Lauren Beckham Falcone, "Tiger Balm: Ivy League Coup for Chua's Cub," *Boston Herald*, April 2, 2011, www.bostonherald.com/news/columnists/view.bg?articleid=1327779.

60. Ericsson et al., *Cambridge Handbook of Expertise*, 695.

61. David Muir and Jo Ling Kent, "No Vacation When You're Michael Phelps's Mom," ABC, August 11, 2008, http://abcnews.go.com/International/China/story?id=5556243.

62. Chua, *Battle Hymn*, 124.

63. Ibid., 138.

64. Ericsson et al., *Cambridge Handbook of Expertise*, 694.

65. Chua, *Battle Hymn*, 29.

66. Ibid.

67. Carol S. Dweck, *Mindset: The New Psychology of Success* (New York: Ballantine Books, 2006).

68. Po Bronson, "How Not to Talk to Your Kids: The Inverse Power of Praise," *New York Magazine*, February 11, 2007, http://nymag.com/print/?/news/features/27840/.

69. Doree Lewak, "I Was Raised by Tiger Mom—And It Worked," *New York Post*, March 28, 2018, https://nypost.com/2018/03/28/i-was-raised-by-tiger-mom-and-it-worked/.

70. Ericsson and Poole, *Peak*, 192.

71. Chua, *Battle Hymn*, 62.

72. California State Department of Education, "Toward a State of Self-Esteem: The Final Report of the California Task Force to Promote Self-Esteem and Personal and Social Responsibility," January 1990, https://eric.ed.gov/?id=ED321170.

73. Roy F. Baumeister, Jennifer D. Campbell, Joachim I. Krueger, and Kathleen D. Vohs, "Does High Self-Esteem Cause Better Performance, Interpersonal Success, Happiness, or Healthier Lifestyles?" *Psychological Science in the Public Interest* 4, no. 1 (May 2003): 1.

74. Roy F. Baumeister, Laura Smart, and Joseph M. Boden, "Relation of Threatened Egotism to Violence and Aggression: The Dark Side of High Self-Esteem," *Psychological Review* 103, no. 1 (January 1996): 5–33; and Brad J. Bushman and Roy F. Baumeister, "Threatened Egotism, Narcissism, Self-Esteem and Direct and Displaced Aggression: Does Self-Love or Self-Hate Lead to Violence?" *Journal of Personality and Social Psychology* 75, no. 1 (July 1998): 219–29.

75. Judith Rich Harris, *The Nurture Assumption: Why Children Turn Out the Way They Do* (New York: Free Press, 2011).

76. Sharon Begley, "The Parent Trap," *Washington Post*, 1998, www.washingtonpost.com/wp-srv/newsweek/parent090798a.htm.

77. Steven Pinker, *The Blank Slate: The Modern Denial of Human Nature* (New York: Viking, 2002).

78. Gary Marcus, *The Birth of the Mind: How a Tiny Number of Genes Creates the Complexities of Human Thought* (New York: Basic Books, 2004), 7.

79. Y. Niiya, A. T. Brook, and J. Crocker, "Contingent Self-Worth and Self-Handicapping: Do Contingent Incremental Theorists Protect Self-Esteem?" *Self and Identity* 9 (2010): 276–97.

80. Quoted in David Glenn, "Carol Dweck's Attitude," *Chronicle of Higher Education Review*, May 9, 2010, http://chronicle.com/article/Carol-Dwecks-Attitude/65405/.

81. David Z. Hambrick and Elizabeth J. Meinz, "Sorry, Strivers: Talent Matters," *New York Times*, November 19, 2011, www.nytimes.com/2011/11/20/opinion/sunday/sorry-strivers-talent-matters.html.

82. Jackie MacMullan, "Preparation Is Key to Ray Allen's 3s," ESPN, February 11, 2011, www.espn.com/boston/nba/columns/story?columnist=macmullan_jackie&id=6106450.

83. Robert K. Merton, "The Matthew Effect in Science, II: Cumulative Advantage and the Symbolism of Intellectual Property," *Isis* 79, no. 4 (December 1988): 606–23, https://doi.org/10.1086/354848.

84. Jeanne Brooks-Gunn and Greg J. Duncan, "The Effects of Poverty on Children: The Future of Children," *Children and Poverty* 7, no. 2 (Summer/Fall 1997): 55–71.

85. Bloom, *Developing Talent*, 5.

86. Jennifer Weiner, "I'll Never Be Rachmaninoff," *New York Times*, December 29, 2018, www.nytimes.com/2018/12/29/opinion/sunday/piano-lessons-mind-focus.html.

87. Ibid.

88. Gary Marcus, *Guitar Zero* (New York: Penguin, 2012), 102–3.

89. Ibid.

6

MIND GAMES

Musicians devote hours of effortful time and potentially thousands of dollars in the pursuit of technique, that how-to manual initially bequeathed by teachers. This bequest is proffered on the premise that the student musician will actually absorb the teacher's lessons. In many ways this is an act of faith for both parties: learning is a gamble, with no sure guarantees, only probabilities.

As I have shown in the preceding chapters, attention and memory are the dual components that flank the act of learning, a dynamic duo that must attend the early stages of knowledge acquisition, whether in the physical realm (like keyboard fingering) or the mental realm (like learning how to read musical notation).

Once technique is truly learned, it is then honed by practice. And given that approximately ten thousand hours of practice or more is required for true mastery, no musician should be so bewitched by the talent myth as to believe that he can escape this requirement. Remember: even Mozart put in his ten thousand hours (albeit by around age thirteen). Further, this practice must be deliberately effortful enough to produce results; just clocking into the practice room will not suffice. Research from the cognitive and neurosciences validates the age-old values of effort and hard work while revealing that learning difficulties should not be avoided or simply endured but actually embraced as desirable. In our so doing, the critical juncture between exposure and learning is fused, the synapses strengthened, the technique hardwired.

At least, that is the hope and even the expectation that undergirds adherence to practice.

A major premise of this book is that the musician's understanding of the cognitive substrates of learning and practice is crucial since, over the course of a lifetime, training and practice hours far outweigh the time a musician actually spends onstage performing before a live audience. While, for avocational musicians, public performance may not ever be an objective, for professional musicians, polished performance is the ultimate goal. This chapter will consider live public performance as the apogee of intense musical training and practice.

BREAK A LEG! AND OTHER MIND GAMES

Performing before a live audience affords many musicians the same kind of exhilarating challenges and enticing rewards that motivate ski jumpers and other thrill-seeking athletes to publicly display their mettle, and thus it evokes a unique set of resources that are simply not needed in the privacy of the practice room during a music lesson or while jamming with friends. For musicians, the thrill of victory can include nailing a tough scale passage, finding the acoustic sweet spot on a high note, or bowing before a cheering audience compelled to rise to its feet. Conversely, the agony of defeat is equally visceral and can leave a negative memory trace so severe in a musician's brain that it cripples all future performance experiences.

You have seen the mental controls necessary for successful public performance; now it is time to consider what goes awry in the brain when those controls falter. And lest it seem like schadenfreude to closely examine the inner workings of musicians' performance flubs, this inspection has both a higher purpose and a venerable history. Regarding the former, cognitive science may offer new clues to help ameliorate performance anxiety. Regarding the latter, an inspection emulates a standard research method in neuroscience, namely the study of damaged parts within hobbled systems, for it is believed that, by closely examining what happens when things fall apart, normal function can be conjectured, bringing brain researchers one step closer to understanding optimal function.

I will begin with an overview of performance anxiety, then consider some irksome subtypes, all the while keeping cognitive science in mind in an attempt to both plumb the mysteries of self-defeating behavior and offer hope for ways to mollify these destructive demons of embodied cognition.

MUSIC PERFORMANCE ANXIETY

Almost all musicians have experienced *music performance anxiety* (MPA). Within this one, unifying experience, individual variations abound, from the variety and severity of the symptoms to the regularity and the conditions under which they appear. The prevalence of MPA is hard to pin down, for the numbers range widely: 15–25 percent of orchestral musicians (in a series of studies that considered only "severe and persistent" MPA among orchestral musicians) to as high as 59 percent in a Dutch study of orchestral musicians. In the United States, several studies have documented a similarly wide range of results among orchestral musicians (24–70 percent), while a Canadian study of professional orchestral musicians found the number astonishingly high: 96 percent.[1]

Musicians who wield instruments with shaking limbs and sweating palms are not the only performers who suffer the deleterious effects of MPA. In one study, said by its authors to be "the first of its kind," professional opera choristers exhibited much higher *trait anxiety* (a part of their personality that shows up in multiple situations and not just in performance venues) when compared to a normative sample (i.e., regular, nonsinger folks).[2]

The many coping mechanisms practiced by performers vary widely as well, from the healthful (exercise, meditation) to the destructive (slamming back multiple shots of alcohol backstage). Dianna Kenny, professor of psychology and professor of music at the University of Sydney, literally wrote the book on MPA. She notes that MPA "is no respecter of musical genre, age, gender, years of experience, or level of technical mastery of one's art."[3] MPA afflicts children, students in training, and legions of professional musicians; it has even struck such musical luminaries as pianists Frederic Chopin and Arthur Rubenstein; cellist Pablo Casals; singers Maria Callas, Luciano Pavarotti, Barbra Streisand, and Tatiana Troyanos; and pop icons George Harrison and Donny Osmond.

Yet despite MPA's prevalence, the current knowledge base in both academic and clinical psychology regarding MPA is still slim, and much of the research is uneven. What is known about MPA—both the disorder itself and the state of the field—is owed to Kenny's meticulous work, which traces the troublesome way in which research on this disorder has been conducted as well as the ill-considered conflation of MPA with social anxiety and social phobia.

Before Kenny took on the study of MPA, most MPA research was based on studies of professional orchestral musicians, leaving out other types of musicians, such as singers, solo instrumentalists, and student musicians. Subsequent studies simply built on these flawed studies, which was problematic enough but particularly so due to psychology's current "reproducibility crisis," in which many studies, especially landmark ones, have failed on a second go-around.[4] Particularly flawed, in Kenny's judgment, are these studies' assessment tools, which are also reused.[5] In response, Kenny developed new measures, the *Kenny Music Performance Anxiety Inventory for Adult Musicians* (or K-MPAI) and the *Music Performance Anxiety Inventory for Adolescents*. The K-MPAI is in wide use internationally and has been translated into several languages.[6] It is hoped that the dissemination of Kenny's assessment tools will do much to advance the knowledge base of this vexing disorder.

Despite this advance in MPA research, an impediment that remains is the mash-up of terminology that surrounds it. *General performance anxiety*, *stage fright*, *social anxiety*, *social phobia*, and even simple *shyness* are interchangeable terms assigned to MPA, which has not allowed it to claim its own distinctive set of traits. Therefore, one of Kenny's greatest contributions to MPA research was to disaggregate MPA from these terms, particularly *social phobia*, and contrast the significant differences between MPA sufferers and social phobics.

These differences start with each cohort's starkly diverse self-expectations and self-evaluation. For example, professional musicians generally hold very high expectations of themselves due to the years of training, expense, and self-sacrifice that it takes to achieve mastery, so they experience proportional levels of self-castigation when things go wrong in performance. By contrast, social phobics generally do not expect much from themselves at all in settings they find challenging, and low expectations can be self-fulfilling prophecies that cause social phobics to shrink ever further from anxiety-producing situations. But musicians march toward the fearful situation, resolute like the bear hunters in chapter 5, believing that there is no way around a performance—they have got to go through it. Consequently, when things go wrong, musicians are more prone to a higher degree of *postevent rumination* than social phobics, who probably exit a cocktail reception just relieved that it is over, while MPA-prone musicians are likely to obsessively gnaw on the memory of a performance blunder for weeks afterward.

These differences are crucial to eventually establishing effective treatments and coping mechanisms, a process heretofore hindered by MPA's entanglement in the psychiatric literature with more general social anxiety disorders and social phobia. This entanglement was encoded in the fourth edition of the venerable *Diagnostic and Statistical Manual of Mental Disorders* (DSM-IV), a reference work published and periodically updated by the American Psychiatric Association. The DSM is considered the definitive reference work for current classifications of mental disorders, so one could argue that the inclusion of performance anxiety as a separate and distinct disorder is an improvement over previous editions: before 1994, performance anxiety was not classified at all.

The most recent edition of the DSM (DSM-V) does not distinguish performance anxiety from other social phobias.[7] Nevertheless, this influential tome at least includes general performance anxiety in its important diagnostic criteria, which are those criteria required to be present in a patient in order to rate a diagnosis. Still, as Kenny notes, there remains "a debate in the literature as to whether music performance anxiety represents a form of social phobia" or if it should, in future editions, be lifted from that category and given a place of its own.[8] As if pointing toward that future, DSM-V appended these "specifiers" below the diagnostic criteria:

> Individuals with the performance only type of social anxiety disorder have performance fears that are typically most impairing in their professional lives (e.g., musicians, dancers, performers, athletes) or in roles that require regular public speaking. Performance fears may also manifest in work, school, or academic settings in which regular public presentations are required. Individuals with performance only

social anxiety disorder do not fear or avoid nonperformance social situations.[9]

Importantly, clinicians are also directed to specify if the anxiety occurs in performance situations only: does the person exhibit a trait anxiety (a part of their personality that shows up in multiple situations) or a *state anxiety*, in which MPA occurs only in very specific performance situations? This distinction is key to untangling the multiple threads that often (though not always) weave through an individual's experience of MPA. Therefore an MPA sufferer's first step should be to determine whether their MPA manifests itself only around music performance or if it is tied to a deeper psychopathology, such as excessive perfectionism. A strong working theory is that people exhibiting certain other psychopathologies may be more prone to MPA, leading to the observation that symptoms of general anxiety can occur together with MPA. Unfortunately, this comingling can also cloud accurate diagnoses of MPA.

A related distinction between state and trait anxieties involves the fear of real versus imagined audiences, the latter being a symptom of general social phobia. Imagined derision and illusory social censure are fears that isolate social phobics in the first place and keep them stuck at home. But for musicians, audiences are real—and so are the judgments and negative, real-world consequences that can accompany audience criticism. One bad review can send a performer's career spiraling southward, along with her confidence.

The importance of these distinguishing factors (trait versus state and imagined versus real), while obvious to performers, has apparently not occurred to researchers with no performing experience who have not seen the need to separate MPA from general social phobias. These and other variables are partly to blame for the dearth of clear definitions of, diagnoses of, and treatments for MPA, but thanks to the work of Kenny and others, clarification of MPA as a separate and distinct disorder seems to be coming into view. A decisive step in that direction was Kenny's authoritative definition of MPA:

> Music performance anxiety is the experience of marked and persistent anxious apprehension related to musical performance that has arisen through underlying biological and/or psychological vulnerabilities and/or specific anxiety conditioning experiences. It is mani-

fested through combinations of affective, cognitive, somatic and behavioral symptoms. It may occur in a range of performance settings,
but is usually more severe in settings involving high ego investment
and evaluative threat (audience) and fear of failure. It may be focal
(i.e. focused only on music performance), or occur comorbidly with
other anxiety disorders, in particular social phobia. It affects musicians across the lifespan and is at least partially independent of years
of training, practice and level of musical accomplishment. It may or
may not impair the quality of the musical performance. [10]

Consider each part of Kenny's definition by first acknowledging that,
overall, it accounts for both nature and nurture—that is, genetic contributions ("underlying biological and/or psychological vulnerabilities")
plus a person's early life experiences ("specific anxiety conditioning experiences"). For example, a performance trauma in adolescence can
feed recurring MPA.

The second clause of the definition contains a laundry list of symptoms through which MPA manifests itself. They are, in order, *affective
disorders*, roughly translated as "mood disorders," such as depression
and anxiety itself. Mood disorders play out in MPA as the sufferer's
uncanny ability to infect the present with worry about a future performance. Many a musician can attest to days or even weeks of panic-
inducing worry leading up to an important performance. *Cognitive
symptoms* might include racing thoughts or an inability to remember
texts or scale passages. The term *somatic* in Kenny's definition refers to
physical symptoms, such as queasy stomach, sweaty hands, and faint-
ness. *Behavioral symptoms* are how the anxiety manifests itself in the
musician's actions; examples include drug use, hostility toward cowork-
ers, and self-harm.

That bona fide MPA is "usually more severe in settings involving
high ego investment and evaluative threat" also points to the unique-
ness of the disorder, in that the judgment of an audience is real (not
imagined) and ratchets up in direct relation to the importance of the
performance and the validity of its assessors (the critics): professionals
are much more likely to become anxious about a career-making debut
in a major venue (Carnegie Hall) with a large audience and a music
critic in attendance than they would be in their hometown theater.
Likewise, student musicians are understandably more anxious about

degree recitals required for graduation than they are for weekly studio masterclasses.

Kenny's definition importantly cites the timeline of MPA, which must be present as an ongoing threat to qualify as a disorder. Otherwise, if MPA appears like a party-crasher—it visits, flames out, and then departs—it can be labeled *situational* and should be analyzed in light of the circumstances that allow it to show up uninvited.

Kenny's last component (a bout of MPA "may or may not impair the quality of the musical performance") is a nod to a phenomenon familiar to many performers, whereby their gaffes are keenly felt and heard by themselves but go virtually unnoticed by the audience.

CAUSES OF MPA

Kenny conducted two studies on self-reported causes of MPA among two different populations, the first being a group of university-level music and dance students in New Zealand, and the second being 357 Australian professional orchestral musicians (see table 6.1).[11] The participants were given a list of possible performance anxiety triggers and asked to rank them. The list of triggers was long (twenty-one in all), but a side-by-side comparison of the first five is enlightening, insofar as it is possible to infer that performance stressors may change as one progresses from novice to master and may also change over a lifetime.

As can be seen, "Pressure from self" was the number one reason given by both students and professional players. It seems we humans can truly be our own worst enemies. Interestingly, "Inadequate preparation" was the number two cause among students, while with professionals, it moved down to number three. One possible takeaway from this is that we realize the importance of deliberate practice as we age, and this wisdom strengthens on the road to mastery.

One of the most intriguing differences between these two populations is revealed on the question of physical arousal, such as elevated heart rate, breathlessness, weak knees, and sweaty palms. The adult professionals ranked "Not knowing how to manage physical arousal" as the second most important cause of their anxiety, while the student musicians did not choose this trigger at all. However, students did note "Excessive physical arousal" as number five, while the professionals

Table 6.1.   Performance Anxiety Triggers Ranked

Causes of MPA in Music and Dance Students	Causes of MPA in Professional Orchestral Musicians
1. Pressure from self.	1. Pressure from self.
2. Inadequate preparation for performance.	2. Not knowing how to manage physical arousal.
3. General lack of self-confidence.	3. Inadequate preparation for performance.
4. Attempting repertoire that is too difficult.	4. Tendency to be anxious in general and not just in performance.
5. Excessive physical arousal before or during performance.	5. Health problems.

Source: Dianna Kenny, *The Psychology of Music Performance Anxiety* (Oxford: Oxford University Press, 2011), 91–93.

ranked this lower, at number eight. What might we make of this? Kenny only notes that more longitudinal studies are needed to ascertain whether these triggers change over time.[12] Yet one simple explanation may be that, while students are alarmed by the primal nature of physical arousal symptoms themselves (yucky sweat!), professionals are not unnerved by them per se or particularly surprised at their manifestation, just aggravated by their inability to control them. Pros may grudgingly anticipate the symptoms' arrival, seeing them as the party-crashers mentioned earlier, while feeling simultaneous dismay at their failure to eject them. This is actually an apt way to describe the two sides of our human *alerting network* that alternately ignites and calms the physiological fires of MPA.

THE PHYSIOLOGICAL BASIS OF PERFORMANCE ANXIETY

The alerting network is best understood as an attentional filtering system, called the *autonomic nervous system* (ANS), which incessantly sifts the information that bombards our senses every second, parsing the important from the trivial. The ANS is essentially distributed between two systems, the *sympathetic nervous system* (SNS) and the *parasympathetic nervous system* (PNS). Stanford neuroendocrinologist Robert Sapolsky describes these two opposing systems as the body's gas pedal and the brakes, respectively.[13] (It may be helpful here to refer to table 3.1 in chapter 3, bearing in mind the differences between automatic and controlled processing.)

The SNS, operating from the bottom up as an automatic response, is primed to alert us in the presence of danger (for example, a vicious animal) or excitement, such as sexual arousal. The actions of the SNS are abetted by a cocktail of hormones (primarily epinephrine, norepinephrine, and the glucocorticoids), which Sapolsky calls "the workhorses of the stress-response."[14] Somatic symptoms, in addition to those already noted (increased heart rate and sweat), include muscle tension; dilation of the eyes; constriction of the GI tract; and, in extremely horrifying situations, sudden vomiting and diarrhea.

In the case of a clear and present danger, the SNS operates not only outside our conscious awareness but so swiftly as to be actually *ahead* of it. For example, if we are peacefully strolling down our neighborhood sidewalk, we do not pause to muse over the source of a sudden and tremendously loud crash that sets our SNS ablaze and sends us fleeing in the opposite direction. This accounts for a common experience of accident victims who state that the velocity of the event left them "no time to think."

As scientists like Sapolsky have taught us, we humans were originally structured for living among the dangers in the wild. Our fight-or-flight reaction is a deeply hardwired instinct responsible for the critical choice between standing our ground to fight an oncoming predator or fleeing the situation entirely. And while it is true that giving a public violin recital is not perfectly analogous to being chased by a lion (no savannah, no heaving, four-hundred-pound animal hot on your heels), as far as our bodies are concerned, the threat of a lion and the threat of an audience are similar. Thus the SNS floors the gas pedal in times of purely psychological stress, which leads to the disturbing experience of MPA.

In addition, we humans have an exasperatingly unique ability to turn on our SNS purely through imagination: either through anticipation of a future performance or while reliving the memory of a cringeworthy performance flub—the postevent rumination that distinguishes MPA from social phobia.

By contrast, the parasympathetic nervous system (PNS) operates from the top down, beginning in the executive control center of the brain, and it hits the brakes to calm our body after arousal, fear, or flight and restore it to a resting state. Thus a large amount of stress research is devoted not to the activation of the SNS or even to stress itself but to how quickly we are able to recover from the stress response. Indeed, much of Sapolsky's celebrated research is based on the observation that animals recover incredibly rapidly after bursts of stress but humans, by comparison, do not (hence the cheeky title of Sapolsky's award-winning book *Why Zebras Don't Get Ulcers*).

Worse than our relatively slow recovery from stress is the chronic malingering of elevated stress hormones in the human body, which can cause a host of human afflictions including hypertension, heart disease, diabetes, and memory loss. Worse still, because the SNS and the PNS cannot operate at the same time, if our SNS is chronically flooring the gas pedal (anxiety before, during, and after a performance), the calming operation of the PNS is necessarily idled. In a state of chronic anxiety, the PNS becomes so rusty with disuse that, in Sapolsky's words, it becomes "harder to slow things down, even in those rare moments when you're not feeling stressed about something."[15] Anxiety becomes an awful, normalized habit, and it makes us sick. Therefore, remedying chronic stress is a worthy aspiration for all of us, not just musicians. But before considering remedies, let us consider what other variables besides MPA can make hard-won technique go awry.

BEYOND MPA

If a musician goofs up in front of an audience, is it always and only because of chronic MPA? The answer is probably not. Through its multiple channels and interactions, an organism as complex as the human brain is bound to trip-wire itself in a variety of equally fascinating and aggravating ways. In fact, the performance failure phenomenon you will learn about next is actually a product of cognition, springing from precisely the way human beings process information. It will be helpful here to recall several cognitive processes from chapter 3. The first element to bear in mind is the difference between automatic and controlled processing.

Controlled processing is what we do when inputting new knowledge (following a recipe, for example), while automatic processing is what we do when we've just brushed the hot stove burner with our elbow on the way to pick up the salt shaker—ouch! In the time that it would require the brain to control process that stinging sensory information, the would-be chef would incur a second-degree burn. Fortunately, our brains do not need to compute the precise temperature at which flesh will burn in order to rescue us from such blunders. Humans come equipped with an auto-control button that sounds the alarm when danger is near, and this is generally a very good thing, in both everyday life and in evolutionary terms; we humans would not have survived without this built-in alarm system.

It is also helpful to recall the fluid period that occurs within working memory (which is learning itself), called maintenance plus manipulation. In this phase of learning, the accumulated sticky notes of practice and experience are tossed within the brain. Learning in this phase is in flux until those sticky notes are pinned down in long-term memory. With these essential brain processes now in mind, let us consider the particularly vexing performance gremlin known in the expertise literature by its full and proper name, *choking under pressure*.

CHOKING UNDER PRESSURE

Choking under pressure ("choking" for short) is what happens when well-trained performers in the physical realm (athletes, musicians, dancers, etc.) inexplicably bungle their performances in public. There are two main reasons that make choking "inexplicable": (1) It happens to motivated individuals who are masters of their craft; and (2) These masters typically perform well or even perfectly in practices and rehearsals. Choking, as noted by researchers who study it, is not merely poor performance but a performance that goes markedly poorer than expected given the performer's abilities and preparation. Thus a significant hallmark of choking is that it is the province of experts and near-experts. This invites another question: If experts choke, what do beginners do?

Beginners, through lack of training, simply panic and flounder, and mistakes are made. The consequences range from the truly mortal to the psychologically mortifying. A novice surgeon who panics, maims; an inexperienced airplane pilot who panics, kills both himself and his passengers; a beginning musician who panics may lose it so badly mid-performance that there is no way out but to crumple and start over. Bach is notorious for his M. C. Escher–like musical mazes, for example. If the musician fails to strike the one pivot note needed to vault the music into a new key, she hopelessly spins around in the previous one, aware that she is lost yet without a roadmap to guide her out of perdition—unless she practices her roadmap along with all the other aspects of her upcoming performance. Granted, mindful practice—practicing how to think, not just what to do—is typically not the province of beginners. And this is unfortunate, for a panic-driven performance gaffe is the perfect seedbed for planting an MPA that, if unaddressed, can grow to chronic and obsessive proportions as the learner matures. This is one motivation behind the cultivation of performance cues (see chapter 5), which serve as lamps to guide one's way out of the abyss of a memory lapse. Cellist Tânia Lisboa demonstrate that even young student musicians can benefit from the kind of mindful practice that includes the installation of performance cues. [16]

Other reactions to panic are fleeing—simply walking off the stage in the middle of a performance—or even fainting, which is an extreme version of panic and fits into the "fleeing" paradigm as a way of taking the path of least resistance. Yet it is notable in the MPA literature that these and other nightmares of the utter breakdowns that distinguish panic are actually quite rare among professional musicians. According to Kenny,

> one of the puzzles about music performance anxiety is that despite intense pre-performance distress, performance breakdowns are relatively infrequent occurrences in professional musicians. [17]

But note that Kenny is speaking of *professional* musicians. As previously noted, most of the musical populations studied for MPA have been adult professionals. Thus we might assume that one reason full-on performance breakdowns are so rare is that childhood experiences with performance panic simply culls those unfortunate kids out of the herd of budding musicians. If so, a caution to music teachers and parents is in order here, but not in the form of a total ban on early performance experiences. Rather, we ought to acknowledge MPA as a real phenomenon even among the very young and provide developing musicians with tools similar to Lisboa's to cope with it. Some of the techniques listed in this chapter can certainly be adapted for the young.

Even though full-on breakdowns are rare among professionals, choking can and does happen. By definition, the special hell of choking is reserved for moderately to very accomplished performers who have pursued hours of training and practice time. Indeed, the degree of mortification due to choking (mildly red-faced to full-on horror) seems directly proportional to the choker's prechoke ability. This exposes a conundrum: Aren't we supposed to improve with more training? And isn't the grand payoff for our investment in training supposed to produce a graceful performance, unburdened by technical thinking—in popular parlance, a performance on autopilot?

In recent years, choking has been the subject of serious scientific research due in part to the financial losses incurred by the business of professional sports when star athletes mess up in front of their fans and in part to the psychological terror that grips chokers and keeps performance psychologists in business. While a choking event may occur only occasionally or just once in isolation, it is more commonly experienced as part of a chain of repeating events: a nasty symptom of choking is its penchant for clinging to the choker like a pall of doom, spawning a series of macabre command performances that can endure for months or even years. One of the most infamous cases of chronic choking was that of major league baseball player Steve Blass. His two-year choking spell as a pitcher for the Pittsburgh Pirates forced his early retirement in 1975 and ignominiously attached his name to the phenomenon of choking in baseball: Steve Blass disease is the curse that dare not be named aloud in the dugout.[18]

As to what causes the mysterious ailment of choking, there are essentially two competing theories: *explicit monitoring theory* and *distraction theory*.[19] The stage has been set throughout the preceding chapters of this book to understand both of them.

Explicit Monitoring Theory. Monitoring one's physical movements while in action is thought to spark choking. This is known as "overthinking." Exactly how this might happen is explored below. The popular remedy? Stop thinking and just do it.

Distraction Theory. Being so distracted that one is unable to attend to the task (the opposite of explicit monitoring) is another hypothesized cause of choking. Top culprits that cause distraction in performance are anxiety (about the performance), personal worries (e.g., over finances or health), and recent devastating news (e.g., the death of a loved one). The popular remedy? Stop thinking and just do it.

Now we'll consider both of these theories and then consider whether Montero's just-do-it principle is a viable strategy for battling the dreaded choke.

Explicit Monitoring Theory

The theory of explicit monitoring springs from attentional focus theories that (recall from chapter 4) currently favor an external focus of attention (on a movement's goal) rather than an internal focus of attention (on the mechanics of the movement). The explicit monitoring theory of choking is based on the premise that, since automatic processing is fast and controlled processing is relatively slow, motor performance is harmed when performers retard their processing speed by overthinking procedural movements that ought to run smoothly on their own by habit gained through practice. This line of thinking celebrates automaticity by espousing the view that, in a well-trained performer, technique must be left to autopilot because once a physical feat is truly learned, it is housed deep within the motor cortex of the brain. Within this pro-automaticity explanation of choking, expert performers who suddenly shift from autopilot to controlled processing leave the land of the learned and take themselves on a time trip back to their raw beginnings, hence the term from ML research: *reinvestment*. By this theory, reinvestment in past training tenets is especially attractive if the way one first learned was by way of mechanical directions, or "rule-based" directives.[20]

Continuing this line of reasoning, the more expert the performer, the more spectacular the choke. Why? It is thought that the verbiage from a beginner's training manual will compute like a once-well-known—but now hazy—former language. The critical resources needed to attend to the task at hand (making music in front of an audience) will be siphoned off to translate reinvestment commands. (Note that this effect strongly resembles distraction theory as a cause of choking. Indeed, some researchers are making the case for this overlap.[21])

Other connections to the explicit monitoring theory are Wulf's constrained action hypothesis, which in turn supports the interrelated theories of "freezing" and the limitations of language, all discussed in chapter 4. Proponents of these interrelated theories believe that directing attention to the mechanics of movement stifles its fluidity. Here it is important to recall that fluid movement of limbs and fingers is such a hallmark of expert performance in sport, dance, music, and so forth that its opposite—sheer clumsiness—is a substantial concern.

These interrelated theories—explicit monitoring theory, the constrained action hypothesis, and distraction theory—are all based on the belief that physical sensation is nearly impossible to adequately capture in words, so language itself is deemed rigid and inflexible. The concept of a cognitive argument between brain regions illuminates these entwined beliefs. It is thought that verbal directions, primarily processed in the brain region known as Broca's area, and sensory commands, primarily processed in the motor cortex, involve such incongruent brain regions that verbal directions are destined for the no-man's-land of the choke. The most dominant explanation as to why this might occur is, again, one of processing speed. Verbal commands are slow to translate into bodily action; they simply take too much time to make their way through our controlled processing system (recall the hot burner analogy), and by the time they have run their course, the action we were attempting has been compromised, even wrecked. If this sounds familiar, I described the phenomenon in which mechanical directions issued during motor learning can become "lost in translation" in chapter 4.

These theories regarding language processing highlight the limitations of language in the re-creation of high-degree motor skill and support the popular belief that choking is the result of thinking too much during a performance rather than thinking too little. Arthur Koestler in his 1964 book *The Act of Creation* (described as "a massive attempt . . . to examine the psychological process underlying both artistic and scientific creation") captures this cognitive argument perfectly by first acknowledging the necessity of words as "essential tools for formulating and communicating thoughts, and also for putting them into the storage of memory," then immediately cautioning that "words can also become snares, decoys, or strait-jackets."[22] As Koestler admonishes his readers,

> words are a blessing which can turn into a curse. They crystallize thought; they give articulation and precision to vague images and hazy intuitions. But a crystal is no longer a fluid.[23]

Distraction Theory

Distraction theory is the second most prominent explanation for choking. Early proponents of distraction theory situated this explanation diametrically opposite explicit monitoring theory. Explicit monitoring theory says that we are bewitched toward the task to our choking doom; distraction theory says that we are pulled devastatingly away from the task.

To understand the cognitive substrates of distraction theory, you must first understand the nexus of working memory, attention, and the upside of automaticity. Recall from chapter 3 that there is an especially fluid period within working memory called maintenance plus manipulation, in which the mixed salad of sticky notes (accumulated while one is paying attention to just about anything) is tossed and recombined in the bowl of the brain. As such, attention in this phase is porous and highly labile. Anything can happen.

Also recall from chapter 3 that one argument in favor of automaticity is its ability to reduce cognitive load, leaving more mental real estate available for other cognitive tasks—this is presumed to be a major bonus of automatic actions. Yet can it be guaranteed that this bonus room in the brain will be filled with positive forces? For if automaticity can create an advantageous opening for creativity, could it not also make room for agitation and worry to take root? This dichotomy is probably the number one reason why cultivating a blank mind is not a viable strategy for warding off MPA or choking. An argument against automaticity might therefore resemble a clever twist on the old proverb "Idle hands are the devil's playground": A performer's idle mind is the choking gremlins' playground. Montero makes a sensible suggestion on this point: "When acting automatically, at any moment, it seems, the mind might jump back into the picture and thus . . . [i]t may be best to have the mind present all along."[24] If a blank mind in performance is not a realistic possibility, why would we not want to be in charge of what is installed there?

The White Bear Problem and the Ironic Effect

A third theory adds another layer to the phenomenon of choking by illuminating why humans sometimes will perversely "think, say, or do precisely the worst thing for any occasion."[25] The propensity for humans to do the opposite of what they intend has been observed for well-nigh two centuries, but it was the late Harvard psychologist Daniel Wegner who named it *ironic processing theory*. It is also known colloquially as "the white bear problem" after a passage by Russian novelist Fyodor Dostoevsky: "Try to pose for yourself this task: not to think of a polar bear, and you will see that the cursed thing will come to mind every minute."[26] The perversity of this challenge inspired Wegner's research into not only thought suppression but behavior. Why, for example, is it not only difficult for a dieter to eschew fantasy thoughts about cheesecake but also for a performer not to physically trip when walking onstage or for an instrumentalist's fingers not to flub a chord progression? Wegner found that, in certain situations, the very action that we intend to do is thwarted by its exact and humiliating opposite—that our intentions for an excellent performance can sometimes be accompanied by an "ironic monitoring process" that attracts failure.[27]

By the tenets of ironic processing theory, the attempt to control one's actions in performance is not beleaguered by explicit monitoring or constrained action or the sensory system's mutinous reaction to verbal commands but by the imps of doubt and failure that routinely accompany the pursuit of success.

Wegner observed that people are most at risk for ironic processing when depressed, stressed, sleep-deprived, or otherwise operating under undue mental load. Considering that public performances are accompanied by heaps of both stress and mental load, it is somewhat remarkable, seen through the lens of the ironic processing theory, that musicians are able to succeed in performance at all.

But succeed we do, in spite of the notorious bogies of performance jitters. While a lucky few have never experienced performance anxiety, research reveals that MPA, choking, and other ironic processes are experienced by most musicians at one time or another. Indeed, these phenomena have likely been around for as long as performing artists have been plying their trade before critical audiences. What else is the traditional admonition "Break a leg!" (or, in the opera world, *In bocca al lupo*, "Into the mouth of the wolf") but a reverse charm to ward off the well-known specter of choking? These and other backstage talismans are examples wherein human experience predates scientific exploration. Now that science has acknowledged the phenomenon of ironic processing as truth experienced (and not just "all in the mind"), it is a subject deemed worthy of scientific study. Such research may offer performers some insight into and even some antidotes for age-old phenomena that have bedeviled performers for centuries. As a prelude to such hope, let us first consider whether there is any advantage at all to performance anxiety.

THE UPSIDE OF ANXIETY

It may be difficult at this juncture to believe there is anything remotely positive about anxiety's effect on music performance. But the fact that most musicians seek a performance experience that is both compelling to the audience and joyful for the doer implies that performers care enough to make it so—that they have (as is said in sports) some skin in the game. This emotional investment, even among the most grounded and experienced performers, is often tinged with a tiny frisson of worry over the quality of the outcome—otherwise, we would not be able to summon enough care to make good music. This symbiosis between arousal and performance is known in psychology as the *Yerkes-Dodson Law*, which states that performance quality generally increases with arousal; that is, our skills get better the more we care about them—but only up to an optimal point. When desire exceeds its tipping point, excitement becomes infected with anxiety, and performance crumbles.

Seasoned musicians know that to feel zero anxiety is either abnormal or a perilous sign that a flat performance is in the offing. Therefore many successful performers have learned that, instead of aiming to extinguish anxiety altogether, a more fruitful strategy is to tame it and bring it under control in order to ride the wave of exhilaration that only a public performance can offer. This strategy comes about through deliberate practice, which is only potent if practiced onstage and in public, and it strengthens with experience. Therefore a practical treatment for MPA is to play music under performance conditions—that is, play and sing in front of people—as often as possible. Practice feeling nervous.

This commonsense strategy is referred to in the psychology literature as *exposure therapy*. Indeed, gathering up some friends (and a few strangers) to make up an audience seems both simple and a real no-

brainer. Ask each friend to bring two or four others, and add entice-
ments: Free coffee! Cookies! Another simple way to generate an audience is to perform in local retirement communities, which often house
a community gathering hall with a decent piano. Even hospitals are now
potential places in which to both give and receive the gift of music.[28]

When performing for an audience is not possible, simulating the
effects of anxiety can be an equally powerful tool. Self-described "peak
performance psychologist" Don Greene uses just such simulations with
his clients. For example, he has musicians run or climb stairs to the
point of breathlessness then immediately play their instrument or sing
to habituate them to performing under the weight of such classic somatic symptoms as elevated heart rate, lack of oxygen, sweaty hands,
and tight abdominal muscles.[29] It is thought that in this way the somatic
symptoms of performance anxiety can be deliberately triggered and
experienced ahead of time, defanging them a little in the process. These
are some commonsense approaches to defying MPA. Let us now turn to
the current state of psychological and neuroscientific research on bona
fide treatments for MPA.

RESEARCHED TREATMENTS FOR MPA

MPA has been studied for over four decades, yet due to the problems
and challenges in the research already mentioned, many questions
about MPA remain unanswered, none more so than the question of
effective treatments for MPA. The few treatments that have shown
some benefit in one study or another still require verification through
repeated trials. As Kenny notes, "there has been an almost alarming
proliferation of treatment approaches to the problem of living, and
these are developing ahead of the capacity of the research community
to empirically validate their effectiveness."[30] This is surely all the more
true for a disorder that is still not entirely understood.

The most important systematic reviews of MPA treatments include
Kenny's as well as those of the team of psychologists Anne McGinnis
and Leonard Milling (2005); a meta-analysis of nonpharmacologic
psychotherapies (Laurie Goren in 2014); and a book-length review of
the relevant literature by physician, violinist, and author Ariadna Ortiz
Brugués.[31] Findings culled from these varied sources are briefly sum-

marized here, although the efficacy of pharmacologic interventions are not, due to the fact that these drugs must be prescribed by a physician after he has first thoroughly analyzed the performer's MPA situation and considering the possible side effects. Some side effects reported in the literature are worth noting, however: excess salivation with beta blockers and disruption of fine motor control with antianxiety medications. While the former might not trouble a string or percussion player, wind players and singers could experience deleterious effects when dealing with excess saliva, and the disruption of fine motor coordination would be a concern to all instrumentalists.

Standard Psychotherapies for MPA

Psychodynamic or Psychoanalytic Therapy: This is the oldest form of psychotherapy (think Freud). The patient is led to consider their past history (for example, childhood relationships and experiences) in order to understand how their past might influence present behavior. As such, this therapy may be relatively more time-consuming than other types, playing out over months or years. This approach may be most fruitful for musicians who have a long, complicated, or fraught history in music—for example, those groomed as child prodigies. However, there have been no controlled studies on the efficacy of this approach for MPA, so Kenny, Goren, and others suggest that future research is needed in this area.

Behavioral Therapy: Behavioral therapy aims to alter the client's behavior when they feel anxious or to ameliorate distressing somatic symptoms such as muscle tension. Goren considers such strategies as *relaxation training, exposure therapy*, and *desensitization therapy* "classic" behavioral techniques. Participants in one study in this category showed some improvement when using *behavior rehearsal*, which involves practicing the desired responses to a future performance situation via play-acting and role-playing. The effect of this particular therapy was stronger when combined with *cognitive therapy*.[32]

Cognitive Therapy: The essence of cognitive therapy lies within its name; if *cognition* means "thinking," then the aim of cognitive therapy is to alter the way that patients think. A more nuanced explanation is that cognitive therapy helps patients interpret their emotional response to situations and, presumably, flip from self-defeating or so-called catastrophizing thoughts to more self-supportive ones. How this might play out in the management of MPA is explored by Kenny, who notes that there are three main focuses in music performance: the self, the audience, and the music. Using cognitive therapy to address MPA would involve directing one's limited human attentional resources to one aim—the music—and away from the self and the audience. This is achieved through directed thinking.

Cognitive Behavioral Therapy: As its name implies, this type of therapy is a combination of cognitive therapy and behavioral therapy. The aim is to change both the way the patient thinks and the way they enact that thinking. Cognitive behavioral therapy (CBT) has been a remarkably robust therapy and has recently gotten a boost from cognitive neuroscience—that is, we now know that the reason CBT can be so effective is that it can actually change the brain via the doctrine of neural plasticity. As such, CBT has been shown to be one of the most effective psychotherapies for MPA.[33] As in cognitive therapy, CBT typically trains a person to rethink a situation by reframing it in a more positive or efficient light then actually practicing that thought while simultaneously engaging in changed behavior around the thought, even if the behavior is not exactly the one that feels instinctive in the moment. Here is an example of a CBT technique for a performer: Backstage just before your performance, you note how nervous you feel via typical somatic symptoms (increased heart rate, sweaty palms, shallow breathing). Instead of allowing negative interpretations of those feelings to enter your mind, you consciously and assertively practice a word or a sentence that translates the word *nervous* to the word *excited*. Similarly, you transform physical sensations to positive signs that you cannot wait to bound onto the stage. This is the cognitive component of CBT. For the behavioral component of CBT, you stride strongly out on the stage, head held high with a glowing smile pasted on your face, even if this is not an accurate portrayal of how you really feel on the inside. (Note: The behavioral component of this technique resembles a recent fad called *power posing*, which will be reviewed later in this chapter.)

ALTERNATIVE THERAPIES FOR MPA

There are other treatments for MPA, both non-Western and alternative therapies, that are promising. Still the following comment by Brugués reflects the caution in the medical and scientific literature about such strategies: "There are too few studies performed to fully support the evidence reported by them."[34] Nevertheless, an overview of two of the most popular modalities among performing artists is offered here. And while Brugués' assessment may be correct about the first one, the second alternative method now offers compelling bona fide research on the question of its effectiveness.

Alexander Technique

Alexander Technique (AT) is

> a method of kinaesthetic re-education, in which a new postural model is associated with verbal instructions; bad habits are inhibited and replaced by consciously directed action. Movements in accordance with the technique are characterised by economy of effort and a balanced and appropriate distribution of tension (not an absence of tension, but no more than is necessary).[35]

AT is taught through a series of lessons by a certified AT teacher. According to the American Society for the Alexander Technique, "people study the Technique for a variety of reasons. The most common is to relieve pain through learning better coordination of the musculoskeletal system," but the society also notes that AT is an especially popular method "to enhance performance. Athletes, singers, dancers, and musicians use the Technique to improve breathing, vocal production, and speed and accuracy of movement."[36]

According to singer, AT teacher, and independent researcher Marisa De Silva, "the current literature on the question of whether Alexander Technique may mitigate MPA is scarce, but the most notable study was conducted by Valentine et al. in 1995."[37]

In this study, a sample of twenty-one music students enrolled in a performance class in a UK university (both vocalists and instrumentalists) were divided into two groups: an experimental group and a control group. The experimental group was given a course of fifteen AT lessons (the AT group).

The two groups first completed three questionnaires (on personality, performance anxiety, and interest in AT lessons) and were then subjected to a variety of measures (height, peak air flow, and heart rate) that were administered on four different occasions: (1) at the required audition to get into the class, (2) at an in-class performance, (3) at a second in-class performance, and (4) at the final class recital. Measurements on the first two occasions were taken prior to students' commencing AT lessons, while measurements on the final two occasions were taken after students had completed the full round of AT lessons.

Results showed that the AT group improved significantly relative to the control group in "overall music and technical quality" as judged by independent music experts. These judges did not know if the subjects they were assessing were in the AT group or in the control group. The AT group improved also on measures of "heart rate variance, self-rated anxiety and positive attitude to performance."[38]

Although this study (which included both quantitative and qualitative data) is the most comprehensive study to date on AT and MPA, Kenny considers it to be of "weak design" and concludes that "we cannot be confident in the findings."[39] The authors themselves acknowledge as much, admitting that their sample size was small, the subjects were predominantly female, and the fact that the experimental group knew that the goal of the study was to prove the efficacy of AT for MPA may have primed them to be more positive in their qualitative assessments of mood and anxiety. The authors state unequivocally that

> with regard to the main hypothesis under test, there were no significant effects of the experimental treatment on height, peak flow or mean heart rate. Thus, there was no support for lessons in AT increasing height or peak flow, or modulating the increase in mean heart rate under stress.[40]

Regarding height and peak (air) flow, the authors had initially hypothesized that these parameters might improve given AT's emphasis on posture and spinal alignment. In addition, "misuse" was added to the list of parameters that saw no improvement. *Misuse*, however, is an oddly subjective term for a scientific paper, although the authors explained that by AT standards, "optimal functioning constitutes 'good use' and deviation from it is termed 'misuse' (a technical term in AT)."[41] For this study, the degree of misuse was judged by two independent AT teachers who specialized in teaching musicians.

Yet what remains somewhat peculiar is the authors' disavowal of heart rate variance (as stated in the previous quote) because heart rate is exactly the parameter that showed a clear difference between the control group and the AT group during the two most stress-inducing performance events for the class: the entrance audition and the last event, the public recital. According to the study, the control group's mean heart rate was significantly lower than the AT group's to start with (at audition), but for the final recital, it shot up well beyond that of the AT group. What is more, even though the AT group's heart rate was raised for the final recital, it was only a little bit higher than their first-audition heart rate—and still significantly lower than the control group's recital heart rate. The authors, at another point in the paper, report that,

> in sum, the results suggest that AT may have beneficial effects on the quality of performance, the mental state of the performer, and may help to modulate increased variability of heart rate under stress.[42]

In addition to these oddities, another weakness of the study was the mystery of the parameter of time. Readers do not know over how many weeks the fifteen lessons were administered and can only infer that they took place over an academic semester. If this is the case, then it is equally easy to infer that the AT group actually experienced a significant benefit from their AT lessons in lowering one of the somatic effects of MPA excitement—increased heart rate—when judged against their peers who did not take AT lessons. In De Silva's opinion, because of these and other factors, the study "should not be totally dismissed":

> First, so as not to be labeled biased, the researchers used the grant to hire two groups of experts: 1) independent AT instructors to teach the AT lessons, and 2) expert musicians who used a video analysis to judge the overall musical quality of the participants from pre-class to post-class. The judges concluded that the experimental group's musical quality in performance improved from pre-class to post-class, whereas the control group's musical quality in performance actually declined.

Mood and heart rate variance (the only data collected from the final recital), also showed clear differences: anxiety in the control group rose over time, while the AT group's declined; and while the control group showed a drastic increase in heart rate variance from audition to recital, the AT group did not.

With quantitative data such as heart rate variance, this study at least shows that AT classes had some quantifiable impact and should not be negated. Further research with replicated results would be necessary to strengthen its case. [43]

One final note about this study should be made: in poststudy interviews, while the AT subjects self-rated general benefits from their lessons rather modestly and musical benefits somewhat higher, all the AT subjects mentioned that they felt an increased awareness of tension and noted improvement in their ability to relax. [44] This latter result would be a significant counter to the natural tendency of the SNS to floor the gas pedal of performance anxiety and a hopeful sign that AT training could help musicians consciously apply the brakes of the PNS in times of stress to bring arousal down to acceptable levels of excitement.

Yoga

Yoga is a holistic mind-body practice because it combines both cognitive elements (via meditation, focused attention and concentration) and somatic elements, through the physical postures most people associate with yoga (called *asanas*), breathing, and deep stretching exercises. Because of yoga's all-inclusive nature, both control systems of the body are operating at once: the "bottom-up" system, via yoga's intense physicality, and the "top-down" system via its requirement for focus, attention, and patience. Indeed, one style of yoga (Kripalu) is known as "meditation in motion." [45]

There are four published studies on the effectiveness of yoga as a treatment for MPA. [46] These connected studies are significant for several reasons, not least of which is the biography of the lead author of three of them, Sat Bir Singh Khalsa, who, along with being a practicing yogi himself over many decades, is also an assistant professor of medicine at Harvard Medical School and a research director for the Kundalini Research Institute and the Kripalu Center for Yoga and Health. As editor-in-chief of the *International Journal of Yoga Therapy* and chief editor of the book *The Principles and Practice of Yoga in Health Care*, he is a leader in the yoga-as-therapy movement.

These four research studies were implemented over a timeline of seven years at the Tanglewood Music Center, an annual summer music academy in the Berkshire Hills of western Massachusetts. Because of the collective ages of the research subjects who were studied (young adult professionals, college-age conservatory students, and adolescents), they represented musicians' most crucial training and testing periods. The results of all four studies indicate that yoga is quite promising as an intervention for MPA.

The first one, a pilot study, took a group of nine young professional musicians (average age twenty-five) who had all won prestigious Tanglewood fellowships and offered them regular yoga and meditation classes over eight weeks (a control group of fellows who did not take yoga classes was also assembled). The fellows were allowed to choose their own schedules, so as might be expected, attendance was high at the beginning of the program (four or five classes per week), dwindled somewhat as the intense Tanglewood rehearsal and performance schedule amplified, and then picked up again as the program drew to a close. Measures of "anxiety, mood and flow" were higher in the yoga group than the control group. Flow was defined in this study, following Csikszentmihalyi, as "an optimal psychological state associated with high levels of performance and is a positive, rewarding experience." Even better, performance anxiety scores showed "statistically significant improvements in comparison" to the control group.[47] The authors of this study write that they were not surprised at the outcome regarding performance anxiety, given that yoga practice uses a number of components that are "particularly known to be useful for anxiety, including meditation, breathing, and counseling directed at specific and individual music performance problems."[48]

The second study, built on the previous summer's pilot study, took place in the same location and again involved young adult professional musicians (music fellows at Tanglewood). Yet this study differs from the first one in several ways: it involved a larger number of musicians, and the groups were divided into three cohorts, not two. Groups 1 and 2 both practiced yoga and meditation three times a week (as in 2005), but group 1 volunteered for an additional full-on "yoga lifestyle intervention." The yoga-lifestyle musicians kicked off the study with a two-day intensive retreat, where they learned about breathing and mediation techniques as well as what the researchers called "conscious eating." As the summer progressed, along with regular yoga classes, they added weekly, facilitated group discussions that wove together the challenges musicians face in both practice and performance with how a yogic lifestyle might ameliorate performance-related physical pain and psychological suffering. A third group engaged in none of these practices and functioned as the control. The results of the second study?

> Consistent with the results of our previous study . . . A period of yoga and meditation practice of just over 6-weeks duration tended to reduce performance anxiety and improved mood in a sample of young professional musicians. Participants responded positively to the yoga program and found that yoga and meditation techniques were beneficial to their music performance and daily lives over both the short and long term.
>
> The yoga program showed a statistical tendency to reduce the cognitive and somatic symptoms of musical performance anxiety. The yoga program incorporated several components that were targeted to alleviate anxiety including meditation, breath control, and counseling directed at specific music performance problems and career stressors . . . Participants found that yogic breath control techniques helped them more effectively manage performance anxiety, especially immediately prior to a concert.[49]

The third yoga study, administered during academic year 2007–2008, built on the two previous Tanglewood studies but the subjects were twenty-four college-age student musicians culled from the Boston Conservatory rather than young adult professionals. Students were offered two yoga classes per week over an approximately nine-week period; were asked to practice on their own an additional four days a week using a prerecorded, sixteen-minute lesson; and were to log the results in a home practice log.

Again, results were positive: "participants showed large decreases in MPA" and their "trait anxiety decreased significantly."[50] Nevertheless, the study was somewhat weakened by sample size; gender imbalance; and, most important, attrition: students' attendance and adherence to the program began to erode as the weeks went on. At program's end, only seventeen of the original twenty-four attended a "post-intervention assessment," and of these, only nine returned a follow-up questionnaire.

Still the participants who did stick with yoga practice until the end of the study reported having a positive experience, and some of them continued to practice both yoga and meditation even after the study had ended. The authors therefore make a bid for yoga as "an efficacious and cost-effective addition to the curricula of music schools that can supplement existing methods of coping with performance anxiety."[51] The first clause of this sentence is a sincere call to action. The second clause presupposes that there are, in fact, "existing methods of coping with performance anxiety" already in place in music schools. Given that interest in MPA as a separate disorder arose only in the 1990s and that shame and secrecy still surround MPA, the idea that a majority of music schools provide adequate supports for students suffering with MPA is questionable. This makes it all the more important that musicians with MPA take it upon themselves to find a modality that works for them to ameliorate it—and, perhaps even more importantly, for parents of young musicians to help guide their kids toward practices like yoga and meditation. A suggestion here is the use of what the authors of the third study nicknamed "minis": very brief yoga stretches and poses coupled with deep-breathing exercises to quiet the mind. As already noted, early negative performance experiences as a young musician in training can plant a noxious seed of anxiety that may perennially bloom throughout a lifetime of music performance. Therefore one of the most exciting prospects for yoga as an intervention is that yoga could be woven into the training of young musicians as a virtual inoculation against the most virulent strains of MPA.

Indeed, this is one of the conclusions reached by the authors of a fourth study. Their purpose was to apply similar yoga intervention methods as were used in the previous studies but this time to an adolescent population procured from the Boston University Tanglewood Institute (BUTI), a prestigious, six-week summer program for advanced teen musicians. The goal was to investigate whether both MPA and performance-related musculoskeletal disorders (PRMDs) might be alleviated through yoga, specifically to "prevent the early disruption and termination of musical careers."[52]

The protocol for this study was much the same as for the previous Tanglewood studies, just adapted for BUTI's shorter duration. And like the previous studies, participants evinced lower MPA symptoms (both cognitive and somatic) than the control group. Another finding was that teen participants seemed to genuinely enjoy the yoga practice.

The authors of this final study are to be especially commended for understanding the anguish that attends a musician's struggle with MPA—the pain that the very thing you love can flip to the dark side and become a bringer of psychic torment—and that teen musicians may be especially vulnerable hosts for early-onset MPA, robbing them of the joy of music-making throughout their lives. Thus the authors offer these hopeful concluding remarks: "starting a yoga practice early and continuing to practice may help musicians prolong their musical careers and take increased pleasure in their craft throughout their lives."[53]

EXPERIMENTAL STRATEGIES FOR MPA

In addition to the researched methods to alleviate MPA covered here, there are a variety of other tactics that musicians may wish to try. In order to wring the most benefit from them, it is helpful to bear in mind two fundamental things we now know about anxiety generally: (1) anxiety is a learned response, and (2) the order in which we experience our physical and emotional reactions to stressful situations occurs in reverse order of what most people assume to be the case. Let us consider these characteristics more closely.

Anxiety is a learned response to past trauma. We must have first experienced trauma and have interpreted this experience as a catastrophe in order to anticipate a repeat experience with dread—which goes to the core of what anxiety really is (another reason why zebras don't get ulcers). As Sapolsky describes it, anxiety is not the same thing as fear:

> Fear is the vigilance and the need to escape from something real. Anxiety is about dread and foreboding and your imagination running away with you. Much as with depression, anxiety is rooted in a cognitive distortion. . . . People prone toward anxiety overestimate risks and the likelihood of a bad outcome.[54]

The second thing to know about anxiety (which should now be apparent from reading this chapter) is that people respond to it in two fundamental ways: emotionally and physically (subjectively and objectively). It may seem that we experience these two basic responses in a predictable, linear trajectory that goes something like this: I feel nervous (cause) so my heart starts to pound (effect). But a mind-blowing finding from scientists like Sapolsky is that this trajectory actually plays out the other way around: we do not experience increased heart rates because we feel nervous—we feel nervous because our heartbeat increases. How can this be?

The boundaries of the emotional and the physical are porous, their intersection bound up in a tangle of cause and effect, fooling us into believing that they occur in reverse order. We now know that in moments of fear, panic, or anxiety, the objective stress response of the sympathetic nervous system first activates and then causes us to experience the subjective emotion of nervousness. How might this work? One answer involves timing. Recall that our bottom-up response is primed to alert us instantaneously: in a race, automatic (bottom-up) processing beats controlled (top-down) processing every time.

In MPA, a trigger stimulates a response that is first physical and then is interpreted as the feeling we call "nervousness." In repeat bouts of MPA, any number of triggers can stimulate the stress response (the smell of bow rosin or the sound of applause, for example) if those triggers were learned through connection to a past traumatic performance experience. Once this learned response becomes practiced, just the mere thought of an upcoming performance can unleash the disturbing physical responses of anxiety.

But if musicians can flip their understanding of cause and effect, they might leverage to their advantage the time gap between the physical responses and the emotional ones. One classic suggestion in this regard comes from cognitive therapy, a self-intervention that involves reframing a negative interpretation with a positive one. As I described above, a musician might substitute *excited* as an alternate term for *nervous*. The catch is to do this quickly before the demons of doubt get there. And if you wonder how you might accomplish that feat, well, we have the well-worn answer by now: practice. Just as movement can be practiced, so can thoughts. This is CBT in action.

Regarding the other fundamental characteristic of anxiety (the fact that it is learned), the answer is maddeningly simple: anxiety can be unlearned. Yet while the answer is simple, the doing of it, admittedly, is not. Nevertheless, unlearning does not appear impossible. The following two interrelated strategies work by targeting the intersection of the physical and emotional responses to anxiety and by exploiting anxiety's fundamental characteristics—its acquisition and its timing—to instigate the sequence of unlearning.

Exposure Therapy and Stress Conditioning

Exposure therapy and *stress conditioning* are based on the premise that people can unlearn their dual stress response through habituation. The theory behind exposure therapy is that frequent interaction with anxiety-producing events will lower the physical and emotional responses to manageable levels. Similarly, there is some evidence for the beneficial potential of what Sapolsky calls stress conditioning as a therapy for anxiety. This involves intentionally and regularly scheduling high-arousal situations so (as in exposure therapy) the body eventually habituates itself to the release of those stress hormones that cause the unsettling physical responses so familiar to performers.

But an important component of this stress conditioning hypothesis involves what happens after, not necessarily during, the stressful event. Recall that much stress research is focused on the time it takes to return to equilibrium, or *homeostasis*, after trauma. Performers who schedule a stress-conditioning event will still experience the hormonal jolt and the cascade of physical symptoms, but how soon they return to a state of calm is key. Some studies of parachute jumpers have shown that, with each successive experience, over time the calming effect of the parasympathetic nervous system immediately following the jump moves from hours to minutes to seconds.[55]

One such study measured both the physical (objective) and the emotional (subjective) responses of skydivers (divided into two groups, "experienced" and "first-timers") via three methods: cortisol measures in saliva, self-ratings for the emotions of prejump anxiety, and self-measures of postjump happiness. These were administered at five different time stamps: two at prejump and three at postjump, all at successive time intervals.[56]

One aim of the study is to determine what the investigators call "the shape of the hormonal response" at three key moments: ninety minutes before the jump, at the jump, and after the jump. Another aim was to investigate *coordinated responsivity*—that is, to see whether subjects' emotions about the activity had an effect on their stress-response hormone levels. Among the findings, one was expected: "First-time skydivers demonstrated increased cortisol reactivity leading up to the jump, and slower recovery after landing than experienced jumpers."[57]

More interesting are the findings regarding the experienced skydivers. Unlike previous studies that show marked decreases in prejump anxiety among experienced jumpers (a vote in favor of *habituation*, or why exposure therapy works), this team uncovered the opposite: "Intriguingly, even after hundreds of jumps [the experienced skydivers] still showed increased subjective anxiety and elevated cortisol leading up to the jump." The investigators therefore surmised that "habituation to a naturalistic stressor is complex" because, while "experience alters emotional and physiological arousal, [it] does not extinguish reactivity to an extreme challenge such as skydiving."[58]

For musicians who suffer from MPA, these findings are enlightening. For one thing, they underscore that, while a goal of amelioration is feasible, complete eradication of pre-performance anxiety is unrealistic. After all, strategies to deal with anxiety generally do not involve the word *cure*.

A second finding from this study is equally inspiring for performers: jumpers who were most elated after completing the thrill of skydiving also demonstrated a faster decrease in cortisol after the jump; the higher the happiness quotient, the faster the return to homeostasis. One lesson we might draw from this is that musicians who pursue therapy for MPA might want to focus just as much attention on mitigating what Kenny calls "post-event rumination" as on pre-performance dread. For a musician who suffers from MPA, it is just as acceptable to celebrate a performance as simply over as it is to celebrate its success. For MPA sufferers, these two parameters could be one and the same.

And lest it seem as if skydiving and public performance have little in common, researchers note that the "extreme" activity of skydiving produces a "natural high" that is so pleasurable, it "shows similarities with addictive behaviors."[59] Might it be a helpful mind game for MPA sufferers to channel John Cougar Mellencamp ("Sometimes love don't feel like it should . . . Make it hurt so good"), reframing public performance as a sweet addiction? Who knows. But given that the jury is still out on definitive therapies for MPA, even this thought experiment might be worth a try.

Resilience Training

What exposure therapy and stress conditioning aim to build is *resilience*. This trait caught the attention of psychology researchers in the 1970s who were studying children growing up in extremely impoverished circumstances. Researchers were surprised to learn that, although the majority of these disadvantaged kids grew into adults with crushing social and mental health problems, about one-third did not; this durable cohort not only survived their difficult childhood but grew into competent, caring adults.

Research into the causes and characteristics of resilience continued, greatly nourished by the positive psychology movement in the 1990s, which inverted psychology's focus to what causes people to thrive rather than what causes them to fail.[60] And perennially circling the findings of positive psychology are questions of inculcation and implementation: how might we instill the skills of reframing a problem or the qualities of grit? And once installed, will they take root on their own and become techniques that people can deploy to better their lives?

With the advent of neuroscience and the twin phenomena of neurogenesis and neural plasticity, these questions have taken on greater urgency while simultaneously vindicating the claims of CBT. Rather than accepting resilience as a fixed trait, researchers are beginning to find that resilience, like Dweck's growth mindset, can be taught, learned, and nurtured through practice. And even though researchers acknowledge that "the psychobiology of building resilience is complicated" because it "likely involves multiple behavioral, social, physical-health, and cognitive strategies that work synergistically or additively with one another," the evidence is that it *can* be done.[61]

For musicians, exposure therapy, stress conditioning, and resilience training all hold the potential to calm the dread of future performances, shorten anxiety's duration, and hasten the return to a state of equilibrium following a performance. If this is true, then resilience training and its ilk are strategies that the mindful musician should consider not only as an antidote to MPA but more broadly as a defense against the rigors of the performing life.

Power Posing

What is power posing? Is it the scientific finding that using strong body positions inculcates feelings of power? Or is it a pop-psychology fad? The tale of power posing follows a strikingly similar plotline to that of the Mozart effect. In the tale of power posing, a seemingly credible scientific study got a massive boost from Oprah, a TED Talk, and a best-selling book because its lead researcher spoke in messianic terms about delivering this news for the empowerment of the people.[62] But the study's high profile (and, some say, the female gender and success of its promoter, Amy Cuddy) fatally intersected with psychology's reproducibility crisis and was outed in the academic press for shoddy research protocols and discredited as pseudoscience—but not before Cuddy became rich and famous by it. Unlike the saga of the Mozart effect, whose authors disavowed the hype from the get-go (yet did not have the megaphone of digital media with which to deny it), Cuddy promulgated her theories using the most visible, popular, powerful, and financially rewarding platforms of the day. For all this, she was pilloried in the digital court of online science blogs.[63]

But just as the Mozart effect retained its core finding (listening to music makes you happy so you perform better), after time passed and the dust had settled, power posing (if not Cuddy herself) rose from the ashes as a more somber version of its former self and sporting a new name, *postural feedback effect*, while retaining the essential elements of its original hypothesis.[64] Strong and assertive stances make people feel not only strong and autonomous but, even more importantly, happy.

What performing musicians need to know about power posing are two things. First, a key criticism of Cuddy's original study involves a fundamental debate in science over quantitative versus qualitative data, or that which can be measured versus what people report they feel. Ardent materialists in science will never accept qualitative data as "real" because, they say, it cannot be measured (and this is the attitude undergirding the equally inflexible opinion that psychology as a whole is not a real science).[65]

Second, while Cuddy's initial and unilateral claims that power posing can rock your life may have been hyperbolic, there are many studies on the postural feedback effect (which Cuddy maintains in an online database) that display an array of results: some weak, some average, and some quite promising.[66]

So what does it all mean for the performing artist? The veracity of the postural feedback effect probably depends mightily upon the context. If you lead the life of an introverted knowledge worker with little human interaction and almost no call to publicly present your work, the benefits of power posing are likely nil. If, however, you are a performance artist whose livelihood depends upon delivering reliably self-assured music-making, power posing may indeed be a life-changer.

Meditation

One study known to date to test meditation alone as a strategy for MPA found some positive effects among a group of student musicians who pursued an eight-week course of meditation classes, as opposed to a control group who did not. In addition, the meditation group reported "moments of relaxed pleasure" even in the period immediately before public performances.[67]

Holistic Word Cues

Some research shows that one-word, or "holistic," cues may act as condensed reminders to help prevent choking in trained practitioners.[68] It is important to note that a one-word cue (as distinguished from an entire sentence of technical instructions) seems to be regarded by the brain as a picture, and therefore the cue does not get tracked into the left prefrontal cortex, the brain region responsible for processing verbal information. Imagine, as a preventative for choking, a cue word such as *loose* scrawled on a card in a nonthreatening ink of inspirational blue and posted on your dressing-room door. But beware of posting explicit directions, for example, "Keep your jaw loose, your palate raised, and your throat open." According to explicit monitoring theory and the constrained action hypothesis, these admonitions are processed so slowly by the brain that they could end up choking off the best-laid plans.

"Avoid Avoiding"

Two succinct admonitions from Daniel Wegner may be helpful: "Avoid avoiding" and "Orchestrate your circumstances for success."[69] In other words, respect the medium (performance) by not avoiding pre-performance jitters; rather, embrace the fear! To orchestrate your circumstances for success means to allot the necessary time for mental preparation. This may sound simple enough for experienced performers, but it must be taught to young students and their parents. Here is my illustration of that point.

In my early years of teaching, I noticed that my inexperienced recitalists would do exactly the opposite of avoiding avoiding in just about any way one could imagine, from last-minute shopping to a boisterous lunch with friends to a late-afternoon visit to the nail salon on the day of their recital. And it was not just my students who did not orchestrate their circumstances well. Their relatives arrived on the day of the big event, often expecting to spend preconcert social time with their son or daughter. At worst, they treated it like a beauty pageant, bar mitzvah, or wedding party.

One parent hauled my soprano student off to the beauty parlor for an "updo" of her hair, a procedure that took over three hours to complete (and two cans of hairspray to cement). The resultant contraption, though beautiful, rode like a five-pound turban atop her head, with every movement a source of terror that the thing would unravel and tumble out into a mess of tresses. Bowing was out of the question.

I recall a couple who arrived the afternoon of my student's recital with two younger siblings in tow, depositing them with my student for some quality one-on-one time while they decamped to the golf club for an afternoon of adult play. I only learned of the babysitting gig *after* the performance, during which I had observed my student acting uncharacteristically flustered and making inexplicable mistakes.

In an effort to help everyone orchestrate their circumstances for success, I wrote a generic "Letter to Friends and Family," posted it on my studio's website, and now require all first-time recitalists to keep the basic template but rewrite it in their own words and share it their friends and family.

Orchestrating Circumstances for Success:
Letter to Family and Friends

Note: Italicized elements are changeable.

Dear Loved One,

Thank you for your support on this very important day! (*Add a lot more thanks here, such as "Thank you for paying for my tuition!"*) I am *excited/nervous* about my performance, so I'd like to pass on some information about how you can help me be successful. First, please remember that this performance is a requirement for *my degree/my studio* and I must pass it in order to earn my *credentials/grade/credit/admittance to graduation.*

Second, a solo performance is both a mental and physical effort. It requires my complete concentration. Therefore, I must do everything possible to clear my mind of unnecessary distractions and activities and must spend much of the time on the day before and all of the time on the day of my performance in quiet, by myself. I will be happy to greet you briefly when you arrive, but I cannot do any of the following: (*edit as necessary; however, do not take for granted what your people know or don't know. All examples are stories from real life!*)

- talk/chat/visit/catch up
- go on an extensive shopping trip with you
- make restaurant reservations for my family
- get my hair done
- get my nails done
- take my younger siblings off your hands for some one-on-one time
- other items can be added here

I know you will be proud of me on this day and will want to record it for history. However, please understand that if you *photograph or video-record* me as I am performing, it may destroy my concentration, and the project for which I have worked so hard may suffer. Therefore I ask you, please do not

- videotape me. Knowing you would want me to, I have arranged to have that done by a professional.

- take any photos of me during my performance, whether flash or nonflash. If you wish to photograph me, you may do so at the very end, while I take my final bow. I will also happily pose for you after my *concert/recital/performance* is over.

STORIES OF MPA

Finally, a commonsense and rather obvious treatment for MPA is the sharing of stories by seasoned musicians and teachers. Kenny devotes an entire book chapter to the voices of professional orchestral musicians, wisely noting that, beyond the research studies and statistical analyses, the collective wisdom of experienced musicians offers its own, unique insight into coping with MPA. What follows here are yet more accounts of coping with the stress of performance from experienced musicians, loosely organized under common themes that attend MPA.

Importance of Venue and Evaluative Threat

As Kenny notes, MPA "is usually more severe in settings involving high ego investment and evaluative threat (audience) and fear of failure."[70] The following three quotes reflect these common anxieties:

> "My level of performance anxiety is usually in direct proportion to the importance I place on the event. If I believe it really doesn't matter, I will likely be pretty relaxed. But if I believe it's a 'do or die' event, the probability for anxiety is much higher."—Rod Gilfry, baritone[71]

> "I had a teacher who once said that only stupid people never get nervous. In other words, ignorance is bliss. I believe there is some truth to that. I think that most of us suffer from performance anxiety because we are overly concerned about what others will think of us and our ability."—Stephen Pierce, pianist[72]

> "I decided to pursue music because I loved it, but for introverted 'little me' the idea of performing was not in the bargain. A month

before my junior recital, I was so jaundiced from anxiety and lack of sleep that my piano professor sent me to the doctor for tranquilizers. The turning point came during my recital when I distinctly realized that no one was going to shoot me!—I can't believe that those thoughts actually formed in my head, that on some level, I was anticipating a life-and-death situation! I eventually enjoyed a rich and fulfilling performing career. If I could do it, anyone can."—Antoinette Perry, pianist[73]

An Antidote to Perfectionism

Dianna Kenny also devotes a considerable amount of her book to perusing the etiology of performance anxiety as rooted in traumatic childhood performance or training experiences. She cautions both parents and teachers of musically gifted children to be especially aware of planting the toxic seeds of MPA by enforcing unrealistic standards of perfection. Percussionist Peter Erskine recounts this story in his autobiography, which illustrates the point:

> Professor George Gaber would prove to be a lifelong friend, a man whose wisdom, advice and love for music has accompanied me every day, and in most every circumstance, musical or otherwise. . . . He also showed me perspective, and this during our first lesson at band camp in Kentucky, my parents in attendance.
>
> Professor Gaber, intuiting and clearly sensing my post–jazz camp trauma and inherent insecurity, instructed me to play a snare drum étude on the practice pad, and to be sure *not* to play any of it correctly—to do otherwise would result in his walking over to the pad and hitting me with a drumstick. "Excuse me?" I asked. "You heard me," he answered, "I want you to play that piece of music, but if you play any of it correctly, or as written, you're going to get hit with a drumstick. Hard. Now play it." I glanced over at my mother, and she had a puzzled (if not horrified) look on her face, as if to say, "Who is this madman?" But I did as instructed, and played the snare drum étude on the practice pad, playing the notes upside down and completely out of rhythm, rendering that piece of music unrecognizable. When I felt that I had done this long enough, I stopped, and Gaber then took a satisfied puff on his cigar, said, "Good," and continued, "Now, I want you to go over to that window, look outside, and tell me what you see." I followed these instructions, and he prompted me while I

was at the window: "Is the sun still shining? Are there clouds up in the sky? The trees are still there, and it seems like the earth is still spinning, right?"

My mother was smiling now, getting the point of where Professor Gaber was going. "Now, come back to the practice pad." I did as he instructed. "You just played that snare drum piece as badly as it will ever be played. In fact, it could not be played any worse than how you played it. And yet, what happened? Absolutely nothing. Now, let's begin."

Now, if THAT'S not a life lesson then I don't know what is. In other words: it's *okay* to make mistakes. And by knowing this and acknowledging this, we remove the bogeyman who is always lurking around the corner of any difficult musical passage. That *and* practicing.[74]

Embody the Fear

Guitarist William Kanengiser says he has learned to "let the fear flow!" from the work of *body mapping* pioneer Barbara Conable. According to Conable, performers should

embody the fear. . . . Any attempt to not feel the fear splits the performer psychically into two persons, the feeler and the repressor. It is the splitting, not the fear, that limits capability. Worse, performers will reduce their body awareness in an attempt to reduce their fear. . . . It is the attempt not to feel rather than the feeling that impairs performance.[75]

Kanengiser adds,

One of my favorite approaches to the onset of performance anxiety comes from Spanish guitar virtuoso Pepe Romero, my long-time teacher and friend. Pepe once commented in his heavily perfumed Andalusian accent: "Do you know the feeling you get backstage, right before you go out? The feeling that you have butterflies in your stomach, that your knees shake so much that you can hardly stand, and that you feel like you're about to throw up?? I LOVE that!! It's because we're like a rechargeable battery: those sensations tell us that energy is flowing into our bodies, energy that we need to give to the music and to the audience. So, I don't fight those feelings, I let them flow right into me, and when I step on stage, I let them flow out to the public so that they become energized too!"[76]

Deliberate Practice Redux

Coping strategies noted throughout the expertise studies literature include the importance of being prepared. Recall that the number one anxiety producer among students in Kenny's study was inadequate preparation, but it was the number three ranked stressor among adult musicians. We may deduce several lessons from these results. First, the gap between rankings suggests that students (at least the ones in this study) had not yet developed sturdy practice habits. This gap further suggests that, as musicians progress from student to professional, they eventually learn the critical importance of practice. In fact, without practice, becoming a full-fledged professional probably will not happen:

> "In reviewing the times in my career that performance anxiety has compromised my performances—even to the point of crashing and burning onstage—I finally concluded that every failure was caused, in one way or another, by lack of preparation, in a perfect storm of procrastination and perfectionism. When these two personality traits conspired, they kept me from even starting some projects, with the rationalization 'I want to prepare perfectly, but I don't have enough time today, so I will start when I have more time.' With gathering success, I also believed more and more that I could rely on my 'talent' instead of hard work. These experiences have shown me that thorough preparation is my best protection against performance anxiety. When I am thoroughly prepared, I know that even if I make a musical or vocal mistake, I can find my way back to an optimal performance."[77]

The simple truth and power of deliberate practice also helps explain why young musicians' initial zeal can peter out when faced with the work of practice. Enthusiasm can power this work, but on its own, enthusiasm is probably only enough to sustain music-making as a hobby. And just in case a reminder is needed, as already noted throughout the preceding chapters, not just any practice will do: practice that is organized, regular, and designed to be effortful—Anderson's deliberate practice—has proven to be the most effective type of practice.

Routines and Rituals

Many performers find peace in so-called ritualized behaviors, such as wearing special jewelry, saying prayers, or reciting mantras—ditto certain pre-performance rituals or routines, such as the commonsense practice of rehearsing in or even just visiting the performance space:

> "For me, the use of reinforcing mantras (e.g., 'I can do this!'), performance scripts, visualization techniques, and performance simulation (recording myself frequently and playing for others regularly), have been the most helpful to me."—Stephen Pierce, pianist[78]

> "Regardless of the event, it helps me to repeat the mantra: 'I will do the best I can with what I've got, in the situation I'm in. And that's enough.'"—Rod Gilfry, baritone[79]

Developing positive self-talk in order to remove one's self as the center of attention and judgment and placing the shared experience of the music at the center of everyone's attention can be very liberating:

> "I have learned that anxiety can be diminished by imagining a movement outwards from me to the audience (giving, loving them, and the music) rather than inwards from the audience to me (them judging me)."—Antoinette Perry, pianist[80]

A technique similar to Perry's is to cultivate a sense of appreciation for the venue. After all, we musicians request—nay, expect—every person in the audience to give us their undivided attention. In popular music, the audience may be invited to join in by dancing, for example, but at a classical music concert, the audience is expected to remain seated, mute, and rapt throughout the entire performance. A chant of gratitude, whispered to oneself while taking the initial bow, can work to ward off the curse of performance anxiety. But more importantly, it serves as both a reminder and an invocation of what a live performance is: a shared space where audience and performer agree to intersect and fix all of their attention on the work of the omnipresent third party in this collective: the composer.

"Deliberate Calm"

Even though, as noted earlier, MPA can afflict anyone regardless of musical genre, age, gender, years of experience, or level of technical mastery, the type of performance anxiety, or "flavor"—panic or choking—is directly proportional to the degree of training. Total inexperience results in outright panic, so as already noted, the simple answer to curing panic is training. Airline pilots train to such an extent that they practice what they call "deliberate calm." The story of Captain C. B. "Sully" Sullenberger's management of deliberate calm is a case in point.

On January 15, 2009, just two minutes after US Airways flight 1549 took off from LaGuardia Airport, it hit a flock of Canadian geese. Many of these big birds were sucked up into the engines, immediately blowing the engines out (and killing the unfortunate birds). After alerting the control tower, Sullenberger and copilot Skiles first attempted to return to LaGuardia, then decided to try a nearby airport in New Jersey. However, Sullenberger quickly determined that was not possible and announced his intention to ditch the plane in the Hudson River. The flight ended there, only six minutes after takeoff, and the lives of all 155 people onboard were saved. In the many interviews following the incident, Captain Sullenberger repeatedly named education and training as the reason he did not succumb to panic:

> One way of looking at this might be that, for 42 years, I've been making small, regular deposits in this bank of experience: education and training. And on January 15th, the balance was sufficient so that I could make a very large withdrawal.[81]

Did Captain Sullenberger log his ten thousand hours? Yes, and then some: at the time of the birdstrike, he had logged 19,663 hours of pilot experience to destinations across North America, Europe, and South America.[82]

The Upside of Quitting

The topic of this chapter—performance and performance anxiety—brings us to the nexus of music-making and mental health, which requires confronting the downside of trying too hard, or what psychologists call *nonproductive persistence*.[83]

Since the advent of the positive psychology movement, the goals of happiness and well-being—that is, thriving at life and not merely surviving it—have been at the forefront of much psychological research, reviving several perennial and ultimately unremarkable assumptions: the more happiness in one's life, the more well-being, so identifying the source of one's happiness is a worthwhile pursuit. Continuing this line of reasoning, an assumed source of happiness is the development of one's strengths (or, in college-application speak, "passions"). But according to psychologists Adam Grant and Barry Schwartz,

> positive psychologists have recognized that the deficiency of a strength or virtue can harm well-being and performance, but they have paid little attention to understanding when, why, and how the *excess of a strength or virtue can harm well-being and performance.*[84]

Let us suppose that all accomplished musicians believe that their musical skill is one of their greatest strengths. Can they all therefore state that their musical skill is one of their greatest joys? The answer may not necessarily depend upon the intrinsic worth of one's skill but upon the heights one attempts with it.

Grant and Schwartz observe that "all positive traits, states, and experiences have costs that at high levels may begin to outweigh their benefits" and calculate those costs by applying previous research to the following luminaries in the pantheon of human virtues: wisdom, knowledge, courage, humanity, love, justice, temperance, and transcendence. They report the discovery of "clear evidence" for the high cost to human well-being of overweening strengths in a category that concerns us here: wisdom and knowledge, taken together.[85] People who value these twin virtues, they observe, "tend to seek out complex jobs, which provide opportunities for learning, challenges, skill development, and growth." But contrary to the popular notion that rigorous challenges always nourish health and vigor, jobs that feature high complexity can also generate high stress, disillusionment, and burnout. They surmise that, for a majority of people, well-being is highest in jobs that feature only moderate, not high, levels of complexity: a just-right Goldilocks ratio of challenge to contentment.

Similarly, by the foundational assertions of positive psychology, the perfect ratio of persistence to attainability begets a fulfilled life of purpose—provided that the seeker is capable of reaching his goals. But what happens when he is not, for various reasons, capable? What should such a person do when pressing on exceeds his capacity for inspiration and meaning and morphs instead into a soul-crushing marathon? A burgeoning line of research thus parries the assumptions of positive psychology by investigating the high cost to human health and well-being of *maladaptive persistence*, that is, persevering despite clear evidence that doing so is causing harm. One study not only shows harm to psychological health but also demonstrates an alarming rise in biological "systemic inflammation" in chronic "persisters" that, if untreated, could heighten the risk for diseases such as diabetes, osteoporosis, and atherosclerosis.[86]

One sensible solution to the problem of maladaptive persistence is starkly simple: just quit. Research on the upside of quitting has shown that

> people who can disengage from unattainable goals enjoy better well-being, have more normative patterns of cortisol secretion, and experience fewer symptoms of everyday illness than do people who have difficulty disengaging from unattainable goals.[87]

Other benefits to quitting include freed-up resources, like time and money, that can be reinvested in other pursuits. Quitting is probably not ever easy or simple; it appears especially difficult for people who are highly invested in their vocation. Yet one study (which uses the gentle euphemism *withdrawal* instead of *quitting*) finds that quitting is especially beneficial to those who have the hardest time doing so. The heavier the chains, the greater the sense of relief once they are removed.[88]

If the effects of extreme MPA are ruinous enough make musical goals unattainable, musicians should give themselves permission to at least explore the option of disengaging from those goals. The upside of quitting professional music performance in favor of the joy of avocational music-making may mean the difference between overall health and well-being versus a life filled with dread and vulnerabilities to the plethora of physical symptoms that Sapolsky's zebras distinctly do not get.

GOOD LUCK—AND BREAK A LEG!

Research in cognitive science will continue to illuminate the peculiar darkness of music performance anxiety, hopefully replacing such talismans as garlic and the reversed good-luck wishes of "Break a leg!" with proven strategies to ameliorate it. The good news is that what we can look forward to on this front comes in the twin phenomena of neurogenesis and neural plasticity. It is not a fantasy to claim that healthy brains can learn new habits of mind, retraining negative responses to music performance from a torrent of anxiety to at least a shot at a manageable onrush of happy excitement.

NOTES

1. Dianna Kenny, *The Psychology of Music Performance Anxiety* (Oxford: Oxford University Press, 2011), 85–107.

2. Ibid., 87.

3. Ibid., 12.

4. Open Science Collaboration, "Estimating the Reproducibility of Psychological Science," *Science* 349, no. 6251 (2015): aac4716.

5. Kenny, *Psychology*, 86–87.

6. Dianna Kenny, "Identifying Cut-Off Scores for Clinical Purposes for the Kenny Music Performance Anxiety Inventory (K-MPAI) in a Population of Professional Orchestral Musicians in Australia," *Polish Psychological Bulletin* (2015): 3.

7. American Psychiatric Association, *Diagnostic and Statistical Manual of Mental Disorders: DSM-V* (Arlington, VA: American Psychiatric Publishing, 2013),

8. Kenny, *Psychology*, 60.

9. American Psychiatric Association, *Diagnostic and Statistical Manual*, section 300.23 (F40.10).

10. Kenny, *Psychology*, 61.

11. Ibid., 91–93.

12. Ibid., 91.

13. Robert Sapolsky, *Why Zebras Don't Get Ulcers* (New York: W. H. Freeman, 1994), 20–23.

14. Ibid., 30–32. Sapolsky notes that the terms *noradrenaline* and *adrenaline* (with which many Americans may be familiar) are actually the British terms for *epinephrine* and *norepinephrine* (22).

15. Ibid., 48.

16. Tânia Lisboa, Alexander P. Demos, and Roger Chaffin, "Training Thought and Action for Virtuoso Performance," *Musicae Scientiae* 22, no. 4 (2018): 519–38.

17. Kenny, *Psychology*, 9.

18. Stephen M. Weiss and Arthur S. Reber, "Curing the Dreaded "Steve Blass Disease," *Journal of Sport Psychology in Action* 3, no. 3 (2012): 171–81.

19. M. S. DeCaro, R. D. Thomas, N. B. Albert, and S. L. Beilock, "Choking under Pressure: Multiple Routes to Skill Failure," *Journal of Experimental Psychology* 140, no. 3 (2011): 390–406, http://dx.doi.org/10.1037/a0023466.

20. R. S. W. Masters, "Theoretical Aspects of Implicit Learning in Sport," *International Journal of Sport Psychology* 31 (2000): 530–41.

21. Peter Gröpel and Christopher Mesagno, "Choking Interventions in Sports: A Systematic Review," *International Review of Sport and Exercise Psychology* 22 (2017), doi:10.1080/1750984X.2017.1408134.

22. Arthur Koestler, *The Act of Creation* (New York: Macmillan, 1964), 176.

23. Ibid., 173.

24. Barbara Gail Montero, "Is Monitoring One's Actions Causally Relevant to Choking under Pressure?" *Phenomenology and the Cognitive Sciences* 14, no. 2 (2015): 393.

25. Daniel M. Wegner, "How to Think, Say, or Do Precisely the Worst Thing for Any Occasion," *Science Magazine* 325, no. 5936 (2009): 48–50.

26. Daniel M. Wegner and David J. Schneider, "The White Bear Story," *Psychological Inquiry* 14, nos. 3–4 (2003): 326–29, doi:10.1207/s15327965pli1403&4_24.

27. Daniel M. Wegner, "Ironic Processes of Mental Control," *Psychological Review* 101, no. 1 (1994): 34–52.

28. See, for example, Hearts Need Art, www.heartsneedart.org/.

29. From Don Greene, presentation on performance anxiety, USC Thornton School of Music, February 2016. See also Don Greene and Melinda Marshall, *Fight Your Fear and Win: Seven Skills for Performing Your Best under Pressure* (New York: Broadway Books, 2001).

30. Kenny, *Psychology*, 167.

31. See Dianna Kenny, "Systematic Review of Treatments for Music Performance Anxiety," *Anxiety Stress & Coping* 18, no. 3 (2005): 183–208; Kenny, *Psychology*, 167–231; and Ariadna Ortiz Brugués, *Music Performance Anxiety: A Comprehensive Update of the Literature* (Newcastle-upon-Tyne, UK: Cambridge Scholars, 2019).

32. See Kenny, *Psychology*, 181.

33. Ariadna Ortiz Brugués, "Music Performance Anxiety—Part 2: A Review of Treatment Options," *Medical Problems of Performing Artists* 26, no. 3 (2011): 164–71.

34. Ibid., 168.

35. Elizabeth R. Valentine, David F. P. Fitzgerald, Tessa L. Gorton, Jennifer A. Hudson, and Elizabeth R. C. Symonds, "The Effect of Lessons in the Alexander Technique on Music Performance in High and Low Stress Situations," *Psychology of Music* 23, no. 2 (1995): 129.

36. American Society for the Alexander Technique, "The Alexander Technique," 2019, www.amsatonline.org/aws/AMSAT/pt/sp/what_is.

37. Marisa De Silva, "How Alexander Technique May Mitigate Music Performance Anxiety," unpublished research paper, December 2018, www.marisadesilva.com.

38. Valentine et al., "Effect of Lessons," 129.

39. Kenny, *Psychology*, 198.

40. Valentine et al., "Effect of Lessons," 138.

41. Ibid., 129.

42. Ibid., 139.

43. De Silva, "How Alexander Technique May Mitigate."

44. Valentine et al., "Effect of Lessons," 138.

45. Janna Delgado, "Meditation in Motion," Kripalu, 2019, https://kripalu.org/resources/meditation-motion.

46. Sat Bir S. Khalsa and Stephen Cope, "Effects of a Yoga Lifestyle Intervention on Performance-Related Characteristics of Musicians: A Preliminary Study," *Medical Science Monitor* 12, no. 8 (2006): CR325–31; Sat Bir S. Khalsa, Stephanie M. Shorter, Stephen Cope, Grace Wyshak, and Elyse Sklar, "Yoga Ameliorates Performance Anxiety and Mood Disturbance in Young Professional Musicians," *Applied Psychophysiology and Biofeedback* 34, no. 4 (2009): 279; Judith R. S. Stern, Sat Bir S. Khalsa, and Stefan G. Hofmann, "A Yoga Intervention for Music Performance Anxiety in Conservatory Students," *Medical Problems of Performing Artists* 27, no. 3 (2012): 123; and S. B. Khalsa, Bethany Butzer, Stephanie M. Shorter, Kristen M. Reinhardt, and Stephen Cope, "Yoga Reduces Performance Anxiety in Adolescent Musicians," *Alternative Therapies in Health and Medicine* 19, no. 2 (2013): 34–45.

47. Khalsa and Cope, "Effects of a Yoga Lifestyle," CR329.

48. Ibid., CR328.

49. Khalsa et al., "Yoga Ameliorates Performance Anxiety and Mood," 286.

50. Stern, Khalsa, and Hofmann, "A Yoga Intervention," 127.

51. Ibid., 127–28.

52. Khalsa, Butzer, Shorter, Reinhardt, and Cope, "Yoga Reduces Performance Anxiety," 36.

53. Ibid., 44.

54. Sapolsky, *Zebras Don't Get Ulcers*, 319.

55. Ibid., 413.

56. Vanessa J. Meyer, Yoojin Lee, Christian Böttger, Uwe Leonbacher, Amber L. Allison, and Elizabeth A. Shirtcliff, "Experience, Cortisol Reactivity, and the Coordination of Emotional Responses to Skydiving," *Frontiers in Human Neuroscience* 9, art. 138 (2015): 1–8.

57. Ibid., 5.

58. Ibid., 5–6.

59. Ibid., 6.

60. Maria Konnikova, "How People Learn to Become Resilient," *New Yorker*, February 11, 2016.

61. Golnaz Tabibnia and Dan Radecki, "Resilience Training That Can Change the Brain," *Consulting Psychology Journal: Practice and Research* 70, no. 1 (2018): 77–78.

62. Dana R. Carney, Amy J. C. Cuddy, and Andy J. Yap, "Power Posing: Brief Nonverbal Displays Affect Neuroendocrine Levels and Risk Tolerance," *Psychological Science* 21, no. 10 (2010): 1363–68.

63. Susan Dominus, "When the Revolution Came for Amy Cuddy," *New York Times*, October 18, 2017, www.nytimes.com/2017/10/18/magazine/when-the-revolution-came-for-amy-cuddy.html. See also Daniel Engber, "The Trials of Amy Cuddy: A Feminist Psychologist Was Dragged through the Mud for Her Mistakes, Did She Deserve It?" Slate, October 19, 2017, https://slate.com/technology/2017/10/did-power-posing-guru-amy-cuddy-deserve-her-public-shaming.html.

64. A. J. Cuddy, S. J. Schultz, and N. E. Fosse, "P-Curving a More Comprehensive Body of Research on Postural Feedback Reveals Clear Evidential Value for Power-Posing Effects: Reply to Simmons and Simonsohn (2017)," *Psychological Science* 29, no. 4 (2018): 656–66.

65. See Timothy D. Wilson, "Stop Bullying the 'Soft' Sciences," *Los Angeles Times*, July 12, 2012, www.latimes.com/opinion/la-xpm-2012-jul-12-la-oe-wilson-social-sciences-20120712-story.html.

66. David Biello, "Inside the Debate about Power Posing: A Q & A with Amy Cuddy," Ted.Com, February 22, 2017, https://ideas.ted.com/inside-the-debate-about-power-posing-a-q-a-with-amy-cuddy/.

67. Joanne C. Chang, Elizabeth Midlarsky, and Peter Lin, "Effects of Meditation on Musical Performance Anxiety," *Medical Problems of Performing Artists* 18, no. 3 (2003): 126–30.

68. Daniel F. Gucciardi and James A. Dimmock, "Choking under Pressure in Sensorimotor Skills: Conscious Processing or Depleted Attentional Resources?" *Psychology of Sport and Exercise* 9, no. 1 (2008): 45–59.

69. Wegner, "How to Think," 50.

70. Kenny, *Psychology*, 61.

71. Thornton Musicians' Wellness Committee, "Overcoming Performance Anxiety," University of Southern California Thornton School of Music, March 30, 2016.

72. Ibid.

73. Ibid.

74. Peter Erskine, *No Beethoven: An Autobiography & Chronicle of Weather Report* (Fuzzy Music, 2013), 36–37.

75. Barbara Conable and William Conable, *How to Learn the Alexander Technique: A Manual for Students* (Portland, OR: Andover Press, 1995), 115.

76. Thornton Musicians' Wellness Committee, "Overcoming Performance Anxiety."

77. Rod Gilfrey, personal e-mail correspondence.

78. Ibid.

79. Ibid.

80. Ibid.

81. Katie Couric, "Capt. Sully Worried about Airline Industry," CBS, February 10, 2009, www.cbsnews.com/news/capt-sully-worried-about-airline-industry/.

82. Alex Altman, "Chesley B. Sullenberger III," *Time*, January 16, 2009, www.time.com/time/nation/article/0,8599,1872247,00.html.

83. Dean B. McFarlin, Roy F. Baumeister, and Jim Blascovich, "On Knowing When to Quit: Task Failure, Self-Esteem, Advice, and Nonproductive Persistence," *Journal of Personality* 52, no. 2 (1984): 138–55.

84. Adam Grant and Barry Schwartz, "Too Much of a Good Thing: The Challenge and Opportunity of the Inverted U," *Perspectives on Psychological Science* 6, no. 1 (2011): 62 (emphasis mine).

85. Ibid., 63.

86. Gregory E. Miller and Carsten Wrosch, "You've Gotta Know When to Fold 'Em: Goal Disengagement and Systemic Inflammation in Adolescence," *Psychological Science* 18, no. 9 (2007): 776.

87. Ibid., 773.

88. Ibid., 774.

7

THE DIGITAL BRAIN

By many measures, the effects of the aptly named digital revolution and the information age have been not merely analogous to the effects of such breakthrough inventions as the printing press, the microscope, the automobile, the television, and the birth control pill but have delivered a cultural wallop possibly equal in force to all of those innovations combined. The magnitude of this effect begins with the sheer reach of digital media via the World Wide Web, reflected in such mind-numbing statistics as international Internet use (currently more than 3.7 billion humans regularly access it) and the number of daily Internet searches (Google alone processes 3.5 billion searches per day).[1] Figure 7.1 is a fascinating snapshot of "what happens in an Internet minute."[2]

What might this glut of information be doing to our brains? That is exactly the question that author Nicholas Carr set out to investigate, first in his provocative landmark essay "Is Google Making Us Stupid?" and then in his bestselling book (a finalist for the 2011 Pulitzer Prize in nonfiction), *The Shallows: What the Internet Is Doing to Our Brains.* Implicit in both of Carr's titles is one of the central conclusions he reached: the way we gather information from the Web has not just changed the way we read; it has changed the way we think.

The cornucopia of information now available on the Internet at the click of a mouse is unprecedented in human history, its embedded treasures unquestionably rich. But this bounty comes at a price, for when information exceeds the brain's *cognitive load capacity* (the limit of our short-term memory), our ability to draw critical connections be-

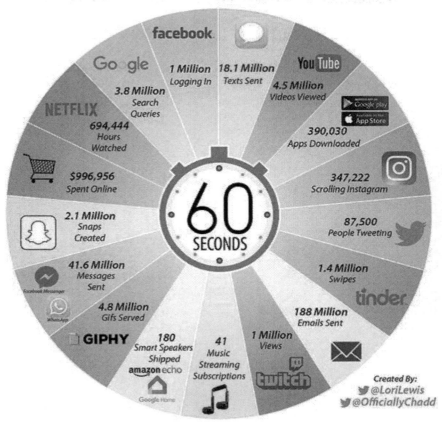

Figure 7.1. Digital Activities in an "Internet Minute."

tween new information and the things we already know—the dynamic core of learning called *constructive memory*—disintegrates. Instead of diving deep into our brains, in Carr's description, we "zip along the surface like a guy on a Jet Ski."[3]

The brain's amazing ability to remodel its operating systems in response to a stimulus is due to its incredibly plastic nature. But the brain has never before encountered the vast and relentless stimuli of digital media; hence there is growing concern that the remodeling of the human mind is proceeding at a scale and pace unique in human experience, regardless if one is a so-called digital native (born into the digital age) or a digital immigrant (a migrant to the digital age).[4]

Understanding the cognitive implications of technology use is essential for both natives and immigrants, for when it comes to the digital revolution, all perspectives are needed. In the words of Sherry Turkle, psychologist and director of the Massachusetts Institute of Technology's Initiative on Technology and Self, "because we grew up with the Net, we assume that the Net is grown up. We tend to see what we have now as the technology in its maturity. But in fact, we are in early days."[5]

While there are many differing opinions on technology's merits and pitfalls, there is broad agreement on one key point: the technological revolution (often referred to in catastrophic meteorological terms as a "flood" or "hurricane") is over. Although some might yearn for a return to a former, less digitally interconnected era, this desire is simply not realistic: we live in a digital age, and technology is here to stay. Nevertheless, just because the floodwaters of this particular revolution have subsided, we need not be complacent about what has washed up on our collective shores. At the same time, while we are yet in the relatively early days of the digital age, we are also, as Turkle advises, "well past the time to take the measure of what the costs are."[6] Let us begin taking those measures for musicians with the good news.

DIGITAL HEAVEN

On the upside, human endeavors as disparate as medicine, marketing, and music have all been enhanced by the ability of their practitioners to harness the riches of the information age.

For musicians, the once-cumbersome and expensive aspects of self-management have all been utterly transformed by digital media. Tasks like producing recordings, printing letterhead and business cards, distributing publicity photos, and networking with other professionals can all be accomplished in record time and with polished results on the slimmest of budgets. For the international musician, smartphone applications provide instant access to online dictionaries, translations, currency converters, and GPS navigation systems. On any continent, we can stay connected with agents, colleagues, and coaches around the clock if we want, and indeed such connection is now practically expected.

For music teachers, the benefits experienced through the use of new technology are many, translating as they do into increases in those two most basic of resources, time and money. Social media group pages make it possible to stay in touch with both parents and clients, advertising upcoming concerts, touting accomplishments, and tagging events of interest. Online scheduling apps have taken the tedium out of booking appointments, while mobile payment and budgeting systems streamline financial record keeping.

For music students, recording lessons is not only simpler than in the old cassette and VHS tape days, but like photos, these data files can be posted and shared immediately. Recorded lessons and rehearsals grant instant access to the augmented feedback they provide, offering heretofore unparalleled opportunities for speeding up the acquisition of the motor skills we call *technique*. The plethora of apps for music practice, education, and just pure music enjoyment are seemingly boundless, since new apps pop up at an estimated rate of over six thousand per day, and old apps are either updated or abandoned by the wisdom of their user crowd. And it is here that the list of digital media marvels shall stop, for, like the apps, these wonders will continue to breed at a rate impossible to tally. Now to exit digital heaven, with the observation that whatever else one believes, the fact that digital media is a potent force is undeniable. Whether that force be turned to good or ill, harnessed for human benefit or revealed to be a cyborg slave master of dystopian fiction, is a central question of the digital age.

TROUBLE IN PARADISE: THE "SCREEN INVASION"

At the start of the new millennium and especially after the release of the first iPhone in 2007, scientists, mental health experts, and investigative journalists began to sound alarms about the effects of digital media on human attention, productivity, safety, relationships, health, and happiness. Countering ecstatic reports from the digital front came unsettling tales, such as *New York Times* reporter Matt Richtel's 2010 Pulitzer Prize–winning series "Driven to Distraction," which was credited by the Pulitzer committee for "stimulating widespread efforts to curb distracted driving."[7] In his series of ten articles, Richtel introduces the evocative term *screen invasion* to describe how ubiquitous our devices had become even then:

> At one time, a screen meant maybe something in your living room. But now it's something in your pocket. So it goes everywhere. And I guess we've all experienced it. It can be behind the wheel. It can be at the dinner table. It can be—(I guess we'll get this interview started off on the right, and slightly off-color note): It can be in the bathroom.[8]

Richtel's work finally got the attention of the insurance industry, which had to take note when a study revealed that texting drivers risked a 23 percent increase in the possibility for collisions.[9]

Around the same time, an alarming uptick in sprained ankles at emergency rooms around the country was sleuthed out as due to texting while walking, eventually spurring the American Academy of Orthopaedic Surgeons to launch its distracted-walking campaign Digital Deadwalkers.[10]

Other experts were more interested in the human brain as the foundational source of these crashes and twisted joints—and more to the point, what was hijacking it? Gary Small, professor of psychiatry and biobehavioral sciences at the University of California, Los Angeles (UCLA), was one of the first to study the effects of digital media on the brain by taking MRI scans of two distinct types of brains—those of digital natives and those of naive subjects (people over the age of fifty who were "new to computer technology, but willing to give it a try")—while carrying out two different activities: reading a book and conducting a Google search. While the scans showed that the two groups did not evince any differences when reading a book, the brains of computer-savvy users showed a twofold increase in activity in their front portions (known as the decision-making center of the brain) when on the Internet as opposed to when they read a book. This finding made sense, in Small's words, "because we know we're making lots of decisions when we're searching online."[11] However, Small's research revealed something else: the brains of the naive subjects showed "little to no activation" in this region when on Google. Why was this?

At the time of Small's study (2008), it was still possible to find enough naive subjects to participate in the project.[12] The brains of these naive subjects were simply not habituated to Web-browsing, so they had not developed the neural pathways needed to surf the Internet. As such, they did not qualify as digital immigrants. So Small and his team had their naive subjects train their brains by searching the Web just one hour a day for five days. After this training interval, they all returned to the lab, where they were retested while performing a Google search. The results were rather astonishing: the exact same neural circuitry in the front part of the brain that in the computer-savvy group had activated during Internet use now had become active in the naive subjects, within only a few days' time. The naive subjects had morphed into digital immigrants. The researchers had captured, in effect, the observable evolution of the human brain. This finding caused Small and his colleagues to wonder,

> If our brains are so sensitive to just an hour a day of computer exposure, what happens when we spend more time? What about the brains of young people, whose neural circuitry is even more malleable and plastic? What happens to their brains when they spend their average eight hours daily with their high tech toys and devices?[13]

The "eight hours daily" figure referenced by Small comes from a 2004 Kaiser Family Foundation study showing that, due to the alchemy of multitasking, eight- to eighteen-year-olds managed to cram eight hours of media content into just six and a half hours of actual time by the clock—a nuanced point not quite accurately captured by Small's description but still a rather stunning statistic. Nevertheless, five years later, the Kaiser researchers reported that those levels of exposure had been "shattered." By 2009, young people were able to stuff a whopping ten hours and forty-five minutes of content into a seven-and-a-half-hour time frame.[14]

Six years after that, a study released in 2015 by the nonprofit organization Common Sense Media found that teenagers between the ages of thirteen and eighteen used an average of nine actual hours of entertainment media per day, and "tweens" (ages eight to twelve) used an average of six actual hours a day of entertainment media. This figure does not include time spent using digital media while at school or for homework.[15]

And herein lies one of the most distinguishing characteristics of the digital age: its ability to perpetually outdistance its own outrageous statistics. And as each new study reveals statistics more disturbing than the last, digital immigrants' concern ratchets up from a creeping sense of unease to full-blown anxiety that the digital natives in their care obsess over their gadgets and, like Tolkien's Gollum who clutches his "Precious," refuse to release their grip on the tiny keyboard beneath their fingertips. Psychotherapist and writer Gary Greenberg relates the following story of what happened when he asked a teen client to relinquish her cell phone:

> Before she could sit down, I asked Kate to hand me her phone. Her parents, already seated, froze as she swung her head around and trained her eyes on me. It was, I realized, the first time we'd made eye contact, and what I saw was a mixture of fear and anger not unlike that of a raccoon cornered in a vegetable patch by an irate gardener wielding a shovel.
>
> "Why?" she demanded. "Because I have a really hard time concentrating when you're distracted," I said. "I keep wondering what's going on your phone, and I figure that whatever it is must be more interesting than what's going on in here."
>
> "Well, that's for sure."
>
> "I'm certain that's true," I said. "Nothing here can compete with what's on your phone. But sometimes we have to pay attention to less interesting things." I reached out my hand, and she put the phone in it. It was warm and moist. I thought I could feel the indentation of her fingers on its rounded edges. "It seems almost like this phone is part of you," I said as I put it on my desk. "Like another limb or something."
>
> "No duh," she said. "It is." She held my eyes. There was no shame or defensiveness in them now, let alone fear. Just contempt.[16]

But these obsessive tendencies are no longer the province of the young; they also occur among their parents and educators, many of whom are as yet digital immigrants. Who says you can't teach an old dog new tricks? As Small's experiment proves, even that old saw has been overturned through the doctrine of neural plasticity, which, as you saw in chapter 3, is a double-edged sword. Although new tricks can certainly be learned at almost any advanced age, they cannot be guaranteed to be healthy tricks. Digital natives and immigrants alike have acquired the new trick of multitasking that, in the information age, has morphed far from its original meaning of managing several manual tasks (minding the children while foraging for food) to juggling two or more cognitive tasks, abetted by technology.

MULTITASKING: "DUMBING DOWN THE WORLD"

The term *multitask* first appeared in the nascent computer-technology field of the 1960s, but after the advent of the World Wide Web in the 1990s, the word was absorbed into the popular lexicon. While pursuing many tasks at the same time has been a part of human activity for millennia, the current manifestation of the term *multitasking* refers to the mingling of two or more technology-based tasks: reading e-mail while listening to music, texting while watching television, or driving a car while following a GPS and talking on a smartphone. Research on human multitasking in the digital environment has zeroed in on the following parameters:

—⟲⟲⟲—

Multitasking Parameters

Attentional Filtering: The ability to successfully filter relevant from irrelevant information while multitasking.

Organization of Thoughts: Keeping the cognitive results of multitasking organized in the brain for later retrieval.

Task Switching: Shifting from task to task and returning to an important task after distraction or interruption.

Task-Switch Cost: The time lapse when changing from task to task and associated costs in cognition, productivity, health, and human happiness.

—⟲⟲⟲—

Multiple studies show that the vast majority of people manage all these parameters extremely poorly when pelted with digital distractions due to our limited attentional capacity—that is, the number of thoughts we can keep in play at one time. That number, famously posited by cognitive science pioneer George Miller as "the magical number seven, plus or minus two," is currently estimated to be about four. The take-home message is it is very difficult for people to pay deep attention to more than one thing at a time. Nevertheless, most of us vastly overrate our ability to do so.

Communications professor Clifford Nass conducted some of the very first studies of multitaskers at Stanford University, and the results were (to quote an adjective that Nass uttered seven times in just one interview) "scary."[17] Nass's team set up two related experiments, choosing as their subjects so-called high multitaskers, that is, students who do "five, six or more things at once, all the time."[18] The first experiment attempted to discover whether multitaskers can focus and not become distracted, and the second considered the efficacy with which multitaskers shifted from one task to another. A significant note at the outset of these experiments is what the three members of the Stanford research team believed they would find. Their hypothesis was that the subjects would be "stars at something," be it filtering (the ability to disregard irrelevant information), task switching, or keeping the bounty of their multitasking searches organized in their brains. Their findings?

> We were absolutely shocked. We all lost our bets. It turns out multitaskers are terrible at every aspect of multitasking. They're terrible at ignoring irrelevant information; they're terrible at keeping information in their head nicely and neatly organized; and they're terrible at switching from one task to another.[19]

Contrast Nass's "terrible" rating with the self-assessments of habitual multitasking digital natives, like this MIT student interviewed for a PBS documentary:

> I feel like the professors here [at MIT] do have to accept that we can multitask very well, and that we do at all times. And so if they try and, you know, restrict us from doing it, it's almost unfair because we are completely capable, moving in between lecture and other things and just keeping track of the many things that are going on in our lives.[20]

In Nass's estimation—before his untimely death in 2013—members of the tribe of digital natives, who constitute the demographic that is most engaged in multitasking, are most certain of its efficiency and are most blinded by überconfidence in their ability to flit between tasks with no detriment to learning. He observed that, while "virtually all multitaskers think they are brilliant at multitasking"—especially digital natives—his findings revealed "one of the big new items here, and one of the big discoveries is, you know what? You're really lousy at it."[21] But Nass also stressed that an impetus for his research was the burgeoning habit of multitasking among people of all ages and abilities around the globe, digital natives and immigrants alike, or what Nass called "made multitaskers." He noted with concern that,

> in a world where multitasking is being pushed on more and more people, we could be essentially undermining the thinking ability of our society. . . . And frankly, we're seeing this across the world, from the least developed countries to the most developed countries. Multitasking is one of the most dominant trends in the use of media, so we could be essentially dumbing down the world.[22]

Because multitasking is toxic to attention, by extension it necessarily degrades learning itself, thus Nass's chilling assessment does not seem far-fetched. Echoing Nass, researchers at UCLA declare bluntly that "multitasking adversely affects how you learn."[23] Not only did their study subjects demonstrate significant decrements in their ability to recall the facts that they had attempted to learn while pelted with distractions, but they were also unable to predict what might happen during subsequent trials based on their experiences in the first trial. The latter result is no small finding for our ability to predict cause and effect based on past experiences is the essence of learning (recall Gary Marcus's admonition that "the ability to learn starts with the ability to remember"[24]). These learning decrements were due, in part, to where the learned items were stored by the multitaskers. It seems that multitasking creates a kind of filing error. How might this occur?

Recall that, as we progress through our day (and indeed, our lives), our accumulated sticky notes of experience pile up in short-term memory, where they are parsed as declarative or procedural, then sent on their way to long-term storage. The UCLA researchers found that the information the test subjects gathered while multitasking (information that should have been stored as declarative learning, or facts) was instead shunted to parts of the brain that encode procedural learning, which is the province of motor skills. This storage error made the learned facts, in the words of the lead researcher, "less flexible"—that is, more elusive for retrieval. And facts that are misfiled in this way are not merely clerical errors. Retrieval is proof that learning happened—a thing cannot be said to have been learned if it cannot be retrieved and successfully repeated. In this light, Nass's catastrophic forecast about the regression of human learning due to the pall of multitasking seems entirely plausible.

What might this information mean for musicians? Given that music teaching, learning, and performance all rely on both declarative and procedural learning, it seems rather obvious that we should, at the very least, be concerned with where our acquired music information is stored and whether we really need neuroscientists to admonish us, as the UCLA researchers did. To "concentrate while [we're] studying" might depend upon the degree to which we allow interruptions from digital media to intrude on our practice time.

INTERRUPTION SCIENCE AND ACQUIRED ATTENTION DEFICIT DISORDER

In the workplace, the twin specters of interruption and stress currently haunting the modern office environment have spawned a specialty niche in personnel circles: *attention management* and *interruption science* are now bona fide subjects and are hot topics in business news and on the lecture circuit. Gloria Mark, a leading researcher in these new fields, has conducted multiple studies on *information workers* (also called *knowledge workers*), that is, those who wield ideas rather than jackhammers for a living. In several seminal studies, Mark and her fellow researchers found that information workers (labeled "informants") switched tasks frequently: on average, every three minutes.[25] Even when these tasks were linked or "thematically connected," the informants spent only eleven minutes focused within what Mark called "working spheres" before switching themselves to a different sphere (an internal disruption) or being interrupted by an external force, like a phone call or a request from a manager. Interestingly, the informants were just as likely to interrupt themselves as to be interrupted externally.

A more alarming component of Mark's research is her finding that, once interrupted, her informants took an average of twenty-five minutes to reconnect to their first, or central, task.[26] This lost time is task-switch cost, and according to multiple researchers who have studied it, the cost is steep. Think of it: if nearly a half hour of productivity is lost each time a worker switches tasks and he changes between working spheres every eleven minutes, is it any wonder that the task-switch cost spent in a cognitive fog of "Where was I?" is estimated to be in the 40 percent range?[27]

If we apply this calculation to a musician's practice hour, the results are an appalling loss of twenty-four minutes of practice time per hour. This lost work time is alarming enough, but with the addition of the UCLA research, we you can see that the quality of the remaining thirty-six minutes of practice time will be degraded as well. Imagine how this might play out. If a musician's paltry, leftover thirty-six minutes of practice attention is divided between figuring out her fingering, answering texts from her partner who left for work and forgot to crate the puppy, and checking her home webcam to make sure that Fluffy isn't ripping up the carpet, there is a good chance her work will be cognitively misfiled, degrading the paltry amount of leftover practice time even further.

There is one obvious solution to both the steep task-switch cost and filing error problems: turn the cell phone off and stow it out of sight during practice and rehearsal stints. There is compelling research to show that the familiar buzz, chime, or chirp of an incoming message, even the silent physical presence of a cell phone, offers temptations to connect that can negatively impact cognition. It also appears that, the more challenging the task, the more likely we are to self-distract, and a smartphone dotted with candy-colored apps provides an enticing escape pod:

> Once attention has been shifted to the smartphone for one purpose (e.g., by virtue of a specific notification source), users often then engage in a chain of subsequent task-unrelated acts on the smartphone, thereby extending the period of disruption. . . . And, some evidence suggests that the more "rich" (e.g., including a visual image rather than just text) the information encountered during an interruption, the more detrimental the distraction is likely to be with respect to primary task completion.[28]

Multitasking results in high task-switch cost, filing errors, and procrastination. If these symptoms are not enough motivation to relinquish our digital devices during practice, perhaps the high cost to human health posed by constant interruptions is.

ZEBRAS DON'T MULTITASK, EITHER

By the tenets of the information age, multitasking seems to be a veritable job requirement for information workers, who may watch a video clip, surf the Web, type a document, and answer a question from the boss all at the same time. In the effort to manage the gush of information coming at them, Mark shows that knowledge workers tend to work faster and thus under greater pressure than if they were to concentrate on just one task alone. So multitasking's signature feature—high-density, high-pressure work—can also beget great gobs of stress.[29]

To test this, Mark and her team measured the effect of e-mail use on information workers by dividing their subjects into two groups: those who gave up e-mail completely for five days (but continued to use computers) and those who continued to use e-mail, unfettered, while at work. All were attached to heart monitors for the duration of the study. The e-mailing subjects switched screen windows, on average, thirty-seven times an hour, while the e-mail-deprived subjects switched eighteen times an hour on average. For the e-mailers, all that screen switching and message processing kept them in a "steady 'high alert' state" (as measured by their heart-rate monitors). As you learned from Sapolsky's zebras, stress that is unabated rather than doled out in spurts only as needed releases stress hormones that, among other evils visited on our vital organs, have recently been linked to the death of brain cells.[30]

By contrast, the e-mail dieters suffered less task-switch cost and also displayed normal heart rates. Thus Mark and colleagues conclude that taking breaks from e-mail is beneficial for both productivity and health—as long as people give up their digital habits of their own volition. However, it appears that being unconnected may generate adult information workers' own version of adolescent FOMO (fear of missing out). An interesting twist in the details of this particular study is that the researchers had trouble finding enough volunteers willing to voluntarily digitally disconnect for five days.[31]

So what are today's knowledge workers to do with this information? In order for them to succeed in the digital environment, they must, by necessity, multitask. A journalist who interviewed Mark conjures Carr's jet-skiing multitasker when he observes that, for knowledge workers like himself, "it seems your attention must skip like a stone across water all day long, touching down only periodically."[32] Indeed, Carr was propelled to study the effects of the information age when he noted with alarm that, as a knowledge worker himself, he was no longer able to maintain sustained attention on his target while fishing in the endless stream of Internet information:

> Over the past few years I've had an uncomfortable sense that someone, or something, has been tinkering with my brain, remapping the neural circuitry, reprogramming the memory. My mind isn't going—so far as I can tell—but it's changing. I'm not thinking the way I used to think. I can feel it most strongly when I'm reading. Immersing myself in a book or a lengthy article used to be easy. My mind would get caught up in the narrative or the turns of the argument, and I'd spend hours strolling through long stretches of prose. That's rarely the case anymore. Now my concentration often starts to drift after two or three pages. I get fidgety, lose the thread, begin looking for something else to do. I feel as if I'm always dragging my wayward brain back to the text. The deep reading that used to come naturally has become a struggle.[33]

Something had changed for Carr, something he initially labeled "troubles with reading" but that he eventually came to recognize as far more worrying: "my inability to pay attention to more than one thing for a couple of minutes."[34] "What the Net seems to be doing," observed Carr, "is chipping away my capacity for concentration and contemplation."[35] Carr informally polled friends (mostly knowledge workers like himself) and found that others were experiencing the same symptoms.

At around the same time, two psychiatrists independently introduced new terms that describe Carr's and his friends' experiences. *Acquired attention deficit disorder* and *attention deficit trait*, put forward by John Ratey and Edward M. Hallowell, respectively, posit that heavy technology use and multitasking may be actually *creating* attention deficit disorders (ADDs) in people not otherwise susceptible to them.[36] Indeed, Nass's early research reveals that, the more chronic his subjects' multitasking habits, the less they can ignore the irrelevant distractions that Nass's team embed in experiments designed to measure distractibility, spurring Nass to theorize that habitual multitasking degrades attentional abilities over time. As you've already learned, brains can be remodeled both for good and for ill.

INTERNET ADDICTION

As if acquired ADD were not enough cause for concern, a growing cohort of experts note the potential for outright addiction to the Internet and other digital media. This view is lent credence by what the late neuroscientist Jaak Panksepp named SEEKING, our hardwired behavior bequeathed by evolution that is motivated, in part, by the dopamine rush that rewards our brain once we crack open what we are seeking— be it a tasty morsel of food contained inside a shell (a nut, an oyster) or an e-message locked inside a link. (Panksepp preferred to capitalize these "genetically ingrained brain emotional operating systems" to underscore the magnitude of their importance.[37])

Panksepp, a founder of the field of *affective neuroscience*, theorized that there are seven foundational instincts that propel human behavior: RAGE, FEAR, PANIC, LUST, CARE, PLAY, and SEEKING, with the latter being the common thread that links them all. Panksepp described SEEKING as

> a general-purpose neuronal system that helps coax animals and humans to move energetically from where they are presently situated to the places where they can find and consume the fruits of this world.[38]

Panksepp believed that this SEEKING system is fueled in part by our body's "dopamine circuits," which

> tend to energize and coordinate the functions of many higher brain areas that mediate planning and foresight (such as the amygdala, nucleus accumbens, and frontal cortex) and promote states of eagerness and directed purpose in both humans and animals. It is no wonder that animals are eager to self-stimulate this system via indwelling electrodes. It now seems clear that many psychostimulant drugs commonly abused by humans, especially the amphetamines and cocaine, produce their psychic appeal by temporarily overarous-

ing this emotional system. To some extent, other drugs such as opiates, nicotine, and alcohol also derive their hedonic appeal by interacting with this system.[39]

But the complexities of our dopamine circuits proved to be just as inconvenient to the news media in the brain-obsessed 1990s as the nuances behind the Mozart effect. Like a teen influencer in the age of social media, dopamine broke free of the fusty confines of science and burst on the scene as "the pleasure hormone," justifying everything from cupcake cravings to sex addiction to Americans' mania for firearms. If the devil made me do it, the devil now sported a biological cloak that excused our naughty behavior, spawning dopamine's kitschy reputation as "the Kim Kardashian of neurotransmitters."[40] Yet as smartly explained by British psychologist Vaughan Bell, by rejecting the complex nature of this neurotransmitter as too complicated, tabloid journalism missed out on "how weird dopamine really is."[41] For while dopamine is indeed one chemical, it has many different functions in the brain depending on which system it is operating within and which of its various receptors receives it.

Scientists who suspected that dopamine was overemphasized in the pleasure-reward cycle expanded their research to a network of other neurochemicals, including naturally occurring opiates and cannabinoids (yes, the human body produces endogenous versions of both). One of those researchers was neuropsychologist Kent Berridge, who began to suspect in the late 1980s that dopamine was not the only player in the SEEKING system and eventually came to the conclusion that wanting and liking are not, neurobiologically speaking, the same thing.

Berridge believes that dopamine does fuel desire but that our actual pleasure center is a much smaller and "more fragile" neural system than our wanting system. He and colleague Terry Robinson have produced substantial evidence from both human and animal studies to show distinctly different brain mechanisms for wanting and liking the same reward to the extent that often the thrill of the chase proves more satisfying than the actual catch. These insights advanced their *incentive-sensitization theory of addiction* to explain how wanting can metastasize from Panksepp's SEEKING to pathological wanting—the well-known phenomenon of chasing a bigger and bigger high.[42] As Berridge explains it, if dopamine provided us with happiness, it would make [drug] addicts happier than nonaddicts, or let them get more pleasure from a smaller dose of drugs. That's clearly not the case. When we looked deeper into this, we found that dopamine provided the wanting mechanism in the brain, rather than the pleasure mechanism. That's why addicts want more and more, whether it be in the form of binge-eating, gambling, or drugs. And when there's an imbalance between wanting and pleasure, such as for addicts, it actually leads to unhappiness.[43]

Of course, not all wanting is excessive or inherently destructive or even sensory. There is, for example, the pleasure of intellectual stimulation and discovery, and it is this that leads many people (particularly knowledge workers) to deny that the hours they spend on their screens transcend the boundaries of ordinary stimulation and descend into full-on *addiction*. This loaded term attached itself to heavy Internet use in the heady decade of the 1990s, and by the 2000s, the idea that digital media could spawn genuine addiction had gained significant traction among experts and ordinary folk alike. In 2008, Small had this to say about it:

I think [digital media] is addictive. There's controversy among experts whether it is or not. In Asia, there's a recognition that teenagers, many teenagers, are addicted to video games. I think we're behind the Asians in terms of focusing on the problem. . . . We're immersed in it. And it's changing so rapidly, we're just beginning to grasp what's happening. So, think of how long it took us to understand that smoking was bad for our health. I think it takes people a while for reality to hit them in the face. It's hard to get people to stop texting while they're driving, although it's a twenty-three times greater risk of having an accident. How do you get people to stop these behaviors? It's very difficult.[44]

A decade later, while more experts agree with Small's assessment, Internet addiction disorder has yet to be officially recognized as a bona fide mental disorder in the most recent edition of the *Diagnostic and Statistical Manual of Mental Disorders*.[45]

The main sticking point is whether "excessive behavioral patterns" (like excessive Internet or smartphone use) can be addictive in the same way that substances like alcohol and opioids are.[46] While the DSM-V authors take a step in that direction with the recognition of *gambling disorder*, citing neuroscience evidence that "gambling behaviors activate reward systems similar to those activated by drugs of abuse" (channeling Berridge's incentive-sensitization theory of addiction), they conclude that there is insufficient peer-reviewed evidence to label compulsive sex, excessive Internet use, or video gaming as outright "addictions" and instead choose the safer path of including them in a list of conditions for further study.[47] This caution is somewhat remarkable given the considerable criticism lobbed at the secretive DSM-V revision committee for its willingness to treat many other problematic human behaviors as true illnesses and addictions.[48] The World Health Organization, on the other hand, has showed no such restraint and has added *gaming disorder* to gambling disorder in the eleventh revision of its own manual, the *International Statistical Classification of Diseases and Related Health Problems* (ICD-11).[49]

Meanwhile, a growing number of people, both experts and ordinary folks, have simply declared the outright existence of Internet addiction disorder and Internet gaming disorder based on direct and often personal experience. And Internet aficionados continue to deride the idea of addiction, citing the paucity of scientific evidence. This schism seems about right for a disorder that began as a farce.

In 1995, a New York psychiatrist named Ivan K. Goldberg posted a sham disorder as a joke on a website that he had founded for fellow psychiatrists, dubbed it "Internet addiction disorder," and dressed it up in DSM language for good measure. To his surprise (and apparently everlasting chagrin), several of his colleagues responded by fessing up to their own struggles with "IAD," prompting Goldberg to cry uncle and set up an online IAD support group, which was soon flooded with hundreds of people seeking help. He later refined his original invention to "pathological Internet-use disorder" but never seemed to own his invention outright, disavowing the term *addiction*—"to medicalize every behavior by putting it into psychiatric nomenclature is ridiculous," he said—recommending instead that people who overuse the Internet should "get themselves into psychotherapy and work out why they hide behind a keyboard."[50]

Neither Goldberg's mockery nor his disavowal of Internet addiction stopped the late psychologist Kimberly Young from officially proposing the existence of it in a formal setting in 1996.[51] Young went on to write several popular books on the topic, founded a center for the treatment of Internet addiction, and in 2013 partnered with a Pennsylvania hospital to cofound the first inpatient treatment center for the supposed disorder—"supposed" because, as news releases at the time noted, the $14,000 price tag for treatment was not covered by insurance due to the malady's nonrecognition by the DSM-V.[52]

So where do things currently stand? Is IAD a real malady or not? This is the question that a largely British group of researchers set out to answer by first sidestepping the addiction question and bestowing the more easily digestible name *problematic Internet use* (PIU) on the affliction. They conducted a meta-analysis of approximately three thousand participants across forty studies to see what might turn up regarding cognitive impairment due to problematic Internet use, reasoning that "confirmation of cognitive deficits in PIU would support the neurobiological plausibility of this disorder." Their conclusion is that the aggregated meta-analysis

> provides firm evidence that PIU (defined broadly and operationally) is associated with cognitive impairments in motor inhibitory control, working memory, Stroop attentional inhibition [a type of executive function test] and decision-making.[53]

While the authors are clearly pleased to be able to claim a "vital first step towards a better understanding of PIU, supporting its existence as a biological plausible entity associated with dysfunction of frontostriatal brain circuitry," they also concede that it is not possible to determine, in this type of cross-sectional analysis, whether the list of cognitive deficits are present in the people represented in these studies *before* the onset of PIU.[54] After all, this particular list of cognitive impairments mirrors those of *attention-deficit hyperactivity disorder* (ADHD), creating a chicken-or-egg conundrum that plagues much psychological research: to wit, does PIU actually *cause* ADHD (as Ratey's theory of acquired attention deficit disorder suggests), or are ADHD folks just more prone to digital media overload due to their poor impulse control and decision-making?

More to the point: where do we go from here—or, as another recent meta-analysis on Internet addiction was (in part) titled, "Quo Vadis?" This study reveals a significant acceleration in the rate of publication on the topic of Internet addiction, from three articles in 1996, to over fifteen hundred articles cited in PubMed on Internet addiction in 2015.[55] And at the time of this writing, a simple search for articles using the phrase "Internet addiction" on PubMed returns just under three thousand results. Clearly something is up and troubling our collective psyche. While experts debate the parameters of addiction, an urgent and relevant question for the rest of us is "Who benefits from heavy technology use?"

WHO IS MINDING THE STORE?

Determined information workers and fervent technology geeks note that there is still, at present, little research that demonstrably proves the negative effects of digital technology on our brains. Even the British meta-analysis team acknowledge the "paucity of rigorous meta-analyses from which to draw firm conclusions and examine potential moderators."[56] But an absence of evidence does not equal proof positive that there is none to be found. A larger question looms: Why isn't anyone studying the effects of the screen invasion on our brains?

One answer lies in the rapid growth of technology itself, which makes the subject matter a moving target and nearly impossible to pin down. Researchers who attempt to study it face a Sisyphean task:

> By the time you design a research study, apply for funding, implement the study, and you publish the results about the technology, what has happened? The technology's obsolete. We moved beyond it. And so the technology and the practices that go with the new technologies, they keep outdistancing the research. The research can't catch up with it.[57]

A second but perhaps more fundamental consideration is funding, which introduces another vexing question: In whose interest would it be to fund research on the cognitive effects of digital technology? And if that research should vindicate the late Dr. Young and others, who warned that, even worse than "dumbing [us] down," digital technology has the addictive power to enslave us, in whose interest would it be for consumers and companies to break the digital chains and unplug?

Surely not in the interest of Facebook, the titan of social media sites, said by *Forbes* in 2018 to be number four of the "World's Most Valuable

Brands" and valued at a total net worth of $94.8 billion in 2018, with 2.3 billion active users monthly.[58] Facebook has estimated that every day, two billion people use at least one of the Facebook "family of services" (WhatsApp, Instagram, or Facebook Messenger).[59] Indeed, the entire business model of social media sites like Facebook and Instagram is built on free access for users in return for the opportunity to bombard those users' eyeballs with advertising.

Yet in 2018 Facebook was revealed not only to be generating the lion's share of its revenue from advertising profits (89 percent in 2017) but also to have granted several high-profile, multinational companies (including Amazon, Apple, Microsoft, Netflix, Sony, and Spotify) access to the personal information of Facebook users without the users' knowledge or consent.[60] This information likely included users' friends, contact information, "likes," and browsing habits. While Facebook founder and CEO Mark Zuckerberg has repeatedly denied that his company blatantly sells users' data, ongoing investigations are revealing that, at the very least, Facebook has leveraged user data as a valuable bargaining chip and has also privately considered "ways to require third-party applications to compensate Facebook for access to its users' data, including direct payment, advertising spending and data-sharing arrangements."[61]

Likewise, the smartphone industry is surely not interested in funding brain research on digital technology when global revenue from smartphone sales in 2018 came to $522 billion.[62] When 77 percent of Americans over age eighteen and 94 percent of Americans ages eighteen to twenty-nine own a smartphone of some brand, the wireless industry has everything to gain by keeping people connected.[63]

The video game industry is equally disinclined to fund brain research when total consumer spending on video games totaled $36 billion in 2017, a number that by the first half of 2018 had already surpassed the 2017 figure by 40 percent.[64]

So given the lucrative rewards that are risked by funding illuminating research, a looming question remains: Who is minding the store? Inundated as we are by what Turkle calls "these techno-enthusiastic times," it is challenging to find research on the cognitive effects of digital media. But in response to this dearth of information, Turkle points out that saying that we know too little to make a judgment about technology has, as its starting point, that we know nothing about human development, or that somehow the game has completely changed now that we have a technology to put in its place.[65]

As Turkle implies, we collectively know enough about human development to make, at the very least, reasoned guesses about the negative effects of technology and equally astute observations about how we think, behave, and interact when we are preoccupied with it. These sentiments have spurred a number of high-profile defections from the tech industry, including former Google engineer Tristan Harris, who became disenchanted with the fundamental business model of practically all digital media, which means usurping users' attention as deeply and as often as possible. Harris left Google in 2016 to found a non-profit organization called Time Well Spent in order to battle the effects of "the extractive attention economy."[66] In 2018, others joined him in a union of tech experts to create the Center for Humane Technology, whose mission includes the lofty goal of reversing "human downgrading by inspiring a new race to the top and realigning technology with humanity."[67]

As to Turkle's second point—has the "game" of human development changed *because* of the screen invasion? Many experts in the brain and behavioral sciences believe that it has. Recall from chapters 2 and 3 that, when the brain is concerned, the word *change* is synonymous with neural plasticity.

THE PLASTIC PARADOX AND DIGITAL TECHNOLOGY

An emphasis on teaching and learning in music assumes the positive side of neural plasticity, but the downside of that same plasticity, Doidge's plastic paradox, must be taken into account. As musicians, we become what we practice, yet on which side of plasticity's double-edged sword we practice is up to us. Without a doubt, music-making, whether in practice or in live performance, requires sustained focus and concentration. But due to the temptations of digital media, these fundamental requirements are under attack like never before by a mammoth industry that traffics in human attention within what writer Cory Doctorow has called "an ecosystem of interruption technologies."[68] And while diversionary tactics—such as roadblocking, as discussed in chapters 3 and 4—can partly address the plastic paradox, musicians who operate in the digital age face stiff resistance when they attempt to roadblock digital habits mainly via internal switches activated by their own human tendencies. Distraction by pretty, shiny objects and dulcet ringtones is not a moral failing; it is our inheritance from evolution.

Therefore, the introduction of digital media into practice and rehearsal spaces is likely to produce a chain of interruptions, task-switch costs, and stress responses similar to those of any knowledge worker. If our constant need to be connected becomes an obsessive cycle, it seems beyond question that this will interfere with all our relationships, including our relationship to our own instrument. Perhaps the only unknown at this point is the degree of that interference—from a slight shade to a total eclipse.

If you are convinced that it is time to exert some control over your digital media habit, you can, of course, go no-tech and simply silence all gadgets for hours or stash them out of sight for days. Some people find creating "no phone zones" in specific locations like at the dinner table and in the bedroom to be very effective. The efficacy of this approach (known as *digital detox*) may rival cold turkey as a treatment for substance abuse: difficult but not altogether impossible. On his website (www.virtual-addiction.com), Dr. David Greenfield, founder of the Center for Internet and Technology Addiction, offers some simple but effective tips for digital detox based on his contention that digital gadgets (and even the Internet) operate as "the world's smallest and largest slot machines," entrapping us with their lure of "intermittent rewards"—a view that echoes Berridge's finding that the thrill of the chase keeps us coming back for more.[69]

Ironically, there is also a high-tech route to digital detox delivered by apps that are now available to help us manage our habits. Some are free, and some, like organic produce, charge extra for what you are not getting (ad content or spyware, for example). Some of the most popular digital detox apps include monitors that track screentime, timers that kick you off social media sites when you should be working, and switches that turn those alluring app colors to a boring shade of gray.

Books like *Digital Minimalism*, by computer-science professor Cal Newport, espouse a values-based approach to digital media use (keep high-quality tools and eliminate mindless Web surfing). Artist Jenny

Odell offers advice in her book *How to Do Nothing: Resisting the Atten-tion Economy* and is praised for her "knack for evoking the malaise that comes from feeling surrounded by online things."[70] That malaise hovers at the nexus of wanting and having, a place of permanent, unfulfilled desire, where obsessive seeking begets a hollow reward.

WHO CARES IF YOU LISTEN? THE PROBLEM OF AUDIENCE ATTENTION

The doctrine of neural plasticity shows that the construction of new neural pathways in the brain is not only possible but surprisingly rapid and powerfully effective. But the plastic paradox shows that we become what we practice—even if what we are practicing is what former soft-ware executive Linda Stone calls "continuous partial attention."[71] And while individual musicians may be able to win the battle for their own attention, all those focused practice and rehearsal hours are built on the touchingly simple assumption that audiences will pay us in kind with their own undivided attention when we open our souls and perform for them.

Historically, this favor has never been guaranteed. The seated, quiet reverence that most modern audiences of Western classical music now deem as expected behavior is a phenomenon that took decades to incul-cate. Up through the late eighteenth century, listening to Western art music, as performed in European opera houses and concert halls, was largely a social pastime indulged in by the upper classes, whose mem-bers viewed music events as arenas for social posturing; political in-trigue; and, of course, *amore*. Tales of audience shenanigans culled from the seventeenth through early nineteenth centuries reveal that inattentive audience behavior surpassed mere talking during perfor-mances and included playing card games, eating and drinking, and ar-riving late and leaving early. In the dark upper reaches of some Euro-pean opera houses, prostitutes even displayed themselves for sale.[72] Besides, musicians were, by and large, of a distinctly lower class than their audiences, so the chatting, drinking, gambling, and strolling about in the theater by the beau monde of the day was not considered unman-nerly (at least not by the upper classes; there are few accounts of what musicians themselves actually felt about this behavior).[73]

As the French Revolution ended at the dawn of the nineteenth century, the nobility retreated to their mansions, and a burgeoning middle class grew ever more affluent and able to afford the tastes, activities, and accoutrements that had previously been out of reach. At the same time, romanticism took root within Western culture, and with its focus on the emotional inner life of the individual, it nurtured, in the words of the late cultural historian Peter Gay, "the modern art of listening as the most privileged form of introspection." Eventually "worshipful silence, little known in the eighteenth century, gradually established itself as the standard in the nineteenth," a standard that holds today, for any behavior that punctures the hush of the theater is now considered déclassé at classical music events.[74]

Yet a new and powerful scourge that could not have been imagined only a few years ago has now infected theaters and concert halls around the world. Audiences were trained for more than two hundred years to quit yakking, sit down, and be quiet please and have obliged by silently retreating into their smartphones—those ubiquitous mobile minicomputers that beam us up and out of wherever we find ourselves bored to be and link us to anyone, anywhere, at any time. When people attending a concert text, swipe, and scroll, they are yanked into an alternate reality (any place other than the venue at hand qualifies), a reality that kidnaps their ears, eyes, attention spans, and indeed their very souls. We have to wonder, if live music or a live performance of any kind is so tedious and uninteresting as to drive an audience member to her phone, why doesn't she just save the ticket price and listen to a recording at home alone? Otherwise, put down the phone already and be in the moment. This sentiment seems to be growing among the concert-going public as well as among some star performers.

Yet in the early, heady days of the smartphone era, some music organizations sought to capitalize on the smartphone craze. Classical music organizations, desperate to develop new audiences among younger generations, actually welcomed phone behavior instead of banning it. In separate and unabashed bids to engage younger customers by appearing hip, both the Indianapolis Symphony and the New York Philharmonic invited audience members to choose the encore they most wanted to hear by text-messaging their votes during the concert, and a small opera company allowed audience members to determine the ending of Mozart's *Così fan tutte* by texting their votes to decide who should marry whom in the final scene.[75]

What the marketing directors of these organizations may not have accounted for was the backlash from stalwart patrons, who generally find the glow from a smartphone screen an annoying detraction from the mood of the experience. As a result, later iterations of these innovations have included the creation of "tweet seats": cordoned-off sections where tweeters can tweet away without disturbing their neighbors. Still, not everyone agrees that this is an improvement.[76]

Whether coupling old art forms with new technology is a clever marketing tool or a tacky gimmick, we must also take the measure of the costs implied because yet another genie has been unleashed from this bottle: audience participation. What happens when audiences express opinions about the quality of their experience on social media? How should artists and management respond when audiences post their displeasure in real time?

Just ask Steve Martin how his 2010 public interview at New York City's 92nd Street Y went down when, unbeknownst to him, viewers who watched the telecast were simultaneously encouraged to e-mail their responses. Reporter Deborah Solomon was in midinterview with Martin about his recently published novel *An Object of Beauty* when the Y's management dispatched a staff member to walk onstage with a note—which Solomon read aloud—asking that Solomon cease her line of questioning and switch to interviewing Martin about his "interesting career." Martin's reaction, as penned in his *New York Times* op-ed about the incident, read in part,

> This was as jarring and disheartening as a cellphone jangle during an Act V soliloquy. I did not know who had sent this note nor that it was in response to those e-mails. Regardless, it was hard to get on track, any track, after the note's arrival, and, finally, when I answered submitted questions that had been selected by the people in charge, I knew I would have rather died onstage with art talk than with the predictable questions that had been chosen for me. . . . I have no doubt that, in time, and with some cooperation from the audience, we would have achieved ignition. I have been performing a long time, and I can tell when the audience's attention is straying. I do not need a note.[77]

After the event concluded, the Y's manager offered the audience a full refund, prompting Martin to tweet, "So the 92nd St. Y has determined that the course of its interviews should be dictated in real time by its audience's e-mails. Artists beware."[78] A columnist for Salon piled on: "Audience whines about an interview being too highfalutin', so refunds are offered. Is all art up to a vote now?"[79]

This is an excellent question, as the fallout from this event made clear. After Martin's op-ed appeared, at least two high-profile news organizations weighed in on the encounter (one of the responses written by someone who did not actually attend the event and the other by a colleague of Solomon's), decrying the Y and its audience as Philistines, its management as craven, and Solomon and Martin as the defenders of high art.

In the aftermath, Martin Schneider, a blogger who in fact *was* in attendance at the Y, offered a completely different account of what transpired, briefly summarized here: Solomon conducted a spectacularly poor interview from the outset. Martin grew visibly uncomfortable, no doubt because (as he himself noted) he is a professional and gets it when the audience senses a dud. Therefore, some twenty minutes in, when management tried to save the sinking ship by sending Solomon a note to change the course of the interview, the audience burst into applause—not as a slam against Martin but in relief that someone had finally thrown the poor guy a rope (although Martin apparently felt he needed a rope as much as he needed a note).[80]

In retrospect, the even bigger story here was that Solomon (a *New York Times* employee) and Martin (a superstar) both had the bully pulpit available to them via the *Times* editorial pages, which they used to salve their understandably bruised egos. In a predigital, presocial media world, their accounts would have been the only and definitive ones. But the Wild West of the Internet has given us a global stage open to all voices, including that of blogger Schneider. It so happens that Schneider is a reputable writer whose account of the Solomon-Martin interview is balanced and nuanced, not to mention witnessed firsthand. But the open-mic of digital media is also its weak spot—like a stage door with no bouncer to guard it. Not only can thousands of articulate, independent writers like Schneider make a space for themselves for whoever cares to read their creations, but the grumps and curmudgeons of society can also post their opinions, along with racists, xenophobes, sociopaths, professional trolls, and bona fide enemies of the state. At the top of this food chain are the corporate executives and autocrats who can harvest all of it—data, opinions, and personal information—for questionable, lucrative, and even nefarious ends.

Performers and management alike must take the measure of the costs. What is the ultimate harm to their organization, their artists, and their audiences of not merely tolerating but actually inviting gadgets into the sanctity of performance space? New technology, like a locking cell-phone pouch developed by Yondr (whose motto is "Be here now") may offer a promising alternative.[81] Still this technology depends on our willingness to relinquish the beloved item for a few hours. For those unwilling (or unable, if one hews to the addiction narrative), a few artists have begun to plead, shame, and insist upon phone-free zones during their live concerts.[82] And when asking doesn't work, there is only one thing left to do: take matters literally in hand, which is exactly what Broadway star Patti LuPone did at a performance in the summer of 2015.

As LuPone tells it, a woman seated near the edge of the stage incessantly texted throughout the show until LuPone (and, reportedly, others in the cast) had had enough. As LuPone took her usual exit, in which she would habitually shake the hand of a random audience member, she reached out for the shake, snatched the woman's phone instead, and handed it to the stage manager for safekeeping.[83] LuPone later issued a statement through her manager:

> We work hard on stage to create a world that is being totally destroyed by a few, rude, self-absorbed, and inconsiderate audience members who are controlled by their phones. They cannot put them down. When a phone goes off or when an LED screen can be seen in the dark, it ruins the experience for everyone else—the majority of the audience at that performance and the actors on stage. I am so defeated by this issue that I seriously question whether I want to work on stage anymore. Now I'm putting battle gear on over my costume to marshal the audience as well as perform.[84]

In this digital age, audience attention—just like general human attention to any task or experience—is under assault as never before. Investigative writers like Richtel have warned of the dangers of inattention, while Maggie Jackson, author of *Distracted: Reclaiming Our Focus in a*

World of Lost Attention, suggests that the same kind of ambitious public health campaign that went after pollution and smoking as major risks to human health must be applied to society's addiction to its gadgets in order to bring about a "renaissance of attention."[85]

DIALING DOWN EMPATHY

The effect of the digital age on both the creation and the consumption of music has been literally overwhelming. Intoxicated by digital treasures, in our never-ending quest to gain audience and fans and attention, many of us rushed to adapt these treasures as tools of our trade, giddy with their exponential powers to connect and delight, to persuade and win over.

Yet digital media overuse seems to be infecting our culture with epidemic proportions of inattention, which is besetting personal relationships, creating health and safety hazards, cutting into productivity, and retarding the critical socialization skills needed by teens and young adults. Clifford Nass, along with worrying that digital media overuse was dumbing down the world, worried that the inattention incubated by it also interfered with the development of empathy, the ability to feel another's emotions.[86] Empathy is so central to the human condition that it is one of the defining differences that sets us apart from all other mammals. Lack of it is linked to a suppression of the brain's mirror neuron system and a host of behavioral disorders, including psychiatric problems and sociopathologies.

A public health campaign in defense of attention will be effective only in direct proportion to society's recognition of the problem. A force as potent as digital media warrants constraint in direct proportion to its power. Musicians and all performance artists must take a stand in defense of attention by taming these powerful tools themselves and pleading with audiences to stand with them.

NOTES

1. Bernard Marr, "How Much Data Do We Create Every Day? The Mind-Blowing Stats Everyone Should Read," *Forbes*, May 21, 2018,

www.forbes.com/sites/bernardmarr/2018/05/21/how-much-data-do-we-create-every-day-the-mind-blowing-stats-everyone-should-read/#3c1e50060ba9.

2. Lori Lewis, "2019: This Is What Happens in an Internet Minute," All Access Music Group, March 5, 2019, www.allaccess.com/merge/archive/29580/2019-this-is-what-happens-in-an-Internet-minute.

3. Nicholas Carr, *The Shallows: What the Internet Is Doing to Our Brains* (New York: W. W. Norton, 2010), 7.

4. The source for these terms is Marc Prensky, "Digital Natives, Digital Immigrants: Part 1," *On the Horizon* 9, no. 5 (2001): 1–6.

5. Sherry Turkle, *Alone Together: Why We Expect More from Technology and Less from Each Other* (New York: Basic Books, 2011), 294.

6. Sherry Turkle, "Interview: Sherry Turkle," PBS, September 22, 2009, www.pbs.org/wgbh/pages/frontline/digitalnation/interviews/turkle.html#4 .

7. The Pulitzer Prizes, "Matt Richtel and Members of the Staff of the *New York Times*," 2019, www.pulitzer.org/winners/matt-richtel-and-members-staff.

8. NPR, "Digital Overload: Your Brain on Gadgets," August 24, 2010, www.npr.org/templates/transcript/transcript.php?storyId=129384107.

9. Matt Richtel, "In Study, Texting Lifts Crash Risk by Large Margin," *New York Times*, July 27, 2009.

10. American Academy of Orthopaedic Surgeons, "Distracted Walking," December 2015, https://orthoinfo.aaos.org/en/staying-healthy/distracted-walking/.

11. Douglas Rushkoff and Rachel Dretzin, "Digital Nation," PBS, 2010, www.pbs.org/wgbh/pages/frontline/digitalnation/etc/script.html.

12. Gary Small and Gigi Vorgan, *iBrain: Surviving the Technological Alteration of the Modern Mind* (New York: HarperCollins, 2008), 15.

13. Ibid., 17.

14. Victoria J. Rideout, Ulla G. Foehr, and Donald F. Roberts, "Generation M2: Media in the Lives of 8- to 18-Year-Olds," January 20, 2010, Henry J. Kaiser Family Foundation, www.kff.org/other/report/generation-m2-media-in-the-lives-of-8-to-18-year-olds/.

15. Common Sense Media, "Landmark Report: U.S. Teens Use an Average of Nine Hours of Media Per Day, Tweens Use Six Hours," November 3, 2015, www.commonsensemedia.org/about-us/news/press-releases/landmark-report-us-teens-use-an-average-of-nine-hours-of-media-per-day.

16. Gary Greenberg, "My Monster, My Self: On Nicholas Carr and William Powers," *Nation*, March 16, 2011, www.thenation.com/print/article/159279/my-monster-my-self.

17. Clifford Nass, "Interview: Clifford Nass," PBS, December 1, 2009, www.pbs.org/wgbh/pages/frontline/digitalnation/interviews/nass.html.

18. Ibid.

19. Ibid.

20. Rushkoff and Dretzin, "Digital Nation."

21. Nass, "Interview."

22. Ibid.

23. American Association for the Advancement of Science, "Multi-tasking Adversely Affects Brain's Learning, UCLA Psychologists Report," EurekAlert! July 26, 2006, www.eurekalert.org/pub_releases/2006-07/uoc--maa072506.php.

24. Gary Marcus, *The Birth of the Mind: How a Tiny Number of Genes Creates the Complexities of Human Thought* (New York: Basic Books, 2004), 99.

25. Victor M. González and Gloria Mark, "Constant, Constant, Multi-Tasking Craziness: Managing Multiple Working Spheres," in *Proceedings of the SIGCHI Conference on Human Factors in Computing Systems*, 113–20 (ACM Digital Library, 2004); and Gloria Mark, Victor M. Gonzalez, and Justin Harris, "No Task Left Behind? Examining the Nature of Fragmented Work," in *Proceedings of the SIGCHI Conference on Human Factors in Computing Systems*, 321–30 (New York: ACM Digital Library, 2005).

26. Ibid. See also Clive Thompson, "Meet the Life Hackers," *New York Times*, October 16, 2005, www.nytimes.com/2005/10/16/magazine/meet-the-life-hackers.html.

27. American Psychological Association, "Multitasking: Switching Costs," March 20, 2006, www.apa.org/research/action/multitask.

28. Henry H. Wilmer, Lauren E. Sherman, and Jason M. Chein, "Smartphones and Cognition: A Review of Research Exploring the Links between Mobile Technology Habits and Cognitive Functioning," *Frontiers in Psychology* 8, art. 605 (April 2017): 4.

29. Gloria Mark, Daniela Gudith, and Ulrich Klocke, "The Cost of Interrupted Work: More Speed and Stress," in *Proceedings of the SIGCHI conference on Human Factors in Computing Systems*, 107–10 (New York: ACM Digital Library, 2008).

30. Robert M. Sapolsky, *Stress, the Aging Brain, and the Mechanisms of Neuron Death* (Cambridge, MA: MIT Press, 1992).

31. UCI News, "Jettisoning Work Email Reduces Stress," May 3, 2012, https://news.uci.edu/2012/05/03/jettisoning-work-email-reduces-stress/.

32. Thompson, "Meet the Life Hackers."

33. Carr, *Shallows*, 5–6.

34. Ibid., 16.

35. Ibid., 6.

36. Ratey, quoted in Matt Richtel, "Drivers and Legislators Dismiss Cellphone Risks," *New York Times*, July 18, 2009, www.nytimes.com/2009/07/19/

technology/19distracted.html; and Hallowell, quoted in Alina Tugend "Multitasking Can Make You Lose . . . um . . . Focus," *New York Times*, October 24, 2008, www.nytimes.com/2008/10/25/business/yourmoney/25shortcuts.html.

37. [37] Jaak Panksepp, *Affective Neuroscience: The Foundations of Human and Animal Emotions* (Oxford: Oxford University Press, 1998), 51.

38. Ibid., 54.

39. Ibid.

40. Vaughan Bell, "The Unsexy Truth about Dopamine," *Guardian*, February 2, 2013, www.theguardian.com/science/2013/feb/03/dopamine-the-unsexy-truth .

41. Ibid.

42. Kent C. Berridge and Terry E. Robinson, "Liking, Wanting and the Incentive-Sensitization Theory of Addiction," *American Psychologist* 71, no. 8 (November 2016): 670–79, doi:10.1037/amp0000059.

43. Franziska Green, "Pleasing Your Brain: An Interview with Dr. Kent Berridge," *Brain World*, December 28, 2018; https://brainworldmagazine.com/pleasing-your-brain-an-interview-with-dr-kent-berridge/.

44. Gary Small, interview on *PBS Frontline*'s "Digital Nation," https://www.pbs.org/wgbh/pages/frontline/digitalnation/etc/script.html.

45. American Psychiatric Association, *Diagnostic and Statistical Manual of Mental Disorders: DSM-V* (Arlington, VA: American Psychiatric Publishing, 2013).

46. Ronald Pies, "Should DSM-V Designate "Internet Addiction" a Mental Disorder?" *Psychiatry* 6, no. 2 (2009): 31.

47. American Psychiatric Association, *DSM-V*.

48. See Allen Frances, "A Warning Sign on the Road to DSM-V: Beware of Its Unintended Consequences," *Psychiatric Times* 26, no. 8 (2009); and Christopher Lane, "Bitterness, Compulsive Shopping, and Internet Addiction: The Diagnostic Madness of DSM-V," Slate, July 24, 2009, https://slate.com/technology/2009/07/the-diagnostic-madness-of-dsm-v.html.

49. World Health Organization, "Gaming Disorder," September 2018, www.who.int/features/qa/gaming-disorder/en/.

50. Quoted in David Wallis, "Just Click No," *New Yorker*, January 13, 1997, 28.

51. Kimberly S. Young, "Internet Addiction: The Emergence of a New Clinical Disorder," paper presented at the *104th Annual Meeting of the American Psychological Association*, August 11, 1996, Toronto, Canada.

52. CBS News, "Hospital First in US to Treat Internet Addiction," September 4, 2013, https://abcnews.go.com/Health/hospital-opens-Internet-addiction-treatment-program/story?id=20146923.

53. Konstantinos Ioannidis, Roxanne Hook, Anna E. Goudriaan, Simon Vlies, Naomi A. Fineberg, Jon E. Grant, and Samuel R. Chamberlain, "Cognitive Deficits in Problematic Internet Use: Meta-Analysis of 40 Studies," *British Journal of Psychiatry* (2019): 1–8, www.cambridge.org/core/journals/the-british-journal-of-psychiatry/article/cognitive-deficits-in-problematic-internet-use-metaanalysis-of-40-studies/486B3C4B1C7B6045161045BCB48D6D82.

54. Ibid., 7.

55. P. K. Dalal and Debasish Basu, "Twenty Years of Internet Addiction . . . Quo Vadis?" *Indian Journal of Psychiatry* 58, no. 1 (2016): 6.

56. Ioannidis et al., "Cognitive Deficits," 2.

57. Mark Bauerlein, PBS, June 9, 2009, www.pbs.org/wgbh/pages/frontline/digitalnation/extras/interviews/bauerlein.html.

58. See Kit Smith, "53 Incredible Facebook Statistics and Facts," Brandwatch, June 1 2019, www.brandwatch.com/blog/facebook-statistics/.

59. See Dan Noyes, "The Top 20 Valuable Facebook Statistics," Zephoria, September 2019, https://zephoria.com/top-15-valuable-facebook-statistics/.

60. Gabriel Dance, Michael Laforgia, and Nicholas Confessore, "As Facebook Raised a Privacy Wall, It Carved an Opening for Tech Giants," *New York Times*, December 18, 2018, www.nytimes.com/2018/12/18/technology/facebook-privacy.html.

61. Olivia Solon and Cyrus Farivar, "Mark Zuckerberg Leveraged Facebook User Data to Fight Rivals and Help Friends, Leaked Documents Show," *NBC News*, April 16, 2019, www.nbcnews.com/tech/social-media/mark-zuckerberg-leveraged-facebook-user-data-fight-rivals-help-friends-n994706 .

62. See Ben Lovejoy, "Global Smartphone Revenue Continues to Rise, Despite Falling Sales," 9to5Mac, February 25, 2019, https://9to5mac.com/2019/02/25/global-smartphone-revenue/.

63. See Pew Research Center, "Mobile Fact Sheet," June 12, 2019, www.pewinternet.org/fact-sheet/mobile/.

64. See Entertainment Software Association, "2019 Essential Facts about the Computer and Video Game Industry," 2019, www.theesa.com/esa-research/2019-essential-facts-about-the-computer-and-video-game-industry/; and the NPD Group, "NPD Group: Total Industry Consumer Spending on Video Games in U.S. Increases 40 Percent to $19.5 Billion for First Half 2018," August 29, 2018, www.npd.com/wps/portal/npd/us/news/press-releases/2018/npd-group-total-industry-consumer-spending-on-video-games-in-us--increases-40-percent-to-19-5-billion-for-first-half-2018/.

65. Turkle, "Interview."

66. Arielle Pardes, "Google and the Rise of 'Digital Well-Being,'" *Wired*, May 9, 2018, www.wired.com/story/google-and-the-rise-of-digital-wellbeing/ .

67. Center for Humane Technology, "About Us," 2019, https://humane-tech.com/about-us/#primary.

68. Cory Doctorow, "Writing in the Age of Distraction," *Locus*, January 7, 2009, www.locusmag.com/Features/2009/01/cory-doctorow-writing-in-age-of.html.

69. David Greenfield, "Tips for Electronic Etiquette and Mindful Technology Use," The Center for Internet and Technology Addiction, 2017, https://virtual-addiction.com/tips-electronic-etiquette-mindful-technology-use/.

70. Jonah Engel Bromwich, "A Manifesto for Opting Out of an Internet-Dominated World," *New York Times*, April 30, 2019, www.nytimes.com/2019/04/30/books/review/jenny-odell-how-to-do-nothing.html.

71. Quoted in Thompson, "Meet the Life Hackers."

72. Peter Gay, *The Naked Heart: The Bourgeois Experience, Victoria to Freud* (New York: W. W. Norton, 1996), 14.

73. See William Weber, "Did People Listen in the 18th Century?" *Early Music* 25, no. 4 (1997): 678–91.

74. Gay, *Naked Heart*, 18.

75. Stephanie Clifford, "Texting at a Symphony? Yes, But Only to Select an Encore," *New York Times*, May 15, 2009, www.nytimes.com/2009/05/16/arts/music/16text.html .

76. Beenish Ahmed, "'Tweet Seats' Come to Theaters, but Can Patrons Plug In without Tuning Out?" NPR, December 12, 2011, www.npr.org/2011/12/12/143576328/tweet-seats-come-to-theaters-but-can-patrons-plug-in-without-tuning-out.

77. Steve Martin, "The Art of Interruption," *New York Times*, December 2, 2010, www.nytimes.com/2010/12/05/opinion/05martin.html?_r=2&ref=opinion.

78. Sammy Perlmutter, "Steve Martin at the 92 St. Y: Book Talk Leads to Ticket Refunds!" Huffington Post, December 5, 2010, www.huffingtonpost.com/2010/12/05/steve-martin-at-the-92-st_n_791667.html.

79. Mary Elizabeth Williams, "92nd Street Y Goes 'American Idol' on Steve Martin," Salon, December 2, 2010, www.salon.com/2010/12/02/steve_martin_92y_fiasco/print.

80. Martin Schneider, "More on Martin and Solomon and 92Y," Emdashes, December 2, 2010, https://emdashes.com/2010/12/more-on-martin-and-solomon-and.php.

81. Yondr, www.overyondr.com/.

82. NPR, "Lock Screen: At These Music Shows, Phones Go in a Pouch and Don't Come Out," July 5, 2016, www.npr.org/sections/alltechconsidered/2016/

07/05/483110284/lock-screen-at-these-music-shows-phones-go-in-a-pouch-and-dont-come-out.

83. Eric Piepenburg, "Hold the Phone, It's Patti LuPone," *New York Times*, July 9, 2015, www.nytimes.com/2015/07/10/theater/hold-the-phone-its-patti-lupone.html?module=inline.

84. Robert Viagas, "Patti LuPone 'Putting Battle Gear On,' Questions Stage Career after Cell Phone Incident," *Playbill*, July 9, 2015, www.playbill.com/article/patti-lupone-putting-battle-gear-on-questions-stage-career-after-cell-phone-incident-com-352959. For a more humorous take on this incident, see Therandyshow, "LuPWNed! (The Patti LuPone Audience Freakout Remix)," YouTube, January 21, 2009, www.youtube.com/watch?v=F5Wh6DAFpW4.

85. Maggie Jackson, blog, "We're All Distracted" (June 19, 2008), http://maggie_jackson.com/2008/06/19/were_all_distracted/.

86. Matt Richtel, "A Force for Face-to-Face Communication," *New York Times*, November 4, 2013, https://bits.blogs.nytimes.com/2013/11/04/a-force-for-face-to-face-communication/.

8

EMOTION, EMPATHY, AND THE
UNIFICATION OF ART AND SCIENCE

Antonio Damasio's somatic marker hypothesis rescued emotion from scientific banishment and installed it alongside reason as an equal partner. Emotion has always been valued by artists, so while we may not necessarily accord it any further reverence now that it has been rediscovered by science, we musicians should be glad that science has turned its lens on the commodity in which we trade not only for its exoneration as an aid to attention but because emotion inculcates one of our greatest evolutionary gifts, empathy, which allows us to step outside ourselves and enter the soul of another. If the eyes are the window of the soul, then surely the ears are one doorway into it.

EMOTION

As I explained in chapter 1, throughout most of the twentieth century, rational thought was exalted as the pinnacle of human wisdom, while emotion was deemed too silly to merit a serious scientific look. Emotion is still popularly viewed as a trait that one must tame, silence, or outgrow. Yet recent research on emotion from the field of cognitive neuroscience reveals that emotion, rather than being a frivolous accessory, is fundamentally entwined with human reason. "Emotion," Damasio notes, "is not a luxury."[1]

But is this news to artists? Do we musicians really need science to tell us that emotion is important, much less that music has the power to induce it? If musicians do not need evidence of music's power, apparently some scientists do:

> The most intense musical experience of my life was on a winter's evening in 1983 when [my wife] took me to hear Fauré's *Requiem* in a candlelit York Minster. It has taken me the last twenty-one years of studying human evolution and the last year of writing this book to understand why I and so many others were moved and inspired by the music we heard that night.[2]

So let us assume that musicians know, through lived experience, that music has the power to induce emotion in both the creator and the listener. This assumption leads to some questions: Why should we care? Is emotion important? From a scientific viewpoint, the work of scientists Damasio, Joseph LeDoux, the late Jaak Panksepp, and others testify emphatically yes. Emotion can no longer be considered a separate or lesser brain function or a distraction from reason. Indeed, Damasio's epiphany was inspired by studying people with significant brain damage in the reasoning areas of the brain. Because these people could attach no significance to their decisions and could not privilege one choice above another, they were forever stuck in a pathological fog of indecision:

> After studying those patients in great detail, we could not explain their failures of decision making and their completely disrupted social life in terms of impaired intellect, impaired language, [or] impaired memory. . . . Something else needed to figure into the explanation, and that "something else" offered itself very clearly to us: [it] had to do with emotion.[3]

Often the worth of a basic human characteristic is revealed by its devastation. Yet artists, the empaths of human societies, have honored the worth and magnitude of emotion for as long as they have lived among us, weathering the mutability of human culture that, as literary critic Edmund Wilson notes, periodically experiences a "swing of the pendulum away from a mechanistic view of nature"; that is, away from rationalism toward something more organic, humanistic, and emotional.[4] After over a century of rationalism, we in the Western world may be collectively riding that swinging pendulum toward living a more emotionally aware existence. Like the Romantics who upended the mechanistic principles of the seventeenth and eighteenth centuries, we have again come to realize that the universe is, as Wilson notes, "not a machine, after all, but something more mysterious and less rational."[5] We have been here before. And yet, this time the change has not been a reaction against science; on the contrary, it was heralded and partly created by the branch of science that undergirds this book.

So be it resolved that music has the power to induce emotion, and emotion is a vital component of human existence. The power of emotion has been recognized for as long as modern humans have existed, and more recently, emotion has been recognized for its role in reason. Yet emotion does not always unleash the better angels of our nature; we can be guided by the emotions of jealousy and hate and fear of the other, as well as by altruism. There are numerous vectors within us, both individual and communal, that spread both positive and destructive emotion. To balance the wide swath of human emotion, we also harbor inborn mechanisms that act as emotional constraints, guiding and regulating the distribution of emotion. Among the most powerful of these is the vital entity we call *empathy*.

UNDERSTANDING EMPATHY

Empathy may be defined very simply as the ability to feel the experience of others. Evolutionary psychologists tout empathy as one of the most critical of our human traits and one that has persisted throughout human evolution. Think of it: empathy is a powerful explanation for why we are all still here. How else might we explain why we have not yet annihilated each other? Empathy is a cornerstone of a civilized society.

Tania Singer, a neuroscientist who researches empathy, states that "there are almost as many definitions of empathy as there are researchers in the field."[6] Singer's definition incorporates the complexities of empathy:

> We define empathy as follows: We "empathize" with others when we
> have (1) an affective state (2) which is isomorphic to another person's

affective state, (3) which was elicited by observing or imagining another person's affective state, and (4) when we know that the other person's affective state is the source of our own affective state.[7]

There are key components in this definition that concern us. First, the scientific term *affective state* encompasses both feeling and emotion. While most of us likely use these two terms interchangeably, scientists recognize them as two distinct human attributes. We may hearken back to the term *proprioception* as a synonym for feeling.

Part three of this definition illustrates the phenomenon whereby we are literally able to experience another person's joy or pain by observing them score a touchdown or be violently tackled to the ground. Thanks to our mirror neuron system, we are also capable of wincing by simply imagining that scenario. All of these effects are amplified if we hold a strong emotional attachment to the person being imagined, such as a parent might feel for a child.

Part four of Singer's definition refers to the distinctly human attribute of *metacognition*, or awareness of one's own thinking; in shorthand, "Knowing about knowing." This is a key component of empathy, namely, our understanding that, while we are experiencing the joy or pain of another, we do so from an objective, safe remove. Without this crucial ability to distinguish between self and other, witnessing someone else's emotions could result in one of two equally disastrous consequences: feeling absolutely zero emotion upon witnessing the pain of another (this deficit is the foundation of *sociopathology*) or being so entirely overwhelmed by empathy that we completely fall apart. Indeed, in its extreme form, too much empathy can be paralyzing (and apparently there exists a tiny percentage of the population that experiences the sensations of others this deeply).[8] For the rest of us, there seems to be a barometer that allows most of us to hover on the edge of feeling, enough to generate a frisson of emotion without pulling us under—that is, enough to compel us to pull out our checkbook in response to a faraway humanitarian disaster and then not give that disaster another thought once the check is in the mail.

But is this true empathy? For while empathy is closely aligned with other attributes, such as concern, sympathy, and compassion, it nevertheless stands apart from each of them. For a grief-stricken widow whose spouse has died, you may feel a range of emotions—concern, sympathy, or compassion—in direct proportion to your relationship to her. If her husband was your dear kid brother, along with fielding your own grief, you would likely also experience empathy for the depth of your sister-in-law's grief. You would experience her pain even as you recognize it is not exactly the same as yours, for empathy can trigger affective symptoms, or mood changes.

But if this widow is a little-known colleague from work, sympathy and compassion are appropriately calibrated. In fact, we may experience no personal sadness at all. We can feel sorry for our colleague but not feel grief ourselves.

Similarly, we may feel sadness when listening to sad music, but most of us, in most situations, will not be overwhelmed to the extent that we are forced to flee in tears from the auditorium. This brings us to an intriguing facet of empathy studies: how much control can we exert over our empathetic responses? In Singer's review of the current state of empathy research, she notes that most researchers agree on the critical role of attention and decision-making in empathic experience:

> Empathy is not a purely sensory-driven process in which affective states are induced in the observer solely by means of bottom-up processes. On the contrary, it has long been argued that contextual appraisal, cognitive processes, and top-down control are important constituents of human empathy.[9]

In other words, while we may have an instantaneous gush of sympathy, compassion, or even empathy for a fellow human, there are also plenty of settings in which we will step back, assess the situation, and then make a decision about whether we care enough to care.

PAYING ATTENTION TO EMPATHY

While many people equate empathy with a purely emotional response ("I feel your pain"), the current scientific understanding of empathy is that it is a complex process wherein bottom-up, or gut, responses collide with top-down cognitive processes (i.e., the rational mind) that appraise the situation while exerting a calming influence on the gut response. Thus empathy is not an all-or-nothing proposition; it is flexible. Researchers like Singer therefore study parameters such as attention, situational context, and relationships for clues as to how our rational mind exerts this flexibility when our empathy is aroused. Recent experiments in attention have shown how important yet malleable attention is in the doling out of empathy. Participants in one study had measurably negative and visceral reactions to pictures showing people in pain. This is good news for the human race. Yet when the participants were distracted by a simple task and shown the same images, astoundingly, they had no reaction at all to the disturbing images.[10]

Music teachers, as they interact with clients and students who are by and large operating in some state of emotional vulnerability, would do well to note this: our capacity for empathy is toggled to our attentional abilities. For example, we can decide whether to glance at a text message or not in the midst of a teacher-student interaction. To choose to ignore the message is to remain open to empathy, while to give in to temptation is to sever the momentary tie that binds us to another human being. Attention, like empathy, is flexible, indeed—and it is also fragile and fallible.

EMPATHY AND GOODNESS

Our ability to appraise situations and choose how to allocate our emotional resources feeds into one of the most intriguing yet controversial aspects of empathy research, that of *prosocial behavior*, or doing right by a person or group of people for altruistic reasons; that is, doing right by doing good. There is currently a keen scientific interest in how the ability to inhabit another person's circumstances affects levels of empathic concern. In fact, a seminal neuroscientific experiment in 2004 showing that experiencing pain and empathizing with the pain of others evoked overlapping brain responses launched a brand-new field: the *social neuroscience of empathy*.[11] Research from this new field suggests that, when people use their imagination to walk in another person's shoes, such an exercise can spark "heightened personal distress and an egoistic motivation to reduce that distress."[12] This sparks the obvious question "If this is so, can empathy be taught to those who do not possess it or heightened in those who do, in order to actually promote prosocial behavior?" Can empathy make a better society as a whole by making us better people individually? The link between empathy and doing good has been touted in both the popular and scientific press and by politicians, activists, and scientists alike. A position paper by two experts in this new field from the University of Vienna examines the link between empathy and altruism:

> In the public, but at times also in the academic discourse, it appears to be taken for granted that empathy can act as a remedy or a stronghold against anti-social phenomena which seem to affect our society to an increasing extent—such as the selfish greed in the financial industry supposedly contributing to the global financial crisis, or the many armed conflicts we are witnessing these days. . . . Such views have certainly been influenced by the folk intuition that empathy motivates prosocial behavior, such as helping others in need. Indeed, this intuition has received widespread support from social psychology as well as more recently from the field of social neuroscience. . . . At first glance, such a link between empathy and altruism might imply that increasing empathy in our society will reduce egoism and selfishness and the social conflicts associated with them. [13]

Due to the potency of the "folk intuition" surrounding empathy, a 2011 study led by Sara Konrath of the University of Michigan, Ann Arbor, attracted widespread attention when it reported an eye-catching 40 percent drop in empathy among college students over the past thirty years. [14] This was alarming news for, as Konrath herself notes, the traits that society purports to value (the prosocial benefits of honesty, compassion, and selflessness) are directly related and proportional to empathy:

> Participants who score higher on the EC [empathic concern] subscale indicate more continuous volunteer hours per month . . . and are more likely to have returned incorrect change, let somebody ahead of them in line, carried a stranger's belongings, given money to a homeless person, looked after a friend's plant or pet, and donated to charity within the preceding 12 months. [15]

So any damage to the prosocial benefits of empathy and missed opportunities to engender it have raised an alarm about an *empathy deficit*. President Obama began using this term when still a senator in 2006:

There's a lot of talk in this country about the federal deficit. But I think we should talk more about our *empathy deficit*—the ability to put ourselves in someone else's shoes; to see the world through those who are different from us—the child who's hungry, the laid-off steelworker, the immigrant woman cleaning your dorm room. As you go on in life, cultivating this quality of empathy will become harder, not easier. There's no community service requirement in the real world; no one forcing you to care. You'll be free to live in neighborhoods with people who are exactly like yourself, and send your kids to the same schools, and narrow your concerns to what's going in your own little circle.[16]

EMPATHY AND BIAS

While humans possess a great capacity for empathy, they also demonstrate strong biases for where they choose to place it. Most disturbing is our propensity to favor those most like ourselves and to withhold empathy from those we perceive to be very different from ourselves. This inclination is seen most nakedly via *ethnicity bias*, a fairly robust finding backed up by numerous studies in social psychology.[17] We seem to readily feel great gobs of empathy for those closest and most like us (relatives), but our empathic concern radiates out in ever-widening and ever-weakening concentric circles until we feel little to no empathy for those who look and act least like us.

Worse, these biases have been shown to result in not just withholding empathy but in actually celebrating others' misfortunes, a behavior known as schadenfreude. The ability to empathize does not always turn itself to good; empathy can be weaponized. The most effective bullies and torturers are shown to be those who possess a great capacity for empathy, for they understand exactly how to inflict the deepest pain. And if the worst psychopathic figures from history just sprang to mind, the social neuroscience of empathy reminds us that, in our roles as lovers, spouses, parents, and offspring, we are similarly capable of striking with surgical precision at the secret targets in our loved ones whose locations we know too well.

LEVERAGING HOMOPHILY

Is empathy trainable? How might we disassociate the parochial and ethnicity biases that can sully our loftier ambitions for instilling empathy? The social neuroscientists from the University of Vienna warn that blindly racing into efforts to grow empathy without coming to grips with our deeply rooted biases risks amplifying our divides even more severely:

> Initiatives simplistically aimed at a generalized increase of empathic sensitivity will likely not promote a more impartial society. Rather, it will likely replace egoism by its twin brother: an in-group favoring type of altruism—thereby widening, rather than diminishing, the boundaries between social groups. [18]

In other words, practicing empathy when it feels natural to do so—with kin and very close friends—strengthens those existing familial and parochial bonds, thereby reinforcing the narrow confines of our understanding. Yet this is not an argument against pursuing easy empathy; after all, caring for one's family is an innate human characteristic. Perhaps easy empathy offers practice for more challenging scenarios.

So how might we look beyond our immediate families, friends, and neighborhoods to cultivate empathy? For this, there is one overarching response that emanates from social science: our best hope in instilling empathy is to practice envisioning others as extensions of ourselves. This egocentric response definitely goes against the grain of such popular wisdom as respecting differences, even celebrating and embracing them. How might this work?

It starts by acknowledging that *homophily*, the tendency for humans to be attracted to those most similar to themselves, is more common than we might like to believe. [19] Once this is accepted, we can leverage this trait as the kindling needed to light the fire of empathy. Stated bluntly, we are least likely to harm those we see as extensions of ourselves; stated more aspirationally, we can turn our inclinations toward developing compassion for others to see that we share more fundamental characteristics in common than those that divide us. If we accept Obama's charge to practice this change in perspective—seeing others as extensions of ourselves within a larger tribe of humanity—is there any more fertile territory available to us than the arena of art?

INSTILLING EMPATHY THROUGH ART

So let us agree that music has the power to induce emotion and emotion is a vital component of human existence, not least of which is emotion's power to instill empathy. We care about empathy because it explains our evolutionary past. We must safeguard empathy, for it can help secure our future. We must reassert that empathy is a cornerstone of a civilized society. Rearranging our perspective to see ourselves in others and others in ourselves instills empathy. Exactly how this change in perspective is realized is by engaging with art.

This sentiment is lived philosophy for intellectual titan Martha Nussbaum, winner of the 2018 Berggruen Prize, awarded annually to a thinker whose ideas "have profoundly shaped human self-understanding and advancement in a rapidly changing world."[20] Among Nussbaum's many pursuits, making music—in her case, singing solo operatic repertoire—is one of her most cherished. She invited an interviewer to observe her weekly singing lesson with the reasoning that "it's the actual singing that would give you insight into my personality and my emotional life, though of course I am very imperfect in my ability to express what I want to express." Music, Nussbaum says, allows her to access a part of her personality that is "less defended, more receptive."[21] As a moral philosopher, she recognizes the critical roles that emotion and empathy play in the collective good and issues calls to action through her writing:

> For a society to remain stable and committed to democratic principles, [Nussbaum has] argued, it needs more than detached moral principles: it has to cultivate certain emotions and teach people to enter empathetically into others' lives. She believes that the humanities are not just important to a healthy democratic society but decisive, shaping its fate. She proposed an enhanced version of John Stuart Mill's "aesthetic education"—emotional refinement for all citizens through poetry and music and art.[22]

This is not a highfalutin string of nostrums from an intellectual elite. It is a rallying cry for saving the culture. As musicians, our calculus for doing so is strikingly simple: we can cull the fruits of science for better music teaching, learning, and performance, and in the process, we will improve our ability to sow the seeds of empathy. Musicians can help save the culture.

Yet does our culture need saving? We humans continually suffer from empathy deficits, from our smallest daily individual interactions to the grandest of scales, when one country declares war on another. There will always be a need for art to mitigate our basest instincts and demonstrate its power to inculcate sympathy; compassion; and, the ultimate soul swap, empathy.

Because empathy is nothing less than a cornerstone of a civilized society, its components—civilization, society—must be vigilantly safeguarded. Those in positions of power must enforce our laws, but reinforcing commonly held beliefs about justice and human decency are the mandate of each and every citizen. Such a mandate will always find common cause with the pursuit of art and beauty. Art and empathy have this in common: both are among our noblest attributes, yet both require deliberate practice.

CODA: THE FOURTH CULTURE AND THE UNIFICATION OF ART AND SCIENCE

There is ample evidence that we are no longer on the verge of a fourth culture but are squarely in it, as envisioned by C. P. Snow in 1959 and as prophesized by Edmund Wilson in 1931:

> Who can say that, as science and art look more and more deeply into experience and achieve a wider and wider range, and as they come to apply themselves more and more directly and expertly to the needs of human life, they may not arrive at a way of thinking, a technique of dealing with our perceptions, which will make art and science one?[23]

The new science of mind offers the most promising arena for a unification of the arts and the sciences because the scientific questions have changed from only those things that can be directly observed and measured to the most ineffable elements of life. While science poses questions, it is the experience of living that raises the deepest questions we wish to ask in the first place. While science proffers answers to those questions, it is only art that can illuminate those results with meaning.

In closing, I urge musicians, as in the beginning, to experiment between the boundaries of art and science; one need not be an expert in cognitive neuroscience to do so, and it will take many creative minds to engage the discoveries made there. In so doing, we will have to choose what to embrace of the mind's new science—this new enchantment. But those choices should be fully informed by the historic trajectory of scientific knowledge as well as its current state, and our choices should be tempered by the wisdom that human knowledge is not ultimately limitless. As we reach the edges of our collective cognitive capacities, what is left to illuminate the human condition is the boundlessness of art.

NOTES

1. Antonio Damasio, *Descartes' Error: Emotion, Reason and the Human Brain* (New York: G. P. Putnam's Sons, 1994), 130.

2. Steven Mithen, *The Singing Neanderthals: The Origins of Music, Language, Mind and Body* (London: Weidenfeld & Nicholson, 2005), ix.

3. Antonio Damasio, "A Conversation with Antonio Damasio and Siri Hustvedt," Big Think, September 21, 2010, https://bigthink.com/videos/a-conversation-with-antonio-damasio-and-siri-hustvedt.

4. Edmund Wilson, *Axel's Castle: A Study in the Imaginative Literature of 1870–1930* (New York: Charles Scribner's Sons, 1931), 17.

5. Ibid., 5.

6. Tania Singer and Claus Lamm, "The Social Neuroscience of Empathy," *Year in Cognitive Neuroscience* 1156, no. 1 (March 2009): 82.

7. Ibid.

8. Jamie Ward, Patricia Schnakenberg, and Michael J. Banissy, "The Relationship between Mirror-Touch Synaesthesia and Empathy: New Evidence and a New Screening Tool," *Cognitive Neuropsychology* 35, nos. 5–6 (2018): 314–32.

9. Singer and Lamm, "Social Neuroscience of Empathy," 88.

10. See X. Gu and S. Han, "Attention and Reality Constraints on the Neural Processes of Empathy for Pain," *Neuroimage* 36, no. 1 (May 2007): 256–67.

11. See Claus Lamm and Jasminka Majdandžić, "The Role of Shared Neural Activations, Mirror Neurons, and Morality in Empathy: A Critical Comment," *Neuroscience Research* 90, no. 1 (January 2015): 15.

12. Singer and Lamm, "Social Neuroscience of Empathy," 90.

13. Lamm and Majdandžić, "Role of Shared Neural Activations," 20.

14. Sara H. Konrath, Edward H. O'Brien, and Courtney Hsing, "Changes in Dispositional Empathy in American College Students over Time: A Meta-analysis," *Personality and Social Psychology Review* 15, no. 2 (May 2011): 180–98.

15. Ibid., 183.

16. Barack Obama, "Obama to Graduates: Cultivate Empathy," June 19, 2006, www.northwestern.edu/newscenter/stories/2006/06/barack.html.

17. Lamm and Majdandžić, "Role of Shared Neural Activations," 20.

18. Ibid., 22.

19. Miller McPherson, Lynn Smith-Lovin, and James M. Cook, "Birds of a Feather: Homophily in Social Networks," *Annual Review of Sociology* 27, no. 1 (2001): 415–44.

20. Jennifer Schuessler, "Martha Nussbaum Wins $1 Million Berggruen Prize," *New York Times*, October 30, 2018, www.nytimes.com/2018/10/30/arts/martha-nussbaum-berggruen-prize.html.

21. Quoted in Rachel Aviv, "The Philosopher of Feelings," *New Yorker*, July 25, 2016, www.newyorker.com/magazine/2016/07/25/martha-nussbaums-moral-philosophies.

22. Ibid.

23. Wilson, *Axel's Castle*, 235.

INDEX

ABOUT THE AUTHOR

Lynn Helding is professor of practice in vocal arts and opera and coordinator of vocology and voice pedagogy at the University of Southern California Thornton School of Music.

Ms. Helding is a thought leader within the dynamic field of contemporary voice science, or vocology, and was thus elected to lead the founding of the first nonprofit vocology association, the Pan American Vocology Association (PAVA). She is an associate editor of the *Journal of Singing* and creator of the journal's *Mindful Voice* column, which illuminates current research in the cognitive, neuro-, and social sciences as they relate to music teaching, learning, and performance. She is in demand as a master teacher and popular lecturer on cognitive topics at universities, conferences, and workshops across the United States and Canada.

Made in the USA
Columbia, SC
02 April 2021

35492605R00191